Voices for Change in the Classical Music Profession

Voices for Change in the Classical Music Profession

New Ideas for Tackling Inequalities and Exclusions

Edited by
ANNA BULL *and* CHRISTINA SCHARFF
with Associate Editor LAUDAN NOOSHIN

OXFORD
UNIVERSITY PRESS

Oxford University Press is a department of the University of Oxford. It furthers
the University's objective of excellence in research, scholarship, and education
by publishing worldwide. Oxford is a registered trade mark of Oxford University
Press in the UK and certain other countries.

Published in the United States of America by Oxford University Press
198 Madison Avenue, New York, NY 10016, United States of America.

© Oxford University Press 2023

All rights reserved. No part of this publication may be reproduced, stored in
a retrieval system, or transmitted, in any form or by any means, without the
prior permission in writing of Oxford University Press, or as expressly permitted
by law, by license, or under terms agreed with the appropriate reproduction
rights organization. Inquiries concerning reproduction outside the scope of the
above should be sent to the Rights Department, Oxford University Press, at the
address above.

You must not circulate this work in any other form
and you must impose this same condition on any acquirer.

CIP data is on file at the Library of Congress

ISBN 978–0–19–760122–8 (pbk.)
ISBN 978–0–19–760121–1 (hbk.)

DOI: 10.1093/oso/9780197601211.001.0001

Contents

Contributors   ix

    Introduction   1
    Anna Bull and Christina Scharff

I. THE MAKING OF CLASSICAL MUSICIANS

1. Class and Gender Inequalities in the Recruitment of Classical Musicians: Reflections on the Case of Italian Music Conservatoires   19
Clementina Casula

2. The Role of Music Conservatoires in the Making of Classical Music Careers   31
Rainer Prokop and Rosa Reitsamer

3. Social Inclusion in Contemporary British Conservatoires: Alumni Perspectives   42
Jennie Joy Porton

4. Inside Looking In: Strategies to Counteract Misconduct in Artistic Teaching within Higher Music Education   54
David-Emil Wickström

II. PROBLEMATIZING INSTITUTIONAL CHANGE

5. (Un)settling Institutional Hegemony: Challenges of Diversity Strategies in the "Western" Classical Music Sector   69
Kristina Kolbe

6. "To Share Music with Children": The LA Phil and Neoliberal Philanthropy in Inglewood   81
Mina Yang

7. A Critical Perspective on Diversity and Inclusion in US Classical Music Discourse   91
Marianna Ritchey

8. Staging a Loose Canon: Scripture, Tradition, and Embedded Exclusion in Opera Production 102
Caitlin Vincent

9. Disability Representation in Opera 112
Charlotte Armstrong

III. MARGINALIZED VOICES

10. Gender and Class: An Account of a Female Percussionist in the Classical Music Industry 127
Beth Higham-Edwards

11. Making Space for Disability and Music to Interact: An Interview with Composer Oliver Vibrans 135
Oliver Vibrans

12. Black on the Podium: An Interview with Conductor Brandon Keith Brown 141
Brandon Keith Brown

13. Creolization, Mixing, and Plurality: An Interview with Composer Hannah Kendall 148
Hannah Kendall

IV. RACIAL INEQUALITIES

14. The New "Yellow Peril" in "Western" European Symphony Orchestras 159
Maiko Kawabata

15. Irreconcilable Senses of Belonging: Transnational Japanese Artists in the Quest for Authenticity in the World of Classical Music 172
Beata M. Kowalczyk

16. [Re-]training Classical Musicians Toward Polymusicality and Hybridization: An Interview with Jon Silpayamanant 185
Jon Silpayamanant

17. Inclusion and Diversity in the Early Music Scene in the US: A Conversation with Patricia Ann Neely 195
Patricia Ann Neely

18. On Leaving Classical Music: An Interview with Anthony Gray 203
Anthony Gray

V. ACTIVISM: STARTING WITH THE SELF

19. (Dis)orient Yourself!: Disrupting White Ontologies in Classical Music 215
    Eleanor Ryan

20. Everyday Bridges: A View from the Field 228
    Cayenna Ponchione-Bailey

21. Illuminating Women's Music: Exploring the Canonic Ethos behind the Illuminate Women's Music Concert Series 234
    Angela Elizabeth Slater

22. Changing Classical Music from the Inside: An Interview with Chi-chi Nwanoku 246
    Chi-chi Nwanoku

VI. ACTIVISM: BUILDING NETWORKS FOR CHANGE

23. (Un)Silencing Blacktivism in Opera: An Interview with Quodesia Johnson about the *Letter to the Opera Field from Black Administrators* 255
    Antonio C. Cuyler

24. Reflecting on the Work of Gender Relations in New Music: Institutional Critique and Activist Strategies 266
    Brandon Farnsworth and Rosanna Lovell

25. Addressing Inequalities in the Music Industry before, during, and after COVID-19: The Campaigning Work of the UK's Independent Society of Musicians 276
    Deborah Annetts, Vick Bain, Chris Collins, Vinota Karunasaagarar, and Dr. Kathryn Williams

26. "A Community of 30,000 Musicians behind You": An Interview with John Shortell from the UK Musicians' Union 286
    John Shortell

Afterword 297
   Gillian Moore
Discussion Questions for Teachers, Students, Reading Groups, and Industry Leaders 305
References 309
Index 341

Contributors

Deborah Annetts is Chief Executive of the Independent Society of Musicians (ISM) the UK's fastest-growing representative body for musicians, with over 11,000 members. She has led a major change program at the ISM covering every aspect of its work from setting up the charity the ISM Trust, to developing a campaigning function focused on supporting the music sector and musicians. Leading the ISM's campaigning and advocacy function, Deborah has devised various campaigns covering Brexit, music education, diversity and inclusion, workers' rights, and COVID-19, with the common objective to protect the interests of those working in the music sector, the music sector itself and wider creative industries. Outside of the ISM, Deborah is chair of the Educational Recording Agency (ERA), Honorary Research Fellow in arts and culture advocacy at Queen Mary University of London and Commissioner with the UK Trade and Business Commission (UKTBC). In 2022 Deborah was inducted in Music Week Women in Music Awards' Roll of Honour and nominated as campaigner of the year.

Charlotte Armstrong is an Independent Researcher whose work explores the politics and practice of disability representation in modernist opera. She also has research interests in digital humanities and was the Postdoctoral Research Associate on the AHRC-funded project "The Internet of Musical Events: Digital Scholarship, Community, and the Archiving of Performance" (InterMusE). Charlotte now works as the Communications Coordinator for the European Network on Statelessness.

Vick Bain has worked in music for 25 years and is a consultant and campaigner for diversity and inclusion in the music industry, training and advising organizations from every sector and genre of music. This is grounded in her work as a PhD researcher at Queen Mary University in the Centre for Research in Equality and Diversity. In addition to this, Vick is the president of the Independent Society of Musicians, representing over 11,000 musicians in the UK. And she is the author of Counting the Music Industry and founder of the F-List Directory of UK Female+ Musicians, which is a not-for-profit organization supporting female musicians. Vick was enrolled into the Music Week Women in Music Awards Roll of Honour and Radio 4 Woman's Hour Music Industry Powerlist and is a regular press commentator on gender diversity in the music industry.

Brandon Keith Brown is a Conductor, Activist, and Teacher, and is a Laureate of the 2012 Sir Georg Solti International Conductors' Competition. Brown gave a celebrated European debut with the Badische Staatskapelle. It led to a debut and re-engagement with the Berlin Radio Symphony Orchestra (RSB). Other orchestras include the Konzerthaus Orchestra Berlin, the Detroit Symphony Orchestra, the Bremer Philharmoniker, and the Cape Town Philharmonic Orchestra. His mentor is David Zinman. He is a violin student of renowned teachers Roland and Almita Vamos. Brown fights to change the racial conscience of society. His writings have been featured internationally including NPR's *Here and Now*, *DIE ZEIT*, *The Medium*, and the *Berlin Tagesspiegel*. Lectures and teaching include Freie Universität Berlin, Humboldt University, and the Berlin University of Art and Music. He is a frequent podcast guest, speaker, and consultant on the intersection of "race" and music.

Anna Bull is a Lecturer in Education and Social Justice at the University of York. A former professional pianist and cellist, her research interests include class and gender inequalities in classical music education and staff sexual misconduct in higher education. Her monograph *Class, Control, and Classical Music* was published in 2019 with Oxford University Press and in 2020 was joint winner of the British Sociological Association Philip Abrams Award. She has also worked with music education charity *Sound Connections* on developing youth voice in classical music education. Anna is also a co-founder and director of The 1752 Group, a research and campaigning organization working to address staff sexual misconduct in higher education.

Clementina Casula is Associate Professor of Sociology of Economic and Labor processes at the University of Cagliari, Italy. She holds a PhD in European studies from the London School of Economics (UK) and a diploma in piano from the State Conservatory of Music of Cagliari. Her research mainly focuses on the regulative role of public policies in different socio-economic fields, such as territorial development, information society, education-to-work transitions, and music and the cultural and creative industries, always paying special attention to the gender dimension of analysis.

Chris Collins is Chair in Music and Head of the School of Language, Literature, Music and Visual Culture at the University of Aberdeen, and was formerly head of music at Bangor University. He teaches and researches 20th-century European music, specializing in the work of Manuel de Falla. He is also a conductor and pianist. A longstanding campaigner for greater inclusivity in music education at all levels, he is a member of the equality, diversity, and inclusion committee of the Royal Musical Association, and was president of the Independent Society of Musicians in 2020–21.

Antonio C. Cuyler is the author of *Access, Diversity, Equity, and Inclusion in Cultural Organizations: Insights from the Careers of Executive Opera Managers of Color in the U.S.* and editor of *Arts Management, Cultural Policy & the African Diaspora*. He serves as the director of the Master of Arts Program and Associate Professor of Arts Administration in the Department of Art Education at Florida State University (FSU), and visiting Associate Professor of Theater and Drama in the School of Music, Theatre & Dance at the University of Michigan. He is also the Founder of Cuyler Consulting, LLC, a Black-owned arts consultancy that helps cultural organizations maximize their performance and community relevance through access, diversity, equity, and inclusion (ADEI).

Brandon Farnsworth is a Swiss National Science Foundation Postdoctoral Researcher in Musicology and Music Curator based at Lund University, Sweden. After studying at the Zurich University of the Arts, he completed his PhD in Dresden with the publication

Curating Contemporary Music Festivals (2020, Transcript). Brandon has worked on projects with Ultima Festival Oslo, Montreal New Musics Festival, Sonic Matter Zurich, and BGNM.

Anthony Gray trained and worked as a classical singer, working in major UK classical music institutions before leaving classical music to pursue a career as a cross-arts producer and programmer. His roles have focused on supporting artists to create work and push their practice across a number of schemes that he has delivered. Currently head of programme at Fuel Productions Ltd in London, Anthony's career to date has primarily been about making the arts sector as accessible to as many unheard voices as possible.

Beth Higham-Edwards is a percussionist who has performed at the National Theatre and Shakespeare's Globe. She teaches percussion at Junior Trinity Laban and has delivered workshops for the London Symphony Orchestra, BBC Proms, and Britten Pears Arts, among others. She is passionate about equal opportunity in music education and is a known advocate for gender equality amongst instrumentalists. She held a roundtable discussion at the Wigmore Hall in March 2019, is a Creative Associate with SWAP'ra (Supporting Women and Parents in Opera), a trustee with the National Children's Orchestra, winner of the ABO RPS Salomon Prize 2021, and founder of *Gender and the Large and Shiny Instruments*.

Vinota Karunasaagarar was the creative content and publications manager at the Independent Society of Musicians (ISM) and Independent Society of Musicians Trust (ISM Trust), where she was responsible for producing publications such as *Music Journal*, the ISM's quarterly magazine, the annual *Handbook* and educational resources in both print and digital formats. The ISM (ism.org) is the UK's largest representative non-union body for musicians and a nationally recognized subject association for music, and the ISM Trust (ismtrust.org) is the ISM's sister charity, created in 2014 to advance education and the arts and to promote health. Vinota works freelance as a publications consultant and continues to work for the ISM in this capacity.

Maiko Kawabata (lecturer in music, Royal College of Music and staff tutor in music, Open University) is an award-winning musicologist and professional violinist. She is the author of *Paganini, the "Demonic" Virtuoso* and a co-editor of *Exploring Virtuosities: Heinrich Wilhelm Ernst, Nineteenth-Century Musical Practices and Beyond*. Her research interests include performance history, performance studies, gender studies, and music and "race." Maiko's research into Japanese composer Kikuko Kanai is supported by the BBC and AHRC. She has played violin in orchestras and chamber ensembles throughout the UK, USA, and Germany.

Hannah Kendall's work has been widely celebrated. She has worked with ensembles including London Symphony Orchestra, BBC Symphony Orchestra, Boston Symphony Orchestra, New York Philharmonic, San Francisco Symphony, Seattle Symphony Orchestra, the Hallé, Ensemble Modern, and London Sinfonietta, but you'll also find her collaborating with choreographers, poets, and art galleries; crossing over to different art forms, and celebrating the impact these unique settings have on sound. She is the recipient of the 2022 Hindemith Prize for music composition and based in New York City as a doctoral fellow in composition at Columbia University.

Kristina Kolbe is Assistant Professor in Sociology of Arts and Culture at the Erasmus University Rotterdam. She previously worked as a Postdoctoral Researcher in the Sociology Department at the University of Amsterdam and has been affiliated with the LSE International Inequalities Institute and the LSE sociology department, where she completed her PhD in November 2019. Kristina's research interests span the fields of cultural sociology, cultural studies, critical "race" and migration studies, and urban studies. Her recent publications include "Playing the System: 'Race'-Making and Elitism in Diversity Projects in Germany's Classical Music Sector" (Poetics, 2021) and "Producing (Musical) Difference: Power, Practices and Inequalities in Diversity Initiatives in Germany's Classical Music Sector" (Cultural Sociology, 2021).

Beata M. Kowalczyk is an assistant professor on the faculty of sociology at Adam Mickiewicz University in Poznań, Poland, and an associated researcher at the Institutions et dynamiques historiques de l'économie et de la société. She has conducted multi-sited fieldwork with Japanese musicians in Warsaw, Paris, and Tokyo, much of which was based at Warsaw University, the Paris 1 Panthéon-Sorbonne, and the University of Tokyo. Her research has focused on Japanese society and culture, precariousness, and racial and gender-related inequalities in the creative and classical music industries, transnationalism, and postcolonialism. She is the author of *Transnational Musicians: Precariousness, Ethnicity and Gender in the Creative Industry* (Abington, Routledge, 2021).

Rosanna Lovell is a musician, educator, performer, radio maker, and sound artist based in Berlin. Her practice focuses on feminist and postcolonial perspectives in classical and new music, which she explores through performance, intervention, sound, and research, as well as critical and self-reflexive approaches in the arts and arts education. She studied classical music performance and languages at the University of Adelaide (Australia) and in 2018 completed a master of arts at the Institute for Art in Context, UdK–Berlin University of the Arts, where she is also part of the feminist collective FEM*_MUSIC*_.

Gillian Moore is Director of Music and Performing Arts at London's Southbank Centre. She also writes and broadcasts regularly about music. Her book on Stravinsky's *Rite of Spring* (*Head of Zeus*) was named as one of the best books of 2019 by the *Financial Times* and she is a frequent contributor to BBC Radio 3 and to print journalism. Early in her career, Gillian pioneered the role of orchestras in education at the London Sinfonietta, working in schools and prisons, and has commissioned and produced work in collaboration with many leading musicians and artists. She was awarded and MBE in 1993 and CBE in 2019.

Patricia Ann Neely has appeared with many early music ensembles as a viola da gamba, violone, and vielle player, including the Washington Bach Consort, Smithsonian Chamber Players and viol consort, Rheinischen Kantorei Köln, and Sequentia, among others. A founding member of the viol consort Parthenia, she is currently director of Abendmusik, New York's Period Instrument String Band. She has been a member of several diversity committees at academic institutions with which she has been affiliated. Her participation on the Mannes College of Music committee culminated in a partnership with Mannes and the Sphinx Organization, creating a full-tuition scholarship for a string player of color who met the criteria for admission to the college. Continued interest in the lack of diversity in historical performance encouraged research regarding representation of People of Color in cultural history. Ms. Neely presented a paper on diversity in classical music and early music at the Historical Performance Conference at Indiana University in 2019, which led to an appointment as chair of the Equity, Diversity, and Inclusion Taskforce of Early Music America, an advocacy organization for musicians specializing in historical performance practice.

Laudan Nooshin is professor of music at City, University of London. Her research interests include creative processes in Iranian music, music and youth culture in Iran, music and gender, urban music studies, and music in Iranian cinema. Her publications include *Iranian Classical Music: The Discourses and Practice of Creativity* (2015, Ashgate), *Music and the Play of Power in the Middle East, North Africa and Central Asia* (ed. 2009, Ashgate) and *The Ethnomusicology of Western Art Music* (ed. 2013, Routledge). Laudan is currently writing a volume on the sounds of Tehran (supported by a fellowship from the Leverhulme Trust) and is co-editor of the Cambridge University Press series Elements in Music and the City. Laudan is a co-founder and currently co-chair of the Equality, Diversity, and Inclusion in Music Studies Network; she is also a vice president of the Royal Musical Association, in which role she leads the RMA EDI Working Group.

Chi-chi Nwanoku is the founder and artistic and executive director of the Chineke! Foundation. Chi-chi was a founding member of the Orchestra of the Age of Enlightenment and held the position of principal double bass there for 30 years. She is professor of double bass historical studies at the Royal Academy of Music, where she was made a fellow in 1998. The Chineke! Foundation supports, inspires, and encourages Black and minority ethnic classical musicians working in the UK and Europe. The Chineke! Foundation celebrates diversity in the classical music industry through its two orchestras, the Chineke! Orchestra and Chineke! Junior Orchestra, as well as its educational and community engagement work. Ultimately, the Chineke! Foundation aims to give classical Black and ethnically diverse musicians a platform on which to excel, and by such methods increase the representation of Black and ethnically diverse musicians in British and European orchestras.

Cayenna Ponchione-Bailey is a UK-based conductor and academic committed to fostering social justice and environmental sustainability within and through orchestral music. Director of performance at St. Catherine's College (University of Oxford), a conducting fellow of the Oxford Philharmonic Orchestra, and a Leverhulme Early Career Research Fellow at the University of Sheffield, Dr. Ponchione-Bailey's research is focused on the social-psychological and socio-political aspects of orchestral music-making with a current focus on the orchestras of Afghanistan. Publications include "The Body Orchestral" (2018), a book chapter exploring the cognitive mechanisms underpinning co-performer communication, "Digital Methods in the Study of the Nineteenth-Century

Orchestra" (2020) in *Nineteenth-Century Music Review*, "Technologies for investigating large ensemble performance" (2021) in *Together in Music*, and "Agency, Creativity and (Inter)action in Orchestra Performance" for *Making Music Together: Analytical Perspectives on Musical Interaction* (forthcoming). Dr. Ponchione-Bailey holds masters' degrees in orchestral conducting, percussion performance, and musicology, and a doctorate in music from the University of Oxford.

Jennie Joy Porton attended the Royal College of Music on the Joint Principal Study pathway, studying clarinet and saxophone. She completed her Master of Music at Royal Welsh College of Music and Drama, also on a Joint Principal Study trajectory. She has a PhD from Royal Holloway University (supervised by Tina K. Ramnarine), undertaken with scholarship. As a freelance musician, Jennie enjoys a busy, varied performance career predominantly in the orchestral and musical theater fields. Dually based in London and Cardiff, she teaches at Royal Welsh College of Music and Drama, and is particularly interested in matters relating to equality, diversity, inclusion, and representation.

Rainer Prokop, Sociologist, is Researcher and Lecturer at the Department of Music Sociology at the mdw – University of Music and Performing Arts Vienna, Austria. His current research focuses on music labor markets, career trajectories, and study-to-work transitions of classically trained musicians, higher music education, and practices of valuation at higher music education institutions.

Quodesia "Quo" Johnson continues to forge a dynamic and exciting space of shared belonging in arts and culture as a speaker, facilitator, collaborator, equity specialist, practitioner, and creative. Quo combines her background in the arts, teaching artistry, and trauma-informed healing methods to cultivate transformational experiences to dismantle systems of oppression and dehumanization. As the creator, content curator, and cohost of *Taking the Stage with Kristian and Quo*, she engages an international audience in meaningful conversations at the intersection of art, community, business, and education each week through the Dallas Opera's TDO Network. The Dallas native currently serves as the education and company culture manager of the Dallas Opera, interim social justice advisor of OPERA America, racial equity coach of Dallas Truth, Racial Healing & Transformation, and founder and space moderator of Black Administrators of Opera. Quo is a proud graduate of Prairie View A&M University.

Rosa Reitsamer, Sociologist, is Professor and Head at the Department of Music Sociology at the mdw – University of Music and Performing Arts Vienna, Austria. Her research interests include the sociology of higher music education and music labor markets, valuation practices at higher music education institutions, and intersectional perspectives on music, gender, and social inequalities. In 2021, she received the Austrian Gabriele Possanner State Award for Gender Studies.

Marianna Ritchey is Associate Professor of Music History at the University of Massachusetts–Amherst. She has written about Berlioz, comedy, music history pedagogy, absolute music, and operatic representations of Steve Jobs. Ritchey's book, *Composing Capital: Classical Music in the Neoliberal Era* (University of Chicago Press, 2019), examines classical music and capitalist ideologies in the contemporary United States. She is currently working on an array of topics having to do with music and political imagining, ideas that have evolved alongside her work on abolition and mutual aid projects in her community of Greenfield, Massachusetts.

Eleanor Ryan is a New Zealand–born violinist, arts educator, and researcher. Her interests span transcultural and transdisciplinary performance and pedagogy, decolonial, feminist, and post-human theories and their application in performing arts. Eleanor holds a master of music degree in performance from the Royal Northern College of Music (2004) and a master of philosophy in arts, creativity, and education from the University of Cambridge (2020). An assistant professor and head of strings at the University of Trinidad and Tobago from 2009–2018, Eleanor is currently a PhD researcher at the University of Cambridge, focusing on decolonizing performance pedagogies in higher education.

Christina Scharff is Reader in Gender, Media, and Culture at King's College–London. She is author and co-editor of several books, including *Gender, Subjectivity, and Cultural Work: The Classical Music Profession* (Routledge, 2018). Dr Scharff's research on the classical music profession, funded by the ESRC and British Academy, has contributed to our understanding of inequalities in the cultural and creative industries, the subjective experiences of precarious work, and the psychic life of neoliberalism. Dr. Scharff's other area of expertise is in engagements with feminism, building on her first monograph *Repudiating Feminism: Young Women in a Neoliberal World* (Routledge, 2012).

John Shortell is Head of Equality, Diversity, and Inclusion at the UK Musicians' Union. John's work spans policy, education, positive action projects, and lobbying on EDI issues of interest to MU members in the music industry.

Jon Silpayamanant, born in Udon Thani, Thailand, is an intercultural multi-instrumentalist, composer, and music educator based in the greater Louisville and Kentuckiana area. As a biracial Thai American with musical families on both sides of the world, he has been navigating musical code switching and bimusicality for much of his life and uses that experience to inform his understanding of how music ecosystems interact, hybridize, and create systems of exclusion.

Angela Elizabeth Slater is a UK-based composer, director of Illuminate Women's Music, and professor of composition at London Performing Academy of Music, having previously taught at Cardiff University. She has an interest in musically mapping different aspects of the natural world into the fabric of her music. Recent significant achievements include being selected to become a 2020–21 Tanglewood Composition Fellow, a Britten-Pears Young Artist through which Angela worked with Oliver Knussen, Colin Matthews, and Michael Gandolfi, developing *Soaring in Stasis*, which received its premiere at 2018 Aldeburgh Festival. In 2019 she received the Mendelssohn Scholarship award, allowing her to further her studies at New England Conservatory with chair of composition, Michael Gandolfi. Angela was the New England Philharmonic's 2018 Call for Scores winner with *Roil in Stillness*, which received its world-premiere in April 2019. As of 2021 she was writing two new works for Royal Scottish Orchestra and writing a series of six new solo works through the Connected Skies project funded by Arts Council England.

Oliver Vibrans has composed music for the concert hall, theater, film, art installations, and radio. His composition *More Up* performed by the BBC Philharmonic, the Halle and the Able Orchestra won an Ivor Composers' Award and was nominated for a Royal Philharmonic Society award. He has worked extensively with disability arts company Graeae including an outdoor opera *This Is Not for You*. Recent commissions include a concert piece *Treading Water* for the BBC Philharmonic and a score for *Oliver Twist* for Leeds Playhouse and Ramps on the Moon.

Caitlin Vincent researches the future of work in the arts. Key areas of focus include opera, cultural labor, performance and technology, and equity and diversity. Her monograph *Digital Scenography in Opera in the 21st Century* (Routledge, 2021), maps the impacts of digital technology on opera's production conventions, both on and off the stage. An acclaimed opera librettist and former professional soprano, Dr. Vincent is on faculty at the University of Melbourne.

David-Emil Wickström studied Scandinavian studies, musicology, and ethnomusicology at the Humboldt-Universität zu Berlin, University of Bergen, and University of Copenhagen. His main areas of research are Norwegian traditional music, post-Soviet popular music, and higher music education. Currently employed as a professor of popular music history at the Popakademie Baden-Württemberg in Mannheim, he is also the program director for the artistic bachelor degree programs in pop music design and world music. He is a freelance trumpet player and a founding member of IASPM D-A-CH where he served on the association's board from 2013 to 2016.

Dr. Kathryn Williams is a Research and Policy Officer in Equality, Diversity, and Inclusion for the ISM. She is co-author of the *Reports Dignity at Work 2: Discrimination in the Music Sector* and *ISM Global Literature Review: Music Performance, Education and COVID-19*. Also active as a versatile flute soloist and recording artist, her solo work focuses on creatively overcoming her experiences of chronic respiratory conditions through commissioning over 100 pieces limited to a single breath in the project, Coming Up for Air. Her recordings include releases on All That Dust, Another Timbre, Huddersfield Contemporary Records, and NMC.

Mina Yang is the author of *Planet Beethoven: Classical Music at the Turn of the Millennium* (Wesleyan University Press, 2014) and *California Polyphony: Ethnic Voices, Musical Crossroads* (University of Illinois Press, 2007) and an academic program manager for Minerva Projects. She has taught at UCSD, USC, and San Francisco Conservatory; she currently teaches at the Colburn School of Music in Los Angeles.

Introduction

Anna Bull and Christina Scharff

Beginnings

Over recent years, inequalities in the classical music profession have become a central issue in scholarly and industry debates. There are now a range of initiatives that seek to tackle exclusions along the lines of "race," ethnicity, class, gender, and disability. In the UK, where the editors of this volume are based, the double bass player Chi-chi Nwanoku (see Chapter 22, this volume), launched the Chineke! Foundation in 2015, which provides career opportunities to established and up-and-coming Black and ethnically diverse classical musicians in the UK and Europe. An earlier example of this work comes from the Sphinx Organization, based in Detroit, Michigan, in the US, set up in 1997, which aims to increase representation of Black and Latinx artists in classical music. Internationally, the Keychange campaign encourages music festivals and conferences to sign up to a 50:50 gender balance pledge by 2022, and Bournemouth Symphony Orchestra's Resound is a professional disabled-led ensemble. These and other initiatives have been widely discussed in the classical music sector. Reflecting these developments, policy-makers and funders are also starting to address these challenges. In Canada, the project Re-Sounding the Orchestra has explored relationships between Canadian orchestras, Indigenous peoples, and People of Color (Peerbaye and Attariwala, 2019); in the US, interventions to improve pathways into professional orchestras for BIPOC musicians have been set up (Feder and McGill, 2021), and in the UK, Arts Council England recently published the report *Creating a More Inclusive Classical Music* (Cox and Kilshaw, 2021), which provides a detailed overview of the barriers to entering, remaining in, and becoming successful in the classical music sector in England. However, despite this attention to equity, diversity, and inclusion, there is no book that *specifically* explores issues of inequalities and exclusions in the classical music profession. This volume addresses this gap by advancing our understanding of the nature of current inequalities in the field of classical music production, exploring why they continue to exist, and asking what can be done to tackle ongoing exclusions.

We have curated this collection in order to foreground voices for change—those who are already making a difference in classical music. As such, one of the distinguishing features of the book is the inclusion of chapters from those working in the classical music industry, where they are given the opportunity to reflect on issues of diversity and to share insights and inspiration as well as good practice. As a result, we have gone beyond the usual format for academic edited collections to include interview-based chapters with musicians and activists making change in classical music, and to include voices who are not usually heard, such as those who leave due to the very inequalities that this book outlines (see Anthony Gray's chapter, this volume). As well as these practitioner accounts, we have chapters from industry professionals and organizations, and a wide-ranging selection of contributions from academic researchers. Indeed, our perspectives on the classical music profession are informed by conversations and collaborations with practitioners as well as industry bodies, and dialogue with academics who have critically explored the field of classical music (Baker, 2014 and 2020; Bennett, 2008; Browning, 2019; Curtin and Whittaker, 2021; Green, 1997 and 2003; Kajikawa, 2019; Kok, 2006; Leppänen, 2015; Johnson-Williams, 2015 and 2020; Leech-Wilkinson, 2020; Moore, 2016; Lochhead et al., 2019; Schreffler, 2019; Yoshihara, 2007; Wang, 2015), as well as many of those included in this volume.

In curating this volume, we have drawn on our own scholarly and activist work on the classical music profession carried out over the past decade. Anna Bull conducted sociological research with young classical musicians in England after quitting her own career as a classically trained pianist and cellist (Bull, 2016a, 2016b, 2018, and 2019). This research examined the middle-class culture and gendered norms in this classical music youth scene, arguing that classical music's inequalities are in part created through its distinctive aesthetic, which requires a long-term investment of time, money, and effort that is more possible and feels more worthwhile for middle- and upper-class families. The social and aesthetic conventions and performance norms of this aesthetic form a boundary that keeps out those who are not able to reach the standards of ability that are required to play classical music's instruments and canonic repertoire to the standards of precision that its education and performance institutions require. As a result, classical music institutions maintain an appearance of meritocracy and openness to "talent," while the boundary-drawing that keeps out most of those outside the middle-classes is camouflaged by being part of the aesthetic requirements of the music. The gendered and racialized norms of the White middle classes are also reproduced within classical music's conventions, as observed in the youth music spaces in her study, for example through practices of embodied control and male authority. More recently, Bull has turned her attention to sexual and gender-based violence and harassment in higher education, including classical music education, asking whether classical music constitutes a "conducive context" for such violence (Bull, forthcoming), as well as exploring how classical music education can shift away from its "pedagogy of correction" (Bull, 2022) toward embedding "youth voice" (Mayne et al., 2022).

Christina Scharff has examined gender, racial, and class inequalities in the classical music profession in Germany and the UK. Scharff carried out qualitative and quantitative research to map and bring to light existing inequalities, and to understand why they continue to exist (2015, 2018a, 2018b, 2020, and 2021). Scharff published the report *Equality and Diversity in the Classical Music Profession* (2015), which provided quantitative data that detailed the underrepresentation of marginalized groups in the classical music sector in the UK. The report was widely circulated and provided much-needed evidence to begin a more informed conversation about inequalities and exclusions. Scharff also made a range of qualitative contributions by focusing on the dimension of subjectivity. In particular, she showed that "ideal" musicians are often constructed as middle-class, White, and male (2018b) and that various common practices of getting work in the industry, such as networking and self-promotion, foster racialized, classed, and gendered exclusions (2018a). Her research on "the psychic life of neoliberalism" (2016 and 2018a) employed a Foucauldian framework to critique industry discourses that promote entrepreneurialism and to demonstrate that neoliberal rationality shapes formations of selfhood. Her most recent research analyzes how freelance musicians negotiate sexual harassment (2020) and explores the extent to which current discussions of inequalities and exclusion in the classical music profession pave the way for social change (2021).

Both editors, as well as associate editor Laudan Nooshin, have also been active in trying to make change in classical music, and as such this volume reflects their dual role as both academics and also activists who are deeply invested in the themes discussed in the book. Anna Bull has organized a series of events to help music education institutions in the UK better address the difficult issue of sexual abuse in classical music (Bull, 2016c), as well as running training sessions and talks for music teachers and working with classical music organizations to change practices and embed inclusion. Alongside this, she also co-directs campaign and research organization the 1752 Group, which addresses staff/faculty sexual misconduct in higher education, including higher music education. Laudan Nooshin has had a long-term commitment to bringing about change in relation to the issues discussed in this volume. She was involved in setting up and is currently co-chair of the UK Equality, Diversity, and Inclusion in Music Studies network (EDIMS) as well as chair of the Royal Musical Association EDI Working Group. As outlined above, Christina Scharff has supported industry bodies with research data and theoretically informed analysis to help them improve their approach to tackling inequalities and exclusions.

Scope

The book contains chapters that explore a range of national contexts, including Italy, Austria, Germany, the US, UK, France, Poland, Japan, and Australia. However, a limitation of the book is that it predominantly focuses on the Global North rather than the Global South (as defined by Dados and Connell, 2012). Indeed, as editor Laudan Nooshin has described in her previous work, the term "Western art music" is ideologically loaded, not least in claiming "exclusive ownership of a cultural space whilst denying the existence of 'others' who have been and continue to be central to it and who are rendered invisible by the dominant discourses" (Nooshin, 2011, p. 294; see also Silpayamanant, Chapter 16, this volume). The volume risks reifying the ideology that Anglophone and European voices are central to this tradition and practice by representing authors from these parts of the world, and in this way, it could be seen as complicit in, or reproducing, the inequalities that it seeks to address. We acknowledge that due to this volume being the first to address the topic of inequalities and exclusions in the classical music profession, it is necessarily a partial account. We are uncomfortably aware of the gaps and silences in relation to contributors from the Global South, and we look forward to reading work in this area and collaborating with scholars who we hope will, in future, highlight research and activism from areas in the world we have not included. These issues also bring up questions of terminology. For example, while the terms "West" and "Western" are most often deployed unproblematically in the literature and elsewhere, where the authors in this book have used them, we have put these in quotation marks to indicate that these are historical constructs that should be read critically. It is also important to acknowledge that terminology around racialized groups differs across time and space; given geographical specificities, concepts do not always travel easily from one place to another and terminology changes over time, reflecting transformations in discussions about and understandings of racism. For these reasons, we let authors decide on the exact spelling (e.g., capitalized or not) of racialized identities and there are, therefore, differences across individual chapters. As with "West"/"Western," we have chosen to place the term "race" in quotation marks in order to draw particular attention to the constructedness of the concept and to counter the still widespread popular views of racial categories as biologically rather than socially determined. We discuss the term "classical music" in a separate section toward the end of this introduction.

The book focuses on the classical music profession, including institutional training routes into the profession in the form of conservatoires, but we have not included discussions of under-18s education in the volume, for two reasons. First, this issue has already been covered extensively elsewhere, most recently in the *Oxford Handbook for Social Justice in Music Education* (Benedict et al., 2015), as well as other edited collections (Burnard et al., 2015; Frierson-Campbell et al., 2022; Wright et al., 2021). Secondly, we wanted to explore what the classical music profession itself is doing in this area. There is a tendency to shift the blame for the lack of diversity in classical music onto the education pipeline, implying that the profession itself does not need to change. While there is certainly work to be done in classical music education, in this volume we explore ways forward for the profession within the current circumstances, without expecting the inequalities and exclusions that are described in this volume to be solved by education organizations alone.

In line with our focus on industry rather than education, we do not address the question as to why children of diverse cultural backgrounds should study classical music in the first place. Besides going beyond the remit of this volume, the question itself rests on a problematic assumption of a naturalized link between a person's ethnic or indeed any other aspect of their identity, and the music that they listen to or play, in this case between "classical music" as a genre and "Whiteness" (Bull, 2019; Kajikawa, 2019). As explored by Bull (2019), Stirling (2019), Born (2011), and also Chapters 14 and 15 in this volume, there often exist cultural and historical associations between social groups and musical genres that may form a contingent connection or "articulation" (Bull, 2019, pp. 13–14). However, reifying relationships between genres and ethnic identities can serve to draw racialized boundaries around particular musical styles, thus reinforcing exclusionary processes. The question of classical music education for children from diverse backgrounds is therefore one that needs careful thought and more empirical and theoretical investigation elsewhere. Likewise, this volume does not discuss community and amateur classical music-making, and indeed these practices have been less explored in academic literature in relation to inequalities. There is thus a need for more research and potentially activism in this area. We focus on professional, rather than amateur, classical music here as we suggest that there is a particularly urgent policy imperative to diversify cultural practices that receive high levels of public funding, as does professional classical music in the UK and in many other Global North countries (Bull and Scharff, 2017).

As editors, our aim was to center the voices of those who are marginalized in relation to various, and intersecting, axes of difference. Several chapters, for example, show how conservatoires reproduce gendered, racialized, and classed power relations: Jennie Joy Porton's interviews with conservatoire alumni bring to the fore the ways in which class background shapes experiences of higher music education in the UK. Similarly, Clementina Casula's study of Italian conservatoires demonstrates the presence of a class divide in the selection process, taking the form of an urban-rural distinction, and of gender biases. Drawing upon interviews with music teachers working at elite state-funded higher music education institutions in Austria and Germany, Rosa Reitsamer and Rainer Prokop trace how constructions of the "ideal" classical music student reproduce the association of the classical music profession with White middle-class culture. Lastly, David-Emil Wickström focuses on sexual harassment in higher music education in Europe and discusses strategies for addressing power-based abuse in instrumental lessons.

As demonstrated by the chapters on higher music education, this edited collection mainly focuses on issues of "race," gender, class and, to a lesser extent, disability. Charlotte Armstrong discusses disability representation in opera and focuses on a range of issues, such as inaccessible spaces and education programs to demeaning, stereotypical roles and problematic performance practices (see also the contributions by Oliver Vibrans and John Shortell). Other axes of difference, such as age, body positivity, pregnancy, maternity/parenthood, sexuality, and gender identity are not explicitly addressed. These gaps reflect trends in research on classical music, which has explored some axes of difference—such as "race," class and gender—more than others (see Cox, 2021). While there exist discussions on inclusion around gender identity in classical music (see for example Pullinger, 2020), this work is comparatively recent, and more needs to be done to include the voices that are not represented in this collection. This book is, therefore, part of a longer and ongoing conversation about inequalities in classical music. The gaps listed here as well as others that may become apparent over time highlight that this book does not address all forms of exclusions and oppression. It is, instead, an attempt to center research and activism that tackle inequalities and exclusions.

Challenges and developments

We have noticed a shift in urgency in this work in recent years, most notably since the Black Lives Matter movement gained more public and international attention in 2020. While there have always been reflective practitioners in classical music who are trying to make change, these efforts have now intensified and more radical discussions have started to become possible. Nevertheless, challenges remain, particularly around patchy and poor quality data, the high levels of unpaid labor that such diversity work often involves, and a sense of fatalism among many institutions that classical music will always remain elitist due to the long training period required to learn to produce its distinctive aesthetic. This fatalism is only exacerbated by the high levels of economic and social inequality that characterize some of the countries discussed in this volume, including the UK, where we are based. It is not misplaced; but it is perhaps incompatible with acting to make change in the world. As Scharff's (2021) analysis of discussions about inequalities has shown, fatalist statements can also lead to a sense of a lack of agency, especially in a wider neoliberal context. Instead, we suggest that activists need to chart a course between retaining awareness of the structural inequalities that exist while drawing inspiration and hope from examples of positive change, including some that are described in this book.

The question of how to acknowledge structural inequalities while holding on to a sense of possibility of change also emerges from analyses of initiatives that promote "diversity." Among scholarly critiques of diversity discourses, some have argued that diversity initiatives can "actually serve as an ideological function that sustains the institutional Whiteness of the cultural industries even while they claim (often genuinely so) to do something more inclusive" (Saha, 2018, p. 88; see also Mellinger, 2003). As Sara de Benedictis, Kim Allen, and Tracey Jensen (2017, p. 343) have argued in relation to television production, representation, and consumption in the UK, "while class is now 'on the agenda,' this is not necessarily 'progressive.'" Class inequalities can, for example, be openly acknowledged, but simultaneously downplayed, shutting down critical discussion about the media's class politics. Resonating with wider critiques of diversity (e.g., Ahmed, 2007), diversity discourses (Bell and Hartmann, 2007), and discussions about racial hierarchies (e.g., Hastie and Rimmington, 2014), "doing" diversity does not necessarily lead to structural change. In their contributions to this book, Mina Yang and Marianna Ritchey draw attention to these dynamics in their analyses of the LA Philharmonic and neoliberal philanthropy (Yang, this volume) and diversity and inclusion in US classical music discourse (Ritchey, this volume). Mina Yang's chapter weighs the costs and benefits of neoliberal philanthropy and unpacks the neocolonialist subtext that underlies much of the recent wave of classical music social programs. Similarly, Marianna Ritchey takes a critical look at calls to diversify classical music, highlighting the way they exclude considerations of class and prestige. According to Ritchey, classical music is White supremacist and patriarchal, but it is also elitist, and there is a need to radically reframe how we envision both diversity and the music itself. As these chapters and wider research on the cultural and creative industries demonstrate, there is a need to subject diversity initiatives to critical scrutiny, while also trying to move forward and find ways to make change.

Resonating with this argument, this volume evidences not only much more critical scholarship than there was just five years ago but also a vibrant field of activism in classical music. It includes examples of activism taking place on the levels of individuals, of groups and networks, and established organizations and unions. We see all these levels of activism as important for creating change in classical music. On the level of individuals, some chapters describe how the conditions of the author's life as a musician led them into change. For example, Brandon Keith Brown describes how the racism he faced as a Black conductor led him to start educating himself in this area, speaking out, and setting up his own organization. Maiko Kawabata took as her starting point personal experiences of racism and sexism, and conducted research on the new "Yellow Peril" to discuss the forms of marginalization that East Asian musicians experience in professional orchestras in Western Europe. The labor that is involved in trying to do social justice work is described by conductor Cayenna Ponchionne-Bailey—labor that is not often recognized or supported by the working conditions in the industry. This labor can also involve confronting internalized values and ideals that uphold inequalities; as Eleanor Ryan describes, White classical musicians can engage in critical self-reflexive work to make processes of racialization visible to themselves and others. This includes reflecting on the ways in which Whiteness as embodiment, in hierarchies of cultural value or simply a sense of superiority, can be reproduced within cultures of classical music. As she outlines, this reflexive work is likely to be deeply uncomfortable for White musicians, but it is crucial to challenge the reproduction of racialized forms of privilege through classical music practice. Shedding light on a different form of reflexivity and self-awareness, Beata Kowalczyk draws on empirical material collected through multi-sited research among Japanese musicians based in France, Poland, and Japan to trace how they negotiate and navigate racialized discourses of "authenticity" in classical music.

Other chapters detail the experiences of classical musicians and administrators in building networks to create change within their specific fields. Antonio Cuyler, in conversation with Quodesia Johnson, discusses the work of the Black Administrators of Opera group as a form of "Blacktivism," that is, "Black peoples' use of advocacy, personal agency, and political action to actualize racial equity and justice." They discuss Blacktivism in the context of an opera industry that "continues to call on our stories and experiences, our creativity, our communities, our expertise, and our networks without ceding power, demonstrating a reluctance to progress beyond a White-centered approach to opera." Similarly, Beth Higham-Edwards describes how her own lived experience as a woman training and working as a classical percussionist led her to become an activist, and to organize networks for women in minoritized roles in classical music. Other examples of such networks, as discussed below, include Gender Relations in New Music (GRiNM) and Illuminate Women's Music.

Finally, chapters from the Musicians' Union and the Independent Society of Musicians (ISM) in the UK detail what is possible when musicians come together in their thousands to try and make change and improve working conditions. The ISM's chapter describes three strands of their work in the UK, including gathering data on discrimination and harassment in classical music, campaigning for better legal protections from harassment for freelance musicians, and revealing the conditions for musicians that the COVID-19 pandemic brought about, including inequalities, and describing how they have been fighting for musicians' rights during this time. John Shortell from the UK Musicians' Union describes two of their campaigns, on inclusion strategies for disabled musicians, and the Safe Space campaign around sexual harassment in the music industry. However, despite these vibrant examples, such progress is too late for some. In an interview, Anthony Gray, a former classical singer and education worker in classical music institutions, describes how the racism he experienced in classical music led him to leave the industry entirely. He does not retain the hope described by others featured in this book, in part because of what he perceives as a lack of activism in the classical music world, especially compared to his new professional milieu of theater, where opposition, unrest, and demanding change is much more common.

By bringing these activist and practitioner voices together with academic research, we hope that this book will continue an important dialogue between scholarly research and musicians'/activists' work on these issues. This dialogue also has its challenges, when, for example, the rhetoric that is required in activist work to inspire others and to build commitment does not take the tone or use evidence in the ways that are required for scholarly publication. Editing these chapters therefore gave rise to questions about the kinds of voices that get heard in scholarly publications—a difficult balancing act for us in terms of our aim to publish a wide range of voices, but also doing so while operating within the conventions of academic publishing. Facilitating the dialogue between musician/activist and academic voices also sheds light on the different forms of labor, including emotional labor, involved in attempts to undo existing power relations. Various contributions to this volume discuss—sometimes more centrally and sometimes more in passing—the work involved in making change. This work is often time-consuming and yet unpaid, mentally and emotionally draining, and frequently done by those already marginalized (Shim, 2021), and carries with it a lot of responsibility.

The editorial decisions needed to draw these diverse voices together mean that some of the chapters in this book directly contradict or argue against the perspective of others. Reflecting wider debates about the lack of diversity in the classical music field, some authors advocate an approach to inclusion that provides all, including those from marginalized groups, with the opportunities and means to access classical music training and practice to perform to what is considered a "high" standard. Others, including the editors in their own publications and research, want to push further to analyze, critique, and challenge the exclusionary aesthetics of classical music (Bull, 2019), or the racialized, classed, and gendered constructions of the "ideal classical musician" (Scharff, 2018b; see below). For example, some chapters seek to make change in the classical music industry by devising schemes that support Black and racially minoritized classical musicians to succeed within already established industry conventions. These perspectives can be contrasted with the more structural critique in Antonio Cuyler's conversation with Quodesia Johnson, in which Cuyler opens up the question, "In relation to White supremacy, do you think the opera industry is ready to change?" Johnson responds:

If we were ready to do it, it would have been done by now. We've taken the very compliant approach, which is normal in White supremacy culture of: "Let's name all the things that have happened. Let's attribute it to the art form as opposed to our nation, individual selves, or lack of accountability within organizations. Let's look at the systemic things, as opposed to the intentional, systematic exclusion of Black people in the nation and in the field."

These contrasting viewpoints reflect the discussions ongoing in the classical music industry at the present time and as such, as editors, we have not sought to edit out or soften any perspectives that are inconsistent with the stance of other chapters. We have presented these arguments as they are made in the public sphere today in order to allow readers to make their own interpretations, reading across the volume as a whole, and we hope to serve as a resource for critical discussion by students, musicians, and industry workers, and leaders. In order to facilitate such critical discussion, we have added a series of discussion questions at the end of the book for use by teachers, students, activists, industry leaders, and of course musicians themselves, who may wish to set up a reading group to discuss the chapters using these questions as a starting point.

In particular, it would have been possible to focus the entire volume on the issue of "race," due to the complexity and diversity of the different conversations occurring internationally in this area currently. As a result, the chapters that focus on "race" and racial inequalities only skim the surface of the wider academic discourse in this area. We recognize that there is a well-developed conversation around "race" in US musicology (see for example André et al., 2020; Ewell, 2020; Kajikawa, 2019; André, 2018; Maxile, 2008). This conversation is crucially important. But in this volume, we wanted to avoid focusing primarily on the way "race" is mobilized in the US context, which would risk universalizing this context. Therefore, rather than working as a comprehensive introduction to debates, the volume juxtaposes discussions of "race" in a selection of national contexts including the US, UK, Japan, Germany, Austria, Trinidad, and Poland, offering empirical contexts that will, we hope, provide material to contextualize the wider academic debates occurring in critical race theory within a variety of local, national, and international contexts.

To what extent does the music itself have to change?

It might seem like an obvious statement to say that changing the groups of people who create classical music will change the music itself. That is to say, if more diverse groups are involved in producing culture and a wider range of perspectives and identities are represented, the cultural object itself will surely change by having to incorporate these diverse voices. And yet, this point remains, to a degree, an open question in discussions of classical music and diversity, as evidenced by the chapters in this volume. While it would be hard to argue against diversifying the canon of classical music away from the narrow representation of its core texts, the question of whether the sonic ideals, the genre forms, the listening experience, the instruments and other technologies, and the performance and production practices that create the music, need to change, remains open to discussion. One example of the specific form these debates take in classical music is around performances supposedly being required to be "faithful" to the written score and the composer's intentions (Bull, 2019; Goehr, 1992) even when musicologists have shown time and time again that contemporary interpretations and tastes do no such thing and often differ dramatically from "what the composer intended" (Leech-Wilkinson, 2020; Scott, 2014). These live and ongoing debates around notions of "fidelity" to the score are thus also an important part of any discussion of diversity and inclusion, as are the genre conventions of classical music more widely.

The chapters in this volume contribute various angles on these questions. Angela Elizabeth Slater explores what we mean by "the canon" and looks at practical ways in which we can make meaningful change, using the case study of Illuminate Women's Music, a "touring concert series that seeks to highlight the creativity of women both as performers and composers working today, as well as promoting the rich legacy of composition works written by women composers historically." Chi-chi Nwanoku, in relation to the work of the Chineke! Foundation, and Patricia Ann Neely, discussing early music, describe diversifying the canon through recovering the work of composers of color. For Chi-chi Nwanoku a crucial part of transforming classical music is also changing the audience's experience of classical music by allowing audiences to respond to the music however they wish rather than following classical music's habitual listening conventions. However, other chapters illuminate the backlash or difficulties that can occur when changes are introduced. For example, Caitlin Vincent's discussion of revisionist approaches to classic operas describes how even when the musical text remains exactly as written by the composer, changes to the plot of Bizet's *Carmen* were not well received. Kristina Kolbe outlines other experiments in musical change to address inequalities and exclusions, drawing on case studies from Germany of "the commissioning and performance of two new opera works which were intended to be 'intercultural' and broaden the opera's aesthetic profile beyond a standardized notion of opera by bringing together Turkish and "Western" musical elements." Kolbe's chapter "make[s] visible how the opera house's standardized institutional workings ultimately constrained the transgressive potential of the two pieces, risking the remaking of racialized representations and inequalities." As a result, Kolbe argues, tweaking existing institutional practices to become diverse and to bring in "other" musics is not going to be sufficient; rather we need to "fundamentally rethink the standardized production logics that have been entrenched in the "Western" classical music sector." These standardized production logics are also highlighted by Oliver Vibrans, who notes that the standardization of classical instruments works to disable musicians whose bodies don't fit these instruments. It is not only the instruments that are disabling, but also the expectations of the industry, which is "seeking a very particular, specifically educated musician who can execute the work the way they expect" rather than allowing for people whose musical development doesn't follow the path of early, intensive training.

These arguments all point toward musical change as being necessary for social change. However, it is also important to remember that musical innovation does not necessarily lead to social change, but can still entrench existing inequalities, as discussed in Rosanna Lovell and Brandon Farnsworth's chapter on activist network Gender Relations in New Music (GRiNM). As they argue, "new music's understanding of its own 'newness' is understood as a succession of works by individual geniuses," similarly to the work-concept ideal of classical music more generally. However, this legacy needs to be questioned, as

> focusing too much on music as the creation of one singular individual comes at the cost of thinking about it as the product of a specific set of social, historical, institutional, even technological circumstances. Because these conditions have been ignored while universalizing its appeal and accessibility, the contemporary classical music scene has ignored the fact that it strongly favors the music of white, "Western," bourgeois male subjects. (Farnsworth and Lovell, this volume)

However, other chapters detail how composers and musicians from minoritized backgrounds have indeed diversified classical music and in so doing have changed its aesthetic to give voice to identities that have not previously been heard in its spaces. Composer Hannah Kendall describes how she brings instruments such as the harmonica and music box into her compositions, engaging in "creolization" and mixing to change the way instruments sound by "blend[ing] aspects of the Afrological into the "Western" classical context." Similarly, multi-instrumentalist, composer, and music educator Jon Silpayamanant describes his working practices around creating musical hybridity with classically trained and non-classically trained musicians, arguing that classical music has already, and is always being hybridized in different cultural contexts around the world, and has been for centuries due to colonialism. His description of a very different rehearsal style to that described by Kolbe suggests ways forward for a musical and social practice that seeks to embed musical and social diversity in longer-term, deeper ways. More broadly, this approach points to debates about the extent to which participants from demographics underrepresented in classical music may be expected or choose to assimilate its deeply entrenched and often exclusionary cultural norms and that depend on forms of bodily disciplining that have been argued to reproduce exclusions along the lines of class, "race," and gender (Bull, 2019).

Introducing classical music studies

Throughout the volume, authors and interviewees have not generally defined how they are understanding the term "classical music." As editors, our use of the perhaps taken-for-granted term "classical music" as an organizing category requires explanation. In our previous research, we have used this term because it reflects how our research participants talked about their musical practice (Bull and Scharff, 2021, p. 6). We continue to use it here not only because it exists as a commonly understood term in public discourse, but also because it is recognized in cultural policy (e.g., Cox, 2021) as well as in emerging discussions of classical music as an "industry" (Dromey and Haferkorn, 2018). However, similarly to Beckerman and Boghassian's recent edited volume on the classical music industry in the US (2021), precisely what this term designates varies across the chapters in this volume. Furthermore, as explored above, discussing diversity means calling into question the boundaries of what counts as classical music. This variability is important, as it opens up space for classical music to change over time and space, moving beyond ideals of a transcendent, unchanging "museum" of musical works (Goehr, 1992) toward a living practice that changes according to who is playing it, where it is being played, and the purpose for which it is being played.

It is clear, therefore, that any definition of classical music needs to allow for aesthetic, social, and institutional change. It is for this reason that we argue that rather than specify the particular characteristics or conventions that define classical music,[1] we instead theorize it as a genre, in this way enabling these changes to be captured within our understanding of the term. As outlined in Bull and Scharff (2021), we draw on approaches from popular music studies that use genre

> to understand the relationship between the social and the aesthetic by studying the circulation of common "orientations, expectations and conventions" (Neale, 1980, p. 19) between producers, audiences, industry, and texts. This approach draws together analysis of the conditions of production of cultural objects, the aesthetic properties of the objects themselves, and their reception.
> (Negus, 1999; Toynbee, 2000; Bull and Scharff, 2021, p. 3)

Genre theory affords exploration of "how identities (and inequalities) are formed or mobilized through genre; and the role of institutions in shaping genre" (Bull and Scharff, 2021, p. 4). Indeed, the centrality of institutions to genre theory is a further reason why this approach is helpful; both historically and today, classical music's education and performance institutions have been formative in shaping and reproducing its social and aesthetic conventions. Furthermore, the relationality of genre as a concept (Brackett, 2016) whereby genres and subgenres are understood in relation to each other is important in making visible hierarchies of value whereby classical music's value—educationally, socially—is constructed through what it is not, and through who it excludes. Indeed, in relation to new music in the US, as Anne Shreffler argues, "the claim of boundarylessness"—such as ideas of "genre-free music-making"—"masks the stubborn boundaries that remain in the new music scene, particularly those of gender and race" (2019, pp. 444 and 446). It also masks the ways in which to be boundaryless is a form of privilege (2019, p. 449). Similarly, as Bull argues (in relation to classical music in the UK), "the way in which 'classical music' is defined is important—and contested—because the boundaries drawn around it work to store value in this space" (2019, p. xvii). The lens of genre can make such boundaries and boundary-drawing visible by drawing attention to the processes of categorization that are occurring, whether tacitly or overtly. Therefore, we suggest that genre theory constitutes a fertile theoretical framework for understanding and explaining the origins and persistence of inequalities in classical music practice.

In order to pursue these questions as well as to draw together the field of critical enquiry as represented by the chapters in this volume, we suggest the term "classical music studies." This interdisciplinary field enables the study of classical music to draw on, but also move beyond the fields of musicology and ethnomusicology, as well as music education, and bring it into dialogue with cultural studies, sociology, disability studies, gender studies, critical race studies, and other disciplines that have extensively discussed the questions of diversity and inclusion that we consider in this book. The latter fields have a history of engaging with social justice issues, drawing on a range of theoretical, analytical, and empirical approaches. These are also fields that have evolved from, or in dialogue with, social justice movements and, as such, offer a range of tools to examine existing inequalities, understand why they persist, and point to ways to make change. By issuing a call for the interdisciplinary field of "classical music studies," we argue that questions of diversity and inclusion are not subsidiary or additional concerns within the field but instead are integral to it; in the history of classical music's institutions in the UK, for example, questions of inclusions and exclusions over class, gender, "race," and disability have been central (see Bull, 2019; Fuller, 1998).

Furthermore, forms of hybridization of classical music that have occurred during and through processes of colonization also complexify our understanding of what "classical music" is. As Laudan Nooshin has noted:

> What needs to be folded into an understanding of the term ["Western" classical music] is how a music that was originally European has taken on a multitude of forms and meanings globally; and this applies both to the performance of the Euro-(North) American "classical" repertoire outside Europe and North America, and to the compositional work of composers from "elsewhere." (Nooshin, 2011, p. 296)

In addition to such processes of hybridization, such a term can also take as a point of exploration the relationship between this field and other so-called classical musics outside "Western" classical music, which are not included in this book. Overall, we suggest that to understand the institutional, aesthetic, and social conventions and structures that have shaped the phenomenon we understand as "classical music" today, is to explore—and attempt to address and unpack—these legacies and relations.

We hope that the chapters in this book go some way toward illuminating these questions of what classical music is, what it could be, and how we might make change. The first section of the book, "The Making of Classical Musicians," explores the role of conservatoires and higher music education in reproducing classed, gendered, and racialized exclusions. Looking at a wider range of classical music institutions, the second section, "Problematizing Institutional Change" casts a critical eye on how classical music institutions have sought to implement change, shedding light on the benefits and pitfalls of initiatives that attempt to make classical music more "diverse." Moving away from institutions, the third section, "Marginalized Voices," features those who occupy a marginalized position in classical music, highlighting a range of exclusions based on gender, class, disability, and "race." The fourth section, "Racial Inequalities," takes a focused look at processes of racialization by presenting data, experiences, and insights from a range of geographical contexts. While all chapters touch on what can be done to make change, the two final sections have a more explicit focus on activism. Section Five explores forms of activism that have emerged from individual experience and initiative, whereas Section Six centers on networks, alliances, and campaigning work by industry bodies. In the afterword, Gillian Moore, Director of Music at London's Southbank Centre, reflects on what the volume means for music industry leaders. All in all, the chapters shed light on different forms of inequality and exclusion in classical music, but also point to ways in which these can be addressed and tackled.

Note

1. For example, in their work on equality and diversity in classical music, Arts Council England have defined classical musicians as those learning or playing symphonic classical music instruments (Cox, 2021).

I
THE MAKING OF CLASSICAL MUSICIANS

1
Class and Gender Inequalities in the Recruitment of Classical Musicians

Reflections on the Case of Italian Music Conservatoires

Clementina Casula

Introduction: The role of vocational education in the making of professional musicians

Vocational education plays a crucial role in the making of professionals by initiating them into the knowledge and techniques required to offer expert services, accrediting this knowledge in the eyes of their clients (through examinations, licensing, or registration), and socializing them to context-specific cultural conceptions of the professional role (Hughes, 1956; Abbott, 1988). In the arts field, however, vocational education has received limited attention from scholars, possibly because of its ambiguous formal link with the artistic labor market where certifications are not necessarily required (Frederickson and Rooney, 1990), not to mention the cultural rootedness of the belief that professional success in the field mainly relates to inborn individual talent, downplaying the role of education or other social factors (Bataille et al., 2020).

However, beyond formal requirements for entering artistic fields, there are also "implicit and informal requirements, which in practice makes formal education almost compulsory" (Svensson, 2015, p. 4). Legitimated organizations for the training of artists, such as music conservatoires, socialize pupils to the roles and shared rules and values of the profession, facilitating their access to and staying within the networks defining specific art worlds (Becker, 1982), where artists compete for recognition nurturing their reputations with symbolic capital (Bourdieu, 1992). This holds particularly true for those art worlds, such as ballet or classical music, whose aesthetical canons are culturally deep-seated and their faithful reproduction is kept alive through the initiation of pupils into a tradition requiring the disciplined embodiment of specific techniques, rules, and values from an early age (Laillier, 2017; Scharff, 2018; Bull, 2019). Socialization into these traditions leads future artists to conceive not only the socially built definitions of musical taste, practices, and repertoires as neutral and universal

(Weber, 1992), but also the social inequalities backing the mechanisms of their reproduction (Coulangeon, 2004; Wagner, 2015).

In this chapter, I will consider the theme of exclusions and inequalities in the recruitment of classical musicians trained within Italian conservatoires of music. Drawing on my research (Casula, 2018a) and adopting an approach that investigates the influence of institutional assets on the behavior of individual and collective actors (Powell and DiMaggio, 1991), I will first contextualize the modern evolution of these organizations for the vocational training of musicians—which originated in 16th-century Italy as charities—from their marginal collocation within the national education system at the end of the 19th century to their upgrade to its highest tier more than 100 years later. Then, drawing on official statistics and empirical data, I will discuss the issue of inequalities in the recruitment of conservatoire students, focusing on the dimensions of class and gender. My conclusions advocate that Italian conservatoires, still ongoing a profound reform, consider issues related to inequalities and exclusions a matter of concern for state-legitimized organizations training musicians and operating within a democratic society.

The hybrid status of Italian conservatoires within the national system of education

Despite the strong association of Italian culture with classical music, nurtured by the international fame achieved by Italian musicians of the past and present, the integration of music within legitimate national culture, codified within the system of education, represents a problematic and still unresolved process. The elitist approach of the national education system adopted after the unification of the country (1861) was strengthened by the Fascist reforms of the idealist minister Giovanni Gentile, imbued with dualisms between "culture and labor, education and vocational training, mass education and the education of the ruling elites and, finally, humanistic and scientific knowledge" (Grimaldi and Serpieri, 2012, p. 151). Music education, historically associated with medieval workshop training,[1] was confined to state-funded conservatoires, reorganized under common regulations that defined their operations for nearly a century (Maione, 2005). The consequences of this confinement soon emerged in terms of the standard good technical level, but weak general culture, of musicians exclusively trained within conservatoires, shaped according to the virtuoso profile, and the poor musical culture offered by standard educational paths to other citizens. Since the 1960s, in the face of growing international legitimacy of music training as part of citizens' education, the problem of inadequate opportunities within the national education system was addressed in a lengthy parliamentary debate discussing the possibility of introducing it in all educational levels so as to create an integrated pathway. In the absence of parliamentary agreement, the government found a stop-gap measure with the opening of new conservatoires funded by the state or local authorities, allowing the admission of a large number of students looking at music training mainly in recreational rather than vocational terms (see Table 1.1). This radical change in the characteristics and size of the educational demand, however, was not followed by a revision of the offer: although favorable to staff expansion, conservatoire teachers resisted pressures for a redefinition of their mission, perceiving it as a de-qualification of their cultural capital, and continued to reproduce the model to which they had been socialized.

Only at the end of the 20th century did parliament adopt a reform law (n. 508/1999) inserting conservatoires of music and other state-recognized academies of dance, theater, visual arts and design, within a system of Higher Artistic and Musical Education (AFAM) set in the tertiary level of education which, until then, had been the exclusive realm of the university system. While the original draft law, following the pyramidal model used in many other countries, provided for the advancement of only a selection of the nearly 80 Italian conservatoires to the tertiary level of education, the powerful action of the artists and musicians' trade union (UNAMS) attained the inclusion of all of the institutes, with the aim of upgrading the economic and social status of their teachers to that of university professors. Following the Bologna process promoting the establishment of a European Space of Higher Education, conservatoires gradually adapted to the regulations of universities: they widened their curricular offer to include a variety of non-classical and theoretical courses and adopted the training credits logic required to facilitate the international conversion of undergraduate,

Table 1.1 Italian conservatoires of music: number of institutes, students, and percentage of female (F) students in selected years

school/academic year	# institutes	# students	% F students
1926/27	15	4,659	49.7
1946/47	25	3,032	45.9
1966/67	35	6,026	42.5
1986/87	69	33,884	48.9
2006/07	78	44,927	55.3
2019/20	78	26,546	41.2

Source: Istat and Statistical office MIUR-AFAM (selected years); data for 2019/20 refer to students of the academic (AFAM) level.

graduate, and postgraduate courses. In the absence of an adequate offer of basic music training within the national education system,[2] conservatoires were also temporarily allowed to organize pre-academic courses.

My study on Italian conservatoires (Casula, 2018a) offered a sociological interpretation of the radical change brought by the 1999 reform which, though it managed to break through the institutional inertia that characterized the institutes and adapt them to the rules governing higher education systems in Europe, was unable to integrate them into a comprehensive pathway of music training within the national education system. The debate over the reform—mostly confined within conservatoires—has seen a polarization between those for and against in terms of the efficiency and effectiveness of the reform vis à vis the traditional order. Issues of inequalities in the production of classical musicians, however, have not been discussed, as if they were not a matter of concern for the institutes. In the following paragraphs, I will argue that it is indeed a relevant issue to be taken into account by public educational institutions, in order to actively endorse more integrated and equitable labor markets and societies.

The discussion will be mainly based on the analysis of official statistics and qualitative semi-structured interviews and focus groups I conducted with nearly 100 conservatoire students and teachers and professional musicians trained in Italy. Starting with personal contacts, the interviews proceeded from the spring of 2013 to the winter of 2017 through a snowball sampling, asking interviewees for further contacts, selected trying to give account of the main variables describing the population considered (especially with reference to disciplinary specialization, gender, size, and location of the institution).[3] After obtaining participants' informed consent, interviews were tape-recorded, transcribed *verbatim*, and analyzed following an inductive and comparative approach, based on the coding and assessment of the main subcategories and thematic areas that emerged (Brinkmann and Kvale, 2015). Questions aimed at reconstructing interviewees' musical path, focusing on its main phases, from recruitment to training, entrance, and time spent in the labor market: this also allowed me to identify mechanisms continuing to reproduce class or gender inequalities within an internal conservatoire hierarchy, drawing distinctive educational paths for future classical musicians, which will be discussed in the following paragraphs.

Social class and musical hierarchies in student recruitment

The regulations adopted at the beginning of the 20th century to govern Italian national conservatoires of music were primarily defined to shape the precocious training of selected students exiting from primary schools, who—if planning to become professional musicians—were not expected to engage in standard educational paths, nor in other activities distracting them from musical practice. The curricular offer concentrated around a limited number of courses associated with the main practices and repertoires of the classical canon, presented in a list revealing an internal order of musical prestige, with courses ranging from those strongly associated with artistic genius and soloist virtuosity to those with a more accompanying and subsidiary role: composition, singing, organ, piano, harp, violin, viola, cello, double bass, flute, oboe, clarinet, bassoon, horn, trumpet and trombone, and band instrumentation.[4] These rules remained the same even after the 1960s when, with the creation of new institutes around the country, the student population grew exponentially, widening the proportion of pupils interested in music education more for recreational than professional reasons, attracted by different musical genres and following standard educational paths contemporaneously.

To enter a conservatoire, candidates have to pass a formally meritocratic selection process, managed by an internal committee of teachers often chaired by the director, evaluating their musical aptitudes and their compatibility with the favored course. Our interviews, including various generations of students enrolled within conservatoires from the 1960s to today, allowed us to identify how the committee used its discretionary powers to influence the selection on the basis of social factors.

One of the most influential variables appears to be students' family background: those recruited to the most prestigious and requested courses of the classical offer (such as piano and violin classes) often come from urban upper classes or musical families possessing the economic and cultural resources needed to arrange in advance for private music lessons with teachers connected to the conservatoire network, as illustrated in the following quote.

> **Pianist, female, 35 years:**
> The teacher with whom I had private lessons took me to her conservatoire teacher because there was an opening in her class and she had many requests. I took lessons from her for nearly three to four months. She told me from the start that she was giving private lessons to other children at the same time and, in August, before the admission test at the conservatoire, she would decide who to choose among us. To my great joy she chose me, and I did the admission process already having the indication that I would enter in her class.

Preliminary musical abilities developed by children coming from rural areas, often applying to the conservatoire after having started to play with local bands—ensembles associated with amateur proficiency and all-encompassing repertoires, largely diffused in the rural areas of Italy[5]—were not fully convertible into those appreciated by the institutes. In the following quote from the autobiography of an internationally known jazz musician born in a rural village of Italy, the selection committee refuses the candidate, labeling him as "unmusical," possibly identifying "musicality"—exclusively associated with the classical canon—as a distinctive trait of urban upper classes (Bull, 2019).

> **Jazz trumpet player, male, 55 years:**
> I applied to enter the trumpet class. Each candidate had to take an aptitude test. The test consisted of a series of banal and utterly idiotic rhythmic exercises. I was deemed to be unfit. I was "not musical," was the sentence. The truth was that I did not come from a bourgeois family of [the city] nor did I have influential friends.... My mother and I did not get discouraged, however, and thanks to one of the more open-minded teachers I managed to enter on my second attempt, but the story was actually ridiculous. (Fresu, 2009, p. 45, author's translation)

Candidates from rural areas admitted to the conservatoire are more frequently assigned to the less requested courses, at the bottom of the prestige hierarchy of the classical canon. Those choices, however, are formally justified by the selection committee on the basis of objective musical or physiological grounds, as in the following quote, where a candidate playing several instruments is only allowed admission to the low-enrollment trombone class of his local band director, on the grounds of a supposed physical compatibility with the instrument.

> **Conservatoire teacher, trombone class, male, 45 years:**
> I played the drums, keyboards, and the guitar.... So I told the director of my local band, who was also teaching trombone at the conservatoire: "I want to enroll at the conservatoire for the guitar class"—"No, there's no place for guitar" [he replied]—"Then for the piano class"—"Nooooo, there's no place for piano"—he pretended to be informed.... "Let me see . . ."—he looked at me—"You have the trombone lips!" Do you understand? He needed young pupils in his class.

The musical hierarchy defined through the student recruitment process—often reproduced by social distinction practices separating those from the cities and those from rural areas—might be reversed as students' training progresses. In the following quote, a trumpet player (originally wishing to play the violin) recalls the greater proficiency shown during the orchestral training lessons by his wind session, mostly made up of students used to playing together within local bands, vis à vis the string session, uniting colleagues trained as virtuoso soloists.

Music Conservatoire teacher, jazz trumpet player, male, 40 years:
C.C.—*In your experience [as a conservatoire student], were there hierarchies between the instruments?*

Absolutely! There was a great deal of segregation, not only between violin and wind students, but above all between townspeople and country people—but the things went hand in hand.... Segregation was mainly concentrated in the first years, but by the time we had to follow orchestral training, for us [wind students] it was revenge, because the conductor was pissed off with the strings, who couldn't make two notes in time, while we were thriving because, playing in local bands, we'd been used to do this for a long time.

This "revenge of the lower classes" can be interpreted with reference to the different structuring of musical hierarchies, according to the organizational context of reference. At the educational level, piano and violin rank at the top of the prestige scale because they are positively associated both with the romantic ideal of the virtuoso soloist and upper-class distinction. At the occupational level, however, this hierarchy is often reframed: wind instruments may assume a new prominence within symphonic orchestras, as they are more often involved in solo parts vis à vis the more numerous colleagues of the string sessions (Pegourdie, 2015), or may find positions also within non-classical music ensembles. Given the extremely limited number of pianists or violinists managing to realize a career as concert virtuosos (Wagner, 2015), upper-class families—at first encouraging their children's education in classical music—usually opposed the prospect of a professional path in music, perceived to be at high risk for social downgrading (as in the following quote).

Music Conservatoire teacher, pianist, male, 55:
My grandmother played the piano, although not professionally: in her family, everyone played; it was a habit of the time—seven brothers, each one [playing] a different instrument.... In Vienna, her father bought her a grand piano that we still have since 1901.... They were a wealthy family living in a village in northern Italy with an Austro-Hungarian musical culture.... My mother also played the piano, but no one played professionally.
C.C.—*How was your decision to become a professional pianist received in your family?*
A drama! I mean, they loved it as long as I was the good son who only listened to classical music instead of rock, and so on.... but as I said, "No, I want to be a pianist!"

The influence of social factors in the recruitment process did not end after the 1999 reform, as we can see from the interviewee of the following quote, a young boy from a lower-class immigrant[6] family, who was recruited for pre-academic courses in the horn class (lacking candidates), with the usual pretext of his physical compatibility with the instrument.

> **Conservatoire student, horn class, male, 15 years:**
> I asked [the Commission for admission]: "What instruments are available?" Because if there was the guitar or flute, I would have chosen them.... But they told me that my lips were suitable for the horn, because they are thin, so I thought: "Since I don't know what to choose, I'll do what they advise me to do."

Gradually, however, the influence of teachers in the recruitment for the classical courses seems to weaken, due to a variety of reasons: the more impersonal and bureaucratic role assigned to teachers within reformed conservatoires, the oversupply of traditional classical music training in the face of growing demand for non-canonical and non-classical music courses, the ongoing reshaping of the cultural borders defining career strategies, repertoires, and professional identities of classical musicians (Casula, 2018b). This should not be necessarily taken as a sign of the definitive removal of class inequalities in the informal rules governing conservatoires' recruitment of classical musicians. A new pattern, to be empirically explored, may emerge from the reduced opportunities for young people from the lower classes to access the classical music profession, in light of the national education system's limited provision of the basic musical training required to access conservatoires after the reform and increasingly achieved privately by families possessing the necessary economic and cultural resources.

Female students and classical music education

Since the beginning of the 20th century, women have made up almost half of the student population of Italian conservatoires (see Table 1.1). This data seem to offer a bright picture of the relationship between gender equality and recruitment in classical music education, but further investigation reveals how this balance relies on deep-rooted discrimination.

The distribution of students in curricular courses by gender, in fact, shows how, for most of the 20th century, girls were concentrated within a very limited number of courses of the classical offer, responding to the ideals of feminine gracefulness and respectability corresponding to their condition of submission to masculine authority (DeNora, 1995; Green, 1997). Female students' adherence to the gendered prescriptions of the classical canon was particularly evident at the beginning of the century, but even at the end of the 1960s—in a period of significant socio-cultural changes for Western societies—their educational choices appear to have been guided by traditional gender stereotypes: more than half of them enrolled in piano (57%), followed by singing (14%), violin (9%), or harp courses (5%), with only 8% of them in less predictable instrumental courses (and their participation in composition grew, chosen by 7%).

Only at the end of the century did significant changes in female educational paths emerge: data for the end of the 1990s show how the gendered prescriptions of the classical canon still endured (with 35% of all female conservatoire students recruited in piano and 9% in singing classes) but widened to include instruments originally precluded for women within fully legitimated feminine musical practices: the feminization of violin courses became more noticeable (14%), and the flute became one of the favorite instruments of girls (with 8% of their total preferences); moreover, a significant proportion of female students (34%) accessed a large variety of courses of the classical canon offering higher expectations of insertion within the labor market. This trend seems to have persisted after the reform: 15 years since its launch, female students' choices have expanded to a wider variety of classical canon courses (after violin and flute, also cello and clarinet), although they still avoid instruments at the lower levels of its hierarchy.[7] Male students' choices confirm a greater variety in the choice of classical courses, extending to the new curricula introduced to integrate the traditional canonical offer. They also show a greater presence within non-classical courses and academic courses, holding a more direct link to professionalization, where the participation of female students appears more limited (see Table 1.1).

The issue of implicit gender biases still limiting the recruitment of young generations of female conservatoire students and precluding them from full access to the classical music profession was further explored in the interviews. In the following excerpt, a double bass teacher tells us about one of the few girls assigned to his class for pre-academic courses, who refused to even touch the instrument on the basis of an irrational fear—a feeling often experienced by women having to use artifacts strongly symbolically associated with masculinity (Wajcman, 1991). Although in this case the gender-typing of the instrument relates to the girl's socialization rather than to the organization's prescriptions or teacher's biases, the teacher appears unprepared to recognize it as a matter to be managed at the organizational level, treating it rather as an idiosyncratic reaction of the individual pupil.

> **Conservatoire teacher, double bass class, male, 60:**
> A little girl showed up, poor girl, last year [*he reproduces their dialogue, imitating the girl's whining voice*]: "They put me in this classroom. . . ."; "Come on, let's try [the double bass]"; "No, noo!"; "But, look, it doesn't bite: it's an instrument"—I swear to you, she did not even touch it!—"No, no, I want to play the clarinet!" Thus I took her to my [clarinet] colleague: "I don't know, she must

have the 'doublebassophobia': she hates the double bass, I cannot keep her in my classroom!"

In the interviews with girls from rural areas, a sort of "double standard" emerges where the gender association of instrumental practices seems related to the music world of reference. The girl of the following excerpt was recruited to play the tuba, an instrument she had loved since she was little, in the band of her village: only open to male members until the 1970s, local bands today usually assign instruments on the basis of members' requests and the mutable needs of the ensemble. The same young woman, however, when studying classical music privately or at the conservatoire, felt compelled to follow the conventional prescriptions of the classical canon regarding female gracefulness and respectability (Bull, 2019), opting for piano and viola courses.

> **Conservatoire student, viola class, female, 18:**
> C.C.: *How did you get to the tuba?*
> The tuba is . . . [*she laughs*] a love that I have had since I was little, since I was playing the piano . . . but I saw it as something a bit difficult [to realize].[. . .] I knew that there was a local band [in the village]. . . . I went there and asked how I could start: I did a year with a teacher [of the band] and then I carried on, so now I play there also.

Although adopting formally gender-neutral rules in the selection of students, Italian conservatoires informally endorsed the classical canon's restriction of female students' training to those courses associated with conventional feminine stereotypes and roles, strongly limiting their access to professional paths in classical music throughout the 20th century. In recent decades, these limits have been increasingly widened, following contemporary changes within society that have legitimated women's access to a wider variety of musical practices of the classical canon. The persistence of biases in the recruitment of female students, however, is suggested by their reduced presence both in non-classical music courses and in the higher steps of music education, aspects that deserve further investigation, as do other forms discouraging their full participation in the music profession (Buscatto, 2010; Scharff, 2018; Casula, 2019).

Conclusions: Toward comprehensive, equitable, and inclusive models of music education

With music assigned a limited and marginal role within the Italian public education system, conservatoires have constituted virtually the only comprehensive offer of musical training, attracting a wide range of potential candidates in their early youth and preparing those of them managing to complete a selective course of study to become professional musicians. The candidate recruitment process, although formally adopting meritocratic rules, in practice often reproduced social inequalities naturalized over time within the classical canon. As seen in this chapter, even in the final decades of the 20th century, social variables such as class or gender continued to influence the educational and professional path of candidates aspiring to enter the conservatoire. The recruitment tended to assign candidates from musical or upper-class urban families the more prestigious courses, associated with the ideal of the virtuoso soloist but also a source of cultural distinction; boys from rural and lower urban classes were often assigned to the courses at the bottom of the classic canon hierarchy, with an accompanying and subsidiary musical role, but with occupational perspectives offering a chance of social mobility. Girls were more often associated with courses responding to the ideals of feminine grace and respectability, strongly limiting their professional chances.

Gradually the strength of this logic has weakened, but more as a result of wider cultural and social changes involving new generations of students and families and teachers, than of any internal reflection of the organizations upon their outdated values, rules, and functions.

Only at the very end of the 20th century did a law radically revise the secular order of Italian conservatoires, inserting them alongside other state-recognized academies of applied arts within the tertiary level of education. Their curricular offerings widened to include non-canonical and non-classical courses, and they adapted to the general rules governing the university system. Twenty years later, Italian conservatoires still face several important challenges: the high number of institutions and staff devoted to the specialized training of professional musicians, in front of an artistic labor market offering quite limited and very often precarious employment conditions (for poorly paid, unprotected, and insecure jobs); the problematic recruitment of music students at the academic level, in the face of inadequate pre-academic music training within the national system of education; the need to adopt meritocratic procedures for staff selection, against the resistance of vested interests. Within those challenges, it is fundamental for Italian conservatoires to also include the active promotion of equity and inclusion as a collective responsibility[8] in order to become not only more effective, but also more fair institutions.

Notes

1. The origin of Italian conservatoires dates back to the 16th century, when religious institutes were founded to *conservare* (i.e., protect) orphans and deprived children, hosting them and offering them vocational training. In the 17th century, when music production expanded, music training turned out to be a profitable investment

for conservatoires: the growing quality of teaching increased the amount of private donations and fee-paying pupils enrolling to study music at the charities, whose name became distinctively associated with professional music education (Delfrati, 2017).
2. High schools of music and dance have been recently introduced within the national education system, but their sparse distribution and limited curricular offer has not resolved the issue of the absence of a pre-academic layer of public music training.
3. The empirical part of the study—which also comprised a questionnaire completed by 17% of a population of nearly 6,000 full-time conservatoire teachers—complied in all its phases with the requirements of the ethical codes shared at the international level by the main associations for the social sciences and with the rules set by Italian and European law for the collection, analysis, and protection of personal data for statistical and social research aims.
4. Some extracurricular courses were added in the second half of the century to this original core, which the 1999 reform broadly revised, providing a wide list of courses, presented in alphabetical order within distinct disciplinary areas and going beyond the classical canon.
5. More than 2,360 local bands are recorded in a website dedicated to Italian musical bands (https://www.bandamusicale.it/, last accessed on April 1, 2021). On the contribution of local bands to breaking the gender-typing of instruments, see also Casula (2021).
6. The history of modern Italy was characterized by huge migratory flows of Italian citizens seeking work and fortune abroad. Only from the last decades of the 20th century did Italy become the destination of growing numbers of foreign nationals, and the debate over ethnic and racial dynamics within society started to develop, more recently with reference to "second generation" immigrants, though primarily within the field of pop music production (Thomassen, 2010), not yet in the classical one.
7. During the 2014–15 academic year, boys constituted nearly 77% of the students in horn and bassoon courses, 90% in trumpet and trombone or tuba, 91% in double bass, 94% in percussion courses (Casula, 2018a).
8. This could be realized by the organizations, for instance, adopting specific plans to promote anti-discrimination policies foreseeing measures to promote and grant equality of opportunity (such as blind auditions, quota systems, or mentoring initiatives), the adoption of ethical codes (preventing or sanctioning sexual misconduct from staff), and educational initiatives to develop staff and student awareness of the issue as a collective matter.

2
The Role of Music Conservatoires in the Making of Classical Music Careers

Rainer Prokop and Rosa Reitsamer

Music conservatoires play a pivotal role in deciding which individuals gain access to the classical music profession as they offer artistic training alongside performance opportunities, generally seen as an indispensable prerequisite for entering this profession. However, the course for the classical music profession is usually set in childhood. Most classical musicians begin learning an instrument at an early age and move into intensive training during adolescence to compete professionally, as Wagner's (2015) empirical study on educating young violinists has shown. Research has also highlighted that children of color and/or from disadvantaged socio-economic backgrounds have to a lesser extent access to primary and secondary music education programs and extracurricular music activities (DeLorenzo, 2012) and that classical music practice is associated with middle-class culture (Bull and Scharff, 2017; Scharff, 2018a). Bradley (2016), Hess (2021), and others have theorized the link between music education and middle-class culture from a historical perspective, arguing that music education was employed as a civilizing force within the colonial project to deliberately cultivate the values of the middle class. As Gustafson (2009) explains, in order to convey these values, from the beginning of the 1830s onward songs were taught in schools to foster patriotic sentiments and to impose strict notions of physical comportment and compliance on children, while Black and Indigenous musics were omitted in music curricula and placed as inferior to "Western" art music. This cultivation of middle-class values "served to elevate whiteness and further participate in the minoritizing process [of Black and Indigenous people] inherent in internal colonialism" (Hess, 2021, p. 28). Classical music institutions, including conservatoires founded in the late 18th and during the first half of the 19th century, significantly contributed to cementing the whiteness of music education through reinforcing colonialist epistemologies in music (Bradley, 2016).

The link between white middle-class culture and music education is reproduced until today and affects access to performance-based school ensembles and classical music practice in general. As Elpus and Abril (2011) found in their research on the demographic profile of high school band, choir, and orchestra students in the United States, Hispanic students and students from lower socio-economic groups were underrepresented in music ensembles; Black music students, however, appeared to be well represented in relation to the general student population. Regarding the overall findings, Elpus and Abril (2011) emphasize that "white students were found to be a significantly overrepresented group in school music ensembles" (p. 141) and over 60% of all music students were female. Similar results were found by Scharff (2015) in her study on inequalities in classical music education in England where "women currently make up around half of the student population at five UK conservatories" (p. 7). Despite this feminization of the classical music profession that has been more pronounced than in other music worlds, such as that of jazz, rock, and pop (Casula, 2019, p. 3), inequalities continue to persist in the classical music world. As Bull (2019) notes in her study on class and youth music education in England, the social scene, the continuity between home and school culture, as well as the type of long-term investment required to learn a classical music instrument, tend to support upper middle-class youth in pursuing a career as classical musicians. This support was evident, for example, in the fact that lower-middle-class students in Bull's study generally felt less comfortable and confident and were more likely to experience bullying by instrumental teachers than their upper middle-class peers. Moreover, minoritized groups are required to negotiate racist stereotypes during music education and professional work (Yang, 2007; Leppänen, 2015), and women and gender non-conforming musicians need to conform to the oppressive binary construction of gender and bourgeois notions of heteronormative femininity to advance a career as classically trained musician (Green, 1997; Bull, 2019).

This chapter aims to deepen our understanding of the role of music conservatoires in the production and reproduction of social inequalities by exploring the admissions process, particularly the cultures of valuation at entrance exams. Our research is informed by a constructivist perspective that considers musical performances and desirable personal qualities such as creativity, musicality, and artistic personality not as "facts," but rather as socially constructed and attributed within valuation processes embedded in specific social and local contexts. Consequently, artistic quality and creativity cannot be comprehensively explained from a composition or a musical performance; they are negotiated through the definition of criteria of valuation and the construction and attribution of value.

Theoretical approaches

Bourdieu's theory of fields and his conceptions of cultural and symbolic capital as well as habitus have been widely applied to examine how value is fabricated, evaluated, and attributed to individuals, actions, and things in diverse artistic and musical fields. Studying the production and consumption of 19th-century French literature and art, Bourdieu (1993) emphasizes the role of critics and evaluators as gatekeepers in the production of symbolic capital for specific cultural goods and demonstrates how these actors struggle to impose competing definitions of legitimate literary or artistic work. For Bourdieu, the ability to impose criteria of valuation and to consecrate particular artists and their works is a major stake in the fields of cultural production, as it allows actors to reproduce their own positions in the field. Following Bourdieu's theory of fields, Nylander (2014), in his ethnographic study of admission exams at two jazz schools in Sweden, argues that the outcome of the exams depended on both "the rules of entry" (Bourdieu, 1993) as they were deployed and appropriated by the teachers, and the social and musical dispositions that the candidates bring to the auditions and how they match the former. Similarly, Saner et al. (2016) describe admission exams at Swiss art colleges as a process of "*mutual* coordination between the *organizational* habitus of the selecting institution and the *individual* or *familial* habitus of the candidate to be selected" (p. 61, emphasis in original, translation ours).

For McCormick (2015), Bourdieu's theoretical framework is little helpful to analyze the valuation culture at international music competitions, as to her understanding the actions of the judges as well as those of the competition participants cannot be comprehensively explained in terms of instrumental rationality, position-taking, and status accumulation. McCormick draws attention to the formation of the self as a crucial topic for the study of valuation cultures (Lamont, 2009) by examining the judges' beliefs about the value and purpose of competition, the reasons for participating in this institution, and their shared understanding that the performers should provoke a particular emotional experience for them. In order to capture these intersubjective dimensions in the valuation process, McCormick refers to Hennion's (2005) performative approach to taste (in contrast to Bourdieu's reduction of taste to class position) and his concept of "attachment" to show how judges were attentive to the competition participants' musical performances, connected to their music, and invested in it.

Recently, scholars have also examined the role of subjectivity in (re)producing inequalities in higher music and art education and the cultural and creative industries (e.g., Scharff, 2018b) in general. Drawing upon Foucault's understanding of subjectivity and power, Burke and McManus (2011), in their study on admission practices at art and design schools in England, suggest considering subjectivity as "the relational, discursive, and embodied process of identity formation; of becoming recognized as a legitimate subject" (p. 704). The authors found that "worthy" students were ascribed with characteristics historically associated with white, Eurocentric forms of masculinity such as the "unusual" and "being creative." Consequently, the selection interviews became a space in which subjective constructions of value were played out in ways that "reinforced classed, gendered, and racialized inequalities and mis/recognitions about who is (not) seen as having potential" (p. 707). Allen et al. (2012) identified similarly powerful and tacit mechanisms of exclusion in their study on the discursive construction of the "employable" student and "ideal" future creative worker that circulates within both higher art education and the graduate labor market in the UK. In particular, their study shows how the practice of (unpaid) work placements, alongside normative valuations of success and employability, is located within systems of classification that worked to disadvantage working-class students as they had restricted access to requisite resources, including time, money, and industry contacts necessary for undertaking placement and taking responsibility for organizing these.

Our study is concerned with the valuation practices employed by teachers at admission exams at higher music education institutions in Austria and Germany and sheds light on the role of class and "race" in the construction of the "ideal" classical music student. Lamont's (2009) notion of self-concept is a helpful tool for exploring this construction because it considers both "the formation of the evaluators' subjectivity and how individuals' self-understandings shape their evaluative behaviour" (Beljean et al., 2015, p. 41). In this context, we understand valuation as a practice that is deeply interactional and employed by teachers to give worth to candidates at admission exams by attributing particular musical abilities, identities, and dispositions. The 39 teachers we interviewed for this study teach orchestral instruments, piano, voice, conducting, or composition at an elite state-funded higher music education institution in Austria or Germany. These teachers, who are all white and from (upper) middle-class backgrounds, were afforded institutional power and endowed with critical capacities to impose criteria of valuation and to justify, but also to challenge the ascription of worth and the associated categorization of candidates as "ideal" classical music students. Our analysis of the teachers' valuation practices is divided in three parts. In the first part, we will examine the teachers' self-concepts as classically trained musicians who employ the trope of luck to conceal class privilege they have enjoyed in their childhood and youth to study an instrument and advance in a career as musician. In the subsequent two parts, we draw attention to the role of class and "race" in both the teachers' self-concepts and their valuation practices and the ways in which they inform the construction of the "ideal" classical music student.

The teachers' self-concepts

All the teachers we interviewed for our study talked about themselves in our conversations, including their childhood musical socialization, their careers as professional classical musicians, and their understanding of a "good" music teacher. By analyzing these narratives, it became clear that the teachers' self-concepts share several commonalities. All teachers mentioned that they started to learn an instrument at an early age and had been regularly attending private music lessons throughout their youth, while they performed in youth orchestras or played concerts as solo artists. For example, a female conducting teacher said that she had already sung in her mother's children's choir at the age of two and had been attending flute, piano, and violin lessons together with other children from the age of four. At the age of 13, she was encouraged by her mother to learn the organ and to take additional private music lessons. During her youth, she often performed at the local church and passed the entry exam to an elite higher music education institution in Austria at the age of 17. Similarly, a cello teacher noted that his parents were both musicians and, as a result, he and his siblings studied a classical music instrument at a conservatoire, whereby two became professional musicians.

These forms of musical socialization experienced by the teachers exhibit characteristics of the "concerted cultivation" (Lareau, 2011) of middle-class parenting, whereby parents conceive of their child as a project to be invested in for the future, thus providing opportunities for the child to accumulate resources, skills, and experiences. The investment that constitutes good middle-class parenting is brought about in part by extracurricular activities that include encouraging the child to join a choir and/or to practice a classical musical instrument, and to engage in conversations with music teachers about the child's progress in acquiring musical skills. These activities require a high level of parental time, money, and affective support that non-musician parents and working-class parents can hardly afford (Wagner, 2015). The teachers we interviewed knew about the importance of parental investments in a child's musical education so that he/she/they will pass the entry exam at an elite higher music education institution between the ages of 16 and 18. In our conversations, however, they rarely named the privileges the students from middle-class families and they themselves had enjoyed. Rather, they were taken for granted and concealed by mobilizing the trope of luck. A piano teacher and a cello teacher employed the trope of luck in their narratives about their own musical education in childhood and youth as follows:

> I got my first teacher when I was six, but I began playing the trumpet when I was four because my father is a trumpet player.... But after my parents realized that I never played the trumpet, but always ran to the piano and played melodies from children's programs, they hired a very good piano teacher for me. This was huge luck because I think the first teacher is the most important to learn an instrument properly. [piano teacher, male]

> I've been playing the cello since I was eight, but it wasn't until 15 that I really wanted to do it professionally. And I was lucky because I grew up in a social environment that was good. I had a very good teacher, sure, but I also met cellists as a teenager who inspired me and ... that was the moment when I thought that's what I want to do. That's how it should be ... with the professionalism, the artistic standards, the possibilities and so on. [cello teacher, male]

As Scharff (2018a) notes in her study on young female classical musicians, the trope of luck was employed by her research participants to portray their financially secure family backgrounds as a matter of luck. In our study, the trope of luck becomes a rhetorical means for the teachers to account for their own privileged class position and to render invisible the structural constraints experienced by those who were not "lucky" enough to grow up with the support of parents to learn a classical music instrument and to advance a career as a classically trained musician. These narratives of luck are couched in an individualistic framework (Scharff, 2018a), where access to classical music education and the possibilities for identification with young classical musicians and for developing desirable dispositions and skills such as an intrinsic motivation, the mastery of the instrument, and the commitment to study a classical music instrument become disembedded from social structures because they are regarded as a matter of luck. This individualistic rhetoric is constitutive of the teachers' self-concept as classically trained musicians who often grew up in "musical families" and were encouraged and financially and emotionally supported by their parents to realize their professional aspirations. In what follows, we will investigate how these self-concepts inform both the teachers' valuation practices and the construction of the "ideal" classical music student.

The "ideal" classical music student

The teachers share the idea that the "ideal" classical music student can master the instrument exceptionally well at a young age to meet the high technical and artistic standards required to pass the admission exam at a higher music education institution as a young adult and to pursue a classical music career. This view is emphasized by a violin teacher as follows:

> We do not only want to train good instrumentalists. The students should also grow personally and should be able to find a job. In the case of the violin, this is first and foremost an orchestra position. We therefore select only students [for our classes] who are already fully trained in regard to technical skills and know how to play the instrument at a high level. That's really the most basic

precondition to be accepted and to have a realistic chance to make a living as a musician. [violin teacher, male]

Moreover, the "ideal" student is also expected to be familiar with the canon of "Western" art music and literature, as we learned in a conversation with a conducting teacher. He told us about a candidate from a lower socio-economic background who managed to pass the demanding entry exam, but, as the teacher found out later, he seemed to lack both knowledge about classical music and the abilities needed for producing high quality musical performances. Toward the end of our conversation, during which the teacher repeatedly referred to the student pejoratively as Tarzan, he said:

> Tarzan worries me because his progress is too slow. And in his first year of his study, I had to invest extra time to write lists with symphonies, operas, and novels he had to study.... But I am convinced that studying conducting is one of the greatest achievements in his life because he grew up in a family with poor education.... Certainly, he will never become a great conductor, but if he continues to compensate for his weaknesses, I guess he can find work at a small theater. [conducting teacher, male]

As this quote illustrates, candidates from disadvantaged socio-economic backgrounds were rarely considered as able to pass the entry exam and to pursue a classical music career. If they did, they had to negotiate negative stereotypes about working class students and were expected to work harder than their peers from (upper) middle-class backgrounds. In contrast, candidates from musical families were generally seen as talented and gifted, as the following quote by a voice teacher demonstrates:

> Talented and gifted candidates attend a choir as a child. They grow up in musical families or their parents are instrumentalists or opera singers. [voice teacher, female]

These valuation practices employed by the teachers do not address differential class positions, which provide candidates from middle-class backgrounds with greater access to valuable cultural and material resources necessary to pass an entry exam and to be perceived as "employable" students (see also Burke and McManus, 2011). As a result of this lack of attention to the fact that certain candidates have unfair access to music education in their childhood and youth, teachers tend to be drawn to candidates who resemble their self-concept. This tendency is exhibited in the following quote by a piano teacher:

> I feel most comfortable with really intellectual students with whom I can not only talk about music, but also about book releases, exhibitions, and theater performances because that's also interesting to me. [piano teacher, male]

Similarly, a voice teacher argued that the entrance examination is a situation for determining

> whether the candidate is interesting to me, whether I want to shake his hand when he enters the room and want to welcome him. That's important because I train students artistically for many years and we need to be on the same wavelength. [voice teacher, male]

Puwar (2004) describes valuation practices in which individuals are drawn to candidates who have the same social background, share similar interests, and belong to the same networks as "social cloning." This practice of social cloning amounted to acts of self-affirmation and self-reproduction at entry exams because several teachers attributed desirable qualities to candidates who resonated with their self-concept, thus producing a certain type of classical music student. From the teachers' perspective, this type represented the "ideal" classical music student. These acts of self-affirmation and self-reproduction exhibited in teachers' valuation practices may explain the role of music conservatoires in reproducing social class inequalities, but reveal little about the association of the classical music profession with whiteness. In the final part, we therefore draw our attention briefly to the role of "race" in the teachers' self-concepts and valuation practices as well as the ways they inform the construction of the "ideal" classical music student as white musician.

Artistic personality and potential

Besides the mastery of the instrument at a high level, talent, giftedness, and a strong interest in and knowledge of music, art, and literature, all the teachers considered artistic personality and "potential" to be important qualities for aspiring classical musicians. When we asked the teachers how artistic personality and potential are defined and assessed at admission exams, a voice teacher said: "We don't expect candidates to be perfect singers, but they need to demonstrate empathy toward the music they sing" [voice teacher, female]. Similarly, a piano teacher defines artistic personality and potential as performative self-expression skills and creative use of notated music:

> What we look for at our entry exams is, of course, a very high level of piano playing. What I personally look for is personality. People who fit the big

stage. People who have something to say. I also often look for people who are funny, who are unusual in a certain way because they very often have a personal message. They can bring something new. And that's important. [piano teacher, male]

Regardless of the different terms used by teachers to describe artistic personality and potential, creativity, individuality, artistic self-expression, and the capacity for artistic development in the course of study were considered as central reference points for attributing these qualities. However, the teachers also mentioned experiences of uncertainty and encountering difficulties in assessing these qualities because they cannot be defined "objectively." A violin teacher articulated this view as such:

Potential and personality are the things that are really difficult to define. What is personality? What is potential? Do they refer to the musical expression of a candidate or their intonation or their artistic self-expression or . . . ? That's really difficult to say and if I were to write it down, it's not at all clear because a lot happens unconsciously in this communication. But then . . . it's difficult . . . but I try to look for moments that touch me emotionally. [violin teacher, male]

The teachers perceive the music performed by the candidates as "inherently mediational" (Born, 2005) through a constellation of aural, visual, notational, performative, corporeal, social, discursive, and technological dimensions. Subsequently, a way for the teachers to overcome uncertainties in assessing artistic personality and potential is to forge affective "attachments" (Hennion, 2005) with particular candidates and their musical performances described in the quote above by a violin teacher as "moments that touch me emotionally."

Forging these affective attachments is contingent on the teachers' self-concepts that are structured by whiteness because, as white people, they occupy a "social location of structural advantage" (Frankenberg, 1993, p. 1) and a standpoint, a position through which they look at themselves, at others, and at society. As Yang (2007), Leppänen (2015), Scharff (2018a), and Kawabata (this volume) note in respect to the formation of subjectivity within the classical music world, whiteness manifests itself in the construction of white musicians as musical and creative, and their "others," particularly East Asian musicians, as robotic, mechanical, and technical. In our study, we observed a similar construction in relation to the "ideal" classical music student as a white musician. Several teachers perceived candidates from China, Korea, and Japan as lacking artistic personality and potential and legitimized the unequal distribution and ascription of qualities such as individuality, creativity, and musicality by referring to the musical training of these candidates in their countries of origin. A piano teacher expressed this view in regard to young Korean pianists as such:

I often visit schools in Korea where young top talents are trained. These are twelve- and thirteen-year-olds who play virtuoso pieces like Liszt's *Spanish Rhapsody*. And they play these works technically very well and very fast, but unfortunately relatively interchangeably because there is no individuality and no feeling for the music, but this way of playing is rewarded in this education system. I don't mean to reproduce a stereotype . . . but it's a given fact that it is much more difficult for these young talents to fight their way through at the entry exam, because there are just so many young Asian talents who all play very well, but unfortunately all in the same way. [piano teacher, male]

All teachers referred to the stereotyping of East Asian musicians as performers without individuality and creativity, with some mentioning that they "have heard many young German musicians at admission exams playing like machines" [violin teacher, male] and some arguing that "Asian musicians have finally overcome the robotic way of performing works because they have studied for generations at European music conservatoires" [flute teacher, female]. However, only one teacher rejected the racial hierarchies inherent in the construction of the "ideal" classical music student by questioning the distinction between the technical mastery of an instrument ("technique") and the artistic interpretation of works:

Asian musicians are often perceived as playing like machines because they achieve a very high level of technical mastery [of their instrument]. But we cannot separate technical mastery from artistic interpretation. If I can master my instrument technically very well, I can also express myself artistically very well, and if I can express myself artistically, I also know how to master the instrument technically. [piano teacher, male]

The suggestion to abandon the established distinction between "technique" and "interpretation" aims at establishing alternative criteria of valuation for the assessment of the candidates' musical performances and may help to challenge the construction of the "ideal" classical music student as white musician. In the end, however, several teachers said that they tend to privilege Austrian or German candidates, who were unspokenly thought of as white individuals, over students from China, Japan, or Korea. In so doing, the teachers reproduced the association of the classical music profession with whiteness.

Conclusion

Our study has shown that the teachers' self-concepts as white, classically trained musicians from (upper) middle-class backgrounds can inform their valuation practices to an extent that they result in acts of self-affirmation and self-reproduction, whereby the association of the classical music profession with white, middle-class culture is reproduced. Our study has also shown that teachers are afforded institutional power and endowed with critical capacities that can be employed for developing alternative criteria of valuation and increasing social and musical diversity among students studying an orchestral instrument, voice, conducting, or composition at a higher music education institution. Moreover, we suggest that increasing diversity among music teachers working in schools and music conservatoires can help to disrupt the process of "social cloning" (Puwar, 2004) and, in turn, supports recent initiatives such as #MeToo, Black Lives Matter, and #operaisracist to bring about social change in the classical music profession.

3
Social Inclusion in Contemporary British Conservatoires

Alumni Perspectives

Jennie Joy Porton

As the first generation in my family to experience higher education and having studied at a state school, I was in a demographic minority at the two British conservatoires at which I trained. I had attended a junior conservatoire program for under-18s for eight years and so had been exposed, to some degree, to the environment and had a flavor of the cultural ethos of this type of establishment. Prior to commencing my studies at the senior conservatoire after leaving school, I had assumed a certain level of self-assurance from this musical training. However, upon arriving at my undergraduate institution, almost immediately, I began to question how I fitted into the system and my self-confidence plummeted. My initial entry point to the research considerations central to this study was a concern over my sense of belonging, and perceived social and cultural divides among my conservatoire student contemporaries. My formative conservatoire experiences, unequivocally rooted in issues of class, have since remained a key contributary factor in my musical performing career, directly linked to notions of my own "talent," self-worth, and choice of "appropriate"[1] career paths.

The motivation to undertake this study thus emanates from my own personal experiences and observations as an alumna of the conservatoire system. The issues considered in this chapter have, whether through choice or inadvertently, shaped my musical studies, cultural and social experiences, career expectations, and conception of my self-identity more generally, both within and beyond the conservatoires' walls. These matters arose gradually as my studies progressed and have become increasingly more relevant and important to me as I now work within the music profession as a performer, and reciprocally teach at one such institution. They are, I believe, important issues that need be addressed in the discussion of the contemporary practices of these establishments and the direct effects of these on their student inhabitants.

As I reflect here on my personal experiences, it is also crucial to acknowledge the racial privileges I have likely experienced due to my Caucasian heritage. The notion that my higher education training was seemingly not impacted by my "race" bespeaks the normativity of Whiteness in these institutions. Gendered dimensions were present in certain aspects of my education experience, in a predominantly subtle manner, in line with my collected empirical data. However, this chapter's main contribution is in exploring some of the classed dynamics of classical music education in UK conservatoires; the full-scale study on which this chapter is based also includes some insights into the gendered dimensions of alumni conservatoire experiences, which are not explored here.[2] To avoid any sense of reductivism, from the outset I acknowledge that class is but one element, intersecting with gender and "race," in the discussion of cultural practices and identity. Thus, this research serves as a contribution to a much-needed wider debate.

Narrowing the field

Conservatoires (or "conservatories") are defined as centers for musical excellence at the higher education level, with a distinctive focus on practical and profession-orientated training. Emphasis is placed on one-to-one tuition, traditionally specializing in musical performance in the "Western" classical genre. In the UK, there are presently nine such institutions.[3] Aside from Cottrell (2004), London School of Economics (2012), and Scharff (2018), conservatoire alumni provide a rich though relatively untapped source of data. Yet their critical insights have the potential to inform institutional practices and policies relating to issues of inclusion/exclusion, barriers, and representation, therefore speaking directly to equality and diversity concerns. Perkins (2013, p. 197), whose research was carried out within a UK conservatoire, acknowledges that "in recent years, there has been increasing focus in the music education literature on what and how students learn at conservatoires of music." However, she states that "as educational institutions, conservatoires remain largely unresearched and, crucially, relatively unchallenged. In particular, existing research has paid little attention to in-depth studies of culture, so that not enough is known of the cultural practices that characterize and shape a conservatoire education" (2011, p. 1). Though this claim was made ten years ago, and it should be acknowledged that the conservatoire research field is expanding, it is still appropriate to posit that student perceptions of institutional practices require further research.

This chapter presents a snapshot of a larger study (Porton, 2020), which looked at the practices of contemporary British music conservatoires (in England and Wales, specifically) from alumni perspectives. I begin with an outline of the broader study from which this data is drawn and follow this with a brief exploration of the theoretical framework in which this ethnography is positioned. Building on existing findings (primarily those of Davies, 2004, and Perkins, 2013), the voices of the alumni interviewees are foregrounded to demonstrate that conservatoires are shaped by social concerns and that there are social hierarchies that impact students' embodied experiences of learning and, critically, their identities. These social hierarchies, particularly in relation to type of schooling pre-HE, are shown to typically work in favor of the middle-class students, to the detriment of working-class students. Simultaneously, I consider how institutional practices can affect students' notions of identity throughout the course of their studies, and furthermore, how the conservatoire experience continues to shape the identities of the alumni beyond their time at the institution, as they navigate the profession thereafter.

The alumni accounts demonstrate that the conservatoire experience is layered with cultural and social concerns and that it is deeply connected to issues relating to class. The "musical/non-musical" familial habitus, the label of first-generation to attend HE, and type of schooling pre-conservatoire are shown to be connected to student experiences of conservatoire practices, institutional culture, and subsequent notions of identity with regard to musicianship, ability, and career direction.

The study

This chapter considers alumni responses to conservatoire practices spanning three decades of attendance from 1990 to 2018. Twenty participants shared their testimonies via a semi-structured interview approach. The interviewees' names have been anonymized, while attendance dates are shared for logistical and temporal context in relation to their experiential insights. To provide a snapshot of the testimonies represented in this study, a handful of alumni voices are showcased in this chapter. Their names have been changed to Alumnus 1, Alumna 2, etc., numbered according to the order in which their voices appear in the text that follows.

The 20 alumni represent seven conservatoires in England and Wales, with many attending more than one institution for undergraduate and postgraduate, or swapping from one to another mid-course. When referring generally to "conservatoires" in this chapter, I infer these seven institutions listed here, as attended by this alumni cohort. Of the 20 alumni, there are 11 woodwind players, three string players, three brass players, two percussionists, and one vocalist. There are no pianists amongst the alumni, which was a coincidental outcome of the ethnographic research process and not pre-planned.

As members of the professional community presently, these alumni, at the time of their respective interviews with me, were all full-time performing musicians. This was self-categorized by them in the following ways: two were contracted orchestral musicians, six were freelance orchestral musicians, two identified as orchestral and musical theater freelancers, one participant was a musical theater specialist freelancer, three were musical theater and commercial freelancers, three were contracted musical theater performers, and three identified as "general freelancers." The interviewees were half women and half men (all identified as cis-gender), while eight identified as working class and twelve as middle-class (see "Identifying Social Background" in this chapter for further discussion). Racial background was not discussed, though at times information relating to this was volunteered unprompted during the interviews (thus highlighting the complexity of discussions surrounding identity).

This chapter positions conservatoire institutions as social, cultural, and embodied learning environments. Pierre Bourdieu's concepts of habitus, capital and field, and hierarchies within educational establishments (1979, 1989), and Stuart Hall's concept of identity (1990), can be applied to the ethnographic data to generate both a cultural and class-based analysis. These two thinkers can be brought into conversation with each other on multiple issues. For example, relevant to this chapter's discussion, both figures were concerned with access to culture in relation to issues of class and shared a key interest in the dynamics of power regarding cyclical, reproductive practices. In so doing, they also linked these concepts of class and power to notions of identity. An emphasis on representation through discourse and reflexivity is also a meeting point of Hall and Bourdieu; therefore, the method of discourse analysis is used to critically reflect on the alumni testimonies, resonant with the methodological approach used by both thinkers.

Specifically, in my analysis that follows, I apply the concept of habitus to examine how alumni's social position in wider society affects their experience of educational practices. In its most simple form, habitus (Bourdieu, 1989) is an exposure to a socio-cultural environment (e.g., familial or educational settings), and is connected to social and cultural capital. Capital concerns cultural and social exchange, and exposure to and the accumulation of knowledge and/or accomplishment(s). This chapter also adopts Hall's understanding of identity, in particular his concept of "becoming." Hall considers how difference (cultural, racial, class, gender) is represented through practices and the discourses employed by people and places (e.g., society, media, institutions) and is politically, socially, and culturally constructed:

> Cultural identity . . . is a matter of "becoming" as well as "being." It belongs to the future as much as to the past. It is not something which already exists, transcending place, time, history and culture. Cultural identities come from somewhere, have histories. But, like everything which is historical, they

undergo constant transformation. Far from being eternally fixed in some essentialised past, they are subject to the continuous "play" of history, culture and power. (Hall, 1990, p. 225)

It is this particular understanding of cultural identity on which this study is framed, that conservatoire students share many points of difference as well as similarity, and are in an ongoing process of "becoming,"[4] developing and transforming their sense of identity.

Identifying social background

Measuring and defining social class remains a complex issue, with varying constructs available. This chapter adopts Bull's (2018) broad approach to class definition; in her study of how class inequality shapes the aspirations of young musicians, she draws on an intellectual lineage of class as the "interplay of material and cultural aspects of social life [i.e., cultural taste, leisure practices, morality, aspirations, and ideas of self-worth] to examine how identities are formed around economic inequalities" (2018, p. 80). I position my discussion of class status as central to a wider focus on social background, thus also allowing for a broader reflection on issues including opportunities in relation to music education, and historic familial musical and HE experiences.

While in the UK there has been an increasing focus on how all corners of society may have access to higher education over the past three decades in particular, presently, there remains limited research detailing the class backgrounds of conservatoire students. However, we know that the working classes are underrepresented in the conservatoire system; Scharff (2018) confirms the long-held assumption that conservatoires have traditionally been the home of the middle and upper classes. As with music degrees at universities, this is a higher education subject that draws more students with higher class profiles than the British national average. In relation to schooling before higher education, Scharff's data reflected that across the UK, 6.5% of children are privately educated (rising to 18% from age 16),[5] yet these students make up on average 24.4% of conservatoire student intake (across five conservatoires, with data from 2012/2013) (Scharff, 2018, pp. 46–47).

To commence this discussion of how social position in wider society affected alumni's experience of conservatoire practices, I asked them with which class they instinctively identified, without defining class parameters or categories. This approach was purposefully adopted so as to not in any way lead the participant's response in relation to self-identity and representation. Focusing on the two formative types of habitus, the alumni discourse shows a clear theme of a "them and us" division within conservatoire culture in relation to class background. There were two notable ways in which this was articulated: firstly, in relation to a "musical/non-musical" familial habitus, and secondly, regarding a state school/ private specialist music school educational habitus. Though not consciously articulated, there was also a divisive pattern reflected in the data regarding the experiences of those alumni who were the first generation in their family to attend higher education.

"Them and us"—familial/primary habitus

Of the alumni interviewed, 13 said that they came from "musical" families with varying degrees of musical activity and achievement, from conservatoire-trained parents, active amateur musicians to hobbyist players. The remaining seven had no immediate family members who owned and/or had learned to play an instrument, and shall be henceforth labeled as "non-musical."[6] Of those interviewed, two had parents who were/are professional musicians and were themselves conservatoire-trained.

A "musical" familial habitus was an identifying factor across the narratives, for both those who did experience this and those who didn't. There was also a perceived divide upon first entering the conservatoire, between those from "musical" backgrounds whose parents played traditional "Western" classical instruments and those who did not, as demonstrated by Alumna 1:

> Even though my home life was so full of music, different music, nobody really cared because it wasn't the music they were into, their families didn't play it, it didn't matter [to them]—"How dare she like something else." It does make you feel they look down on you because of it. I think it's a classical thing.
> (Woodwind student, 2006–2010)

Identifying as working class and "first generation HE" (a term used to describe someone who is attending higher education, i.e., university or an equivalent institution, while their parents did not), Alumna 1 did not come from what she described as a "classical musical background." In her interview, she shared her love of rock music, stemming from a childhood bond with her father, and reflected how she rebelled against the "others" at the conservatoire who did not place cultural value on this genre. This feeling of difference has since become an increasingly important part of her identity, as this continues to transform, in line with Hall's concept of "becoming." She considered that the lower value placed on her musical heritage, as part of conservatoire culture that places "Western" classical music at the top of its hierarchy, has directly served to strengthen her "connection to her roots," in resistance to conservatoire tradition. Alumna 1's discourse acutely reflects the multi-layered experience of the cultural and pedagogical conservatoire habitus. Her narrative demonstrates her perceptions of cultural and institutional hierarchy and manifestation of symbolic capital.

Maintaining a focus on the familial habitus, I asked the alumni whether or not they were "first generation HE"; of the 20 interviewed, eight were categorized as such and of these, at the time of their conservatoire studies, seven identified as working-class and one as middle. To reframe this, the working-class alumni were overwhelmingly more likely to also be first generation HE. The 12 alumni who were not first generation HE all self-identified as middle class, except for one. The alumni did not articulate a perceived divide between those who were first generation HE and those who were not, but crucially, in the discussion of identity, there was a clear pattern reflected in the data. When asked whether they felt they were treated as an individual or had to "fit in" to the conservatoire system, all but one of the first generation HE alumni chose the latter, with feelings of struggle with perceived conformity in adapting to the accepted cultural practices of the system. For non-first-generation HE students, this figure was notably lower, at only half.

Interestingly, all but one of the alumni who were first generation HE (i.e., seven of the 20 interviewed) also came from a "non-musical" family habitus and the data suggests that there is a pattern relating to the way this particular cohort processed the "them and us" background divide. That is, the self-confidence of first generation HE students who did not have a "musical" family background was markedly more negatively affected upon arrival at the conservatoire in comparison to their peers who did not share this same background, with instances of poor mental health in response to this environment.[7]

"Them and us"—educational/secondary habitus

There was another "them and us" divide reflected in relation to educational background, which particularly resonates with the issue of class. This divisive feeling was strongest for those who came from a state school background, who felt a key separation between themselves and those from private specialist music schools in particular (e.g., Chetham's School of Music, Purcell School for Young Musicians, Wells Cathedral School[8]) (see also Beth Higham-Edwards in this book). It was not, however, a key point of reflection or an issue the other way around.

This perception of a "them and us divide" in relation to schooling and preconceived ideas of class status in connection with this, was a prevalent theme in the data, which arose frequently in the interviews and related to different thematic discussions, particularly in relation to notions of "talent" and well-being.[9]

Building on the findings of Perkins (2013) regarding the framing of "star" students in conservatoire culture, the alumni perceived that "favorites" were selected by heads of department and principal study teachers based on assumptions and perceptions regarding individuals' cultural and symbolic capital that were unequivocally connected to their social background (e.g., educational habitus, previous instrumental teacher, membership of youth music ensembles). They considered that these two figures of power, specifically, pigeon-holed students according to this capital and that the subsequent hierarchy of "favorites" was largely fixed throughout the duration of their studies. Vitally, alumni from both state and specialist private musical school backgrounds considered those from the latter educational habitus to be more likely to be labeled as a "favorite." There was clear evidence that this directly impacted the alumni's sense of "self" regarding confidence in their abilities and their identity as a musician, and that this impact had the potential to be long-lasting, as they navigate the profession thereafter.

Throughout the discourse, alumni identified more strongly with either their familial habitus (in this case, I refer to "musical/non-musical" family) or their educational habitus (school), that is, no single participant demonstrated that both were of equal importance with regard to notions of identity. These habitus-related identifications were important elements in their reflections on contextualizing their conservatoire cultural experience in the first year of study. This was a reflection across the data regarding notions of identity relating to social background. As an example, for Alumnus 2, it was this latter factor, the "non-musical" family habitus, with which he most strongly identified and this was the dominant factor across his narrative when discussing his background. He is not first generation HE, identifies as middle class, went to a state school, and comes from a "non-musical" family.

> I did notice there were people who were quite serious, who had gone to Chets [Chetham's School of Music]—that Chets group I suppose, who had had music as quite a regular thing—but I didn't feel alienated. I didn't feel at all I wasn't as prepared as them, it was fine. And I felt there was no disadvantage coming from a non-musical family, in actual fact I quite like it because it's "my thing." My parents were so supportive, what was really nice is there was just less of a pressure I found.
>
> (Woodwind student, 2005–2011)

Once at the conservatoire as a senior student, Alumnus 2 felt the environment of the institution provided him with the impetus he needed to work harder, he consciously made use of his social background in a positive way so that he considered it worked "for" him and not "against" him. This sentiment was echoed by three other state school alumni, who stressed the importance—with regard to aspiration and identity—of consciously utilizing their broad musical experience pre-conservatoire, as a means of consciously differentiating their skill set from those who had been to private specialist music schools, whom they perceived excelled predominantly only in the "Western" classical tradition. The alumni who had attended private specialist music schools were markedly more confident of their musical abilities upon commencing their studies at the conservatoire, in contrast to their peers from state school backgrounds.

Socio-economic background and financial support during conservatoire studies

The alumni's main sources of finance alongside conservatoire studies were student loans (through the English, Welsh, and Scottish governments' systems of student finance, which involves loans for tuition fees as well as "maintenance" or living costs), parents and employment (music-related or otherwise). Instruments were viewed as a particular form of symbolic capital and were intrinsically linked to individuals' economic capital. Issues regarding staff perception of the quality of alumni's instruments and the manner in which this was demonstrated, was a concerning point in the data, noted by half of the alumni, as demonstrated by Alumna 3 in a stark manifestation of class directly affecting conservatoire experience:

> A teacher commented that one of my recital marks wasn't higher because of the instrument I had, which I was really sad about because that was all I could afford.... My parents re-mortgaged to help me buy a new one [eventually] for £10,000.
>
> (String student, 2004–2009)

While it is the responsibility of principal study teachers to give honest guidance to students regarding what is required to advance, Alumna 3 was offered no assistance in where she might apply for specialist loan schemes or scholarships specifically for the purchase of a new instrument. She was, therefore, consciously made aware of her social background and class status given that she did not come from an affluent family, and a student maintenance loan would not cover the cost (and regardless, was not intended for such use, as inferred by its title). As such, notable sacrifices had to be made (her parents re-mortgaging the family home) in order to do what was expected of her and, vitally, what it was implied would raise her chances of success at her conservatoire.

The alumni testimonies show that there is clear financial pressure regarding symbolic capital in relation to musical instruments and in retrospect, for the working-class alumni, this negatively affected the way they framed their entire conservatoire experience. All 20 of the alumni articulated a distinct lack of direction from conservatoire staff regarding how to obtain financial assistance (i.e., grants and loans) for new instruments. The collective interview discourse points to ongoing issues regarding staff responses to the matter (in particular, the Principal Study Tutor), across the conservatoire sector, with reports of little understanding and patience offered to students, and an attitude of "It's not my problem, just do as I suggest."

Another area of the conservatoire course in which alumni reported socio-economic issues was with accompanist fees to pay for pianists to play with them for their student recitals. The wider study from which this data is extrapolated showed that some conservatoires set aside provision in their budget for a departmental accompanist and typically allocate a set number of hours per student, so that this is a service provided by the institution. However, over the past three decades, in the time that these alumni subjects attended conservatoires, some institutions did not provide for this. This meant that students had to source and self-fund an accompanist in order to meet obligatory recital requirements and therefore pass their degree. Such practice, therefore, privileges those of a more secure socio-economic status and relies on students finding accompanist peers if they cannot afford a professional; the data suggests that there are discrepancies between institutions, but this has been a systemic issue across the conservatoire network.

Many alumni held a job alongside their conservatoire studies in order to address social and financial concerns. This was more of an assumed and accepted part of independence and the higher education experience for those from working class backgrounds in particular. Across the alumni cohort, there was clear evidence that those who felt they had no choice but to take on employment for social and financial reasons, considered their conservatoire achievements were likely negatively impacted, in retrospect. There was, however, a clear social reward when the job was non-music-related, that working-class interviewees especially described how spending time away from the intense conservatoire "bubble" was beneficial to their well-being.

Reflections

Conservatoires are increasingly aware of the underrepresentation of the working classes at their institutions, and by and large, are attempting to make some headway in this complex issue largely through greater emphasis on their outreach programs, and reflecting on their admissions practices in line with an increased focus sector-wide on equality, diversity, and inclusion. However, these institutions have not yet fully turned this gaze inwardly, to reflect upon and address how their students, from an array of social backgrounds, experience their conservatoire training differently, and how this is connected to notions of identity.

Alumni were questioned as to whether they consciously thought of their social background, or were consciously made aware of it at any point during their conservatoire studies, as a result of institutional practices or culture; the majority said that they were not. However, though they were not all explicitly conscious of it, all of those from working-class backgrounds proceeded to say that they think this was something that had affected their time there in some form or another and that in retrospect, they felt that certain experiences (emotionally, socially, culturally, educationally) had occurred directly because of their class background.

Davies recommended that:

> Music educators at the Conservatoire might thus examine how students' so-called innate musical qualities could be shaped by social factors such as their different social class backgrounds and musical training histories. In doing so, these educators can consider how they can improve the practices that discourage students from developing their capabilities as fully as possible, practices that also prevent the Conservatoire from fulfilling its official story of musical "excellence" as fully as it possibly can. (Davies, 2002, p. 235)

The alumni discourses presented above clearly show that conservatoires across the network have failed to heed her call for more introspective examination to reflect on how students' social backgrounds impact pedagogical experience, and how their practices could/should be adapted in response. Of the 20 alumni interviewed in my study, 18 of them attended conservatoires (or had at least two years of study left) in the seventeen years since Davies's work was published. Yet, every single interviewee considered that if conservatoires were more aware of the nature of their social background, their experience would have been improved, thus suggesting three things: firstly, Davies is right to state that conservatoires need to address this issue; secondly, the continued absence of tailored student support that acknowledges students' social background and how this can shape their embodied learning experiences; and thirdly—and crucially—this is an issue across the conservatoire network, not limited to one institution. This is a key area in which conservatoire practices can be improved and would most benefit those students from lower socio-economic backgrounds, and would go some way toward addressing symbolic capital hierarchies (particularly relating to equipment), among the student body.

This chapter thus highlights an area of interest that requires further exploration for a more generalized research conclusion, and I acknowledge that class is but one element intersecting with gender and "race" with regard to identity and to pedagogic and cultural experiences of institutional practices. The alumni discourses clearly show that the holistic "conservatoire experience" is far more complex than apparent at first glance, and a more nuanced, and arguably, a more targeted approach, would have positively impacted their self-esteem, general well-being, and conceptions of themselves as musicians and artists.

Notes

1. Purposefully placed in quotation marks as a contentious term, but one befitting my experiences with conservatoire figures of power.
2. Doctoral research undertaken at Royal Holloway University of London. The full-scale study uses the themes of notions of "talent," curriculum, and health and wellbeing to explore these research queries.
3. Association Européenne des Conservatoires. "United Kingdom National Overview." Accessed July 27, 2021. https://aec-music.eu/members/national-overviews/united-kingdom
4. Throughout this chapter I frequently refer to Hall's second concept of identity as outlined here, as his concept of "becoming."
5. Page 12, ISC Census and Annual Report 2016. Accessed September 9, 2021. https://www.isc.co.uk/media/3179/isc_census_2016_final.pdf
6. Purposefully positioned in quotation marks for this is a shorthand label used to aid in presenting the data, but playing an instrument is of course not the only way to be musical, or rather, not playing an instrument does not equate to being non-musical (as indeed the immediate alumni quote here, demonstrates).
7. See Porton (2020) for further detail.
8. In the UK context, "private" schools are defined as fee-paying schools for students up to 18 years of age and outside of the state education system, while specialist music schools are private institutions that focus heavily on musical training in addition to mainstream curriculum and typically have an audition entry process.
9. See Porton (2020) for further detail.

4
Inside Looking In

Strategies to Counteract Misconduct in Artistic Teaching within Higher Music Education

David-Emil Wickström

The #MeToo movement has led to a closer focus on sexual harassment, and higher music education (HME) is no exception.[1] While some high profile cases have become public, such as that of Siegfried Mauser, the former rector of the University of Music and Performing Arts Munich, who was convicted of sexual harassment and rape (and similar cases exist world wide—e.g., Gluckman, 2017; Lazar, 2017; Knobbe and Möller, 2018; Midgette and McGlone, 2018; Bartsch et al., 2019; Fetters et al., 2020), many more remain unreported or are known only as rumors that are not publicly discussed. This is not only because the victims fear the consequences to their careers if they report, but also in part since they do not feel like they will be believed, as a survey from 2018 among British music, drama, and dance students showed: 57% of the surveyed students did not report incidents of inappropriate behavior since 54% of them felt that they would not be believed or be taken seriously (Payne et al., 2018, p. 2).

Harassment and discrimination is not a new problem in higher education.[2] This problem not only covers issues of abuse (both verbal and physical), enabled by power imbalances and institutional hierarchies, but is also linked to questions of teaching methodologies and access, including how to make institutions and their degree programs more gender-balanced and inclusive for all students and staff. This has also been on the agenda of the European HME association "Association Européenne des Conservatoires, Académies de Musique et Musikhochschulen" (AEC). Its project "Strengthening Music in Society" (SMS), which ran from 2017 until 2021, was funded by the European Commission through the Creative Europe program. It included a working group on "Diversity, Inclusiveness and Identity," which the author chaired. The working group's aims are to give the AEC members ideas on how to open the institutions to groups of society currently not served by HME as well as to broaden the institutions' focus to musics beyond "Western" art music.[3] In light of the events mentioned above, we as a working group also chose to focus on power relations within institutions since harassment acts as a barrier toward inclusivity (Wickström, 2021).

David-Emil Wickström, *Inside Looking In* In: *Voices for Change in the Classical Music Profession.* Edited by: Anna Bull and Christina Scharff with Associate Editor Laudan Nooshin, Oxford University Press.
© Oxford University Press 2023. DOI: 10.1093/oso/9780197601211.003.0005

This in turn has led to a new project, PRIhME (Power Relations in Higher Music Education) funded by the European Commission's Erasmus + program from 2020 until 2023. In this project, nine European higher music education institutions (HMEI) focus on different aspects of power relations within HME in four stakeholder assemblies. The outcomes from these assemblies will be presented to the AEC council as suggested recommendations for AEC's member institutions. While this chapter primarily focuses on artistic teaching and staff-student interactions, the PRIhME project is important because power relations within HMEI affect *all* stakeholders, both in terms of student recruitment as well as in terms of in-house relationships among students and among faculty, and between students and faculty.

While patterns of abuse across HMEIs appear to be similar as far as the limited evidence suggests, we also must keep in mind that there are national differences in HME due to (among other aspects) funding, tuition fees, legal framework, recruitment, and musics taught. This leads to different sets of student expectations: in Germany, for example, there are no tuition fees for most students in state-funded HMEIs and so institutions are not dependent on these fees for their funding. The pressure to change established routines is thus different than, for example, in the UK or the Netherlands where students, quite bluntly, expect a return on their invested money. One outcome of this is the seemingly stronger focus on power relations in the UK in AEC discussions—coming from, among others, students' unions. Once we move toward Eastern Europe, however, anecdotal evidence suggests that these issues tend to be downplayed by the conservatory leadership.

Another important aspect to consider are changes in the student body. Especially prevalent in Germany and Austria, HME includes students from the former Soviet Union and East Asia. This brings an additional set of intercultural challenges that can amplify existing issues in relation to hierarchies and power abuse. My personal experience suggests that students from more marginalized backgrounds—primarily due to ethnicity or residential status, but also class, gender, and sexuality—are more reluctant to complain about their main instrument teachers than students from more privileged backgrounds. In addition to marginalized backgrounds, students who recently arrived as refugees (e.g., Syrian refugees) or whose parents or grandparents moved to Germany as labor migrants (e.g., German students with Turkish parents or grandparents) can experience added pressure due to personal circumstances that impact on how they deal with hierarchies and interact with staff and other students.[4]

These issues can only be tackled by beginning a discussion within institutions and highlighting the factors involved. This chapter is one attempt at this. After briefly examining the unique challenges HMEI face due to the way artistic teaching is structured, the second part looks at how these power relations can be uncovered and fought by drawing on some strategies different European HMEI are pursuing. In particular, the chapter focuses on different models of tuition besides the traditional master-apprentice model.

What is misconduct?

Previous research into staff misconduct in HE has focused on sexual misconduct. Drawing on Liz Kelly's (1988, p. 41) broad definition of sexual violence, a report on sexual misconduct by UK university staff defines the term as "a continuum of sexualised and predatory behaviours of staff towards students" (National Union of Students and the 1752 Group, 2018, p. 8). For the purposes of this chapter, I extend this definition beyond sexual misconduct to discuss power-based misconduct more broadly, and to include non-sexualized verbal abuse such as belittling students and saying that they are worthless.[5] By framing the behavior as "misconduct," Anna Bull and Rachel Rye argue that the responsibility for ensuring an environment free of harassment is placed on staff or faculty. This is in response to findings that students who make complaints about staff sexual misconduct in UK HE are not taken seriously *and* are made to feel responsible for the behavior of staff. In Bull and Rye's definition, misconduct is used to signal

> that such conduct is a matter of professional behaviour in the workplace, and to ensure that the focus remains on the responsibility of the staff member for maintaining professional conduct in their dealings with students. (Bull and Rye, 2018, p. 9)

The impact of such staff misconduct can have far-reaching consequences on students, including losing confidence, losing access to teaching, loss of networks, dropping out of their degree course, changing career, mental health impacts such as post-traumatic stress disorder, and financial and emotional impacts such as a sense of powerlessness, among others (Bull and Rye, 2018, p. 17).

In what ways are abuse and misconduct specific to HME?

While the studies above are focused on higher education more generally, in HME abuses of power can take further, specific forms. In HME, misconduct can also relate to hierarchies of value between instrument groups, musical traditions, and genres—including the often (perceived) superiority of "Western" art music in HME—as well as between different degree programs and staff/student-hierarchies. Power relations—in particular those between staff and students—also relate to how artistic standards are defined and applied (thus regulating access through admission procedures and assessment criteria) and what musics are included and excluded in the degree programs (thus defining what musics are officially supported in the institution and, in those institutions where state funding is given for HME, by the state itself). While one of AEC's PRIhME assemblies is specifically dedicated to power relations in terms of gender and sexual orientation, the other assemblies not only focus on power in general, special needs, socio-economic and geographical background, but also on artistic standards, since these discussions also affect power relations.

Why is HME so prone to abuses of power? One issue enabling misconduct by faculty within HMEI is the close relationship between the students and their instrumental teachers.[6] This is rooted in the predominant teaching model for main and secondary instruments: one-on-one classes, often described as the master-apprentice-model, which involves a close relationship with the same teacher for the duration of one's studies.[7]

While the master-apprentice model can have its benefits—especially in terms of long-term artistic development—it is a closed relationship, which means that misconduct may not be visible to outsiders. The teachers' influence extends beyond the classroom: they often decide who gets to play where and when during in-house and external recitals, master classes, and concerts. Teachers can provide their graduates with jobs or awards since they often are on the jury of grant-awarding bodies. This makes the students malleable to pressure from their teachers since they know that the teachers can damage or even destroy their career. While these roles shift after a student has graduated, the power relations do not necessarily change since the teachers remain gatekeepers for jobs, grants, and awards.

Since many students also spend a lot of time practicing and not necessarily interacting with other students, their opportunities to share their experiences can be somewhat limited. This anonymity is often aided by the conservatory buildings' architecture and closed spaces, but also poorly lit parts of the buildings and parking spots (Herold, 2006a, p. 63). By literally making the rehearsal spaces and classrooms as well as the office walls transparent and thus the inside visible to the public, the possibility of misconduct can be reduced. This also has to include a policy of not being allowed to teach outside the conservatory walls (or at least to limit this as much as possible).

Solutions

To combat misconduct, awareness about these issues has to be raised. Formal bureaucratic tools and top-down measures initiated and enforced by the institution's leadership are important not only to deal with misconduct once it arises but also to clearly show what the consequences are. On a formal level, this requires institutional policies including staff codes of conduct, provisions in the teachers' contracts outlining what constitutes misconduct and clearly denouncing it, and reporting routes with clear procedures in place for dealing with complaints as well as disciplinary measures and consequences for offenders.[8] However, and perhaps surprisingly, staff codes of conduct are not in place at all HMEIs. According to a report from 2017, only 10 out of the 24 *Musikhochschulen* in Germany had one (RKM—AG "Sexualisierte Diskriminierung," 2017).

In addition, a rethinking of higher music pedagogy is also essential to changing the institutional culture and tackling misconduct brought about through unequal power relations. While the master-apprentice model with its one-on-one teaching focus remains for many the standard of HME, there are calls for a reassessment of one-on-one teaching methods as well as a shift to group lessons (e.g., Daniel, 2004; Lebler, 2006; Lebler, 2007; Liertz, 2007; Gaunt, 2008; Creech and Gaunt, 2012; Carlsen, 2019; Encarnacao and Blom, 2020; Mitchell, 2020a; Mitchell, 2020b; Gaunt et al., 2021). This is also an important step in accommodating different styles of learning (Green, 2002) and giving students different perspectives to draw on. Ryan Daniel (2004, p. 25ff) in his review of previous research, points out that teacher domination, which can hamper students' progress, is minimized in group lessons due to power being distributed among the participants present and their interaction. While in this literature more generally the main arguments have been based on pedagogical and financial reasons, the imperative to tackle misconduct gives further impetus for change.

Toward this end, the working group within the AEC SMS project on teaching and learning have called to shift teaching in HME toward a student-centered approach. Within this paradigm shift, a rethinking of the teacher's role is necessary (Sætre et al., 2019). This follows a general trend in (European) higher education in which HME has been influenced by wider developments linked to the Bologna process in Europe,[9] especially the shift toward instructional design and its focus on learning as "an active process of knowledge construction and sense-making" (Nerland, 2019, p. 56). This includes, among other aspects, moving away from a focus on *teaching* to *learning* as well as giving students ownership in the learning process.

Creating *student-centered learning environments* (Nerland, 2019, p. 54) with a shift to transformative learning is something that Andrea Creech and Helena Gaunt (2012, pp. 703ff) argue for when reassessing individual instrument teaching. One of their recommendations is that one-on-one teaching should form part of a broader portfolio of teaching approaches that include, inter alia, group as well as online lessons (Creech and Gaunt, 2012, p. 707).

One option inspired by Creech and Gaunt (2012, pp. 703ff) is to change the model of the main instrumental/vocal teacher to that of a mentor or facilitator. In this model, the students have a main instrument mentor during their study period who follows the students' artistic development over time. At the same time, the students have regular instrumental/vocal lessons with other teachers. This model loosens the student-teacher relationship and exposes students to different teaching styles as well as artistic perspectives not only to learn from, but also to reflect on.

Morten Carlsen (2019) describes another version of this model, which he labels the "mentor." The focus here is on a collaborative approach both among the teachers and the students employed at the Norwegian Academy of Music. This includes group lessons[10] with peer feedback as well as the option to have two main instrument teachers. An essential aspect of this approach is a different mode of verbal feedback employed in class (Carlsen, 2019, p. 102), where the focus is less on prescription (telling a student what has to be done) and more on teaching through questions and experiments, thus have the student reflect on his/her artistic practice and opening up a two-way dialogue with the main instrument teacher.

Looking outside the world of "Western" art music training, a further option is the model we use at the Popakademie Baden-Württemberg: we disrupt the master-apprentice model by deliberately changing instrumental/vocal teachers (mostly) every year. The reasoning behind this approach is twofold: on the one hand, learning is a life-long process and the input the students get is something that they will continue to work on beyond the time that they study at the Popakademie. The other main reason is that each teacher has their specific methodology and specialties and each student should get different perspectives during their studies on which they can then draw. In addition, the Popakademie uses a mix of group and one-to-one lessons. While individual lessons remain central to a student's artistic development, certain instrumental/vocal techniques such as issues related to micro-timing and groove, sound design, and genre-specific approaches can be more efficiently explained in a group setting. In addition, a group lesson enables the students to focus on peer learning through listening to each other and musically interacting with each other as well as giving each other feedback. In this context, individual lessons can be used to focus on the students' specific needs (see Lebler, 2006 and 2007; Daniel, 2004, pp. 35ff; Mitchell, 2020a, p. 108 for other group lesson benefits and approaches).

The question of group size is also an economic one: one-on-one lessons are the most expensive recurring costs of music education and thus something that teachers and HME leadership defend in part to justify the costs.[11] Despite the pedagogical advantages of also offering group lessons in the main subject and the possibility to use the freed up funds for, e.g., the teachers' professional development or activities focusing on widening participation in HME, such a shift could also be used politically as a cost-cutting measure by the funding bodies. This is something Mitchell (2020a, 2020b) picks up on when describing the shift from one-on-one tuition to a mix of one-on-one and group tuition at the bachelor of contemporary music degree at Southern Cross University in Australia and the resulting underlying change management process and negotiations with teachers and students. While the main rationale for the shift was financial, Mitchell (2020b, p. 120) argues against the superior value of one-on-one teaching. She outlines a holistic model where group lessons supplement one-on-one lessons and that does not only include main and secondary lessons, but also other courses like ensemble and ensemble direction.[12]

While these approaches destabilize the master-apprentice model they do not, however, eliminate misconduct since what happens during one-on-one lessons remains nontransparent to outsiders and the teachers still have the potential to influence their students' careers. One way to alleviate this is to have clear and simple procedures to change main instrument teachers in which the teacher the student wants to move away from is not part of the formal procedure. This means that the student can talk to a staff member or head of department who is not involved with the student's main instrument teacher and get a new teacher without their previous teacher being part of this process. At the Popakademie, the procedure is that the student informs me in my function as the program director and I then talk to the head of that instrument department as well as the new teacher and we formalize the switch.

The teachers' perspective should not, however, be forgotten. Gaunt (2008, pp. 233ff) points out that one-on-one teaching can also be difficult for the teachers. This includes being drawn into the students' problems, not being able to maintain a critical distance, and lacking a forum to discuss these experiences with other teachers as well as the lack of formal structures to help with problematic relationships.

This points to a further area that still is not common within HME (or necessary to qualify for an artistic teaching position in HME): pedagogical training. This not only includes professional development providing the teaching staff with (current) teaching methodologies, which Mitchell (2020a, 2020b; see also Creech and Gaunt, 2012, p. 707) argues is necessary in order to break the reproduction of teaching like the teacher's teachers,[13] but also sensitizing faculty to issues of power abuse and conscious/unconscious bias training. This is especially an issue when the teaching staff consists of many part-time teachers and/or freelancers as well as high-profile artists who are hired based on artistic merit and fame. Getting the faculty to take part in any kind of training is not only a question of finances (are part-time teachers and freelancers paid to take part in the training?), but also finding suitable time slots.

One low-stakes way to encourage a critical assessment of one's teaching approach is through self-reflection and evaluation. The publication "Decentering Curricula: Questions for Re-evaluating Diversity and Inclusiveness in HMEIs" (Guerra et al., 2021, also included in Barbera et al., 2021) is a tool that we, as the AEC diversity working group, developed to address these issues by using questions. Aimed at faculty and staff, the goal is to start a process of thinking through questions that focus on who the students and teachers are, what is studied and taught, how the students and teachers approach teaching and studying as well as where the teaching and studying take place. Structured similarly to an assessment form used at accreditations of degree programs, these questions can be:

- In what ways does your curriculum provide one-to-one lessons?
- To what extent may the student contribute to determining the repertoire/style/genre taught in one-to-one lessons?
- What procedures are in place to combat power abuse and misconduct (sexual harassment, verbal harassment) within one-to-one lessons?
- What provisions are in place if a student wants to change their one-to-one lesson teacher? (Taken from "2.2 One-to-one lessons" in "Section 2: How do we study? How do we teach?" in Guerra et al., 2021)

These questions also provided the basis for the workshops we have held for various groups of AEC members since November 2020 and the response of the participants has been very positive. While we as a working group acknowledge that reaching all teachers is difficult and that there will also be resistance to change, we feel that getting the discussions started within the institutions is a very important first step.

Institutional culture

Formal procedures and a shift in pedagogy (including professional development) are two important components in combating misconduct. A third area is creating an institutional culture that is open to feedback, creates a safe space for complaints from students and staff, does not tolerate misconduct, and creates spaces for students and teachers to share their experiences. This can be through regular meetings between the HMEI's leadership/program directors and student representatives where current issues are discussed. Another important measure is to set up liaison teachers/staff for students where students can share their experiences confidentially with a person not directly involved in the students' teaching and where the students can get advice on how to proceed. Peer feedback e.g., during teachers' meetings, can also provide a valuable space where experiences can be shared and discussed among faculty and senior staff.

An important step in this context is to raise awareness among staff and students of what amounts to harassment and misconduct. Especially in the multicultural environments the conservatories operate in today, both students and teachers are not always aware of what can be offensive to others. This includes acts that are normalized within a specific cultural setting, but can be seen as offensive in another. Shaking hands (or the post-COVID equivalent of exchanging fist or elbow bumps) or hugging students and/or staff can be one such act. Central here is making it clear that consent is necessary. The simple question to ask is whether it is okay for a teacher or another student to make physical contact with a student (e.g., to correct a student's posture). The teacher or other students have to accept "no" as an answer and then find another way to demonstrate what the teacher wants to illustrate. While simple in theory, issues of power and how the student perceives the situation and what is expected of her/him can still influence the student to give an answer s/he is uncomfortable with.

This also touches upon conscious/unconscious bias training, which was an issue raised during a two-day training I led for teachers and students at a European HMEI in 2019.[14] The first day was dedicated to the students where my co-trainer (a graduate student from another European HMEI) and I focused on power relations within the institution. In small groups the students identified areas of concern in terms of general power relations as well as in their experience with teachers. These were then discussed and solutions suggested—first within small groups and then in the plenary. One issue that arose was that the students felt the orchestral auditions were not fair. It turned out that the auditions were conducted by the main instrument teachers, thus neither by external reviewers nor with screens. In this case, industry practices from orchestras can provide a model that tries to minimize both conscious and unconscious bias by having an anonymous review done by external examiners.[15] Blind auditions were subsequently introduced at that institution following the workshop. The second day was dedicated to the staff, where we used a similar approach to identifying issues they were concerned with, in addition to bringing in the issues the students had identified.

Another strategy to uncover and combat existing power relations is by widening participation in HME through actively promoting a diverse staff and student body, which can involve focusing on less-visible staff and student groups and creating awareness for them. Within the realm of popular music and jazz programs, this can help break established expectations and power structures, for example, how band work is structured or what terminology is used when referring to groups less visible both in general and within certain instrument groups (e.g., women, People of Color). Measures include networks for female students and professionals like Delta Frauen[16] and Music BW Women[17] (both initiated by

Popakademie students). Music BW Women is the Baden-Württemberg branch of the Music Women* Germany network.[18] The network's first branch was founded in 2017 in Hamburg as a project of RockCity Hamburg. The aim is to provide a platform to exchange ideas, provide coaching and mentoring programs, and to promote events. One example is their concert series "Club of Heroines," which features at least 50% female musicians performing. Other measures consist of institutional programs like Berklee College of Music, Valencia Campus's activities (Barbera, 2021), and the Elevate project at Leeds Conservatoire (Gilbert, 2021). The latter is a holistic approach focusing on gender within the institution itself:

> [Elevate's] intention is to put gender firmly on the agenda for the institution, giving female staff visibility within the organisation as well as a network of other women and "allies" across the conservatoire and beyond. (Gilbert, 2021)

By focusing not only on increasing and retaining female staff members and students through panel discussions, workshops, and peer mentorship programs, the project also raises awareness for gender issues in general by highlighting books in the library on gender equality and by hosting "Women of LCoM," a photography exhibit showcasing 30 women from the institution. The project also aims to broaden the conversation both by engaging men and reaching out beyond Leeds.

Finally, another important tool is to empower the students to speak up and to establish and encourage a critical student representation. One step is to give the students a neutral and open platform to discuss these issues. In the aftermath of the #MeToo campaign, conservatories in Northern Europe have had discussion and reflection groups with the students within the conservatory to talk about different forms of discrimination (in this case based on gender).

Conclusion

It is important to keep in mind that misconduct operates on a continuum, and that verbal abuse and other forms of misconduct must also be dealt with. In this chapter I have outlined four overarching areas to combat misconduct in artistic teaching in HME:

- creating an overall awareness of power relations, discrimination, and misconduct in HME
- establishing and enforcing formal guidelines on what constitutes misconduct and reporting procedures

- changing the pedagogy used in artistic teaching (especially primary/secondary instrument lessons)
- focusing on ongoing systematic professional development for (artistic) teachers within HME, which involves pedagogical and unconscious bias training. In a further step, this includes re-examining how new teachers are hired and what criteria beside artistic merit (e.g., pedagogical) are deemed important.

Combating misconduct is not easy and a multi-pronged approach is necessary, which involves both policies specific to the individual institutions and a change in institutional culture. The central issue is to raise awareness among faculty and students and to start talking about power abuse. One approach is by using questions as a tool for self-reflection as in the AEC diversity working group's publication "Decentering Curricula" (Guerra et al., 2021).

While these measures will not eliminate the problem, an open discourse about the issues—also within the AEC—will make it much more difficult to conceal. More importantly, by implementing the measures discussed in this chapter, we can not only change our institutions and pedagogical approaches, but also provide the music industry with individuals who are conscious of the issues and who can continue to raise them within the industry setting, thus moving the discussions from the inside to beyond the walls of HMEI.

Notes

1. I would like to thank Clara Barbera, Anna Bull, Jef Cox, Joshua Dickson, Moritz Eggert, Patsy Gilbert, Baptiste Grandgirard, Alfonso Guerra, Miranda Harmer, Stefan Heckel, Deborah Kelleher, Jan-Gerd Krüger, Esther Nass, Mojca Piškor, Katja Thomson, Christina Scharff and all the AEC SMS-working goup members for their valuable input and comments during the writing process.
2. See Feltes et al. (2012) for a survey of five European countries and a review of previous research, and Herold (2006a) for a survey that focuses on forms of sexual harassment, the institutions' reactions, measures taken, and how cases were delt with in 25 German HMEI.
3. The outcomes from the SMS-Project are published on a dedicated website: https://sms.aec-music.eu (accessed March 8, 2021).
4. Besides issues of respect, there are probably also other issues like language, refugee status, and socio-economic background, as well as discrimination experience involved.
5. See Josefson (2016) for examples within a Swedish context.
6. Herold (2006b) argues that the strong connection between the student, music, and her/his instrument makes the musical practice a "körperlich-sinnliche Erfahrung" (embodied-sensual experience) that makes the student/pupil more vulnerable to abuse.

7. Jørgensen (2000, 68) defines the master-apprentice relationship as "the [historically] predominant relationship between teacher and student in instrumental instruction . . . where the master usually is looked at as a role model and a source of identification for the student, and where the dominating mode of student learning is imitation."
8. The AEC provides a guide for a code of conduct on their website written by the AEC Council in 2013 (AEC Council, 2013). It most recently highlighted these guidelines in a post on their website in the wake of #MeToo in 2018 (N.N., 2018). Bull and Rye (2018, pp. 27ff) offer recommendations on what to include in such a code.
9. The Bologna process has as an overarching goal to create common standards and more coherence within the European Higher Education Area and thus to increase both student and staff mobility within European Higher Education. See http://ehea.info and https://ec.europa.eu/education/policies/higher-education/bologna-process-and-european-higher-education-area_en (both accessed 23.09.2021) for more details.
10. While group lessons in form of master classes have been part of HME these have mainly been seen as add-ons to one-on-one lessons and been teacher (or artist) dominated.
11. These costs also provide a justification for limiting access to HME through a highly competitive (and excluding) admission process.
12. Mitchell (2020b, p. 123), however, also points out that they have a two-tiered system where students who passed a competitive entry exam have more one-on-one lessons than students who entered without an audition.
13. Based on their survey of 134 instrumental teachers Mills and Smith (2003, pp. 17 and 21ff), however, argue that while of those surveyed 57% teach how they were taught, they are not clones of their teachers, but that they also draw on other influences when teaching.
14. I am happy to share the training outline if you contact me at david-emil.wickstroem@popakademie.de.
15. Drawing on research by Goldin and Rouse (2000), Criado-Perez (2019) in chapter 4 argues that blind auditions are a success story for meritocracy and gender equality. Fasang (2006), however, argues that blind auditions (as conducted among three elite orchestras in Germany) can remain a form of discrimination.
16. https://www.facebook.com/groups/555645727954154 (accessed May 27, 2021).
17. https://musicbwwomen.de (accessed May 27, 2021).
18. https://www.musicwomengermany.de (accessed October 25, 2022).

II
PROBLEMATIZING INSTITUTIONAL CHANGE

5
(Un)settling Institutional Hegemony
Challenges of Diversity Strategies in the "Western" Classical Music Sector

Kristina Kolbe

"Diversity" seems to be a much-sought-after good these days: from universities to the private sector, from state organizations to the cultural and creative industries—tackling diversity (or rather the lack thereof) appears to be high on the institutional agenda. For the classical music sector, it is particularly the reckoning with its own institutional barriers of access, participation, and representation that are deeply entangled with wider inequalities of class, "race," ethnicity, and gender (among others). Many music institutions, concert halls, or opera houses have hence started to strive toward reviewing their staff structure, broadening their aesthetic program, and widening their audiences in the name of diversity. But what happens when the white elitist space of "Western" classical music seeks to diversify itself? How are discourses of diversity negotiated in a cultural sector so profoundly implicated in hierarchies of class, systems of whiteness, and legacies of imperialism? Does diversity work indeed unmake "raced" and classed inequalities in the cultural sector or contribute to their remaking?

Indeed, the role and function of institutionalized diversity programs in the creative industries are intensely debated (e.g., Banks, 2019; Erigha, 2018; Gray, 2016; Leong, 2013; Nwonka, 2015; Saha, 2018). While some emphasize their possibilities to push for institutional revision and social change, critics on both the practitioner and the scholarly side note that the notion of diversity has become an empty signifier, a term designating everything and nothing and ultimately a lens through which systematic power structures tend to be concealed and reproduced not despite of, but precisely because of the translation of diversity agendas into institutional life. Rather than pushing for a fundamental interrogation of institutions' "raced," gendered, and classed exclusions, a merely formalistic recognition of diversity might even serve as a justification for not addressing more systemic inequalities in the cultural sector. Cultural institutions—especially those that have been criticized for their overt elitism, such as the classical music sector—might thus use the frame of diversity mainly to re-legitimate their social prestige and justify their privileged access to public (or private) subsidies. Subsequently, by being tangled up with commodification processes that derive value (monetary or otherwise) from difference, diversity initiatives in the cultural industries might ultimately sustain endemic logics of "race"-making that keep institutional whiteness in place (e.g., Saha, 2018). Yet, the urgency to address systemic inequalities in and beyond the cultural production sphere persists. And while the cultural production sector has certainly not only mirrored wider social power relations but has actively contributed to their remaking, it has also been a site for resistance, contestation, and social transformation (e.g., Hall, 1996). In times of increasing inequality (e.g., Piketty, 2014) and upsurging white nationalism, which brought fundamental questions of belonging, identity, and citizenship to the fore of ("Western") politics with new force (e.g., Lentin, 2020), the arts and cultural institutions can certainly not sit idly by but have to mobilize their own means to strive toward a more equal, just, and anti-racist (cultural) world.

Against this backdrop, this chapter explores some of the contingencies that diversity work in the "Western" art music sector can entail. To that end, I draw on a year-long qualitative study of a diversity project implemented at an established opera house in Germany, which promoted a "Turkish German" intervention into its institutional workings to broaden the house's aesthetic profile and its staff and audience structure. In this chapter, I first discuss some of the key debates that have informed my study and that help theorize the ambivalences of diversity initiatives in the classical music sector. I secondly outline my case study and methods. I will then turn toward my empirical findings. Rather than focus on one specific question or data set in-depth, this chapter provides an overview of some of the key challenges that diversity initiatives come up against when taking place in the white elitist space of classical music.

Grasping the ambivalence of diversity initiatives in the classical music sector

Whether diversity initiatives in the arts sector have reproductionist or disrupting consequences is a matter of much debate. For example, Gavan Titley (2014) acknowledges the importance of more diverse representations in the cultural industries in the "West." However, he simultaneously recognizes the risk that mainstreaming diversity can ultimately reduce critical debates around racial justice to depoliticized marketing rationales that seek to generate economic value rather than engender structural change. In a similar vein, Anamik Saha (2018, p. 106) observes that in today's "neoliberal conjuncture diversity neutralizes 'race,' and is now more likely to act as a marker of consumer brands, lifestyle choices, and postracial cultural appreciation . . . rather than the lived experience of multiculture." Saha identifies an integrationist agenda in contemporary cultural policy that would not actually address systemic racial inequalities but instead seeks to *manage* ethnic and cultural plurality from a white, hegemonic center. This, he explains, puts considerable constraints on marginalized cultural producers who would be pressured to package their work in standardized ways that appeal to the diversity-seeking mainstream consumer. Nancy Leong (2013; see also Bhattacharyya, 2018) therefore argues that diversity discourses enable the continued commodification of "race" instead of proffering rigorous interventions into racial injustice. By mobilizing and re-inscribing rigid constructions of otherness, diversity thus becomes just another feature of racial capitalism, which she describes as "the process of driving social and economic value from the racial identity of another" (ibid., 2190) for the benefits of predominantly white institutions. As such, diversity discourses present just another way of managing the demands of minorities while keeping white-centered power relations in place, producing what Stuart Hall (1992, p. 24) famously calls "a kind of carefully regulated, segregated visibility." Or, as Sara Ahmed (2007, pp. 245–246) puts it, how deep whiteness runs in institutions shows precisely when they "embrace diversity," as if diversity is what adds spice and color to "mainstream white culture." Saha (2018, p. 22) therefore cautions that diversity agendas may tend to "serve an ideological function that sustains the institutional whiteness of the cultural industries even while they claim (often genuinely so!) to do something more inclusive."

When researching the effects of diversity initiatives in the cultural sector, it is therefore crucial to develop a detailed analysis of the creative, institutional, and political implications of such strategies and to "switch the question from how cultural industries represent race, to how cultural industries *make* race" (ibid., p. 11; emphasis in the original). According to Herman Gray (2016, p. 248), it is this critical focus on the practices of "race"-making, which would reveal "race as a practice of knowledge/power" that is endemic to cultural organizations. From institutions' organizational set-up to the funding systems they rely on, from the cultural policies they address to their specific institutional histories, from the dominant aesthetical parameters of production to practices of performance, critique, and judgment—to develop a keener understanding of the disruptive or reproductive consequences of diversity in the arts, it is about zooming into the very processes of cultural production and into the ways in which "diversity" is negotiated in cultural practice itself.

Such concerns are of special significance for the classical music world. Not only has the institutionalization of classical music been characterized by discourses of European elitism, institutional whiteness, and imperialist expansion but its aesthetic history has equally been shaped by a profoundly troubled relationship with non-eurological music. According to Laudan Nooshin (2003, p. 245), classical music's relationship to other musical systems has historically "draw[n] from a deep-rooted discourse of binary opposition—a language of difference—in order to mark the boundaries between Europe and its 'ethnic others.'" The frames of musical representation did indeed change over time—from integrating imagined ideas of othered musics into "Western" musical parameters to craving authenticity, mimesis, and even hybridity—yet, as Martin Stokes (2004, p. 50) holds, "the hierarchical and exploitative relationships that . . . pertain between centres and peripheries, dominant and subaltern groups" remained firmly in place. Such boundary-drawings have played out not only in the aesthetic musical material and long-standing racialized character depictions but have also underwritten the very study of and discourses around music, cultural value, and legitimacy, with classical music being depicted as a symbol of "Western" civilization.

These long-standing entanglements between classical music and structural inequality are certainly not bygone but, as Anna Bull's (2019, p. 144) elaborates, "classical music's history is present in its contemporary practices, and its classed and 'raced' legacies cannot be dismissed as belonging to the past." Certainly, cultural policy has sought to address these issues by changing the discourse around classical music away from an overt display of elitism and toward a language of cultural participation and democratization. However, Bull holds that such discursive changes have mainly reproduced classical music's prestige as highbrow culture by disguising itself as open and inclusive while leaving its exclusionary legacies, barriers, and biases untouched. All these critical accounts of diversity discourses have crucially informed my own research in that they shed light on how diversity can ultimately lead to the reproduction of inequality rather than to its undoing. It is thus this complex backdrop that contemporary diversity debates in the music sector need to grapple with and against which they need to be assessed.

Case and methods

This chapter is based on an ethnographic study of a diversity project at an established opera institution in Germany, which I conducted between 2016 and 2017. The project specifically aimed at broadening the institution's staff, audience, and aesthetic profile in ways that would reflect Germany's postmigratory and multicultural character with a special focus on the country's population of Turkish heritage. Drawing from production-focused methodologies as exemplified by Saha (2018) and Georgina Born (2010), I explored how diversity as a contingent discourse takes form in the practices of classical music production today, how it links to and negotiates hegemonic representations of difference, and how it constructs concepts of cultural value and legitimacy. As part of my study,

I followed the opera's diversity managers in their day-to-day work, I spoke with administrative staff, musicians, composers, and local participants involved in the project and—to the extent possible—observed rehearsals and performances. I considered the practices of music-making itself but also positioned such creative discussions within a wider analysis of "Western" art music's institutional histories and of the current political context, where the legacies of German imperialism and racialized accounts of citizenship continue to play out.

While having been shaped by various long-standing migration processes, Germany continues to grapple with its widely held image of a "non-immigration country" that has constructed Germans of color and Germans with migratory biographies as eternal others (e.g., Yılmaz, 2015; El-Tayeb, 2016). As demonstrated by the election successes of the extreme-right party *Alternative Für Deutschland* [Alternative for Germany], increasing rates of racist violence, and strong backlashes against recent migration in the context of the "refugee crisis" of 2015, white nationalist views furthermore risk becoming more and more mainstream again (e.g., El-Tayeb, 2016). The arts have certainly played an important role in challenging racist discourses with many activists and artists of color powerfully pushing for the recognition of Germany's cultural and ethnic plurality. At the same time, however, the cultural sector has itself also been a site of deep-seated, racialized inequality (e.g., Kosnick, 2008). It is within this ambivalent context that current diversity discourses in the cultural industries take shape. In the following, I will therefore draw out some of the key challenges of diversity initiatives in the cultural sector, and in classical music specifically, as revealed by my data.

Diversity as contested discourse

First, it is important to note that diversity as a term and an institutional objective is in and of itself rather unspecific, can be interpreted in different ways and, as such, can have very different consequences for the social, aesthetic, and organizational structures of cultural institutions. Whether we are talking about concert halls, opera houses, or music conservatories, cultural institutions are not only organizational and aesthetic but social bodies. They consist of a conglomerate of people with different expertise, skills, and experiences who work together following specific divisions of labor, institutional histories, and hierarchies. The moment in which the discourse of diversity enters into institutional life, it therefore enters into a wider set of social relations and relations of power that stretch beyond the cultural sector. What exactly is meant when cultural organizations seek to "diversify" themselves, how the very term is understood, and how it is negotiated in the different areas and processes of institutional life is therefore not a given but a contingent and contested social process. Whether diversity discourses can address and unsettle institutional inequalities of "race," class, gender, or disability (among others) or whether it ultimately contributes to their reproduction thus depends on "how they get taken up, as well as who takes them up" (Ahmed, 2007, pp. 245–246).

In my own research into diversity strategies in Germany's opera sector, I particularly observed two conflicting accounts of diversity, one that recognized the latter as a call for self-reflexive institutional change, the other focusing merely on bringing more minoritized cultural producers into the realm of classical music without, however, questioning the organizational and aesthetic set-up of the sector itself. Despite following dissimilar logics, these different understandings of diversity were often not made explicit among the opera's staff while repeatedly clashing in practice. One example where such conflicts manifested can be found in the children's choir reform that was part of the opera's overarching diversity strategy. As common practice for many opera houses, the institution trains its own in-house children's choir whose members receive free music education and can gain valuable performance experience (another example is discussed in the interview with Anthony Gray in this volume). Preceding the launch of the opera's diversity project, the choir predominantly consisted of white German children, with the majority being middle-class. Causing concern about access barriers, the opera's directorship therefore decided to push for the broadening of the choir's membership, specifically reaching out to children of Turkish descent. While this strategy has partly proven successful, leading to Turkish German children now making up about a third of the choir, my data also document how it served as a reproductive platform for "raced" and classed inequality. This is partly because the choir managers and members had different interpretations and objectives in reforming the choir, prompting different institutional consequences.

On one hand, the opera's leading diversity managers understood the choir reform as a grounded, intersectional approach to institutional change and championed a revision of the choir's standardized workings in favor of a wider set of cultural practices. In our many conversations, they repeatedly highlighted that, for them, "diversity is not just about access for diverse people, it is first and foremost about us as an institution" because "German high culture" would still act "as a hypocritical ivory tower which only claims that its doors would be open" while continuing to be "a very white and socially elitist space" (interviews and fieldnotes, September–November 2016). These more self-reflexive understandings of diversity also translated into practice with the opera house changing its standardized approaches to the choir's management, casting, and repertoire. For instance, rather than only publishing casting calls via established music schools or via word-of-mouth, the choir was advertised via Turkish media outlets and in collaboration with various local partners, such as schools, youth clubs, and neighborhood centers focusing specifically on working-class areas. Moreover, the opera adapted the casting procedure itself, letting children audition with whichever pop or folk song they wanted and focusing on their vocal potential instead of testing a specific level of "Western" art music knowledge. In line with these approaches, the choir's repertoire also expanded, specifically including pieces in Turkish language. In short, rather than merely integrate diverse voices into an otherwise static musical environment, the opera's diversity team foregrounded a diversity of practices, equipped to rethink the ways in which the opera's aesthetic and organizational workings are entangled with inequalities of "race" and class.

On the other hand, the accounts of some of the choir parents revealed a different take on diversity. Many of them, especially participants of white and middle-class background, framed the choir reform not in terms of institutional change but rather as an opportunity for "intercultural learning," stating that "getting to know about our multicultural society" would be a "useful resource" for their children's generation (interview and fieldnotes, 2016–2017). Simultaneously holding onto the opera's prestigious social status as "one of the best music institutions in Germany," the parents identified the choir as a productive realm in which the children would be exposed to different cultural and ethnic backgrounds while still being part of the highbrow sector. We can therefore again detect an intrinsic connection between the structures of classical music education and the production and remaking of a particular middle-class self-formation. In these accounts, diversity seems to be first and foremost a commodity that ultimately serves the (white) middle-classes to hold onto their social position in today's multicultural yet hierarchized world. Such findings resonate with Diane Reay et al.'s UK-based study (2011) on urban schooling preferences of white middle-class families who sent their children to lower-performing and ethnically diverse schools to encourage an openness toward social difference. Their analysis shows that contemporary middle-class subjectivities not only assign a high value to education but also recognize open and cosmopolitan attitudes as important cultural resources today. However, they nevertheless continue to share certain other class characteristics too, such as "a sense of entitlement, educational excellence, confidence, competitiveness, hard work, deferred gratification" and, connected therewith, a continued "ability to erect boundaries, both geographically and symbolically" (ibid., p. 12). The case of the children's choir speaks precisely to these shifting yet steady markers of white middle-class identities. In this way, the institutionalization of diversity seems to indeed reinvigorate the highbrow sphere as a site of middle-class formation and elite-making.

These reproductive logics also played out in the practices of the choir's management. For instance, while the choir's intercultural reform initially also attracted a number of children of working-class background, whose families were struggling with the choir's intense logistical demands, some of these children had to leave the choir early on again. As a choir manager explained, this was because their parents "weren't really able to provide the logistics," expanding that they "didn't come to rehearsal regularly or were always late. We tried to get in touch with the parents, but there was little response. . . . It's also not our purpose as an opera choir to provide more focused social work" (interview, 2014). This incident documents how, in moments of tension and challenge, the choir's inclusivity appeared to exhaust itself rather swiftly. Instead of allocating sufficient resources to the choir management to rethink its institutional workings and entrenched social biases, it is the children's families themselves who are made responsible for their dismissal from the choir. In essence, diversity, rather than prompting institutional change, is reduced to a (missed) individual opportunity to gain cultural capital and social mobility within an individualist neoliberal society. Overall, the choir project shows how the contingent nature of diversity discourses simultaneously opens up a critical lens through which to challenge classical music's white elitism, while also enabling the remaking of classed and "raced" inequalities.

Diversity and the (re)making of musical otherness

The different ways in which diversity is understood also inform the different ways in which diversity as institutional and creative labor gets organized. It is crucial to consider how institutions structure and divide such work as this is by no means random but often reflects the degree of institutional value assigned to a politics of diversity. This becomes an especially challenging consideration when classical music institutions seek to produce a diverse musical program, one that goes beyond the standardized precepts of "Western" genres and seeks to bring into dialogue different musical systems. The ways in which such creative work is thought of, developed, and structured can illustrate how notions of diversity and difference come into being musically and, as such, take shape as representational practices. Who decides what kinds of music are regarded as diverse and are seen as the unmarked standard? Which aesthetic and organizational parameters influence the musical production process? Whose voices are foregrounded in the creative decision-making while others are pushed to the peripheries? And how do these cultural production dynamics tie in with wider discourses of difference and inequalities of "race" and ethnicity? These concerns then back the question of how and, importantly, under which creative conditions diversity work in classical music can lead to either the unmaking or the reproduction of racialized representations of (musical) difference.

My study of diversity work in Germany's classical music sector gives some insight into these issues. Specifically, part of the opera's diversity project involved the commissioning and performance of two new opera works that were intended to be "intercultural" and broaden the opera's aesthetic profile beyond a standardized notion of opera by bringing together Turkish and "Western" musical elements. One of the pieces was commissioned to a Turkish Kurdish composer living in Germany, the other one to a Turkish composer from Antalya. Troubling "Western" art music's legacies of imperialism in their respective ways, both works indeed unlocked spaces for a critical creativity that challenges hegemonic notions of "Western" genre and unsettles Orientalist notions of difference (see Said, 1978). However, my analysis of their production process also makes visible how the opera house's standardized institutional workings ultimately constrained the transgressive potential of the two pieces, risking the remaking of racialized representations and inequalities. At stake in diversity debates in the "Western" creative industries is therefore also "the question of *authorial agency*" (Born and Hesmondhalgh, 2000, p. 38; original emphasis), which shapes the ways in which diversity is being done.

How the opera institution took on an authorial agency itself is already exemplified in the very framing of the commissioning processes. As one of the opera's curators recognizes, "the terms *interculture* or *Turkish German* of course raise certain musical expectations—internally for us and externally for the audience. They are not very sharp and group many things together, but it was important to communicate to the public that these operas were not supposed to just be contemporary "Western" music but something different. Internally, you also need to justify why you commission a particular work to a particular composer.... So, when we said Turkish German, we needed to find something or better someone who would compose accordingly. We wanted a Turkish sound." The curator also identifies that "the mere fact of commissioning music for a "Western" art institution is that the musical choices are always already skewed to an extent. Both composers integrated Turkish instruments, but they are only a few whereas our orchestra holds over 60 musicians—so the few need to adapt to the many in a sense. It's a numbers game, it's just how it is." It is noteworthy that, while critically recognizing the opera's uses of reductive generalizations, such labels are also seen as necessary for external and internal marketing purposes and for justifying particular commission choices to the institution's in-house management.

However, while it is certainly understandable that musical programming of any kind requires some sort of marketable labeling to mobilize institutional support and audiences, such labels are not innocent descriptions but also *do* something. Within diversity projects, they not only impact the ways in which cultural difference is presented but can also shape creative production in ways that construct certain representations of difference. Here, Saha (2018, p. 138) explains that the "assemblage of processes, apparatus, rationales and logics that are embodied in each stage of production" entrenches a "rationalizing/racializing logic of capital" into the production process precisely through practices of "(self-)formatting, marketing and packaging." The explicit Turkish German framing of the commissioned pieces certainly helped push for their realization. However, such a label also draws a distinction between the opera's "Western" canonized program and such other(ed) exceptions, playing into ongoing processes of othering that Turkish Germans are subjected to in wider debates around citizenship and belonging.

Moreover, while the two works were meant to produce a "Turkish sound," it was the orchestral set-up of a "Western" classical music institution that set the ultimate aesthetic boundary. This created a lot of challenges for the composers who had to create the right degree of musical difference, staying within the boundaries of the institution's standardized aesthetic paradigms. The kinds of power relations at play in the composition of the two pieces also extended into the practices of rehearsal. In particular, issues surrounding notation, instrumentation, and conducting became central sites of tension where the institution decisively shaped the production process of both operas, putting a considerable burden onto the minoritized cultural producers. While both operas included Middle Eastern instruments like bağlama, oud, kanoon, or zurna, their players often recounted that they did not feel that their instruments were being showcased. One of the musicians even said that, rather than feeling like their instruments were central to the opera piece, he felt like he was merely "adding sonic color" to the composition. One of the composers equally expressed concern that they had to largely adhere to "Western" compositional styles and could not, for instance, include elaborate maqam-scales, long improvisation sections, or micro-tonal structures, as this would have overwhelmed the orchestra. The burden to adapt to the musical dominance of "Western" genre concepts was thus relegated to the minoritized musicians.

These reflections seem to precisely illustrate Stuart Hall's (1992, p. 23) cautionary words on diversity discourses risking being reduced to "a bit of the other" instead of really decentering Eurocentric cultural practices. Rather, it seems that the frame of diversity allows the opera institution to draw symbolic value from the work of the *diverse* instrumentalists, while at the same time pushing them—at least to some degree—to the margins of the musical process. Furthermore, being hired only for the production of the intercultural operas, the musicians of Middle Eastern instruments not only had to be virtuoso in their own right but also had to be able to play according to staff notation and conductor's beat, two essential playing techniques of "Western" classical music. Again, the main burden of doing diversity in musical practice was outsourced to the minoritized players, who in some instances were even let go and replaced by musicians who could fulfil such criteria, making the possibility of musical assimilation the baseline for employment altogether. The decision to opt for musicians who were already also trained according to "Western" musical parameters was inter alia made because the opera institution's routinized production schedule did not allow for more rehearsal time to be made available. The scarcity of institutional time and resources thus became yet another factor that further constrained the transgressive possibilities of the intercultural opera productions. Subsequently, the development of the two pieces shows that, for diversity to really challenge reductive representations of difference, attention must be paid to the production process itself. Here, it is crucial to decouple disruptive creative efforts as far as possible from the standardized production logics of "Western" cultural institutions.

Conclusion

This chapter outlined some of the challenges that diversity agendas in the classical music sector can entail. While my research into diversity efforts at a German opera institution certainly showed that diversity can prompt profound institutional change, this chapter focused on unpacking how such discourses can simultaneously enable the ongoing marginalization of racialized and classed others. It specifically cautioned that diversity projects in "Western" highbrow institutions, even when launched with genuine intentions of institutional and social change, proceed within a hierarchical cultural topography and run the risk of reproducing "race"-making and elite-making logics. Building on cultural studies, sociology, and critical "race" scholarship, I first looked into the contingent effects that diversity as a contested discourse can have on institutional practice. Secondly, I drew out how the standardized production practices of "Western" institutions impact the ways in which diversity can take shape in musical practice and discussed the risk of diversity work becoming racialized labor. For diversity work to contribute to the undoing of institutional whiteness and elitism, I would therefore argue that it is crucial to approach it in open-ended creative ways, delinked from potentially limiting hierarchical institutional workings. Moreover, it would be helpful if institutions provided sufficient room for reflection on institutional effects of diversity agendas, so that unintended social consequences can be recognized and addressed. For classical music specifically, it is essential to critically consider the sector's histories of exclusion and to develop an awareness of how their legacies continue to shape the field today. These critical remarks, however, are by no means intended to discourage an active reckoning with classical music's institutionalized social exclusions. Rather, the chapter hoped to open up a constructive perspective for those working toward a more equal and just cultural sector.

6
"To Share Music with Children"
The LA Phil and Neoliberal Philanthropy in Inglewood

Mina Yang

In December 2020, the *Los Angeles Times* music critic Mark Swed opened a column titled "Black Music Matters, and Classical Companies are Misfiring on Diversity" with a description of his visit to the new home of Youth Orchestra Los Angeles (or YOLA for short). Bearing witness to the construction of the gleaming new hall, Swed seemed to have found the saving grace for classical music's ills, averring: "Gehry's reimagining of an abandoned bank building may not be able to satisfy all the demands for systemic change that have been directed toward classical music privilege. But it just may be the single most heartening start." For the bulk of the rest of the article, Swed considered which black composers he thought should or shouldn't be included in the repertoire of professional orchestras as a response to the historical moment of racial reckoning following the George Floyd killing. He then returned to YOLA in the conclusion of the article:

> For real systemic change, we need a real system in place, something solid and lasting. YOLA is that system. It trains talent and attracts audiences. It goes to the core of the issue. It generates enthusiasm, broadens horizons, and inspires commitment. That sounds like advertising copy, but there are YOLA grads to prove it attending college and working for the L.A. Phil. Someday in the not distant future, grads will be playing in the orchestra. YOLA looks to be impervious to the coronavirus. (Swed, 2020)

Swed is not alone in his enthusiastic endorsement of a community youth music program as classical music's answer to a range of social ills. From the mid 2000s to the early 2010s, a spate of documentaries and books sang the praises of El Sistema, Venezuela's ambitious music education system that purported to lift thousands of children out of poverty and into the musical spotlight.[1] International music and human rights organizations showered José Antonio Abreu, the late El Sistema founder, with accolades and honors. In a year of profound crisis for arts organizations, and particularly for Old Guard critics like

Swed (who has been the classical music critic for the *Los Angeles Times* since 1996), the model of El Sistema might seem like a welcome beacon of hope. Such a model promises a future that would draw on the best of humanitarian impulses to provide rich musical opportunities to less privileged youths and possibly even save their beloved musical tradition from the intensifying accusations of racism and elitism coming its way. The Los Angeles Philharmonic has in its internationally renowned maestro, Gustavo Dudamel, whose meteoric career was launched while the music director of El Sistema's crown jewel ensemble, Orquesta Sinfónica Simón Bolívar, a poster child for the benefits of El Sistema, his charms only magnified by his pronounced Spanish accent. LA Phil's YOLA program, spearheaded by Dudamel and inspired by El Sistema, appears to give lie to the contention that classical music is only for rich white people, and the rich white people who give money to the LA Phil can feel good knowing that they are providing the resources needed to help produce more Dudamels, or at least ticket-buying fans who look more like Dudamel, for a rosy future ahead.

What Swed and the LA Phil reps fail to mention are the criticisms of El Sistema that have emerged and grown in volume in recent years. Geoff Baker (2014, 2017, N.D.), for example, revealed how Abreu manipulated the packaging of the program, staging extravaganzas meant to impress politicians at home and the media abroad. Alums of the program described a culture of abuse and exploitation that rewarded the most talented students—often from middle-class families—at the expense of everyone else. Abreu famously refused to provide any data about the welfare of El Sistema students and graduates and downplayed the tremendous expense of the program, paid for by Venezuela's dirty oil money. Even for the El Sistema–inspired programs in North America and Europe, where there is far more transparency and accountability, initial enthusiasm has become somewhat muted.[2] Still, in the US, where socioeconomic inequality is all too often coupled with racial inequity, El Sistema–inspired programs have at least partially mitigated the increasingly troubling optics of the almost exclusively white, wealthy audiences who patronize the symphony and opera. But as Marianna Ritchey argues elsewhere in this volume, including a few brown and black bodies in promotional photos or inclusion-oriented programs does not necessarily signal the arrival of a more equitable culture. And giving money to nonprofit outreach efforts that support music education in underserved communities, possibly resulting in a few of these youths of color being absorbed into the classical music fold, turns out to be more complicated and ethically slippery than it may first seem.

Against the backdrop of the COVID pandemic crisis in arts institutions and the growing influence of the black Lives Matter movement, the LA Phil's construction of the new Beckmen YOLA Center, designed by Frank Gehry and underwritten with funds ($23M at the time of writing this chapter) from the founder of Roland Corporation and LA Phil board chair Thomas Beckmen, provides a timely case study with which to unpack the intricacies of arts philanthropy, classical music, and social change. Rather than simply revel in the generosity of the multimillion dollar gift, we should carefully think through what such a building actually means for the YOLA students as well as for other youths in Los Angeles and elsewhere. Does the gleaming new concert hall in the heart of Inglewood in fact support Swed's claim that an extracurricular music program for kids from underserved communities offers the best hope for a systemic change that will begin to dismantle classical music's racist legacy? Or might we instead critique the Beckmen Center as a concrete instantiation of neoliberal philanthropy, white savior discourses, and the (mis)use of "starchitecture"? As more establishment arts organizations and institutions launch similar community programs, we should take a moment to pause and ask who these program administrators and deep-pocketed donors are really saving.

Neoliberal Philanthropy

The kind of philanthropic giving that is underwriting the YOLA program and the building of the Beckmen Center is becoming more common today. As David Callahan observes in his 2017 book, *The Givers: Money, Power, and Philanthropy in the Gilded Age*: "Philanthropy is becoming a much stronger power center and, in some areas, is set to surpass government in its ability to shape society's agenda. To put things differently, we face a future in which private donors—who are accountable to no one—may often wield more influence than elected public officials, who (in theory, anyway) are accountable to all of us. This power shift is one of the biggest stories of our time" (Callahan, 2017). Callahan's book traces the recent growth of philanthropy, which, perhaps not surprisingly, is directly intertwined with the increasing influence of neoliberal ideologies around the world. As business interests take precedence over social welfare and the wealthy dodge paying taxes through ever more sophisticated means, individual wealth for the .1% has ballooned and state coffers have shrunk. With more money than they can possibly spend in their lifetimes, many billionaires are turning to philanthropy as a way to make a big impact and leave a lasting legacy.

Programs that use arts for social change (AFSC), particularly those located in underserved neighborhoods, have experienced significant growth as a result of this increase in philanthropic activity. Adam Saifer sees a direct link between the ascension of the neoliberal state and the increase in spending on AFSC programs in underserved communities since the 1990s. At the same time that neoliberal policies leached money and other resources out of communities of color, these communities became attractive sites for investment through the expansion of

AFSC programs. Saifer's critique zeroes in on AFSC philanthropy's use of impact metrics from the venture capital world, which calculates the social return on investment of these programs using language that reinforces the racialized dynamics of white saviors and grantees of color. In particular, he bristles at venture philanthropy's role in "shift[ing] AFSC organizations from racial justice organization to a metaphorical caulking gun responsible for filling in the gaps of the retreating racial neoliberal state" (Saifer, 2020). Successful in lowering their tax liabilities, the über-rich have signed giving pledges and have tethered their success as philanthropists to funding nonprofits with clear social missions. Whereas earlier philanthropists gave to established educational and arts institutions, today's philanthropists seek to achieve more morally satisfying social returns on their investment, without relinquishing their power to decide who and what should be the beneficiary of their largesse.[3]

Orchestras, long dependent on philanthropic money, are all too aware of this sea change in giving. Some of the foremost orchestras in the "Western" world, including the Boston Symphony Orchestra, Philadelphia Orchestra, and the Berlin Philharmonic, among others, have jumped on the music-for-social-change bandwagon in a bid to be socially relevant, enhancing their diversity portfolio by starting or expanding their own youth programs and attracting the notice of AFSC philanthropists.[4] The LA Phil and its well-heeled benefactors are at the forefront of this trend. In 2007, the LA Phil, newly headed by the proud El Sistema alum Gustavo Dudamel, launched YOLA in South Los Angeles with 80 students. The program now boasts four locations (South LA, Ramparts District, East LA, and Westlake/MacArthur Park, all neighborhoods with populations that are majority black and brown), and it currently provides free music lessons and orchestral training to over 1,300 students. YOLA has become a flagship outreach program under the wing of the LA Phil, with the orchestra's website prominently featuring photos of happy children of color playing little violins and clarinets.

Public Education Under Neoliberalism

As impressive as YOLA's growth is, it is clearly not enough to reach the almost 560,000 kids in Los Angeles County who live below the poverty level (Public Policy Institute of California, 2017; Austin, 2019). In the 1960s, public education in California was considered among the best in the nation, and music classes constituted a part of the normal fare for public school students across the Southern California region. Under the assault of neoliberal policies—including the passage of Proposition 13, which dramatically reduced tax revenues that fed into school funding, and the charter school movement, which is attempting to privatize public education—public schools in California have struggled to survive and balance the books, slashing any non-essential programs, such as music, in the process.

The devolution of public education has had an especially devastating effect on minority-majority neighborhoods. The Inglewood Unified School District, for example, found itself mired in mounting debt, with diminishing funds tied to a smaller student population due to the decrease in birth rate and the siphoning away of students into charter schools. In 2012, the school district was taken over by a state-appointed superintendent. The white superintendent Don Brann, who chose to move to the neighboring predominantly white city of El Segundo, got himself into trouble with his Inglewood constituents soon after the start of his tenure. In explaining why he needed to use taxpayer funds to beef up his personal security detail, he spoke of his fears for his safety in Inglewood, which is a largely middle-class city in LA's tony South Bay region, but is often lumped together with Compton, Watts, and other storied hoods that are likewise black and brown (Kaplan, 2014). As Damien Schnyder details in his study of public education in LA, there is a long history of outsiders imposing their educational agenda in black neighborhoods in California. The downward trend of public schools in communities of color has intensified with the corporatization of public education wherein poorly performing schools have been converted into charter schools—for the most part run by outsiders—that are not accountable to their communities even as they divert public funds away from public schools (Schnyder, 2012).

White saviorism

So why not accept the goodwill of organizations like the LA Phil that is filling a gap? It seems curmudgeonly, at best, to find fault in Dudamel's quote, featured prominently on YOLA's website: "To share music with children—who might not otherwise have access to it—is to share beauty, to share a different way of being. It can change their definition of what is possible for themselves" (Los Angeles Philharmonic, 2021). How can we find fault with any effort to bring music into the lives of our youths?

We can find fault because where there once were regular music classes, marching bands, and jazz ensembles for any students who were interested, we now have mostly white teachers and program staff coming into underresourced school districts to teach Beethoven and Tchaikowsky to a select group of students, purportedly saving their young charges with the civilizing influence of "Western" culture. Instead of having all students enjoy the benefits of music education for a few hours a week, a handful of kids get up to eighteen hours of instruction a week after school from LA Phil–approved teachers. Although orchestras are relatively rare in communities of color in California, music-making is not at all a scarce commodity. At Jordan High School in Watts, for example, generations of dedicated black music teachers have shaped the lives of young musicians, among them Buddy Colette and Charles Mingus. Down the street from the new YOLA Center, the Inglewood Park Cemetery holds the remains of Chet Baker, Ray Charles, Pee Wee Crayton, Ella Fitzgerald, Lowell Fulson, Etta James, Big Mama Thornton, and T-Bone Walker. Inglewood is also the home to the Southeast Symphony Orchestra, the longest running predominantly African American orchestra in the country. Mariachi musicians are currently organizing protests against the city's plans to develop affordable housing in East LA's Mariachi Plaza, displacing them from their site of nightly music-making.[5]

Recently, while reading about a black classics professor at Princeton who is challenging the very foundations of his discipline, this author was reminded of the YOLA kids. In the article written by Rachel Poser, Professor Dan-el Padilla Peralta compares his education to that of Frederick Douglass, concisely and devastatingly articulating the problem at the heart of white saviorism:

> Padilla, like Douglass, now sees the moment of absorption into the classical, literary tradition as simultaneous with his apprehension of racial difference; he can no longer find pride or comfort in having used it to bring himself out of poverty. He permits himself no such relief. "Claiming dignity within this system of structural oppression," Padilla has said, "requires full buy-in into its logic of valuation." He refuses to "praise the architects of that trauma as having done right by you at the end." (Poser, 2021)

Likewise, these exceptional kids who "escape" their impoverished communities are being asked to absorb the values of the culture that is offered to them by YOLA—values that celebrate dead white male composers rather than living poets, the sanctity of fixed texts rather than the excitement of improvised performances; a hierarchy that puts Euro-American culture above all others, that preserves an enduring canon with the money of the elite even if only a small segment of the world actually listens to it; that asserts its cultural supremacy and uses this claim to supremacy to keep others—these kids and their families, for example—down and out. As cultural historian Lawrence Levine so brilliantly demonstrated, and as musicologists like Loren Kajikawa have more recently reminded us, institutions like the symphony orchestra were founded with the express purpose of exclusion, as a means of drawing clear lines between the power elites—who were and are for the most part wealthy whites—and everyone else (Levine, 1988; Kajikawa, 2019). Discourses around diversity—meant to allay the concerns of those who care about social and racial equity—do little to challenge the power dynamics that inhere in these institutions (see Ritchey in this volume).

This is borne out by those on the ground. Rachael Marissa Edwards, who worked for OrchKids, another El Sistema–inspired program in Baltimore, wrote about her decision to resign from her job: "Often times, nonprofits are created and predominately [sic] funded by white people and they come into our communities and do not want to get to know who we are. Instead, they come into their jobs with pre-conceived notions and want to 'save' us when really they are killing us" (Edwards, 2016). Edwards detailed the degrading language some of the staff members used about the students and the racist incidents she herself endured. After she reported these incidents to human resources, the organization retaliated by demoting her. Although those working in nonprofits may have the best intentions, the core missions of AFSC programs are framed in ways that reinforce the dynamics of white saviors saving "troubled" youths of color, getting in the way of moving beyond racialized interactions.

The LA Phil and Starchitecture

Finally, let us turn our attention to the building. There is nothing like an expensive building, especially one designed by a (no, *the*) star architect Frank Gehry, to signify importance and permanence. The LA Phil PR department is making sure everyone recognizes this milestone of the YOLA program. In an impeccably produced video released on the occasion of the breaking of ground for the construction of the concert hall, one after another of the Phil's top administrators touts the significance of the building for the YOLA program. With music swelling in the background, YOLA alum Liliana Morales, a smiling young Latina, gushes, "For the students, and for the community, for their parents, for the city of Inglewood, having a space built specifically for YOLA students, it really shows that they care about all of us" (LA Phil, 2020). At the groundbreaking ceremony, Simon Woods, the CEO of the LA Phil, proclaimed: "I can tell you that there is no prouder day than this morning. . . . There is nothing which is more meaningful than what we are doing here, what we're launching here in Inglewood. It's a historic day for the LA Phil" (Carter, 2018). The message is clear: The LA Phil cares, the people who give money to the LA Phil care, and this building is the concrete proof of how much everyone cares. All this caring about the youth and diversity serves to legitimize the main mission of the LA Phil—the perpetuation of a Eurocentric musical tradition—and erases or at least hides from view the checkered history of classical music and "Western" colonialism.

Never mind that with the Beckmen Center, the LA Phil is deploying starchitecture, a type of monumentality that captures and celebrates the money, tastes, and status of the elite, of the top.1%, on a global stage. Starchitecture, in the form of a sleek Gehry-designed concert hall, will inevitably attract media spotlight and reflect it back brightly on the LA Phil. Rather than hire local black or Latinx architects, which would have significantly boosted the reputations of those architects, the LA Phil board went with the internationally celebrated nonagenarian starchitect. Rather than spend $23 million paying for music teachers' salaries for all the kids in the neighborhood or to fight for the passage of Prop 15, which would have at least partially reversed Prop 13, the LA Phil chose to build a state-of-the art concert hall for a few kids and get a lot of credit for doing so. To borrow from the parlance of social media, the Beckmen Center is the LA Phil virtue signaling in concrete, steel, and glass.

And the LA Phil has much to gain with the growing visibility of the YOLA program and the perpetuation of neoliberal policies that necessitate such programs. In 2018, $56 million, almost half of the $125 million annual budget of the LA Phil, came from individual donors. The biggest donation was made by the late Dudley Rauch, one of the longest-serving LA Phil board members, who said of his $25 million donation:

> When you make a financial commitment to any organization, you are essentially voting your values, and at the Philharmonic, the values here are right, in my opinion. We are not just preserving orchestral music, but we are making the Hollywood Bowl a better, more welcoming place; we are voting for the values that Gustavo has brought to us about youth education. (Los Angeles Philharmonic, 2018)

While other traditional orchestras watch helplessly as their funding from public sources and donors dwindle to a trickle, the LA Phil is riding on the success of its music-for-social-change program, convincing donors like Rauch that they are paying for a lot more than just old music.

In an era of seemingly irreversible audience shrinkage, the LA Phil has fared notably better than its peers, largely because it understands that orchestras cannot survive on appeals to the ear alone. The LA Phil earned the label of the "most important orchestra in America" by no less than the newspaper of record, the *New York Times* (Woolfe, 2017), by reinventing itself with a photogenic new hall (the $265 million Disney Hall, also designed by Frank Gehry), a media-savvy music director from the Global South, and a community outreach program that demonstrates its dedication to the principles of diversity and inclusion. Its administration understands the marketing fundamentals of this millennium, that eyeballs first hook audiences, and then a tug of their hearts makes them stay. With the construction of the Beckmen Center, the LA Phil is repeating their successful formula, if on a less grand scale: a design by an architect who guarantees media attention, a photogenic object, and lots of heartwarming stories showcasing multi-hued kids. Following the financial disaster of the COVID shutdown, other orchestras are no doubt studying the LA Phil playbook.

There are certainly a number of ways that the YOLA program can be improved to bring more value to the community it serves. Students might be given more opportunities to bring in music from their own communities or peer groups, penning their own hip-hop verses or performing corridos on stage instead of practicing scales. The program could recruit and hire more teachers and staff who come from the communities of color they serve, perhaps even alums of the program. YOLA could start a collaboration with members of Inglewood's own Southeast Symphony Orchestra. But at the end of the day, this can only be a program for a select few, many of them from families that are more inclined to have the resources to support their children in such endeavors, and their "success" is defined by the LA Phil and the Eurocentric culture they represent.

Conclusion

For the kind of systemic change Mark Swed was talking about, we need to re-evaluate our whole neoliberal taxation system and its devastating impact on public education, not just in California, but everywhere that neoliberalism has become the dominant ideology and policy. Public schools still offer the best hope for kids from underserved communities for upward mobility. Why not offer every child music education—one truly based on diversity and inclusion—and have them use dedicated music spaces in their own schools with the support of their own teachers to practice and show off their varied musical heritages in the ways they see fit? As numerous articles on philanthropy's limits during the pandemic have shown, even the best-intentioned philanthropists cannot spend enough or make enough of a positive splash to offset the damage they have wreaked by minimizing their tax liability and starving public coffers (Sammon, 2019). Nonprofit administrators have been only too happy to go along, stroking their benefactors' egos and feeding them feel-good stories about how they're saving black and brown children. It is time to acknowledge that in actuality, these community programs, with the support of their wealthy patrons, are doing much more to prop up institutions that perpetuate the status quo power structure rather than changing a meaningful number of lives for the better (Vu, 2021).

A revision in the tax code would certainly be far less Instagrammable than a shiny new building with Gehry's name attached to it, but that is what would actually create systemic change for the youths of Inglewood, East LA, Watts, and beyond.

Notes

1. See, for example, *Tocar y Luchar*, 2006; *The Promise of Music*, 2008; *El Sistema: Music to Change*, 2009; Turnstall, 2012.
2. I myself wrote about the early years of YOLA with tremendous hope in my last book, thinking that it was the one area of the classical music world that offered optimism. I have since become much more gloomy about the prospect of any one thing saving this musical culture. See Yang, 2014.
3. See, also, Sammon, 2019.
4. See, for example, the list of 116 members of the El Sistema USA umbrella organization (El Sistema USA, 2021).
5. See Vasquez, 2019; Zanfagna, 2017; *Boyles Heights Beats*, 2020; *LAist*, 2021.

7
A Critical Perspective on Diversity and Inclusion in US Classical Music Discourse

Marianna Ritchey

Today in this-is-2018-WTF?! news, the Metropolitan Opera has announced several new ventures intended to draw in audiences, including commissioning women to write operas for the first time ever. Yep, that's right: As the *New York Times* reports, composers Missy Mazzoli and Jeanine Tesori are "the first two women commissioned to write operas for the Met." The performing arts organization has existed for over 130 years. (Montpelier, 2018)

Classical music in contemporary US practice is widely perceived as having a diversity problem. Its orchestras, opera companies, conductors, and boards of directors are overwhelmingly White and male; similarly, the number of compositions by women, People of Color, and other minorities that get commissioned or programmed at performance venues is vanishingly small. For years, articles with titles like "Opera Can No Longer Ignore Its Race Problem" and "Sexism Is Rife in Classical Music" have proliferated, along with an accompanying discourse outlining ways to address these inequalities (Barone, 2020; and Rhodes, 2014).

There is no need to rehash all the statistics and trot out all the graphs again; the institutional world of classical music simply is White supremacist and patriarchal, and indeed, as many scholars have recently argued, White supremacist patriarchy is part of the whole point of how this particular set of musical sounds and styles coagulated into a "tradition," how and why certain types of it became canonized, and how and why we continue to teach it, play it, and talk about it the way we do (Taylor, 2007; Kajikawa, 2019; Attas and Walker, 2019; Ewell, 2020). Within such a context, the outrage many musicians and composers express toward classical music makes sense and is perfectly valid. And yet, the discourse aimed at "diversifying" this musical culture deserves careful critical scrutiny, lest such efforts end up reiterating the inequalities they seek to dismantle. In this

Marianna Ritchey, *A Critical Perspective on Diversity and Inclusion in US Classical Music Discourse* In: *Voices for Change in the Classical Music Profession.* Edited by: Anna Bull and Christina Scharff with Associate Editor Laudan Nooshin, Oxford University Press. © Oxford University Press 2023. DOI: 10.1093/oso/9780197601211.003.0008 chapter, I will address one of the core problems I see in the mainstream case for diversifying classical music, which has to do with the liberal political perspective that shapes much of the classical music discourse in the US.

Political theorists use the term "liberal" to gloss the set of perspectives that, while originally emanating from 18th-century British political economy, swiftly came to dominate social and economic policy and discourse in the US and, over time, much of the rest of the industrialized world as well (Appiah, 2001). In the economic sense, liberals' orientation toward society is rationalist, individualistic, and elitist, in that it naturalizes capitalism and the social inequality that capitalism relies upon (Mouffe, 2005; Gilbert, 2014). Yet many liberals also see themselves as caring deeply about social problems like poverty and oppression—in everyday US parlance, to be "liberal" is to self-identify as someone who is tolerant of difference and sympathetic to the plight of the marginalized. Unlike leftists, however, liberals do not see capitalism as a prime driver of poverty and oppression; rather, they tend to identify such problems as stemming from poor personal choices or lack of opportunities for individuals (Brown, 2005). Thus, US liberals tend to identify "diversity" with the raising up of individuals from various marginalized identity categories into existing institutions and power structures (for further critical discussion, please see: Davis, 1996; Melamed, 2011; Ahmed, 2012). This individualistic perspective often has the effect of rendering class hierarchy, the main issue with which this essay is concerned, invisible. The following arguments are specific to classical music practice in the United States, although they may have wider relevance for musical contexts in the UK and Western Europe generally.

Diversifying programming

In addition to the kinds of outreach programs Mina Yang diagnoses in this volume, which are intended to build audiences and create better avenues of access to this music, activists also level demands at institutions to change their programming and commissioning practices, in order to make what's put on stage more representative of the communities these entities claim to serve. Within these demands, there are slippery aspects that require critical attention.

For example, the Metropolitan Opera has become a target in this discourse, because its programming statistics are simply so stark and indefensible. It hasn't commissioned a single opera by a woman, in 130 years? Such a statistic truly is a "WTF" moment, as the quote at the beginning of this chapter puts it. When women composers demand more representation at the Met, it makes sense, and such demands certainly are well-intentioned. It is also easy to be sympathetic to demands that a powerful cultural institution like the Met should "reflect" or "represent" the actual diversity of people in a community.

And yet, there are also major problems with representational identity politics of this kind, problems that emanate from the liberal political framework that shapes this orientation. Within a liberal politics of representation, inequality will be resolved by more diverse representation within the existing institutions that shape our public discourse and give us access to "culture." This politics frames institutions themselves (like the Met, or like the US government) as eternal and essentially benevolent. Nothing needs to change about their structures or the way they function; rather, they must simply insert a certain percentage of individuals with marginalized identities into their existing networks, in order to more accurately reflect the diverse population they supposedly represent. At best, these kinds of commentators believe that changing the "race," gender, or sexual identities of the people with power will somehow automatically transform that power into a force for good instead of bad; at its worst, though, this discourse doesn't seem to care about outcomes at all—simply changing the face of power is the only real goal.

Dylan Robinson (2020) critiques this orientation toward diversity, focusing on the ways music institutions and White composers use the "inclusion" of certain aspects of indigenous musicking to "enrich" the existing system. At one point, Robinson analyzes a work by a White composer that incorporates Inuit throat singing into a composition. This incorporation was meant "to bring two worlds together," but in reality it stripped the throat singing from its normal context and mode—from its world, in other words. For example, the piece required the singers to stand side-by-side, facing the audience, rather than holding one another's arms and looking into one another's faces. Additionally, since the classically trained musicians who played the orchestral parts were not able to improvise, the composition was fully notated, whereas traditional Inuit throat singing is collectively improvised. Robinson says that such works and performances are celebrated as diversifying classical institutions and compositions, and yet they alter nothing about institutional structures or functions. Indigenous people are offered space onstage, but not allowed to determine the venue, how the space should be arranged, how the audience-performer dynamic should be designed, and so on. In short, what Robinson calls "inclusionary" music "on the surface *sounds* like a socially progressive act," whereas in reality it "performs the very opposite of its enunciation" (p. 6). (See also Kristina Kolbe's essay in this volume).

Powerblindness

The way inclusion-oriented diversity initiatives render systems and structures invisible precisely by not challenging them is a common lacuna in the conversation about US classical music's gender problem. The outreach work of one of the composers mentioned in my opening quotation, Missy Mazzoli, can serve as an example of what I mean by this. Mazzoli has become a poster child for women in classical music, and a much-lauded example of an activist working to diversify its institutions. Not only is she the first woman ever to be commissioned by the Met, but she has also started a widely-publicized program, called Luna Composition Lab, aimed at encouraging and supporting young women in working toward the goal of becoming professional composers. Luna Lab is underwritten by the Kaufman Music Center, and works in partnership with Face the Music, an after-school program for high-school-aged musicians. Luna Lab's and the Kaufman Center's language explaining and promoting this program centers on the fact that women aren't well represented in classical music, and foregrounds the need for mentorship and role models in addressing this representational deficit.

The extreme sexism of the classical music world is obvious, and the statistics these commentators cite are legitimately infuriating. And yet, mainstream classical music discourse in the US is notable for the way it lacks any kind of structural critique, fixating instead on an individualistic politics of identity-based representation—a type of diversity that Dylan Robinson notes is all about content rather than systems. This ethical orientation means that such diversity programs and demands are in danger of reiterating what I see as the "powerblindness" that's at the center of the "Western" classical music ideology (Tomlinson, 2019). The problem with classical music isn't just that it's White supremacist and patriarchal; the problem is also that it is *elitist*, and its elitism is entwined with its other bigotries. Furthermore, it's elitist in more than a merely superficial way—critics sometimes point to the fancy dress codes or unique concert decorum of classical music as examples of its elitism, and fixate on spaces and venues as a means of overcoming this issue, as though if we can listen to Schubert in a bar while eating nachos, it won't seem so exclusive.[1] But this musical culture's commitment to propping up class privilege goes much deeper than mere appearances or decorum. As Anna Bull (2019, p. xvi) points out, classical music's boundary-drawing around itself isn't limited to mere taste paradigms, it also has "moral, economic, or cultural content," and thus a major aspect of classical music's institutions and traditions has to do with "recreating classed identities." In fact, I would say that this is the subtext of the discourse celebrating outreach programs to underserved youth or to young women; classical music is seeking fresh ways to keep reproducing class power by estheticizing it, and by making it seem available to anyone who wants to join.

To reiterate: US classical music institutions like the Met represent the institutional enshrinement of Whiteness and maleness, no doubt, but also of money and class privilege. This musical culture's various inequalities cannot be adequately explained by "race" and gender marginalization alone; they must also be understood within the framework of class and prestige that has shaped the classical music tradition in the US, its training methods, its audiences and patrons, its venues and where those venues are built, and the sounds, styles, and instruments it has tended to prioritize. While some commentators may refer vaguely to this issue, it is not a major aspect of how political demands for diversification are shaped in the mainstream conversation in the US.

Barbara Tomlinson (2019, p. 176) discusses the way this kind of "powerblindness" works within liberal feminist discourses generally, noting that "the reward structures of neoliberal institutions [like the Met or a corporation or the government] cultivate experts who are unwilling or unable to identify power or to challenge it." Institutions obviously do not reward people who may truly destabilize institutional power, but this fact is disguised by rhetoric like "breaking the glass ceiling," which implies that some aspect of an institution is being shattered or destroyed. For Tomlinson (p. 177) an important tactic in resisting powerblindness is "to discern in any given social and historical situation *which difference makes a difference.*" In the case of "Western" classical music, particularly in the US, it is obvious that gender and "race" make a difference in who gets to participate, and yet discussions of diversity that fixate only on gendered and racialized hierarchies and only on individuals make it impossible to see that class is another type of difference that makes a difference.

The philosopher Olúfẹ́mi Táíwò (2020) also takes up the issue of powerblindness, criticizing the way liberal constructions of representational identity politics homogenize diverse life experiences by obscuring questions of class and access to power. Táíwò describes the way White colleagues often respectfully defer to him when the need to speak about racism comes up. For example, a White woman journalist offers to give him a freelance opportunity, because the story is about racism and she has "no idea what it's like to be Black." He notes that this gesture makes sense, is well meaning, and stems from her comradely desire to give up something for him in the spirit of racial justice, and yet moments like these—when his White colleagues defer to him as a means of "centering" the voices of "those most affected" by racism—also make him uncomfortable. Of course, as a Black man living in America, he is affected by racism, and yet in reality the people "most affected" by racism "are disproportionately likely to be incarcerated, underemployed, or part of the 44 percent of the world's population without Internet access" (paragraph 10). In other words, the vast majority of Black people are not even close to the networks of power and privilege that Táíwò himself (a tenure-track professor at an elite university) inhabits. In theorizing this more nuanced understanding of the intersections of multiple identities, Táíwò suggests thinking not only in fixed terms of White privilege and/or male privilege but also "being-in-the-room privilege." Who is in the rooms where things get decided, discourses get shaped, and legislation gets handed down? This is a kind of access to power that is not reducible merely to "race" or gender identity.

Táíwò's essay brings the calls to diversify classical music's institutions into sharp relief. When we issue demands for greater representation of "women" at the Met, for example, *which* women are we talking about? This year's Luna Composition Lab fellows manifest a great deal of gender, racial, and ethnic diversity, and yet they also seem to come from class-privileged backgrounds, backgrounds that have included specialized study with renowned pedagogues and composers, access to private schools, elite summer camps, expensive instruments, and social and familial contexts capable of supporting them in pursuing their musical goals. Furthermore, these are young people who do not seem to have to perform wage labor in order to help their families survive, and as such they also have sufficient free time in which to develop musical skills. These particular class and lifestyle factors are a huge part of what make participation in classical music in the US possible. In short, as Táíwò puts it, these are primarily individuals who have (or whose parents have) successfully made it past "the various social selection pressures" that "filter out" the individuals who actually experience the vast brunt of negative outcomes of "race"- or gender-based inequality. "That is, they are most likely to be in the room precisely because of ways in which they are systematically *different from* (and thus potentially unrepresentative of) the very people they are then asked to represent in the room."

But—due to the liberal politics classical music culture is closely associated with in the US—even when classical music initiatives do attempt to address class-based inequality they risk reiterating this exceptionalist worldview, in addition to maintaining the centrality of Whiteness, maleness, and wealth. As Mina Yang puts it in her essay for this volume, programs like El Sistema, or like the BSO's diversity initiatives, make it possible for "exceptional" kids to "escape" their unfortunate circumstances by absorbing the values of the culture that is offered to them by these orchestras. This is the classic liberal approach to inequality I glossed above, wherein the conditions that *cause* inequality are rarely cited as the problems that need solving; rather, carefully gate-kept, means-tested pathways to personal betterment (with "personal betterment" always figured in economic and cultural terms that ascribe to liberal norms) are made available to certain individuals, individuals who are willing or able to jump through the various hoops the liberal bureaucracy puts into place as barriers against the vast majority of the working class.

When individual representations of exceptional individuals are then celebrated for somehow empowering everyone from a given identity category, it helps emphasize the fallacious notion that American culture is a meritocracy that simply rewards hard work and excellence, and that this individual excellence in turn is somehow good for everyone from those identity categories. In radical feminist discourse, this version of empowerment politics is referred to with the interchangeable terms "mainstream feminism," "bourgeois feminism," "liberal feminism," "White feminism," or "trickle-down feminism" (hooks, 1984; Jaffe, 2013; Lewis, 2016; Davis, 2017). Sarah Jaffe (2013, paragraph 2) dissects some of the ways this version of feminism manifests in mass-market empowerment treatises like Sheryl Sandberg's *Lean In*, or in people's "hand-wringing" over the sexism faced by female CEOs or presidential candidates, noting that "while we debate the travails of some of the world's most privileged women, most women are up against the wall." For example, even here in the relative comfort of the imperial core (the United States), women make up 60% of the minimum wage workforce, and in most employment sectors they earn around 83 cents to every dollar earned by men. Indeed, in New York City—home of the Metropolitan Opera, which is now triumphantly promoting the feminist cause by programming one woman composer—fully 95% of low-paid domestic workers are women. Despite all the celebration in this country about the first woman vice president and the first woman director of national intelligence, this labor condition is only getting worse. A recent study found that 100% of the jobs lost due to the pandemic in December 2020 were jobs held by women, specifically low-paid women of color (Aspan, 2021). "And yet for much of mainstream feminist discourse," Jaffe writes, it's as if "there's nothing about [the economy] worth examining from the standpoint of gender" (2013, paragraph 5). The diversity initiatives in American classical music aimed at uplifting and empowering individual women artists seem similarly uninterested in the plight of "women," full stop. Are the material conditions of the women who scrub the Met's toilets or clean its patron's houses or are worked to death as slaves in the mineral mines that feed the portfolios of the tech executives who fund its productions in any way altered by the performance of an opera by a woman? Representational identity politics—which ignores wider structural questions about the differing conditions of different kinds of women—implies that this is so, and yet it is difficult to imagine what evidence could demonstrate the connection.

Diversity and institutional health

Calls to address classical music's "race" and gender inequities in the US are often formulated in marketing terms. An editorial about the Boston Symphony Orchestra's diversity outreach programs notes for example that for such institutions, "attracting new audiences that look more like the communities in which they are located is absolutely essential if they are to stay in business as vital cultural institutions" (*Baltimore Sun*, 2016). Within this neoliberal framing, people are seen in terms of their identity as consumers, "diverse" people (meaning, people with underrepresented identities) are seen as resources that can bolster perceptions of an institution's relevance, and it's taken as a given that the financial health of institutions is paramount.

Attaching demands for racial and gender liberation to the project of "saving" classical music becomes even more problematic in this light. The notion that diversifying classical music will save it from market extinction is probably somewhat true. Indeed, much like US imperial capitalism generally, the system does have to be seen to respond to the demands of marginalized identity groups who have been traditionally left out of its project, lest the population grow too restive. Thus, as scholars as well as activists have been pointing out for decades, such carefully managed representational diversification actually strengthens the system, by making it seem like it is flexible enough to address all our demands and give us all the things we want—in short it underscores the fiction that everyone can have a "seat at the table" if they just ask nicely enough, and work hard enough in the right ways (Davis, 1996; Boltanski and Chiapello, 2005; McRobbie, 2009; Crispin, 2017; Ahmed, 2012; Warner, 2012; Lewis, 2016). As such scholars have argued, capitalism actually allows for the expression of a wide array of difference and is able to make space for a plethora of identity categories, so long as such diversity is never figured in terms of opposition to the system itself. Thus as James Currie (2011, p. 161) points out, institutional "diversity initiatives" can often serve a disturbing propaganda function, as once existing institutions (like the US government) have triumphantly uplifted individual people from marginalized identity categories into positions of power within those institutions, it communicates "the message that difference can be acknowledged without the world economy having to be disturbed."

Countless radical thinkers and activists all over the world have demonstrated that oppressive hierarchies of "race" and gender can't be abolished without also abolishing capitalism (Marx, 1867; DuBois, 1903; Goldman, 1911; Luxemburg, 1913; Robinson, 1983; Federici, 2004). This is obviously not to say that capitalism is the original cause of racism or sexism, nor that ending capitalism will automatically end racialized and gendered hierarchies. What such radicals argue is that all forms of oppression must be theorized together, and that one cannot end without all of them ending. So long as our society is organized in accordance with a system that requires mass exploitation in order to function, it will not be possible to bring about a true end to any form of domination or hierarchy.

But if racism and sexism can't end unless capitalism is also destroyed, then where does that leave classical music, with its opulent million-dollar gentrification architecture, its lucrative art holdings and investment portfolios, its service as a discreet tax shelter for billionaires (INCITE!, 2007; Drennan, 2017; Horning, 2019), its array of skills that require years of sustained, focused, expensive study to acquire, its tuxedoes and champagne? It is frankly difficult to imagine how the *institutional* world of classical music could ever adequately resolve the inequalities caused by racist, sexist, elite class hierarchy, even if this were a thing that prominent artists and institutions were actually calling for, which they aren't. Whether "Western" classical music in anything like its current form could survive the social transformations the end of capitalism would generate thus seems unlikely, but we cannot pretend that simply replacing rich White men with rich women and minorities, or even with individual poor people "lifted up" out of poverty thanks to their exceptional talent and the intercession of benevolent charitable programs, will bring about a fundamental reordering of classical music, or of the world in which it functions as a potent symbol of (and machine for reproducing) wealth and power.

Conclusion

As rationalists, American liberals are impatient with critiques of institutions that don't present a roadmap for how those institutions can easily and efficiently solve the problem being pointed to (Head, 2016); in this sense, my essay may be unsatisfying to many readers steeped in a liberal political ethos that centers institutions, celebrates exceptional individualism, displaces the responsibility for political action onto elected officials and authority figures, and still adheres to a progressive understanding of history in which things automatically get better with time. Nonetheless, I believe my critique does offer a solution, which is simply to look outside existing institutions for answers to our problems. I do not mean to suggest the kind of anti-institutional activities supposedly represented by the "entrepreneurs" of contemporary US classical music, who have constructed brand identities based on the way they are perceived as challenging status quo methods of performance and programming (Moore, 2016). In my opinion, entrepreneurship in classical music was always a political dead end, a piece of capitalist flim-flam carefully deployed to strengthen elite power and further the meritocratic fallacy; indeed we see that some of the entrepreneurial artists celebrated for tearing down institutions in the early 2000s are now comfortably ensconced inside those very institutions, earning salaries at Harvard (Claire Chase) or the LA Phil (Yuval Sharon), or reaping major commissions from elite venues (Missy Mazzoli).

The kind of anti-institutional orientation I wish we would develop is one that refuses to see institutions (classical music venues, corporations, universities, the state) as the benevolent distributors of rights and freedoms that we might one day receive if we ask nicely enough. Instead, we should orient ourselves toward people, and toward constructing autonomous forms of musicking that don't require institutional patronage. There are people in classical music who are working toward creating this new world, but their ideas are not likely to be featured in solution-oriented articles or in the kinds of demands for greater representation that are most likely to be boosted and profiled in the media (and listened to by institutions). The composer Nebal Maysaud (2019), for example, recently published a manifesto in *New Music Box*, proclaiming that "it's time to let classical music die," and offering instead a new vision of musical practice founded on collective care and autonomous coalition building. They propose a new musical community (or communities) that will be run "not by the ones with the most institutional power, but those with the least," and proclaim that "we will no longer depend on White elites to fund diversity initiatives and hope it trickles down. Instead, we will be guided by the belief that when our most oppressed are liberated, we are all liberated" (paragraph 35). This is a vision of freedom that is grounded in a fierce politics of radical democracy, one that has no use for the exceptionalism and tokenism of liberal identity-based diversity initiatives, "White savior" programs like the ones Mina Yang discusses, or the idea that meaningful change occurs when previously-marginalized individuals seize power from White men only to wield that power in the exact same way.[2]

An orientation like Maysaud's points to a radical re-envisioning not just of classical music but of the social world itself. When you stop formulating your conception of a good life primarily in terms of the possibilities that are offered by existing institutions and practices, surprising new ideas, connections, and activities can begin to bloom. In fact, Maysaud's comments make me think of mutual aid, the core ethos of anarchism, an anticapitalist philosophy strongly opposed to liberalism in the way it centers collective identification as the foundation of individual freedom. Joining a mutual aid crew retrains you to see that collective goals can be accomplished without the guidance of institutions or hierarchies. Identifying a problem in your community and working with others to solve it directly—without appealing to the city council or the police or a nonprofit, and, perhaps most importantly, without needing to ascribe to a profit-motive—reshapes the contours of the world, and opens up new possibilities for living, making, and doing things together. Furthermore, in my experience such work is often more conducive to a wider array of diversity than is possible within most institutional contexts. For example, a mutual aid crew might include people with PhDs as well as people who never went to high school; legal citizens and undocumented immigrants; middle-class people, working-class people, homeless people living in total poverty; and so on. Notably, it is this very diversity that shapes mutual aid projects, as group practices are informed by a multiplicity of perspectives that the group constantly works to synthesize in consensus decision-making, which is very different from the top-down decision-making of liberal institutions.

Adopting this kind of radical orientation may or may not help a musician succeed at the Met, but it certainly would represent a move toward a more emancipatory politics. This new ethical framework also points toward a way the arguments in this essay might apply to contexts beyond the US: wherever you are reading this, you are probably embedded in an institutional context similar to the one I have diagnosed, in terms of the way such contexts shape and limit our epistemological frames. In a future like the one Maysaud imagines, all kinds of music would exist, including "Western" classical music, surely, as well as music we haven't even imagined yet. What wouldn't exist would be the kinds of privileged positions, platforms, and inspirational narratives that put individual success above collective flourishing, and that use examples of individual identity-based empowerment as a means of strengthening the White supremacist, patriarchal, elite power hierarchy, by repackaging it as capable of providing us the liberation we yearn for.

Notes

1. This idea undergirds the proliferation of alternative music venues across the last decade in America, like (Le) Poisson Rouge, National Sawdust, or the various "site-based" operas of LA opera company The Industry.
2. See for example bell hooks (1984, p. 15). She argues that so long as a group "defines liberation as gaining social equality with ruling class White men, they have a vested interest in the continued exploitation and oppression of others."

8
Staging a Loose Canon
Scripture, Tradition, and Embedded Exclusion in Opera Production

Caitlin Vincent

In July 2019, American soprano Tamara Wilson made headlines for refusing to wear blackface makeup for a production of Verdi's opera *Aida* with the Arena di Verona in Italy. Wilson's decision broke 106 years of tradition at the opera company and spurred furious debate on social media and arts journalism sites (Lunny, 2019). In a series of now-deleted Instagram posts, Wilson, a White woman, explained she had not known her costume for the role involved a dark body suit, dark makeup, and dreadlocks until shortly before the production's premiere, and it "was wrong" (Salazar, 2019a). After singing a second performance without the production's customary makeup, Wilson canceled her remaining appearances with the company and announced she would be retiring the role of Aida from her repertoire (Salazar, 2019b).

The controversy highlights a major challenge facing opera companies in the 21st century: how to stage historical operatic works in the face of modern-day cultural norms. The Arena di Verona is one of many companies worldwide that continue to employ outdated staging practices—including blackface and yellowface—for their productions of canonical works. The operas *Madama Butterfly*, *Turandot*, *Otello*, and *Aida* are regularly staged with White performers wearing racialized makeup and costumes, and these artistic choices are frequently supported by companies, audiences, and performers alike. Indeed, just weeks before Wilson refused to darken her skin for *Aida*, soprano Anna Netrebko defended the practice for her performances of the role with St. Petersburg's Mariinsky Theatre. Posting an Instagram selfie of herself in brown face makeup, Netrebko wrote, "I am NOT gonna be White AIDA!" (Giovetti, 2019).

As questions of inequality, racism, and sexism come to the fore in the cultural sector, opera's continued reliance on historical repertoire and traditional staging practices is under increased scrutiny. Faced with uncertain funding and high market competition (Holton, 2020), opera companies need to modernize themselves to more closely align with current cultural developments. At the same time, companies need to retain their primary audience base of conservative operagoers who prefer traditional productions of canonical works. This chapter examines the degree to which companies find themselves in an ideological conflict between operatic tradition and contemporary social expectations. In the course of the discussion, I consider how the nature of the operatic canon and the resulting rift between different opera audiences is forcing companies to address the art form's institutionalized racism and misogyny.

The chapter begins by outlining the underlying tension between an opera's material score and its stage interpretations and the resulting rift between opera traditionalists and more progressive operagoers. Next, the chapter considers the challenges posed by the operatic canon as both a defining aspect of the artform and a risk management strategy for companies. Drawing on examples of recent productions, the chapter then discusses three strategies being used by companies in an attempt to resolve the problematic aspects of popular canonical works: 1) revision or reinterpretation, 2) education and contextualization, and 3) casting. The chapter concludes by discussing the long-term implications of these strategies in practice.

The score versus the stage

Opera is the combination of a tangible musical score and an ephemeral live performance. The musical aspects of an opera (e.g., notes, rhythms, and text) can largely be preserved through notation, allowing the score to function as a historical artifact of the time in which it was created, as well as the intentions of the composer and librettist. In contrast, the stage interpretation of an opera is unfixed and can vary depending on the performers and the artistic vision of the stage director and their creative team. The tension between the stage and the score, or what Abbate (2001, p. ix) terms "the transcendent and the material," is a defining aspect of the operatic genre and establishes an underlying conflict between the work that is preserved in the score and the work that is performed on stage.

Opera must also contend with the complications posed by its archival capabilities. While the stage interpretation of an opera is a product of its time, the material score is potentially the product of a time long past. Rosen (2001, pp. 28–29) describes this as the paradox between the "timeless" score that is "frozen in every detail" and the "historical" stage interpretation, which is shaped by its creative team, performers, audience, and surrounding cultural context. The notes, rhythms, and text of a work like Mozart's *Don Giovanni*, for example, are preserved within the material score, which functions as a historical artifact of the opera as it premiered in 1787. However, in the centuries since *Don Giovanni*'s first performance, the possibilities for its stage interpretations have remained fluid, evolving alongside the artistic movements and cultural developments of modern-day society. The result is an ever-expanding rift between an opera's creative origins and its ephemeral manifestations on stage.

Abbate (2001, p. xi) highlights a common concern that canonical operatic works, as preserved in musical scores, can be undermined by their stage interpretations and acquire "alternative histories." The fear is that if such histories achieve a canonical status equal to that of the material score, they could potentially sully the work for future generations. Accordingly, Weber (1994, p. 118) refers to the premise of a fixed operatic "truth," in which the musical score is seen as "a meaningful self-contained reality—which enters time, as it were, only to await realization by inspired but faithful interpreters." The assumption is a kind of operatic custodialism, whereby the "truth" of an operatic work must be protected from "irresponsible management and producers bent on desecration" (Ridout, 2012, p. 170).

Disagreements about the relationship between stage and score and how operas should be interpreted has led to what Cooper (2016) terms the "opera wars." On one side are opera traditionalists who ascribe to the premise of Weber's operatic "truth," which is either upheld or violated by a given stage production. On the other side are more progressive, concept-driven advocates who "dismiss traditional stagings as stodgy re-enactments that lack dramatic vitality" (Cooper, 2016). While proponents are equally outspoken on both sides, traditionalists are generally more outraged by seeming violations in stage interpretations. Consider the Facebook group, "Against Modern Opera Productions," which boasts more than 61,000 members and posts diatribes against untraditional opera productions (Against Modern Opera Productions, 2021).

The material score is key to the traditionalist viewpoint because it represents a tangible artifact of the intentions of the original authors. However, traditionalists also draw on opera's long-standing production conventions to justify their criticism of untraditional stage productions. Littlejohn (1994, p. 57) describes this as the "joint and equal authority of Scripture and Tradition." Here, "Scripture" denotes the written text of the score and libretto, and, to a lesser extent, other written sources such as staging manuals and performance notes. "Tradition" describes the way in which an opera has "always" been done, including the traditions established by the major European opera houses between 1880 and 1940 and the stage directions associated with the material score.

The combination of Scripture and Tradition allows traditionalist audiences to establish a benchmark of practice for ephemeral stage interpretations. However, the reliance on Scripture and Tradition as the means for establishing operatic "truth" is deeply problematic. While a strictly traditionalist approach can provide a way to seemingly recreate the artistic intentions of a composer and librettist, it can also be used to justify the racism and misogyny in historical works. This leads us to a necessary discussion of the operatic canon.

The problem with the canon

Over the past century, operatic programming has become increasingly reliant on the canon, or what Till (2012, p. 240) terms a "museum repertory." The canon is essentially a collection of opera's greatest hits: works written by White European men in the 18th, 19th, and early 20th centuries that remain the mainstay of opera companies worldwide. While the exact make-up of the canon has a certain flexibility, operas by Mozart, Verdi, Wagner, and Puccini are reliably represented. Consider Operabase's record of the top 20 most-performed operas in the world in the 2017–2018 season: included are six works by Verdi, four by Mozart, and four by Puccini.[1] The most recent opera listed, Puccini's *Turandot*, premiered in 1926 (Operabase, 2021).

From a management perspective, opera companies have a vested interest in programming canonical works. As public subsidies for the arts decrease worldwide, opera companies are increasingly reliant on box office revenue to sustain their operations, and canonical works have been shown to appeal to opera's traditionally conservative audience (Holton, 2020). A 2000 report on the Royal Opera House in Covent Garden identified a 10 to 20% premium in audience members' willingness to buy tickets for canonical works (Caves, 2000, p. 235). Since these operas lead to the highest return on investment in terms of box office sales, they are produced and revived at much higher rates than any other type of repertoire (Sgourev, 2013).

However, the nature of the operatic canon as a "museum repertory" presents serious challenges. Returning to Operabase's list of the top 20 most-performed operas in the 2017–2018 season, more than half feature racist elements or examples of gendered violence. This includes *Madama Butterfly*, *Turandot*, *Aida*, *Così fan tutte*, and *Nabucco*, which rely on ethnic exoticism and racial stereotypes, as well as *Tosca*, *Rigoletto*, *Carmen*, *Die Zauberflöte*, and *Don Giovanni*, which depict rape, femicide, and other forms of violence against women. To this list, we can add numerous other operas that are frequently programmed despite their problematic narratives, including *Lakmé*, *Les pêcheurs de perles*, *Die Entführung aus dem Serail*, *La fanciulla del West*, and *L'italiana in Algeri*.

We can acknowledge the "Scripture" of these canonical works as historical artifacts. In addition to reflecting a particular time and social context, these operas were shaped by the perspectives of the White European men who created them. Yet the difficult elements of these works are exacerbated by their associated "Tradition," or the way in which they have "always" been done. This is particularly problematic in operas that rely on ethnic exoticism and racist stereotypes, which have traditionally been staged using blackface and yellowface.

The practices of blackface and yellowface involve performers changing their appearance to "pass" as characters of a different ethnicity. In addition to theatrical makeup, concomitants of blackface or yellowface can extend to "dialogue... posture, and costuming," as well as the musical language of a work itself (Moon, 2005, p. 6). Both practices have strong ties to 19th century North American theater, where cultural caricatures were used to frame non-White bodies as racial others (André, 2016; Moon, 2005; Morrison, 2020). Importantly, both practices also set expectations for how performers of color would be perceived for and on the stage. As André, Bryan, and Saylor (2012, p. 3) argue, minstrel stereotypes "provided a coded norm for how Blackness was performed in a musico-dramatic setting and thus became potent models for depicting Blackness on the operatic stage." We can similarly frame yellowface as a means for "inscribing stereotypes onto the performers' bodies" and establishing a caricaturized model of performance (Moon, 2005, p. 40).

In the United States and England, as well as other countries, the use of blackface and yellowface is widely accepted as offensive by broader society. Yet the opera industry has been slow to adapt to these cultural developments and abandon its long-standing production practices. Instead, opera remains one of the only performance genres where "such overt racial imitation is routinely performed without comment or query" (André, Bryan, and Saylor, 2012, p. 2).[2] Indeed, up until recently, opera companies were more likely to receive news coverage for productions that deviated from these traditions. Consider the Metropolitan Opera's 2015 production of *Otello*, which made headlines for its decision to costume its White Otello without blackface makeup (André, 2016).

Opinions about the use of blackface and yellowface in opera generally break along the same lines as the opera wars. Traditionalists in favor of operatic "truth" argue that the combined authority of Scripture and Tradition should be upheld, even if this means using blackface or yellowface on stage. Similarly, any staged instances of rape or violence against women are justifiable as part of the historical artifact of the operatic work. Meanwhile, more progressive audiences argue that, in the era of Black Lives Matter and #MeToo, operas that promote racial stereotypes or include gender-based violence should be revised, updated, or even retired from the repertoire.

Thus, opera companies find themselves caught in an ideological conflict with major implications for both their financial viability and their cultural relevance. Companies need to program canonical works in order to retain their traditional audience base and maintain their box office revenue. Yet they also need to attract new and younger audience members who have come of age when racial discrimination, violence, and sexism are at the forefront of social concerns. With the rise of social media, opera companies are also now increasingly visible to a global audience and must protect their brands from controversies that might disaffect potential audiences. Given this challenge, opera companies are employing a number of different strategies in an attempt to salvage problematic canonical works and retain one kind of audience without alienating the other.

Strategies to bridge the divide

Revision or reinterpretation

One of the most common strategies used to resolve problematic operas is based on revision or reinterpretation. This approach varies in terms of degree, ranging from minor textual edits to more significant narrative displacements. A company might, for example, update the supertitle translation of an aria in order to edit out racist language. A more invasive editorial approach could involve extensive cuts or complete rewrites of a canonical work.

In 2018, the Canadian Opera Company presented a new production of Mozart's *Die Entführung aus dem Serail*, directed by Lebanese-Canadian Wajdi Mouawad. Aiming to counteract the opera's racist portrayal of the Muslim character Osmin, Mouawad elected to "approach the text in a new way" (Opera Canada, 2018). This involved making extensive revisions to the opera's dialogue, reframing the narrative structure to incorporate flashbacks, and adding invented background for key characters. Italy's Maggio Musicale Fiorentino employed a similar strategy to remove the gendered violence from its 2018 production of Bizet's *Carmen*. Instead of Carmen dying at the hands of Don José at the end of the opera as per the opera's stage directions and traditional performance practice, director Leo Muscato had Carmen steal Don José's gun and shoot him in self-defense. "It was just the last 30 seconds and we wanted to draw attention to one of the plagues of our society," explains company superintendent Cristiano Chiarot (Politi, 2018).

Both productions received mixed receptions. Mouawad's reimagining of *Die Entführung aus dem Serail* was deemed to be largely unsuccessful, with critic John Terauds (2018) noting that the editorial revisions "pitted words against music and arias against dialogue in ways that created nonsense on many levels." A critic for Opera Canada declared that the revised production was "so far removed from the original text that one has to question, why bother staging *Abduction* at all" (Opera Canada, 2018). Muscato's changes to *Carmen* were even more controversial, with an immediate outcry against the production's revised ending as "an example of political correctness going too far" (Politi, 2018). "Bizarre Bizet: A #MeToo Carmen Doesn't Die" exclaimed the title of a review in the *Daily Beast*, while reports described enraged audience members shouting "Kill her! Kill her!" during the final scene (Latza Nadeau, 2018).

The response to both productions highlights the divide between audience perspectives. On one side, the progressive viewpoint—in this case, led by each production's creative team—favors revising problematic repertoire in order to better reflect modern-day society. On the other side, the traditionalist perspective—represented by the critics and audience members—perceives *Die Entführung aus dem Serail* and *Carmen* in terms of a fixed operatic "truth" that has been violated by the directorial revisions. Mouawad's production was seen as being so detached from the "truth" of Mozart's opera that it was no longer recognizable. The backlash to *Carmen* reveals an even more explicit rift. Because the production deviated from both the Scripture and Tradition of the work by allowing Carmen to live, the production was seen as a desecration—even though, as Muscato emphasized, "We did not touch a single note of Bizet's score" (Gentile, 2018).

Education and contextualization

Another strategy used by opera companies when programming problematic works is education and contextualization. Indicative activities generally include lectures or panel discussions that are scheduled alongside productions and provide audiences with cultural and historical context for the particular work. This strategy also gives companies an opportunity to engage directly with community groups or cultures that are misrepresented in a given opera and frame their programming around contemporary responses.

In 2017, Seattle Opera programmed a series of educational initiatives to coincide with its production of Puccini's *Madama Butterfly*, a work that draws on stereotypical representations of Japanese culture and has been frequently performed with White performers in yellowface since its 1904 premiere (Midgette, 2017). These included a panel discussion with local Asian arts leaders, a series of blog interviews designed to "elevate Asian voices," and an exhibition about Japanese culture in the venue lobby (Seattle Opera, 2017). In the weeks following the production, Seattle Opera also produced an evening of plays by Asian American women playwrights and premiered a new opera, *An American Dream*, by composer Jack Perla and librettist Jessica Murphy Moo, about the internment of a Japanese-American family during World War II (Seattle Opera, 2017).

The following season, Seattle Opera used a similar approach for its productions of *Aida* and *Porgy and Bess*, two works widely criticized for their depictions of Black characters and outdated staging traditions (André, Bryan, and Saylor, 2012). The company hired a private consultant to lead community outreach efforts, including an open forum with members of Seattle's Black community to "express their feelings about the art form" (Karras, 2018). As with their production of *Madama Butterfly*, Seattle Opera designed exhibitions for the venue lobby and published program notes about Black misrepresentation in opera.

An organizational strategy based around education allows companies to program canonical works without appearing to champion their problematic elements. Activities that specifically contextualize the racist or sexist elements of an opera's Scripture and Tradition are used to remind audiences that the works are historical artifacts that reflect outdated viewpoints. Because this approach does not explicitly revise the works, but merely contextualizes them, it functions as a less invasive strategy than an approach of revision or reinterpretation. As such, the strategy is less likely to prompt backlash from traditionalist operagoers. Indeed, Seattle Opera's Communications and Public Engagement Manager, Gabrielle Kazuko Nomura Gainor, highlighted the positive responses to the company's efforts around *Madama Butterfly*, noting that approximately half of their patrons found the various initiatives had "made them think about the piece in a different way" (Karras, 2018).

Casting: color-blind and color-conscious

A third strategy employed by opera companies when programming canonical works centers on casting. Companies must decide which singers will be hired to perform problematic roles like Cio-Cio-san in *Madama Butterfly*, Aida in *Aida*, and Otello in *Otello*, among others. This challenge extends to casting for chorus members and deciding how the large ensembles in *Lakmé*, *Turandot*, and *Madama Butterfly*, for example, will portray the respective Indian, Chinese, and Japanese characters specified in the scores.

Opera companies have generally relied on the premise of "color-blind casting," or casting without regard to the ethnicity of the performer. The rationale is that companies will cast the best performer for a role, regardless of their appearance or cultural background. In 2019, Opera Australia used this approach when casting a White soprano as the Puerto-Rican character Maria in Bernstein's *West Side Story*. "We're committed to colourblind casting, and we don't cast any role based on ethnicity or skin colour," noted a statement by the company following criticism of the cast announcement (Boland and Lloyd, 2019). Lyndon Terracini, then artistic director of the company, confirmed that "it is about finding the best people" and reiterated that the casting choice had been approved by the Bernstein estate (Boland and Lloyd, 2019).

André (2016, p. 14) argues that the premise of color-blind casting is flawed because "there is no blindness today regarding Black and non-Black casting of roles or roles of any racial/ethnic identity; race and gender are always noticeable: people do not *not* see race and gender." Moreover, any attempts to achieve color-blind casting can easily be undercut by the artistic choices of the creative team or even the narratives of the works themselves. A traditional production of *Madama Butterfly* that incorporates kimonos, Japanese wigs, and Geisha-style makeup is not in itself "color-blind" but actually relies on an explicit ethnic reading of the text. In the same way, *West Side Story* requires the ethnic distinction between its White Tony and its Puerto-Rican Maria to establish the fundamental conflict of the narrative. By casting White performers as Cio-Cio-san and Maria in productions that are not themselves designed to be "color-blind," companies risk accusations of cultural appropriation or worse.

Color-blind casting also fails to address the reality of the long-standing discrimination against performers of color in the opera industry (Elliott, 2016). While certain operas have traditionally been sung by performers of color—Gershwin's *Porgy and Bess* is one example—the bulk of roles in the canon have remained largely closed to all but White performers (André, 2016; Elliott, 2016). By choosing to cast White performers as Asian, Black, or Latino characters and then using makeup and costumes to help them assume the ethnic identities of these underrepresented groups, opera companies can be seen as actively perpetuating these inequities in practice (Hopkins, 2018).

As a result of these issues, the concept of "color-blind casting" is gradually being replaced with so-called "color-conscious casting." This refers to casting decisions that acknowledge the implications of skin color in certain roles, as well as the historical discrimination in the sector (Hopkins, 2018). In this context, any decisions about "the best performer for a role" must consider ethnicity and cultural background, alongside vocal quality and skill.

Still, color-conscious casting remains a controversial strategy for opera companies because it plays into traditionalist concerns about productions that break from Scripture and Tradition. The approach is also complicated when applied in practice. Should Bizet's "Spanish Gypsy" Carmen only be cast with a mezzo-soprano of Romani descent? Or, as critic Anne Midgette (2017) asks, is it better to have a Korean soprano perform the role of Cio-Cio-san over a White soprano, or does that imply that "all Asians look alike"? More generally, there are concerns that a shift to color-conscious casting might have unintended consequences and further pigeonhole performers of color into certain kinds of roles.

Conclusion

Each of the strategies discussed above has been designed to help opera companies salvage canonical operas for 21st century consumption. Yet each encounters obstacles in practice because of the rift between traditionalist and progressive viewpoints. Attempts to revise or reinterpret canonical works are perhaps most vulnerable to criticism because they actively deviate from an opera's Scripture and Tradition. While the ending of Maggio Musicale Fiorentino's *Carmen* only involved changing a single stage direction in the material score, the interpretation violated the way the opera had "always" been done and thus prompted an extreme reaction from traditionalist audience members. Strategies relating to casting are also likely to prompt backlash, with strong opinions both in favor of and against casting decisions that align with modern-day expectations for equity and diversity. Consider Anna Netrebko's vehement declaration not to be "White AIDA" or the controversy surrounding Tamara Wilson's refusal to don blackface makeup for the Arena di Verona. Even strategies based on education and contextualization can present a challenge. While initiatives such as those promoted by Seattle Opera help to frame problematic works as historical artifacts, the works themselves remain steeped in racism and misogyny, which no amount of panel discussions or lobby exhibitions can counter.

Ultimately, these strategies are little more than stopgaps. As modern-day society continues to grapple with issues around discrimination and gendered violence, the classics of the operatic canon will only become more problematic. As André (2016, p. 206) notes, "music is not "innocent" of political content—these works carry cultural meaning." This points to an unavoidable reckoning in opera's future, in which companies must decide whether they wish to continue programming these works for the sake of opera's artistic legacy or whether modernization requires abandoning the canon, once and for all.

Notes

1. In the 2017/2018 season, the top 20 most performed operas in the world were (in order): *La Traviata, Die Zauberflöte, La bohème, Carmen, Il barbiere di Siviglia, Madama Butterfly, Tosca, Rigoletto, Don Giovanni, Le nozze di Figaro, Turandot, Hansel and Gretel, Aida, Così fan tutte, Nabucco, L'elisir d'amore, Il trovatore, Eugene Onegin, Un ballo in Maschera,* and *Lucia di Lammermoor* (Operabase, 2021).
2. Like opera, classical ballet is facing increasing criticism for its long-standing use of blackface and yellowface in performance. See Chan, 2019.

9
Disability Representation in Opera

Charlotte Armstrong

Some six years on from the publication of the *Oxford Handbook of Music and Disability Studies* (Howe et al., 2015) music and disability studies can no longer be thought of as an academic subdiscipline in its infancy. Yet, while revisionist discourses of disability in musicology reflect a vibrant and still evolving scholarly perspective, there remain some largely overlooked areas of inquiry, including opera. As an art form, opera has much to contribute to critical and cultural disability studies scholarship. Its multimodal nature provides manifold opportunities to engage with the meeting points between disability and literature, drama, dance, design, and performance. In this way, opera provides a vantage point from which to explore key issues in disability representation: from inaccessible spaces and education programs to demeaning, stereotypical roles and problematic performance practices. This chapter begins to unpack some of these issues, firstly, by exploring the data gathered in the Musical Representations of Disability Database—which sheds light on the recurrence of disability in opera narratives—before highlighting operatic works and practices that interrogate and extend the creative possibilities of opera's engagement with disability.

Opera's narrative prosthesis: Exploring the musical representation of disability database

Stories about disability permeate literature, film, theater, and television narratives across a wide range of genres, time frames, and geographical contexts, from fairy tales to horror films. The disability theorists David Mitchell and Sharon Snyder (2001) have coined the term "narrative prosthesis" to describe not only the frequency with which we see disability represented in literature, but also the absence of portrayals of disability that reflect real lived experiences. Instead, they point to the use of disability by writers as a "crutch upon which literary narratives lean for their representational power, disruptive potency, and analytical insight" (p. 49). Indeed, related to disability's prevalence in all narrative arts is its often predictable or formulaic representation: its adherence to representational tropes, stock characteristics and narrative formulae. Foundational cultural disability studies scholarship (Garland Thomson, 2017; Kriegel, 1988; Michell and Snyder, 2001) has identified the use of disability as a symbol for moral deficit and evil, social transgression, divine intervention, and punishment for sin within cultural narratives, where disabled characters have been depicted variously as malevolent villains, naïve victims, and bearers of spiritual insight. Many of these tropes and trends can also be found in musical depictions of disability.

Established by members of the Music and Disability Interest Group of the Society for Music Theory (SMT) and most found the Music and Disability Study Group of the American Musicological Society (AMS), the *Musical Representations of Disability Database* (Howe and Armstrong, 2021) includes over 200 crowdsourced entries detailing depictions of disability in musical texts composed between 1400 to the present day. The data gathered suggests that the frequency with which we encounter disability in other narrative art forms is mirrored in music. Each example is categorized according to the nature of the impairment it depicts, enabling users to explore representational trends based on time frame, geography, and genre. Because the database relies on crowdsourced user contributions, there are likely many unlisted depictions of disability across a range of musical genres, however, the data suggests that depictions of disability are most commonly found in text-based music genres (Figure 9.1). Indeed, of the database's 266 entries, over 60% occur within opera.

As the range of critical attention given to opera's "mad" characters might suggest (McClary, 2002; Rosand, 1991), mental health and cognitive disorders (including

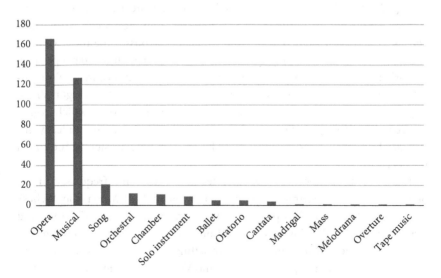

Figure 9.1 Representations of disability in music by genre (Howe and Armstrong, 2021).

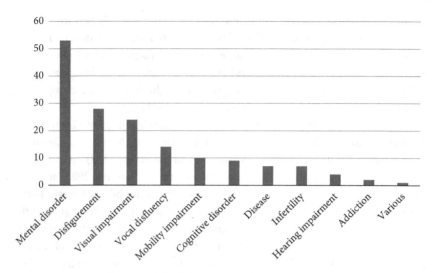

Figure 9.2 Representations of disability in opera by category of impairment (Howe and Armstrong, 2021).

addiction) are most frequently represented among the listed categories, accounting for 38% of the entries (Figure 9.2). The second most common type of disability, accounting for 20% of the entries, is visual impairment. Blind and visually impaired characters often appear in the form of the stereotypical "blind seer" (as in several adaptations of the *Oedipus* myth) or are depicted as having remarkable musical capabilities (as in Kancheli Giya Alexandrovich's *Muzïka dlya zhivïkh* [1984]). The depiction of blind characters as possessing these kinds of extraordinary abilities ties into the wider representation of disabled people, particularly those with sensory impairments, as possessing almost magical or "superhuman" abilities as if to compensate for their loss of hearing or sight. Visual impairment is also utilized in opera narratives as a means through which to generate comic confusion. In Fromental Halévy's *L'éclair* (1835), for example, Lyonel is struck by lightning and becomes blind before regaining his sight at the end of the opera.

This kind of "temporary" disability features with some frequency in the operatic canon. For example, the title character in Carl Maria von Weber's *Silvana* (1810) "begins the opera mute, but then regains her voice" (Howe and Armstrong, 2021). The loss and restoration of sanity is another common narrative device and can be found in comic settings (as in Giamoco Meyerbeer's *Dinorah* [1859]) and in opera seria (Antonio Vivaldi's *Orlando* [1727]). Related to this is the trope of "feigned" disability, particularly madness, which occurs predominantly in Baroque era operas such as Francesco Sacrati's *La finta pazza*

(1641), Andrea Ziani's *Le fortune di Rodope e Damira* (1657), and Domenico Freschi's *Helena rapita da Paride* (1677). The "redemption" of disabled characters through heroic acts can also be identified as a recurring dramatic theme in opera plots, for example, in Robert Schumann's 1849 opera *Genoveva*, which features a young boy with a hearing impairment (deafness) and vocal disfluency (muteness), who saves the title character from death.

Twenty-two percent of the opera entries in the database fall into the "mobility impairment" and "disfigurement" categories. Among them, we find examples of what Martha Stoddard-Holmes refers to as the "afflicted child" stereotype, who finds their contrast in "a host of terrifying, leering old men with avarice, deception, and a smoggy sexuality hovering about them" (Holmes, 2009, p. 9 and pp. 95–96). In conceptualizing these stock categories of characterization, Holmes touches on the long-established tendency of disability narratives to frame disabled characters as either victims or villains. In opera, villainous disabled characters often have either spinal deformities or dwarfism, including several examples of the "evil dwarf" stereotype, such as Alberich, who can be found in Wagner's *Der Ring des Nibelungen* (1874). Characters with dwarfism are also frequently depicted as having supernatural abilities, as in Ignacy Jan Paderewski's 1898 opera *Manru*, in which the dwarf, Urok, is an evil sorcerer.

In addition to highlighting the presence of stereotypes and trends, the database also brings a number of representational patterns into focus, with certain types of disability appearing more often in operas composed during certain periods. For example, the depictions of "madness" that predominated on opera stages in the early nineteenth century gave way to a newfound fascination with a more physical (and indeed visible) manifestation of the "abnormal" with the emergence of musical modernism. Among the 63 operas listed in the database between 1890 and 1930, there is a distinct prevalence of physical impairments such as dwarfism, spinal deformities, absent limbs, facial disfigurements, and debilitating wounds. This is perhaps because, in relation to the wider shifts, progressions and transformations of the time, disability was a striking and prominent theme in the modernist zeitgeist, with disabled people occupying a space as a kind of universal other (Poore, 2007; Siebers, 2010). At this time, medically imbued narratives of degeneracy and decline were particularly widespread in popular discourse, contributing to the rising social and cultural anxieties that eventually became the central premises of national socialism (Poore, 2007, pp. 51–59). But attitudes toward disability were not wholly disparaging. Tobin Siebers (2010) explores the parallel emergence of a celebratory "disability aesthetic," in which creators drew upon the visual rhetoric of the disabled body to celebrate difference and counter traditional notions of aesthetic health, beauty, and normality.

Emerging from within these contexts, works such as Tchaikovsky's *Iolanta* (1892), Janáček's *Jenůfa* (1903), Strauss's *Die Frau ohne Schatten* (1919), and Shostakovich's *Nos* (1928) reflect and have shaped a prevalent modernist fascination with the anomalous bodily form. Crucially, however, these operas do not exist in a historical vacuum: they have seen 1190 live performances in the past decade (*Operabase*, 2021), demonstrating their broad international reach even before accounting for their dissemination beyond the stage (via live broadcasts and DVD releases, for example). As frequently performed repertoire, these operas are constantly transformed and updated for the contemporary stage. Here, disability takes on new meanings in light of dramaturgical (re)interpretation, resulting in some transformative, but also often problematic, representations of disability. Examining depictions of disability in a performance context opens up new avenues for critical exploration, with crucial questions about representation, embodiment, and casting remaining unaddressed in the context of opera.

Performing disability

Perhaps one of the most repeatedly visited issues in discussions around disability representation in performance is "disability mimicry," when non-disabled performers are cast in disabled roles and mimic the features or characteristics of a specific impairment. Disability mimicry has been most vociferously discussed in relation to film, with much less critical discussion having been afforded to similar depictions of disability in opera. Nonetheless, the discourse around the use of this practice in film has much to contribute when considering disability's representation on the operatic stage. From *My Left Foot* (1989) to *Music* (2021), disability mimicry has been ubiquitous in Hollywood narratives about disability for decades, with many non-disabled performers winning awards for their portrayals of disabled characters. As of 2018, 16% of all best actor and actress Oscar wins since the awards started in 1929 were awarded to non-disabled performers for their portrayals of disability (*Hijinx*, 2018). This statistic is more striking still when taken alongside the fact that there has been just one disclosed win for a disabled performer in Oscars history (Parrott, 2019). While criticisms of disability mimicry have become more commonplace in public discourse, its prevalence remains largely unaddressed.

The year 2020 saw the UK release of *Come As You Are*, which tells the story of three men who embark on a road trip to a brothel that specializes in providing sex services for people with disabilities. In the film, all three of the central characters (two wheelchair users and a visually impaired man) are played by non-disabled actors. When asked about this choice in an interview with *Forbes*, producer Grant Rosenmeyer cited a lack of time and resources, stating that "[a]s artists we can't really be afraid of [criticism]. Not enough stories are going to get told that way and this one was so worth telling. People are entitled to their opinion" (Lopez, 2020). Rosenmeyer seems to suggest here that the production team would have preferred to cast disabled actors in these roles, but he implies that telling this story was more important than allocating the necessary time and resources to casting. In fact, this urgency for the film's story to be told seems somewhat misplaced given the fact that *Come As You Are* is a remake of the 2011 Belgian film *Hasta la vista*.

For many advocates of authentic and inclusive casting, balancing narratives about and performances of disability cannot be a "one or the other" issue. Certainly, creating an accessible working environment for a range of different needs and requirements can take time, but so too does honing the physical characteristics of a specific impairment. In addition to producing the film, Rosenmeyer in fact played one of the central characters, Asta Philpot. As the real-life figure who inspired the original Belgium feature, Philpot was involved in the making of *Come As You Are* and coached Rosenmeyer on the physical and gestural aspects of the role: "We would drill the physicality every day... spending time in the chair, getting the position" (Rosenmeyer, quoted in Lopez, 2020). For some critics, particularly those in the disability community, this was simply not enough: Charlotte Little described the film as "another link in the chain of the systematic exclusion of disabled talent from the film industry" (Little, 2020). Others (particularly those writing for more "mainstream" publications) appeared to include somewhat tokenistic objections to the film's use of disability mimicry. For example, *Variety*'s critic (Harvey, 2019) wrote that "[r]eception in real-world disabled communities may be somewhat muted by the casting of able-bodied actors in the lead roles. Nonetheless, it's hard to entirely resist," while the *Guardian* reviewer (Ide, 2020) remarked: "The film loses points for its decision to cast able actors in the central roles, but explores its theme of sexuality and disability with admirable candour."

The public discourse around *Come As You Are* is representative of a wider trend in which a flurry of disapproving publications emerges following the release of a film or television show featuring a non-disabled actor in a disabled role. These pieces rarely move beyond reductive judgments of "authentic" (and therefore good) or "inauthentic" (and therefore bad). But authentic casting is not a panacea for the inherent misappropriation and misrepresentation bound up with the practice of disability mimicry, and nor would "fixing" disability mimicry gloss over the myriad challenges and opportunities of disability representation in the performing arts.

While much of the discourse on disability mimicry in both scholarly and activist contexts focuses on film and television, issues surrounding this kind of embodied representation are further complicated by live performance. Without the same availability of computer-generated imagery (CGI) and other special effects, for example, non-disabled performers' attempts to depict disability's physicality on stage (and, increasingly, on our screens) are often sensationalized and unconvincing at best. As an inherently embodied art form, opera is no stranger to run-ins with issues around representational politics. Recent examples include Russian soprano Anna Netrebko's unapologetic use of blackface and fake braids in a 2019 production of Aida, despite the company's supposed banning of the practice as late as 2015 (see Caitlin Vincent's chapter in this volume), and the Hungarian State Opera's decision (in the same year) to stage Gershwin's *Porgy and Bess* with an all-White cast, despite the composer's requirement for all performances to feature an all-Black cast. While problematic portrayals of disability have seen somewhat less attention from the opera-going community, disability mimicry is a pervasive practice, even within high-profile companies that have made public gestures toward increasing diversity and inclusion. However, in some corners of the industry, companies are (albeit slowly) beginning to adapt to broader calls for more inclusive casting practices.

In 2019, Deutsche Oper Berlin mounted a new production of Alexander Zemlinsky's 1921 opera *Der Zwerg* (The Dwarf). In a short documentary released to accompany the online streaming of the production in 2020, dramaturg Sebastian Hanusa (Deutsche Oper Berlin, 2020) explains:

> [A] challenge posed to anyone mounting Zemlinsky's *Der Zwerg* is clearly the question of whom to cast in the title role. . . . You really need someone who's not just a brilliant singer and actor but also capable of pulling off such difficult and demanding vocals. And there's the little matter—and it's there in black and white in the text—that this man, this tenor, is a person with dwarfism.[1] Which raises the question: as an opera house or as a director, do you spend ages searching for a great tenor who's also small in stature, or do you go down another path?

On the surface, Hanusa's words chime with the defense of the *Come As You Are* producer Grant Rosenmeyer: "[Authentic casting] takes time; it's a very long casting search. You can absolutely do it; it just takes time and resources." (Lopez, 2020). But in fact, Deutsche Oper Berlin did "go down another path," casting both the German actor Mick Morris Mehnert and British tenor David Butt Philip as Zemlinsky's protagonist. The cynic might note that, as an actor with dwarfism, Mehnert's performance lends a certain "authenticity" to the production without stifling the company's ability to put an acclaimed, able-bodied tenor front and center. However, this casting choice cannot be solely attributed to the company's desire to avoid the use of disability mimicry: it is a particularly elegant solution in the context of Zemlinsky's opera, in which the protagonist increasingly grapples with his imagined self (embodied by Butt Philip) and his physical reality (reflected by Mehnert). Nonetheless, this particular example does prompt us to consider the rarity with which we encounter physically disabled performers on the opera stage. Hanusa appears to point to a dearth of disabled talent, but in fact, the availability of opportunities for disabled performers and practitioners in the opera industry seems a more probable culprit for this lack of visibility.

In his memoir, the German bass-baritone Thomas Quasthoff recalls the barriers to education and musical training he faced during his youth during the 1970s (Quasthoff, 2008, p. 88). Born with severe birth defects caused by thalidomide, Quasthoff was denied the opportunity to audition for music academy because of his physical inability to play the piano. Today, of course, disability protection acts in many countries prevent this kind of overt discrimination from happening, but other barriers remain in place for disabled performers (see the interview with Oliver Vibrans, in this volume, for the perspective of a disabled composer). Research undertaken by the charity Youth Music points to significant disparities in access to music education and instrument sales for young disabled musicians in the UK (Youth Music, 2020), and even those who can access the requisite materials and training to become a professional musician are likely to face discrimination during their professional careers, particularly in relation to casting. The American baritone Weston Hurt has described a period of time at the beginning of his career in the early 2000s when he was frequently overlooked for roles based on his disability (Hurt, quoted in Brigolin, 2017). Born without a right hand, Hurt was offered a festival contract with a high-profile opera company in Germany on the condition that he acquire a prosthesis. Having done so, he recalls: "Boom! I started getting gigs and gigs and gigs" (Brigolin, 2017). The prosthesis, it seems, enabled Hurt to "pass" as non-disabled, allowing him to obtain more roles. This calls to mind Sandahl's observation that disabled performers lack the requisite bodily "neutrality" to be considered for roles perceived as non-disabled, and are often "told that their impairments would detract from the playwright's or director's intent for a non-disabled character" (Sandahl, 2005, p. 255).

Further issues surrounding disability's (in)visibility in performance are highlighted by Quasthoff, who resisted participating in staged opera productions for many years, writing that it "seems an unnecessary display of my disability" (2008, p. 128). Here, the singer seems to suggest that his presence on stage would render him as a spectacle to be consumed by the audience. This issue is defined by David Church as "freakery," a process whereby "non-disabled audience retains the power to subject a non-normative body (traditionally, that of a person with disabilities) to the ableist gaze as entertaining spectacle, enjoying a mixture of shock, horror, wonder, and pity" (2011, p. 3). Quasthoff also notes the frequency with which he was offered the role of Verdi's Rigoletto during his career (2008, p. 135), echoing Sandahl's suggestion that the number of demeaning, stereotypical roles is one of the most persistent barriers to disabled performers (Sandahl, 2005, p. 257).

Despite Quasthoff's reluctance to be defined by his disability, his musical achievements have often been talked about in terms of "overcoming," with Quasthoff unwittingly cast in the role of the "supercrip" or "saintly sage" (Straus, 2011, pp. 138–142). This speaks to the way in which reductive narratives about disability can begin to inform public perceptions of disabled figures like Quasthoff, who, despite declining opportunities to perform in "canonical" disabled roles, still fails to evade being associated with disability stereotypes. What is more, representations of disability in the narrative arts can influence and shape wider attitudes toward disability. For example, if the public are frequently exposed to disabled characters who are only notable for the extent to which they overcome or triumph over their impairments—a phenomenon known as "inspiration porn" (Young, 2014)—figures like Quasthoff are at risk of continually being defined by their disability, and not by their artistry on its own terms. In short, the dilution of disability to superficial stock characters and narrative tropes can result in a problematic cycle of misrepresentation.

One solution to this particular problem is to make a range of roles available to disabled performers. Hurt (2018) discusses the merits of this approach as he explores how the ability to choose whether or not to "display" his disability on stage allows him to create unique theatrical moments:

> I am at a place in my career now where I am able to make the decision alongside the director whether or not my character would have one hand or two and reviewers, for the most part, have stopped mentioning it. I find, as it always has, that it brings greater depth to the character should we decide to not wear my prosthesis for Nabucco, Sharpless, or Rigoletto or to start the role of Valentin with the prosthesis only to return in Act 3, home from war, without it. Or better yet, in my Houston Grand Opera debut as Scarpia in Puccini's *Tosca*, the brilliant director John Caird had the idea for me to remove my prosthesis on stage during Act 2 to heighten the level of drama with Tosca. These choices are unique to me and are simply there to add to the drama of the storytelling which allows me to create a character which is four-dimensional.

Hurt suggests that there are rich interpretative and creative opportunities when exploring disability critically on stage, but he also stresses the need for opera companies to consider disabled performers for roles often assumed to be able-bodied ("Who's to say that any of these characters had two hands to begin with?"). Here, he speaks to the fact that "fixing" the problematic nature of many portrayals of disability in opera does not solely depend on authentic casting of roles assumed to be either disabled or non-disabled. Fox and Sandahl (2018, p. 122) summarize this as follows:

> If we discuss the implications of casting only as an absence or presence of disabled people, we risk reinscribing disabled/non-disabled binaries, and acting as if our engagement with drama only exists in relationship to non-disabled people and the extent to which they wish to assume disabled identities for fun, profit, or as an example of their supposed actorly virtuosity.

In fact, the representation of disability in opera does not begin and end with individual performers at all. Instead, I would argue that solutions to the "problems" of disability in performance lie in exploring the multifaceted aspects of disability's representation in opera, leading us, perhaps, to stop seeing disability as a "problem" at all.

Contemporary encounters with opera and disability: A way forward?

When considering the performance of disability, disability studies and performance studies challenge and complement one another, revealing a host of so-called "representational conundrums." This is a term used by Sandahl to describe "challenging, puzzling, or paradoxical issues that are unique to or complicated by disability's presence" on stage (Sandahl, 2018, p. 130). One such conundrum can be found in the challenge of reconciling contemporary debates around casting and "authenticity" with historical depictions that are far removed from the realities of disability as a lived experience (see Caitlin Vincent's chapter in this volume; Bull, 2019; Johnston, 2016). It can be easy when discussing disability representation in the arts to find ourselves choosing between tradition and innovation, but embracing innovative modes of disability representation needn't necessitate the removal of older, more problematic works from the repertory.

Outdated representations of disability often reveal and underwrite the cultural moments in which they were created, acting as "magnets" to which an era's primary social and political concerns are secured (Garland Thomson, 1996). As such, they can provide opportunities for critical reflection and radical interpretation. Taking this idea a step further, Naomi André suggests that opera "is not inherently flawed with racist, sexist negative stereotypes. Instead, it works as a mouthpiece, a conduit, through which a reflection of a society's cultural ideology—which may include those stereotypes—can be heard and seen" (2018, p. 159). Engaging with opera as a "site of critical enquiry, political activism, and social change" (p. 195), opera creators might think more carefully about how we both mobilize and contextualize disability, forming productions that interrogate the social, historical, and political contexts in which these scenes were conceived.

Nonetheless, meaningful engagement rarely happens without real-world perspectives (in this case, the perspectives of those with a lived experience of disability). Much of my emphasis in this chapter has been on both "canonical" operas and so-called "mainstream" opera production. Today, however, disabled-led opera companies are creating innovative works that address challenges in narrative representation while also embedding a so-called "aesthetics of access" into the creative and practical aspects of their performances. This concept has been developed by Jenny Sealey and the Graeae Theatre Company over the past decade. It refers to the integration of access measures and considerations for practitioners, performers, and audiences into all stages of theatrical production, from planning, to casting, to performance (*Disability Arts International*, 2017; Graeae, 2021). We find pertinent examples of this approach in Graeae's forthcoming opera, *The Paradis Files*, and in Amble Skuse and Toria Banks's digital opera *We Ask These Questions of Everybody* (2021). Performed by a cast of entirely deaf and disabled artists with music by Errollyn Wallen, *The Paradis Files* tells the story of Maria Theresia von Paradis (1759–1824), a blind composer and musician from the 18th century. In September 2020, a short documentary about the making of the opera was screened as part of the *Tête à Tête* opera festival. It revealed how *The Paradis Files* is incorporating signing and captions alongside opera's amalgamation of text, dance, drama, and music to fully explore the creative potential of accessibility's artistic aesthetic and push the already multimodal boundaries of opera. *We Ask These Questions of Everybody* also brings together an all-disabled cast and creative team to dramatize the transcript of a real-life Personal Independence Payment (PIP) benefit interview (PIP is a form of state welfare support in the UK). These two operas place disability at the center of their narratives, depicting both historical and contemporary experiences of disability while navigating present-day representational politics in real-time. This careful balance between nuanced narrative and accessible process avoids perpetuating negative disability stereotypes and creates richer dramaturgical engagements with disability in the process. Therein, perhaps, lies the way forward.

Conclusion

Like many depictions of disability in the arts, operatic responses to disability reveal and underwrite the cultural moments in which they were created. Yet, older works that depict disability problematically do not exist in a historical vacuum: they are frequently transformed and updated for the contemporary stage. Here, problematic staging practices often go unquestioned by production teams and audiences alike. Moreover, the sustained use of offensive stereotypes and tired stock characters in the fictional world of a production can influence real-world perceptions of disabled people, which in turn can have negative ramifications on employment prospects for disabled performers and practitioners. My intention here—and indeed, in this chapter as a whole—is to demonstrate how the problems surrounding opera's engagement with disability cut across aspects of its representation in both text and performance. By pushing the boundaries of accessibility and inclusion in the opera industry and breaking new ground in terms of disability representation in the genre, contemporary works like *The Paradis Files* and *We Ask These Questions of Everybody* may set new standards for disability representation in the genre.

But what can researchers, practitioners, and administrators do to ensure these the steps these projects have taken are the rule and not the exception? First, there is a need to further develop new critical frameworks that facilitate meaningful collaboration between academics, disability activists, and operatic performers and practitioners. This will enable us to ensure that positive steps being taken in one context do not continue to exist within a silo. Secondly, quantitative and ethnographic research is needed to establish the current state of play in the industry. Only when we understand the scale of the problem can we begin to address systemic inequalities and move toward a more equitable culture for disabled performers and practitioners. Thirdly, and perhaps most importantly, there is a need to engage in dialogues with and acknowledge the voices of those with real-world lived experience of both disability and operatic performance. Without their insights, questions raised in this chapter about casting, performance practice, and the real-world impact of opera's thorny relationship with disability will remain unaddressed.

Note

1. Hanusa uses the term "Kleinwüchsige," which is the German medical term for dwarfism, as opposed to the more outdated and derogatory "Zwerg."

III
MARGINALIZED VOICES

10
Gender and Class
An Account of a Female Percussionist in the Classical Music Industry

Beth Higham-Edwards

At time of writing, England is in its third lockdown as a result of COVID-19, and any resemblance of normality or of the industry returning feels very far off. The media being shared among musician colleagues is about how Brexit might impact UK musicians, and news on how the pandemic is affecting the industry, disproportionately women and parents (PiPA, 2021; Venvell, 2020). Currently, none of my income is from performing and it is therefore hard to still identify as a musician. However, this feeling is not necessarily new to me as I have never felt that my place in the industry is secured. In this chapter I will be writing from my own perspective about barriers I have experienced due to my gender and familial background. I am acutely aware that my positioning as White, living without a disability, and being heterosexual, will have undoubtedly privileged me in many ways, and I would like to acknowledge this.

How my identity and background led me to activism

The role of family and access

I was born in the early 1990s and grew up in a working-class area of South East London. My parents worked for local authorities and I am the only musician in my family. My parents are from working-class backgrounds and were the first and only of their generation to go to university. While my upbringing was middle-class, my extended family remains working-class and my parents retain socialist values. My childhood memories include my mum attending a monthly working women's group. My dad was a town planner who believed in equal access to transport for the whole community, as well as eradicating barriers, whether physical or financial.

This upbringing, strongly routed in values of fairness, often jars with values I see upheld within the classical music profession—nepotism, elitism, and exclusivity. I did not realize how deeply I had imbibed my parent's socialist values, until I saw the contrast between my reactions when I experienced prejudice, to the reactions of some of my peers experiencing the same thing who often did not even recognize these things occurring.

My music tuition was given to me by my parents, who wanted me to have opportunities that were not available to them. Recorder was my main instrument until I went to university, as group recorder lessons were offered by my primary school. I attended a non-fee-paying grammar secondary school and while my school was academic, it had a strong science focus and the music department was neglected. Only three pupils, including myself, took music to A Level. Classical music was not accepted within my school student culture. You would be embarrassed to be seen carrying an instrument case and playing the recorder, which was seen as either a children's instrument or an instrument played by hippy historical enthusiasts. Even within classical music circles the recorder is often seen as uncool, and so you can imagine how strange an interest in the recorder was considered among my school friends. I kept it hidden at school, and as a teenager was more regularly seen at indy gigs and Reading Festival than any classical venue.

In my second year at secondary school, I gained a place at Junior Trinity Laban, a conservatoire junior department that took place on Saturdays. Junior Trinity is the reason I continued music through my teenage years. If I had not grown up 20 minutes from it, I most likely would not be in the profession. The locality of Junior Trinity was why I auditioned; we did not know what a conservatoire was. My parents were also recommended a Saturday music center in London Bridge, just under an hour away. This journey, however, felt too long to make every Saturday. We were shocked to find students traveling to Junior Trinity from as far as Devon and this started to show a cultural difference between coming from a musical family, and not. My parents' parenting style in general seemed different to parents more embedded within the classical music scene and upper classes. I remember my mum finding it strange and overbearing when parents would come into their children's music exams, spend their Saturdays hanging around their teenagers between music lessons while berating Trinity Laban staff and music teachers, and criticize their children after a performance. I remember my mum feeling initially concerned about the added time pressure of doing music on a Saturday. However, this worry disappeared when she saw how much I enjoyed it.

Throughout my education, I did not approach music with the view that it might become a career. My family and I were oblivious to the fact that other children were being prepped for the industry from the age of four. I started learning percussion at age 13, and while it is more usual for percussionists to start learning later than other instrumentalists, it was a knock to me when I discovered in my early 20s that several music schools existed where children were being trained in percussion from the age of eight.

The microcosms of privilege that are bred in environments where talented young musicians mix, only became apparent to me later when I was surrounded by people in the profession who had known each other for decades and had no doubt that they deserved their place in the industry. Almost all my work is obtained from organizations rather than other musicians. There is a whole network of percussionists who give work to each other. I am not part of this network due to my education and my career progression not being a linear path from music school to conservatoire, concert society orchestral gigs, and working within the professional orchestral scene.

Despite gaining a place at the Royal College of Music (RCM) for my undergraduate degree, I chose to study music at the University of Birmingham, a decision that made my piano teacher's nose wrinkle. I was put off by the competitive culture I had observed at the RCM and wanted to have the first-year university social experiences my friends were going to have on their courses. My motivations were not career-led, and I was not aware that other musicians my age were making career-led choices.

In my final year I decided I wanted to be a performer. I asked for an additional percussion teacher who performed in a prestigious UK orchestra. He was shocked to find that I did not know what an orchestral excerpt was, and I was shocked to find that excerpts made up the majority of the audition requirements to study percussion at postgraduate level at conservatoire. I felt that the prospect of a career in performing percussion was over despite having a music degree, fantastic tuition at Junior Trinity, and being only 21.

After a lot of hard work learning books full of orchestral excerpts within a few months (compared to the four years of preparation other candidates received on their conservatoire undergraduate courses), I gained a place at a prestigious London conservatoire. While waiting to take up my place, I applied for administrative internships in music education departments. I was fortunate to gain a place on the Trainee Music Leader Scheme at Spitalfields Music. This experience introduced me to the field of community music, an area I have a huge amount of passion for as it is generally targeted at those excluded from regular arts provision.

During the second year of my master's degree, I was offered a job performing in the National Theatre's production of *Amadeus* as part of Southbank Sinfonia. I was the only one in the *Amadeus* orchestra who was not an alumnus of the Southbank Sinfonia training orchestra. The fixer told me that he needed someone for the production who was trustworthy: unlikely to drink on the job, able to respond to a director, and work well within a big cast. It was one of the few times that not being the archetypal laddy percussionist worked in my favor. I had done a short internship with Southbank Sinfonia's orchestra manager in the office before I started my master's. While I am proud of the reasons they hired me, it does show that hiring practice is about who you know and who likes you, which is a barrier for those who enter the profession through a non-traditional route. As of now, I have enjoyed a few successful years performing. Since the pandemic has hit, I have taken a temporary job as a nanny, a concession some musicians around me do not seem to have had to make.

The role of gender

When I was exposed to the classical percussion environment, I felt thwacked 'round the head by the misogyny, lack of respect, and marginalization of women. At the conservatoire where I studied for my master's, there were ten teachers in the percussion department teaching different disciplines, all of whom were male. We had weekly classes with visiting professional percussionists and not a single woman was booked during the two years that I was there. There were six female students and 12 male students in the department. The teaching staff did not reflect the student body.

While I was benefiting from wonderful teaching from my main teacher and most of the other teachers in the department, myself and the other female students felt that we were not receiving the same quality teaching from one of the professors, and some of the visiting professors, as the male students. I had comments on my appearance when playing, saying I looked like a secretary, or receiving feedback after a mock audition, which was entirely about my attire, rather than playing. A teacher told me sexually explicit stories at the expense of the women he worked with in his professional orchestra. This teacher even told me that he "wouldn't allow *his* daughter to play percussion." I was discouraged from taking an audition by a well-meaning teacher, as he knew that the lead percussionist on the audition panel was "unlikely to submit a girl, especially an intellectual one." These are examples of instances when teachers treated me and the other female students in the department differently. It was clear that some teachers could not see past the fact that I was a woman, which negatively affected their ability to teach me and marred the whole experience.

I sometimes hear the argument that sexist men will eventually die out. However, there was little about the student culture to support this view. The male students idolized the male professionals and this created a self-perpetuating cycle of behavior that marginalized women, included a huge amount of drinking, and a prevalent "lad culture" (a British subculture). I observed female students allowing themselves to be the butt of the joke, and joining in with sexist/homophobic/racist banter in order to fit in. The backdrop to this behavior was a "survival of the fittest" mentality: not joining in would affect your chances of getting work. This is a huge barrier to change, as challenging this behavior, for a freelancer, is very risky business. When I started my gender advocacy work, I felt that I was saying goodbye to the chance of working in many, largely orchestral, settings.

Since speaking openly about issues facing women in our sector, I have had women reaching out to me and they often refer to their time at conservatoire with a sense of shock at how stressful and pressured student life was for them, alongside terrible stories of mistreatment. I feel particularly saddened when I think of the number of stories of sexual harassment I have heard from other female instrumentalists, many about men in leadership positions such as teachers and conductors. This is an area that our industry needs to pay some serious attention to (please see ISM, 2021).

Other female students and I complained to staff about the problematic teacher, and I raised the issue of women's underrepresentation among the teaching staff. The conservatoire now has one female percussion teacher and the department has invited some female visiting professors. And yet, the most problematic teacher still teaches there and was not put under investigation. While it did not feel like anything was achieved at the time we complained, I wish that more conservatoire students would complain about the negative environments that are upheld in conservatoires and inappropriate choices of teaching staff. Unfortunately however, and based on conversations with other women of my age, these realizations often seem to come years after the fact.

While studying for my master's, my performing career began. I was performing at the National Theatre and subsequently at Shakespeare's Globe where I found many female percussionists on the books. I found a freelance scene where skilled female percussionists were well represented and it made me question why they weren't teaching in conservatoires. Arguably, conservatoires have a hierarchical attitude toward different career paths: being a freelancer is not held in as high regard as having a permanent orchestral position. While conservatoires do increasingly promote the idea of a "portfolio career," this is undermined by the fact that it still appears relatively easy for a principal player of any major orchestra to gain a teaching position in a conservatoire regardless of their ability as an educator. With female percussionists and brass players underrepresented in orchestras, and with the conservatoires still favoring teachers with orchestral seats, the issue of representation among teaching staff continues to self-perpetuate.

In November 2018, I collected data by tallying how many men and women had percussion seats within the member orchestras of the Association of British Orchestras. I found that among a total of 104 percussion positions, eight posts were held by women (8%). I also surveyed the percussion teaching staff at UK conservatoires as listed on their websites. Out of 93 positions, 10 posts were held by women. Including visiting professors, there were a total of 142 positions, 15 of which were held by women. In short, 90% of the percussion teaching posts in UK conservatoires seem to be held by men. Incidentally, I wrote to an industry organization asking for data on which orchestras run screened auditions. I received an email reply from the CEO saying he did not know, and that there was not a gender problem in orchestras.

I compiled this data into a report, circulated it to industry representatives and hosted a roundtable discussion at Wigmore Hall in March 2019. This was well attended by major music organizations and percussionists. In my discussions with some of the percussionists after the event, they told me that a conservatoire representative present at the event informally had taken the line of "Oh, but we don't have that sort of behavior at our conservatoire, do we?" However, that attendee was in the minority as after the event; I received numerous invitations for meetings with high profile organizations. The people I met with were extremely encouraging. However, the meetings rarely resulted in any concrete targets or measures. I got the sense that the industry wanted to change but did not know how.

Being an activist in classical music

In 2019, I was asked to join the charity SWAP'ra (Supporting Women and Parents in Opera). SWAP'ra is an artist-led charity that is run by a group of freelancers. During the pandemic, I launched a program called *SWAP'ra Makes Space*. This was a series of gatherings for women who do not get the opportunity to engage with other women in similar professional roles and was inspired by my mother's Working Women's group. It was also a direct response to the pandemic, worked well online, and I was able to get it up and running during a time when other gender equality projects I was involved in were canceled. I wanted to do something that fostered a sense of community and improved quality of life in order to help women stick with the profession during this difficult time. Challenges involved in being a freelancer, such as isolation and fear of losing work, are grossly underestimated and I am keen to do what I can to keep women interested in staying in the industry.

I have recently taken a smaller role with SWAP'ra as creative associate in order to give me the capacity to create a group that is dedicated to gender and instrumentalists not just in opera or classical music, but across the music industry in general—which more accurately represents my career and interests. Founded in 2021, the name of the group is Gender and the Large and Shiny Instruments.

My motivation to start a dedicated group came as a response to three things I learned during my time in advocacy. Firstly, I have attended countless events about gender in the classical music profession and find that often I am the only instrumentalist there, among other regular faces who routinely attend events on diversity and inclusion. Discussions at these sessions rarely relate to the nuanced issues I face, as a female percussionist. Having a group specifically about instrumentalists means we can dig down. I have found it fascinating speaking to brass players and finding that the social cultures and performing pressures can differ greatly, even between trumpet and trombone.

Secondly, one of the most valuable things that came out of my roundtable in 2019 was not necessarily meeting high profile members of the industry, but the impact that openly speaking about the issue had on some of the percussionists who attended. A year later, I saw one of the female percussionist attendees at a gig. We were two of three women booked to play in a section of 11 percussionists. It was the second time we had met and she came over to me with a look of relief and said, "I am so happy you are here." I had not foreseen the empowering effects of identifying the issues in a group and agreeing that they do exist and are systemic. Making her day at work feel a bit safer was a huge win and I hope to create that for others.

Finally, I have seen multiple events for female conductors, composers, and women in leadership, but not much for women in roles that are not necessarily named on the concert program such as instrumentalists, technicians, and backstage staff. While I understand the need for women in leadership roles, I find it important to consider women at all levels of an organization, as everyone's lived experience is of equal value.

Reflections on my activist work

While diversity and inclusion is now a huge topic of conversation within classical music, there still exists a barrier for freelancers getting their voices heard. I have many female instrumentalists keen to speak with me about issues they have faced, however this feels whispered and there seems to be a fear of being "outed" or of comments being passed on and heard by male colleagues. In fact, one of the guest speakers who spoke at one of the *SWAP'ra Makes Space* network meetings told us that her partner had questioned whether it was a sensible move for her to accept our invitation, even though she no longer works in the industry.

There are plenty of conversations happening, but they often include the same people, and while there is a lot of talk, change feels slow. I attended an industry conference in 2020 and saw a lack of freelancers, instrumentalists, and young people. The conference fee was high and I could only go because SWAP'ra paid for my ticket. I also lost work on the days I was there and, in general, my time working in advocacy has left me out of pocket. At the conference, I felt a sense that people were defending their organizations and that this defensiveness got in the way of progressive conversations and change. I raised a couple of points and was surprised to find numerous people personally thanking me for my contributions, saying that I was raising things that they felt they could not.

Equally important, the many conversations that are being held around diversity and inclusion are not reaching those on the ground. I believe there is sometimes a disconnect between unnamed freelance performers (i.e., those in the ranks—not soloists) and artistic planning teams in general. Most instrumentalists I speak to have no idea about the conversations that are happening in the industry, and are not necessarily encouraged to join them. I think performers are much more likely to engage with a movement set up by someone with lived experience and knowledge, for people to trust it and feel it is really being made for them rather than to make an organization look good.

A final thought

My dad told me that when he first started reading town planning reports—which include various sections on roads, financial considerations, environmental impacts, and so on, the section on disability and access was always last. When he wrote his first report, he flipped this and put accessibility at the front. By making a town accessible to someone in a wheelchair or someone with lost sight or hearing, you by default make it accessible to many more people: someone pushing a buggy for instance, or someone who can read English better than they can hear it. I have the feeling that diversity and inclusion has been pushed to the back in the classical music sector, or left as something for education departments to tackle. The gender issues I have discussed do not just affect women; they are cultural issues that affect all sorts of minorities, non-drinkers, and even just men who do not want to be a part of a lad culture. By tackling the cultural issues that exist within classical music, and by putting diversity and inclusion first in all planning, the industry may become an inhabitable place for more people, and more people will have a good day at work.

11
Making Space for Disability and Music to Interact

An Interview with Composer Oliver Vibrans

Oliver Vibrans

ANNA: Maybe you could start off by telling me how you got into composing classical music.

OLIVER: Well, my dad was a composer who worked in theater and my mum is an actor and also works in theater, so I was exposed to people being creative. Then I won some composition competitions when I was really young that my piano teacher put me up for and I became interested in the fact that I could do it. I applied to some specialist secondary music schools when I was around 11 and didn't get in because I couldn't read music at that point. I think that was probably for the best in the long run. I did the Sound and Music Summer School, a week-long residential course for young composers,[1] which was quite a significant thing. That was my introduction to the proper world of music and music education at a high level, and it was a very intense experience. I started working in concert music or classical music—I'd been working in theater before—and I'd not had a massive interest in concert hall settings because they could be quite alienating to a lot of people, and to me to some extent, as my education was more based in jazz theory. I had a fantastic composition teacher when I was a teenager, Andy Stamatakis-Brown, a jazz musician and composer. I had a difficult relationship with music theory but Andy met me where I was and taught me in a way that allowed me to develop my own technical relationship with music.

ANNA: I came across you because you were speaking at the Association of British Orchestras conference and you were quite critical of the classical music world in relation to inclusion of disabled people. Could you reflect on how inclusive the classical music world is of you as a disabled person?

OLIVER: My sense is that the classical music world has this way of hiding behind the idea that it's a meritocracy. I think it's very clear in places like conservatoires, and in my experience of applying to music schools when I was 11, that they have a very clear idea of what they value and what they want you to be as a musician to fit into their institutional mold. For people who are kind of "other," it feels like we only get to succeed in classical music if we succeed on industry terms—if we can speak their language and produce work that the industry can look at and say, "This is quality." But I think when you present the industry with something that doesn't fit what they term valuable, then I think they'll just go, "This person just doesn't have x." There's also a huge primacy put on the sanctity of the musical score and being able to audiate—that is, to be able to hear music based on looking at it. But if you're visually impaired you have a totally different relationship with music. So it can be frustrating—you can go to a big educational institution like a conservatoire, or a big organization like an orchestra, and you can ask, why are there so few disabled people? And they'll say, it's so competitive, so what can we do? But the reality is that the exclusion is happening before you get to the audition. Discrimination is happening at various stages—it's to do with existing opportunities, existing instruments, the way that certain pedagogies aren't going to suit people with different bodies.

ANNA: Can you give any examples of the ways that existing instruments or pedagogies might be disabling?

OLIVER: I play the drum kit, which is not a classical instrument, and the history of the drum kit is a wonderful example of the social model of disability. You adapt the environment (the drum kit) to suit the individual (the drummer). The drum kit was created out of the necessity for percussionists needing to play multiple pieces of marching band percussion all at the same time. Every player essentially customizes their drum kit to suit their own body and their own way of playing and as a result there is such a plethora of ways that drummers put together their instruments. . . . So the idea of a correct technique is a bit more fluid in the world of the drums, so I was able to find my own way with it. Whereas if you start out playing the violin, you have to play in a certain way. You're going to have to have solved that before a conservatoire or professional orchestra will look at you.

ANNA: That example of how people have to find their own individual solutions to these structural issues reminds me of when I was carrying out research with young people playing in youth orchestras. Some people disclosed to me that they were dyslexic, but their dyslexia existed totally under the radar in these settings—there was no provision for it in the teaching and learning, and so any young dyslexic musicians just took it for granted that they had to manage this privately, on an individual basis.

OLIVER: Also, in the way that disability interacts with professional music, initially the idea that a disabled musician is playing music at all is seen as an extraordinary thing so there isn't much critique or scrutiny of the nature of that music—asking: Is it actually good? Is it expressive? That's not seen as important. And then there's this extraordinarily difficult process of having to push through people's expectations of you as a disabled person, for your ability to be able to make music in a way that is valuable, that is quality, that is professional. But then, I think when you get to a certain point as a musician where people are looking at you and thinking that is professional, it's high quality, and it doesn't matter that you are disabled, then it can be the case that your disability is inaccessible to you as part of your music-making because people make no connection between your disability as your identity and your creative output. Instead, it is something that you've dealt with and you've overcome. As a disabled person, it can often feel like the best you can hope for is to be as non-disabled as possible, rather than people being interested in the nuance of what disability is. As a teenager growing up I'd not met any disabled people— I'd never been able to occupy a space with other disabled people where it felt positive to talk about disability. You internalize that and you want to minimize your disability. I've become politicized thanks to disability studies. I did my dissertation as an undergraduate on disability and performance practice. For me, discovering disability studies was one of the most empowering experiences I'd ever had. It was so exciting to see people having intelligent and nuanced thoughts about disability. The quality of the discussion at the moment is really poor; the discussion is still dominated by a small group of harmful narratives of disability and it's so much work having to constantly push through that. So discovering this body of research was so amazing to me. And I've met amazing disabled artists who have empowered me to access disability as an identity in my work. But at the same time I want to be able to make that a choice—to choose when disability is important or not important to the work I make. An additional challenge is that there currently don't exist any cultural scripts that allow you to do that in a way that is empowering. An odd side effect of becoming a professional musician is that part of my professional work is in disability arts as well as outreach projects, working with young disabled people, that kind of thing. So a condition of the professional work you do is that it's got some connection to your disability. That can sometimes feel trapping and oppressive—what if I don't want to be a professional disabled person, I just want to be a musician? Disabled people are never empowered to make that choice for themselves and furthermore, the nature of a competitive industry compounds the problem. Musicians are rarely in full control of the work available to them and if that work pushes you to frame your identity in a certain way, you're still likely to take the work to further your career.

ANNA: Could you say something about the type of work you've been involved in toward making change in classical music, and what type of work needs to happen?

OLIVER: I do a lot of voluntary Equality, Diversity, and Inclusion (EDI) work; I'm on the EDI steering group for Brighter Sound, which is a music education organization based in Manchester in the UK. I'm also on the EDI steering group for the Ivors Academy, a professional association in the UK representing music creators, as well as a board member for the Ivors Academy Trust. Such groups can be really wonderful spaces, particularly the Ivors Academy, where there's a subgroup that looks specifically at disability. It's amazing to occupy a space with other professional disabled musicians, to get to have a properly nuanced discussion of different people's experiences—that space is a rare one. Most scenarios where music and disability come together exist in the realm of outreach and music therapy. These spaces and the work that happens in them are immensely valuable but they can come to dominate the narrative of disability and music. When working on an outreach project the music itself is not the most important thing but rather the experience of the participants, and thus disability becomes associated more with "participating in" rather than "making" music. In addition, one of the biggest challenges in doing this work is that a "disabled person" can be someone in their 80s, someone with a learning disability, someone like me, so it's almost impossible to create a sense of shared experience because it's such an umbrella term. This makes it doubly important that spaces like the Ivors EDI disability group exist; it allows a community of disabled people to exist and empower one another through nuanced discussion and shared (and differing) experience.

ANNA: I know you work across genres, and you've talked about some of the specific challenges to making classical music accessible to disabled people, but what would you say are the biggest challenges for the classical music profession in doing this work?

OLIVER: I think in the classical music world everyone is trying to jump through a pinhole. There's a very specific kind of musician that the classical music industry wants. Everyone's trying to be that and orchestras are seeking very particular, specifically-educated musicians who can execute the work the way they expect, and speak the language the way they want to it to be spoken. That's a problem that exists beyond disability. I taught in a state school music department for a year and class is a huge boundary as well. But specifically with disability, I think first off—and this isn't something I've had direct experience of—if you're approaching an orchestral instrument with a body that doesn't accommodate how it should be traditionally played, it's incredibly hard to get support to develop your musicianship. There's just no mechanisms or language in the classical music world that will support people in that position. And I think the biggest boundary is the expectation, the fact that we're used to classical musicians being discovered as prodigies at the age of eight, doing grade eight when they're ten. I think if you want to change that pipeline as a disabled person you're pushing through your disability to get there. Because gatekeepers aren't going to look at you and think, "Brilliant, yes, that's what we want." I think my experience is quite odd because as a composer, my disability doesn't have any practical, direct impact on my work. As a young person I found that extremely empowering and important because it allowed me to sidestep my disability. It allowed me to feel more powerful and to be a musician, to be something that is valued in our social consciousness, to get past the negative semiotics of disability. But as I've got older, I've come to identify as disabled, and to see disability as part of my identity beyond just the physical medicalized manifestation. For example, what is my disability in relation to my music-making? People's relationship between their disability and their music-making isn't something other people are particularly excited to explore at the moment. The challenges that I've faced as a disabled person, as a composer, are not so much in the foreground, and that is both a negative and a positive, I think. It very much speaks to the way the industry looks at you—"You're doing something in a way that I understand, so you're in." It's not that simple, of course. As a performer, the challenges are a bit easier to see.... I think the key is having an ability to see past the way that things have worked for 200 years and being able to see value in a range of music-making.

ANNA: This brings me to a question I'm really interested in, which is whether you think classical music itself needs to change to allow it to become more inclusive.

OLIVER: Yeah, definitely, but I don't think it necessarily has to be a painful process. I think big institutions like orchestras in classical music operate in a very specific way that can be alienating to a lot of people who do not understand their language. They will only accept you if you do something in the way that they value. I don't know how to fix it. I think the big thing for me—and it is to do with disability—what I want is for the aesthetic, the expectation, and the culture of the music to change, but not at the expense of quality. I think that's what people fear—if we stop doing it in the way we've always done it, we will start to lose the quality. I think that's bollocks. I think the biggest challenge for me as a disabled person is that people think you're not going to be able to do it properly. I have the highest expectations for the music I make. I'm all about the music. And I think it can be difficult for the industry to know how to have those expectations of disabled people. You need to have a pedagogy of classical music that can empower disabled people to be making work to a high standard. But I think at the moment disabled people are counted out of being able to do this properly in that pedagogy. And I think the disabled people who do succeed do so under their own steam, finding ways to make their practice valuable to the people holding the keys to the kingdom. My practice is pretty standard, in terms of composing. I think it is both empowering and problematic as a factor because I'm just playing the game, I guess.

ANNA: What would you say to people who want to bring about change in the classical music profession, whether that's activists, or people wanting to make their institutions more inclusive?

OLIVER: That's quite hard. I think for change to be truly successful it has to come from the very top and very bottom. You have to empower disabled people to have a place in classical music and that needs to be visible at the highest level of music-making and the work has to be of the highest quality. Showcasing outreach projects is great but it's not enough on its own. From the bottom, you've also got to change the way music pedagogy works for disabled people because it's incredibly difficult even to get started. We need to have higher expectations of disabled music making and not consign it to the realms of "outreach." I was extremely fortunate because my dad, who was also disabled, was a professional composer and so the expectation and the opportunity was there. But I think for so many people, you're excluded before you even start, because of the assumption that people with that body can't do x. There are wonderful examples of people who have shattered expectations to become musicians, but they are rarities. You have to make change from the grassroots so you are enabling disabled people to progress as musicians and to aspire to be professionals, and to give those people the tools they need, the training, adaptations to the instruments. People have also got to see that it's happening, it's got to be more visible. And it's got to be excellent work.

Note

1. Sound and Music is a UK-based charity whose mission is to maximize the opportunities for people to create and enjoy new music.

12
Black on the Podium

An Interview with Conductor Brandon Keith Brown

Brandon Keith Brown

ANNA: Could you start by telling me how you got involved in activism in classical music?

BRANDON: Yes. I had a really awful experience in academia in the US, where I was told I was hired because I was Black. Before meeting me, students emailed they were scared and nervous and anxious to attend auditions, and this swelled up into a racial hurricane, so to speak, and I ended up being released from this position, a position that I had thought that I would really be able to make change from. And in that process of coming to terms with why that happened, I began to reach out and speak to a lot of other Black people, and it turns out that other people have been through the same situation, regardless of occupation. I started to reach out to some sociologists and reading sociology as well to get an understanding of why this happens and why this keeps happening, why in- and out-groups don't get along and what is keeping out-groups from being in-groups. Until this point, I hadn't realized that I'm Black first, before I'm a conductor. Through this process, I began writing about my experiences of racism and writing about the challenges of not being White and being considered an outsider. What I've come to realize is that people who are in the in-group, people who are White, have to learn to become comfortable with being uncomfortable with discussing racism, and really have to learn to get along and to understand and be willing to understand Black people, and to understand that it's a different lived experience.

ANNA: Your career has been quite international—you've predominantly worked in the US and Germany. Could you reflect on your experiences of being Black in classical music across those international contexts?

BR: I should first say I have worked very little in the US. I've worked mainly in Germany and other places throughout the world, and it has to do with a lot of stigma. The US still has an idea of Black History Month concerts for Black conductors, Fourth of July, special concerts that are outside of the main "masterwork" series. But in Germany, I've been able to do a lot more of the so-called canon; I've been able to do the core repertoire here.

Because I won a prize in the Solti Competition in Germany, they've taken me much more seriously and I've been able to get more opportunities. Having said that, I've had some really horrible experiences in Germany too, including racism from members of orchestras I've been conducting. Some of these experiences are pretty common among Black conductors, such as not being let in your dressing room because they don't know you're the conductor. Every Black conductor will tell you that story. But the more people that look like me are on the podium, the more comfortable the musicians will be. We have to remember that musicians can go through their whole lives never experiencing a Black conductor and never feeling any sense of loss about it. This is very important, to make sure that Black conductors are on the podium, that we're being seen, that we're being heard in front of the musicians. This is how they're going to become more comfortable working with us, both in the orchestra and in society.

ANNA: Having had these experiences of racism, what do you think the biggest challenge is in making classical music more inclusive of Black people and People of Color generally as well?

BRANDON: So-called diversity initiatives, focus on getting individual musicians into orchestras, but a lot of these musicians don't share the same cultural repertoire as the White musicians that are in the orchestra. And, as you know, cultural repertoire is all the information that we send out about who belongs and what is valued in society. For instance, if you come into an orchestra and you have an Afro and people complain that they can't see the conductor and they ask you to cut the Afro, that's a misunderstanding of the cultural repertoire of Black culture. But I propose a top-down approach, which is to get more Black conductors—who understand the cultural repertoire of Black musicians—onto the podium. This is not to say that Black conductors will automatically hire Black musicians. But when it comes time to give tenure to a musician, that falls more heavily on the shoulders of the conductor, and if we get more Black conductors on the podium, I know that we're going to get more Black musicians in the orchestra and we won't have this tokenism of Black musicians. Particularly in US orchestras, we have this tokenism, by which I mean one Black musician at a time. Having one at a time is because that's all that White people can actually handle. If you get more Black conductors as music directors, this tells the orchestra, audience, community, and industry that we actually belong in the genre, that we're a part of it, that we're leading the production of music. And that's something that I would like to explore with training Black conductors and getting more Black conductors on the podium.

ANNA: Could you say a little bit about any activist projects or work that you've been involved in to try and make change in classical music?

BR: I've just started an organization called All the Black Dots. I haven't started to get funding for it, but what I want to do is develop a training program for Black conductors to come during the summertime to train with me and then give a concert with an orchestra of underrepresented minorities. This will be not only a source of, I think, inspiration and training for Black conductors, but this will be a chance for audiences to see that we can be producers of sound. You have to remember that when you invest in a conductor, it's usually the largest financial investment than an organization makes. And for them to take a leap of faith and to invest in a Black conductor and to give us large sums of money is not something that boards of directors, particularly in the US, are going to be willing to do. So it's something I want to take place in Germany because I think they're more open to the idea of doing it. This is the type of project that we need. We have to be working in extremes. We can't allow ourselves to say, oh, well, we've got an Asian, we've got somebody from Southeast Asia, we've got Latinx. Those groups are, in the US, markedly advantaged over Blacks. In the States there are fellowship programs for Black musicians' programs—not everywhere else—but Black musicians are not getting in the orchestras full-time and staying there. Why? And we've proven to play just as well as other groups. And when they get in the orchestras, a lot of them aren't getting tenure, they're getting pushed out after the probationary period. Why is this happening? Focusing on developing Black conductors is one way forward toward Black musician tenure.

ANNA: One question that you probably know that I'm interested in is, to what extent do you think the music itself needs to change to become more inclusive of minoritized people and groups? One example would be expanding the canon and the repertoire, which is discussed in chapters in this book for example the chapter by Angela Elizabeth Slater. But as well as that, I'm thinking of the ideals of beauty that we aim for in classical music. For example, Ruth Gustafson (2009) talked about the bel canto classical music voice being at odds with how a lot of African-American singers learn how to sing. Another example might also be rehearsal practices, and whether the musical result we want justifies oppressive rehearsal practices, which tend to be experienced more intensely by those who are already marginalized. This also extends to the hierarchies of authority that are normalized in teaching and learning or that are required to produce some of the more large-scale classical music repertoire.

BRANDON: These are wonderful questions. One of the things that needs to change is we need more Black composers, but a lot of selective programs for composers are not including Black composers because their particular idiom or the way that they speak—through sound—isn't understood by the

White mainstream. And if their voices aren't being heard, then the audiences aren't going to get to know them. It's a prime example of White supremacy. Conductors can bring in Black composers. We need conductors who are going to come in and say, this is a great work, it's by a Black composer. But coming in and giving Black composers a voice doesn't mean that the audience is going to come. The problem is within the communities—and this speaks to London as well—Black people feel alienated from the concert hall. The concert hall itself is this foreboding sonic space of Whiteness that Black people feel that they're not a part of, that they can't be a part of.

ANNA: In the UK, sociologist Ali Meghji's work on Black middle-class people's experiences with "high" culture in London explores this point. (Meghji, 2017)

BRANDON: Yes, so that's my first point, and second, why would you want to go to a place where all of your oppressors are there? Particularly in the US, you go inside a place and the police are there as part of the audience. I'm talking about a city like Baltimore, for instance, which is two-thirds Black. They've got one Black person in the orchestra, not very many Black conductors, except this season they're having quite a few Black conductors come conduct the orchestra. But a large Black community, obviously, has a lot of problems with policing, so what can the orchestra do to help bridge the cavernous gap between their community and the orchestra itself? I think the orchestra has to become an agent of social change within their community. What orchestra has ever had a town hall meeting between the police and the citizens of the city, that's actually saying, "Hey, we recognize that there's a problem with police brutality, that there's a real problem with this"? And this is something that we need to do, to reach out to the people of our community, to bring them together with the police so that they feel more comfortable with the police. The orchestra has to be an instrument of social justice. If the orchestra's not an instrument of social justice, then the orchestra has no reason to survive. Orchestras in the US are fully privately funded for the most part, and the majority of these organizations and the people who privately fund them are White. I think the finding by sociologist Michele Lamont is that 75% of all White people in the US don't live around Black people, which makes the self-reporting of racism suspicious (Lamont et al., 2016). They don't understand the racial dynamics of being Black and what it's like. I think that it's really, really important that the orchestra is brought together with the community in trying to be an agent of change.

ANNA: In this meeting between Black people in Baltimore and the police and the orchestra, would music lead the meeting, or would it primarily involve talking, in your vision?

BRANDON: In my vision, I think it should start with talking. Of course, my romantic part as a musician is wanting the music to speak for togetherness, but people aren't there yet. The fact is that people are dealing with lack of housing, they can't pay their electric bill, they don't have health insurance. These are the real problems that people are dealing with in a city like Baltimore. In any metropolitan city, these are the real problems that Black people are dealing with. In Detroit and Philadelphia, when you look at the orchestra, you'd have no idea that these cities are majority Black. When you look at the audience, you'd have no idea. I think that, first, it's a matter of talking and showing interest, and building trust in the community before we say, hey, look at what we're doing. I think that that would be much more powerful than forcing music on people that they're not used to hearing, that they're going to say that they don't understand in any way. There's the proverbial adage, being "invited to the barbecue," which is a statement that Black people use. The Black barbecue is a very intimate sort of affair. If you're invited to the barbecue and you're a White person, it means that you're really down with Black people. But having an open barbecue with an orchestra in a Black community, that's something that I don't think has been done with any US orchestra, to really go out into the Black community and say, hey, we're here, we're with you. If the orchestras aren't with them, then why in the world would they want to go into the concert hall?

ANNA: Yes, and this is a real contrast to projects where the philosophy is that people will play music together and this is a route to peace, reconciliation, or social justice. Moving onto other recent events, do you want to say anything about how the COVID pandemic has affected these challenges?

BRANDON: I think COVID has shone a light on the fact that classical music audiences are fairly limited, and that classical music lacks utility in the daily lives of people. We think that what we've been doing is so important and so great that it'll survive anything, and then we find out that people really want to hear Beyoncé or Adele, they really want to hear other artists. I think COVID was a really great opportunity for orchestras to reflect on who they *don't* serve. Unfortunately, it hasn't been as successful as I'd like to have seen, but they've certainly felt it in their pockets in all the money and support that they've lost. I wish that COVID would have been an opportunity to remind orchestras of their communities, but I think what's most likely going to happen is that a lot of the orchestras are going to go right back to doing what they were doing before, to serving Mozart to the mostly White communities, because that's all they've known to do, that's what they're most comfortable doing. They're not used to actually going out into the communities and connecting with people who are different to them. And the orchestras are going to keep on counting on these White audiences to sustain them, even though COVID has happened, even though they've found out that these White audiences are not going to be able to sustain them always. And I believe if they had had Black audiences and Black patrons, they would have been in less of a dire financial situation than they're in now. But they've been tuned to playing for Whiteness for all this time, and this has gotten them into serious trouble during COVID.

ANNA: And do you think Black Lives Matter has made any difference so far in classical music?

BRANDON: No, not at all. I've talked to administrators in the UK and in the United States, and in the United States, they understand it, they get it much more. In the UK, they're very uncomfortable discussing racism. These are people who are in power and are going to have the opportunity to hire me, and so this puts me in a real pickle, so to speak. The way that I walk through the world, the way I'm treated, the way that I'm perceived on the podium, there's a difference in this, and you have to come to terms with that if you want to hire me. If you want to hire me, you have to understand that I'm Black before I'm a conductor. I'm actually a Black person that's treated differently. Not all of your conductors have had police run up to their car and put guns to their head. I've had that happen for no reason at all, sitting in my car. These are real common traumatic experiences that are "race"-related experiences that not many conductors are going through. In Germany, I discuss it, and I've found that one of the great things about the Germans, although I get on their case about many other things, is that they're able to reflect on their history. The US can't reflect on its history. They ignore the forever-negative ramifications of slavery and the deficits Blacks still face. It's a real problem. But Germany can, and so they've been a little bit more open to talking about these situations. And this is still one of the things that I bring up, one of the first things that I bring up. With new artistic administrators that are in Germany, I discuss with them, hey, when's the last time you hired a Black conductor? Never? Why is that? I ask them, would you ever wake up in the morning and think of me doing a Bruckner symphony? And normally, they laugh. And I say, well, it's because you can't imagine a Black conductor doing something like this. And they're like, okay, that's true. But there's yet to be a major orchestra that has come out and made a big statement about Black Lives Matter and really done it in a proper way, saying what needs to be said and what needs to be done and explaining how they're going to actually change this. And this circles back to my Black conductors point. To my knowledge, there's never been a Black conductor of a top-15 US orchestra. I know that for a fact. Either we're inept or something in society needs to be changed.

ANNA: To wrap up, what messages or advice would you give to activists, musicians, or organizations who want to make change in classical music?

BRANDON: I think in terms of activists, you have to decide whether you're going to play the White people game, or you're going to go against the grain and be honest. And it's a real fine line. You can be on one side of the fence or the other or you can try to walk the fine line between when to speak out and when not to. There aren't really any superstar Black conductors, but if you were a superstar Black conductor, it would be much easier to speak out about these issues. And even then, some of the bigger Black conductors, they've made their money on adapting to and playing the game of Whiteness, and trying to blend into White culture—in-groups—and not rock the boat. We have to have people who are going to rock the boat, who are going to call White people on their lack of diversity, on their unwillingness to be diverse within classical music. In terms of organizations, the United States has really started to do a rash of hiring across executive directors and people who are Black. I think Louisiana is the first orchestra of its class or of any class, that has hired a Black executive director. This is a rather big deal, and it's somebody who actually comes from the dance community who's been hired. This is important. But to get Black conductors on the podium is most important. In a paper I wrote called "Black Concert Trauma" (Brown, 2020), I talked about how I went to sit down at a concert at the Lyric Opera and a lady told me to go sit somewhere else. And I think if she saw a Black conductor on the podium, she wouldn't have had that reaction—she'd understand that I belong in the room. That's a big message that orchestras need to send and organizations need to send: that Black people belong physically and sonically in this space, that we're good enough to be in this space. Organizations need to teach their audiences and need to learn that Black people deserve and belong in the classical music space.

13

Creolization, Mixing, and Plurality

An Interview with Composer Hannah Kendall

Hannah Kendall

CHRISTINA: How did you get involved professionally in classical music, broadly defined?

HANNAH: I did a music degree at the University of Exeter but fell into composing by mistake. I didn't go to university thinking that I would specialize in composition or anything like that. I didn't really know that I could be a composer. I'd never played any music by women or people of color or women of color. So, I had honestly never really considered that it was a possibility. And then I had a great teacher, Joe Duddell, at Exeter who really encouraged me and pushed me to take it further and to apply to do a master's and I ended up based at Royal College of Music and things went on from then. It's almost a fluke, really, and I felt quite behind and had to work really hard to catch up with my peers at college. Now I'm at Columbia doing a doctorate in composition.

CHRISTINA: And you've also done other work during your studies, is this correct?

HANNAH: Yes. I first worked at the Barbican Centre and started there as an intern because before my master's in composition I did a master's in arts management at the Royal Welsh College of Music and Drama and as part of that I had to do an internship somewhere. And then after that I stayed on at the Barbican for a couple of years in the media relations department. Because the composing thing felt really new, I didn't know whether it would work out and I certainly wasn't making any money from it. Right up until 2018, I was always working part-time to make things work financially, otherwise it would have been completely impossible.

CHRISTINA: In terms of the organizations you worked for, could you tell me a bit more about the work you did for organizations to make the classical music sector more diverse? How did you get into this? Was this because of experiences you personally had as a Black woman working in composition?

HANNAH: Yes. I suppose certainly with UK Music Masters,[i] the whole premise of that organization was about broadening those who enter the classical music industry through musicianship and violin lessons

Hannah Kendall, *Creolization, Mixing, and Plurality* In: *Voices for Change in the Classical Music Profession*. Edited by: Anna Bull and Christina Scharff with Associate Editor Laudan Nooshin, Oxford University Press.
© Oxford University Press 2023. DOI: 10.1093/oso/9780197601211.003.0014

in socio-economically deprived areas of London and so that was the first actual positive steps and positive actions that I have been involved in within the industry to try and make a change. I suppose from that I started to think about how I could do that within my practice as well. So, producing *The Knife of Dawn*, my chamber opera, which was specifically for a Black singer, a lot of the conversations that we had were trying to think how people could make changes individually as well as structurally. And so, yes, a lot of my work within my practice and within my writing stems from there, really. I'm still thinking today how I can diversify not only where my music's performed but also the outcomes of the music itself, and that's a lot of my research here at Columbia.

CHRISTINA: Could you talk about this a bit more? What do you mean by "the outcomes of the music itself"?

HANNAH: I'm thinking more about creolization and this mixing and, certainly, being a Black British composer/European composer and recognizing how my experiences and my inspirations are a blend of completely different things from my African Caribbean heritage and my British/European heritage. I am thinking about how to combine the Afrological with the Eurological. For example, preparing a violin by wrapping dreadlock cuffs or hair accessories for afro hair around the strings of a "Western" instrument that is the icon/the epitome of the "Western" classical but distorting the sounds or combining the sounds by something that's very much associated with African heritage. So, things like that, and trying to create new sounds through that combination.

CHRISTINA: And is this something you are currently working on or is this something you've already done? I know that your more recent works have drawn from a range of influences.

HANNAH: It certainly featured in works for the past couple of years, since I came to New York, really. It's interesting that I had to leave the UK and Europe to have some perspective and be able to look back on the environment that I was working and writing in there and coming away to New York and, certainly, working with George Lewis who is an incredible musicologist and composer whose work focusses on the Afro diaspora, music of Afro diaspora/Afro modernity, which is something that I don't think I would have really been able to do to that extent in the United Kingdom. And so works such as *Tuxedo: Vasco "de" Gama*, that opened the Proms in 2020, and where I embedded harmonicas into the orchestration. It's about bringing the other into the "Western" classical idiom. Harmonicas are often associated with music of the Blues, which is an Afro diasporic music, as are African American spirituals. And I transcribed "Wade in the Water" for music box, and worked it into the piece. I started using music boxes because they're seemingly innocuous, these tiny things that people think are very childlike. But by putting spiritual tunes in those boxes, it's a way of polarizing the concept. For such a long time, I felt as though people didn't really want to hear about that side of my heritage within my music and so I would start putting it in music boxes and it's grown from there. So, it's trickery and actively trying to polarize the context that the music's being performed in. More broadly, the Tuxedo series is a series of pieces that started off with *Tuxedo: Vasco "de" Gama* at the Proms in 2020 and it's inspired by Jean-Michel Basquiat's artwork called Tuxedo. I was incredibly taken by the work, which involves his sketches and writings where he references things such as explorers like Vasco Da Gama and police brutality, things to do with the climate, all sorts of things. It's incredibly rich. He was interested in this notion of creolization, plurality, and something that he spoke of about himself being an American artist of Haitian and Puerto Rican heritage. Before I even read about this, I was drawn to the work. In this series of *Tuxedo* pieces—I think I'm working on my sixth one now—it's really trying to focus on this idea of creolization that I was talking about and how I can blend aspects of the afrological into the "Western" classical context. For example, with "Tuxedo: Crown; Sun King," which is for violin, I try and challenge what the idea of a piece for solo violin is by the violinist actually playing music boxes first, using tunes that are traditionally associated with "Western" classical idioms, such as Beethoven's "Ode to Joy" and "Amazing Grace," which was an important Christian hymn. So, as soon as the performer comes on stage, they're not actually performing their violin, this "Western" instrument, but it's kind of mixing up the context in which they're working and what you expect from a piece for solo violin. Also in this piece, the strings are prepared and restricted by dreadlock cuffs. So there's a lot of that going on in the whole series and my primary focus is how can I mix up the sound world or the context of the space, which is as a result of creolization.

CHRISTINA: I was wondering whether you could say a bit more about "Tuxedo: Hot Summer No Water" as well and your use of a Metropolitan Police whistle?

HANNAH: Yes. That's the same thing as well. Basquiat mentions the presence of police in his artwork *Tuxedo* and "Tuxedo: Hot Summer No Water" was commissioned in the summer of 2020. I was living in New York and the death of George Floyd had just occurred and there were protests going past my apartment for at least a couple of weeks and it felt as though I really had to comment on that in this piece as well. I wanted to use a historical sound with police presence and Black communities, so the whistle jarring up against the sound of the cello, which is the instrument in that work, and have those sounds jar and rub together, just how police in Black communities have jarred and rubbed together.

CHRISTINA; And was this piece performed in 2020 itself?

HANNAH: Yes, Louise McMonagle from Riot Ensemble performed it at King's Place and it was recorded for online stream.

CHRISTINA: Your use of historical sounds in contemporary classical music seems to relate to the wider question of whether you think that "classical music" or "Western" art music itself has to change to "diversify" it, as it were?

HANNAH: I don't think so, actually. I think it's more about context and where the music is playing. I don't think it's about specifically the music itself. I think anyone can engage with and enjoy it. I think it's about context and who's welcome into the spaces, who's invited, who feels comfortable. I still think it's a lot about that and I think we still have work to do with that. I don't think it's about the music itself.

It's something that I'm focusing on particularly but it's because my main focus at the moment is on this idea of creolization and blending. But, yes, from all the experience I have as a composer, I think it's about context and simple things, how we even tell people about what's happening, who gets to hear about it and who gets to know what's happening.

CHRISTINA: So, I guess taking the music out of intimidating 19th century concert halls, for example, is one way, or making tickets cheaper?

HANNAH: Yes. Taking it out but also how do you get people in? How do you make people feel comfortable in these spaces? And people who we wouldn't ordinarily assume to enjoy classical music in those spaces, why shouldn't they be a part of that history as well?

CHRISTINA: Yes, I agree. And in terms of the work you've done, either in terms of your own compositions or in terms of arts administration, could you tell me about a particular project or aspect of this work on diversity that you are most proud of?

HANNAH: I think it has to be the opera. I think that is the thing I'm most proud about because it just wouldn't have happened had I not self-produced it. And especially at that time. I know in the past five years, even the past year, there's been changes to try and diversify programming. In 2020, the opera was the first opera at the Royal Opera House to ever be performed on the main stage by a Person of Color. But had I not produced it myself in 2016, it wouldn't have existed. There wouldn't have been anything for them to even look at, to even try and put on stage. I'm proud of myself for having the foresight and also the skills, through my work in arts management as well as composition to be able to fundraise for it, to get the right people involved. And, quite frankly, I shouldn't have had to do that. But this is the thing: the more I go on, I just feel as though the industry is minimum ten years behind what artists are thinking about and what they're producing and yet they still hold so much power, obviously, and money. So I can have a brilliant idea but I feel as though I've got to convince all of these people to support it, back it, pay for it but then however many years later the work is there and they're able to use it for reasons that might include trying to mix up their programming and what they present.

CHRISTINA: That's an issue that's been raised by various contributors to the edited collection, the work that goes into diversifying classical music, as it were, and that this still often rests on marginalized groups and people and by having to do this work, which is also often unpaid, it might exacerbate their marginalization.

Following on from that, what—for you—have been the biggest challenges in making change in classical music?

HANNAH: I suppose the main challenge is that people come to realization in their own time, For example, you can talk about this for years and years and it feels like it's not really registering and then for some reason, ten years or so down the line there seems to be a click or a shift and then, "Oh, right, actually we have to do something about this." And the challenge is being patient whereas those in power, the gatekeepers, can have this gradualism rather than thinking that there's any urgency to try and change things. That's what I find frustrating. And seeing people in the past year making concerted efforts to shift things but remembering what they said about the topic however many years ago to the contrary of what they're doing now, makes me think, "Well, what's really changed? And how do we know that this is here to last"? Tonight, I'm going to see the first opera ever by a Black person at the Met. It's nearly 2022. It's October 2021. And, also, how is it going to be maintained? Because has there been a consistent support of Black composers, and opera in this case, up until now? No, so, how do we have consistency?

CHRISTINA: I was interested in something you mentioned earlier, when you implied that going away to New York enabled you to take certain perspectives and to do this creolizing work. Thinking more broadly about the industry and the lack of diversity and the challenges that we just discussed, to what extent do you think are these challenges specific to the national and local contexts you were working in? Or are they challenges for classical music internationally?

HANNAH: It's not just contained in the UK. There are international challenges, but I think they might just be different challenges, depending on the location and the history of that nation and who's involved in artmaking/musicmaking. I suppose what I was talking about, coming to America, coming to New York, it gave me freedom and almost permission maybe, to challenge my music in ways that I wouldn't have felt as comfortable in the UK. The challenges are not only about the industry but also about how performers/musicians of color are allowed to acknowledge their non-European or "non-Western" side of themselves. In the US, this is less of a big deal. It just feels as though the talk and the discussions are a lot further down the road than it is in the United Kingdom.

CHRISTINA: Is that, do you think, one of the main challenges, that it feels like a relatively recent discussion, at least in the classical music sector in the UK?

HANNAH: Yes, absolutely. I think that people maybe feel as though it's something that now needs to change, which I think is right, but they might not know why exactly and so mistakes are being made. I've certainly been on the negative end of those things and it takes a lot of grace and patience. To a certain extent you have to code-switch or do whatever to fit in and now this shift has tumbled everything up, so how do we fit into this new mould? For example, I have so many requests for speaking on panels with different industry meetings about diversity and I haven't said yes to any of them because it's just exhausting, and also it's really annoying that when we were talking about this, no one was really interested.

CHRISTINA: Yes, you were definitely talking about it for years before then.

HANNAH: It's frustrating. I'm not sure everyone has had requests like this but, as you were saying earlier, it falls onto the people who are the minority to, again, do all the work.

CHRISTINA: So, perhaps leading on from that, if you could change one thing about the classical music profession or field, what would it be?

HANNAH: This might be unusual. It's something to do with money. There needs to be better access for artists to money. I've been thinking about it a lot and, as I was saying, artists who are working on the ground, they need the resources and the support to make their work, because, can we just wait for people to catch up or cotton on or engage or whatever? If I was waiting for that, I wouldn't have done half the things that I've done and I think there needs to be some sort of agency for artists to support them making their work and then maybe the industry will catch up and present it. This is very much about new music but it could be about performing musicians/classical musicians, for them to have access to just get on with it.

Because even though this huge, monumental shift needs to change the industry, it's honestly hundreds of years behind. We might not see it in our lifetime and we can't let that hinder musicians or music creators doing their own work.

CHRISTINA: It relates to the issue of precarity, doesn't it? And who can afford to be working as a musician or artist in that sector where a lot of work remains underpaid and then how this impacts marginalized groups in particular.

HANNAH: Exactly, yes.

CHRISTINA: And speaking of precarity, it's the year 2021. We are still in a pandemic, so I did want to ask about your thoughts on how the COVID-19 pandemic has affected the dynamics we just talked about, in terms of diversity and inclusion in the classical music sector.

HANNAH: I think that the pandemic shifted a lot of things because I felt as though before there was this huge risk assessment that industries and concert halls or whatever were taking and if we challenged anything too much it would be too much of a risk and we might not do things that take big and bold decisions to the same extent. But COVID took all of that away and I think it opened up access to things that. . . . Personally, I saw and engaged with things I would never have seen had the pandemic not hit. With regard to performances online, I had so many performances and commissions throughout the pandemic and I think a lot of that is to do with the fact that, "Oh, well, it's not as huge a risk to include you on something because there aren't audiences anyway." I think it's incredibly sad that it took a major external event to shift things and to mix things up but I think to a certain extent that's what happened. I know, obviously, that so many performing musicians were unable to perform and to work and that's a huge tragedy, but I think that things like Brexit will do more damage than COVID because of travel restrictions and visas. Obviously, the pandemic is a nightmare and disastrous but it's interesting to see how musicians and organizations made quick changes to make things work and it seems as though because of that, they were able to include more people that they might not have included before.

CHRISTINA: And what messages or advice would you give to activists or musicians in the wider sense—also including composers and conductors—who want to make change in classical music?

HANNAH: To develop a network within the industry. Something that really helps me is I have a network of people who are also people of color, women working in the industry, and that we can talk openly about the difficulties and the challenges and how we might make changes in our own area. It's a completely informal thing but you find people who have an understanding of what it is that you're talking about because obviously the majority of musicians working who aren't minoritized might not even have any idea or clue or notion of what the difficulties that we face even are. And so rather than it being an activist piece of advice or something that can help to drive change in the industry, because, as we've already said, a lot of it does fall on us. It's to find a space where you can find comfort and support and a good solid foundation, because it is really difficult, but having other people who have an idea of the industry, in working the same spaces and in the same ways, it's really important to have that network of people you can talk to.

Note

i. UK Music Masters, formerly known as London Music Masters, is a charity that aims to make music education available to all.

IV
RACIAL INEQUALITIES

14
The New "Yellow Peril" in "Western" European Symphony Orchestras

Maiko Kawabata

I. Why are there comparatively few East Asian musicians in Western European symphony orchestras?

The conductor Zubin Mehta once said, "Where would the great American orchestras be without the Asian input?" (Wu, 2002, p. 241). Has any comparable statement ever been made about the great orchestras across the Atlantic? Readers accustomed to seeing orchestras, especially string sections, populated by East Asians in New York or San Francisco may be surprised to compare the percentages with Vienna or Berlin.[1] In Table 14.1, the American orchestra with the fewest East Asians trumps the European orchestra with the most. While screened orchestral auditions have increased female orchestral membership on both sides of the Atlantic (albeit more slowly in Europe) and ethnic minority orchestral membership from 3% to 12% between 1980 and 2014 in the US, Europe still lags behind (Doeser, 2016, pp. 2–3).[2] Why?

First, no comparable history exists of East Asian immigration; although the Chinese diaspora in France and Britain combined is quite sizeable (ca. one million in total), the Japanese, Korean and Taiwanese diaspora in France, Germany, and Britain combined is relatively small (ca. half a million in total) (see, among others, Latham and Wu, 2013).[3] Second, European orchestral salaries rarely exceed five figures, whereas six-figure starting salaries are expected at top American orchestras, making them more attractive to transnational musicians.[4] Third, the difficulty of obtaining work visas presents obstacles to non-EU applicants; e.g., British orchestras restrict applications to citizens or visa-holders (except for some principal positions, which are recruited internationally). But these factors alone do not explain why opera choruses and dance companies are significantly more diverse than orchestras (Table 14.2).

To make transatlantic comparisons oversimplifies the complexity of the very different histories of migration in Europe and the USA, of course, but offers an opening gambit, heuristically, to my discussion of racialized identity as experienced by East Asians in European orchestras today. Scant academic attention

Table 14.1. East Asians in Orchestras (2020)

United States	Europe
11% Cleveland Orchestra	0% Wiener Philharmoniker*
15% San Francisco Symphony	1% Staatskapelle Dresden
15% Boston Symphony Orchestra	2% Berliner Philharmoniker
18% Los Angeles Philharmonic	3% Deutsches Symphonie-Orchester Berlin
23% Chicago Symphony Orchestra	3% London Symphony Orchestra
27% New York Philharmonic	7% London Philharmonic Orchestra
28% Philadelphia Orchestra	10% Bamberger Symphoniker

*includes four half-Japanese members

Table 14.2. East Asians in European Opera and Dance Companies (2020)

Opera Companies	Dance Companies
0% Royal Opera Chorus	5% Wiener Staatsoper Ballet (corps)
10% Wiener Staatsoper chorus	8% Wiener Staatsoper Ballet (soloists)
20% Deutsche Oper Berlin Chorus	10% Royal Ballet
	14% Staatsballett Berlin
	25% Birmingham Royal Ballet

has been paid to when and why they began to enter European orchestras in the first place; this historical background, yet to be established, is beyond the scope of this present study.[5] Today, more East-Asians populate European orchestras than perhaps ever before—evidence of success, to a degree, in entering racially homogenous spaces that admit much fewer other ethnic minorities. That said, the proportion of East Asians has remained low compared to proportionally high enrollments at European music conservatoires (particularly in string departments),[6] raising the question of why East-Asian musicians continue to be underrepresented in these contexts.

II. To what extent are the experiences of East Asians in Western European orchestras racialized?

To investigate this question, I interviewed 35 professional orchestral musicians (11 male, 24 female; aged 20s–50s) of East Asian descent in Western Europe in 2019–2020.[7] Violin, viola, cello, bass, flute, bassoon, horn, trombone, and tuba were represented, with stringed instruments the majority. All spoke to me under cover of anonymity. My method was modeled on recent developments in analytic autoethnography (e.g., Anderson, 2006), whereby the researcher is numbered among the research subjects, and that relies on analytic self-reflexivity.[8] As a professional freelance orchestral violinist of Japanese origin based in the UK and Germany, I was positioned not as "external researcher" but rather as "insider."

The origins of this empirical study lie in informal conversations among my personal network, which I later documented through a series of unstructured interviews. These covered topics of racialized (and gendered) identity in aspects of orchestral-playing encompassing training, auditions, trials, rehearsals, concerts, and tours. I began by interviewing friends and colleagues I knew personally; as news of my project spread by word of mouth, my sample pool extended to musicians in Austria, Holland, Luxembourg, and Switzerland.[9] Five musicians I approached declined to be interviewed, saying that they had no "race"-specific experience, that they could not be sure if they had and did not wish to speculate, or without stating a reason.

In terms of research ethics, I obtained verbal consent to publish what interviewees told me. No issues of distress, vulnerability, or trauma came up during the interviews. Although recalling racist/sexist experiences can be upsetting, interviewees remarked on their sense of relief and empowerment by participating in a study that would highlight hitherto hidden issues. My own first-hand experiences of racism/sexism, which I divulged in interviews where relevant, were similar and in many cases shared. The interviews revealed five main points, summarized below, using quotes from interviewees—the "voices for change" that this volume seeks to make heard.

The orchestral application process is biased against East Asians

Nine interviewees had sent out resumes that they explained were comparable to those of white colleagues/classmates but did not receive invitations to audition even as others received theirs. Nearly all cases happened in German orchestras, where the application process does not automatically pre-select citizens and residents (unlike, e.g., Britain). Interviewees said: "I felt discriminated against that audition invitations just weren't coming in" or "I couldn't get invitations for some orchestras" or "German boys get more invitations" or "I sent my C.V. everywhere and only got one or two invitations. I felt angry." One said, referring to the obligatory photograph on some German C.V.s, "if you're not from a famous teacher or school, your chance for being invited is very small. If you have an Asian face then it's even smaller." A female violinist recalled:

> When I first started applying for jobs, I was applying for the same jobs as a friend of mine who was [white], with the same resume, identical, and she had a German-sounding name, and she was being invited left and right and I didn't get invited anywhere.

A male violinist who knew that his C.V. was stronger than a certain white woman's noted that "she was invited to audition for the Concertmaster position and I wasn't even invited for Principal Violin II."

Orchestral applications bearing East Asian names are deselected

Five interviewees reported German orchestras passing over East Asian names in the selection process, saying things like, "Sometimes they just see thirty Lees or Kims in a row and don't read them," or, "They now decided not to give auditions to Asians any more. . . . They don't want to have too many Asians," or, "A friend in the orchestra said, 'We have too many Asian players already.'" Women who acquired European surnames upon marriage found that suddenly they received more invitations. This accords with the subheading "Too many Asian names" in a recent exposé piece (Morlang, 2021) and echoes biases favoring "white"-sounding names reported in a UK Department of Work and Pensions study of job applications (Wood et al., 2009).

An East Asian female violinist who served on the audition panel for a certain orchestra gave this insight:

> The invitation list goes around, and you tick who to invite. A colleague of mine, an elderly [German] lady, said to me, "Oh, you know we invite Germans first, just so you know." I said, "Oh great, thanks for letting me know." This person never gave me a chance. It's usually unspoken but here it was spoken with no hesitation whatsoever, "Don't tick the wrong people, keep it German." I've concluded that it's in their culture. They have a strong identity, they are very proud of their musical heritage (as they should be), so we're seen as contaminating their orchestral culture.

It appears that the (fictional) idea of maintaining the purity of European orchestral culture highlighted here may account for the deselection of East Asian applicants.

Orchestral auditions are biased against East Asians

Ten interviewees reported discrimination at screenless auditions: after passing the screened first round, they lost the unscreened second round to white Europeans. A male violinist recalled:

> The first round was behind a curtain. I played well. My friend in the orchestra said afterwards, "You did well, you are in first place, by a clear margin of points." Only four advanced: me, another Asian guy, and two Europeans (white). The second round was without a curtain. I think I also played well in the second round but me and the other Asian guy were eliminated. Afterwards some members of the orchestra I knew, because we had studied together, told me that the level of all players were very high and they certainly would have had enough time and been interested to listen to all in the third round, which was to play as acting concertmaster and also play the solo from Brahms Symphony No.1. If that is so, why did they cut out the two Asians, and among them the one—with curtain—they liked most in the first round?

While discrimination affects both genders, more women than men experienced unfairness and discomfort because they were criticized afterward for their lack of personality or for their looks. East Asian women, particularly those who play larger brass instruments, report having been ridiculed for their diminutive stature during their auditions. Nearly all cases happened in the German system, where only one applicant wins a year-long trial (unlike Britain where a handful of winners may play on trials lasting weeks or months) and thus enjoy less latitude in testing potential colleagues' ability to assimilate. There is an assumption behind this firstly that East Asian musicians need to assimilate—that is, that we are culturally different—and secondly that orchestral culture requires assimilation, rather than accommodating difference, if indeed East Asian musicians do bring musical, social, or cultural differences with us (which seems unlikely if we have trained in Europe).

Two violinists complained about a specific orchestra; one woman said: "Well, many of my teachers at the music academy were members of [a prestigious European orchestra]. After my diploma, it was hard to understand and believe that all my effort was 'wasting time' because all I actually had to do was to change my sex and face to get a job at the orchestra." Another described how hopeless he felt it would be to audition for the same orchestra: "I knew that even if I would have played like Kreisler, Paganini, and Heifetz combined, I wouldn't make it because I know they would not take an Asian guy."

At a German orchestra's violin audition, an older white male colleague was overheard saying backstage, "We're taking no Asians this time," and the comment relayed to the candidate later by another colleague in the orchestra. A violinist who actually won an audition at another orchestra described the peculiar aftermath:

> I had a very strange experience where I auditioned and did get the job but they had a long discussion. The conductor asked me to go speak to him. He said, "Are you going to stay if we take you, if we give you the position?" At that time

(1990s) there were not so many Asians, mostly Japanese women. I was the only [non-Japanese] Asian male musician and I was young. They took a long time and they did decide to take me, but they were worried about something. This question of racism could be expressed in an explicit way, or it could be something they don't say but it just happens in their actions.

Racism at auditions can range from blatant to implied, and strikes most obviously when screens are removed. We know it happens because friends and colleagues in orchestras tell us. Wenzel Fuchs, the Berlin Philharmonic's solo clarinetist, told a reporter "Asians rarely get into the last rounds of auditions" for an article reporting anti-Asian racism in German orchestras (Wiegelmann, 2009).

East Asians experience racism in orchestral rehearsals and beyond

Thirteen interviewees reported being professionally and/or socially branded as different by orchestral and managerial colleagues by means of racist behaviors ranging from racial slurs to microaggressions such as being denied certain perks of the job afforded to others in the same position, or assumptions that we don't speak the language. A violinist said, "Some colleagues always used the term '*Schlitzaugen*-tour' for Asian tours, even to my face." (*Schlitzaugen* is the German term for "slit eyes.") Another violinist said, "People will say things like, 'I'm glad we don't have a load of Chinese people in our orchestra.'" Another violinist said, "One of my [white] friends started a professorship and I asked him how's it going and he said "Shit Koreans," and I looked at him and said, "You do realize I am Korean?"

Many of us have been mistaken for one another; this appears to happen more frequently to women (including myself) than to men. Being reduced to our phenotype and seen as indistinguishable from one another while making music is particularly problematic since it denies us our individuality in a field where individual expression is paramount. Though this may sometimes happen unintentionally, often, white colleagues view cases of mistaken identity as funny rather than offensive. Similarly, in the following instances white colleagues are oblivious to their racism. A violinist said:

A good German friend who works in the [X Orchestra] recently said, "I will not hug my Chinese colleague any more; I don't feel comfortable doing it, I never did." I wanted to tell her, "You can't say these things!" She doesn't think for a minute that it's racist or would be a problem for the person on the receiving end.

The same violinist said, "As a young Asian woman in [Orchestra Y], I had an older Asian colleague. Other colleagues thought her playing was not up to standard, and said things like, 'Asians are good when they're young but they deteriorate very fast,' implying that I would get weak as I age. Shameless!"

Reports of anti-Asian racism by the conductor in orchestral rehearsals include: being ignored while acting as concertmaster even though the conductor spoke to all the other principals; being picked on as a short Asian woman while standing as part of a violin section by repeatedly being asked, "Can you see me?" Racism against conductors is rare because East Asian conductors are rare, yet I have witnessed an East Asian woman conductor being mocked by white orchestral colleagues suggesting that she might find it easier to beat in 2 rather than 4.

Some female interviewees reported overlapping sexism and racism. A cellist in a German orchestra said, "It was normal [for older European men] to hit the bottom of the girls. There was one guy, he hit my bottom with a book. I told him, 'Stop it, it's not funny, if you do it again I will go to a lawyer.' I was very angry. It also happened to another Asian female colleague. Disgusting men!" I have witnessed young East Asian women politely warding off unwelcome advances from older white men in positions of authority in professional settings (as also mentioned in Scharff, 2018, pp. 107–108). Meanwhile, many white members of orchestras that discriminate against East Asian women have East Asian partners or wives, thereby normalizing their domestication; the "yellow fever" sexualization of East Asian women (see Yoshihara, 2007) goes hand in hand with the emasculation of East Asian men.

East Asians are branded "automatons"

Six interviewees reported hearing the tired, widely documented stereotype that East Asians are technically proficient but expressionless (Yang, 2014; Yoshihara, 2007; Leppänen, 2015). A female violinist who sought feedback after unsuccessful auditions said, "More than once, I heard the comment with the undertone of 'You Asians are always so perfect but I didn't feel it.'" Several violinists reported hearing variations on the "automaton" theme during training. One teacher, expecting conformity to stereotype, told a female student, "You have to play like a good modest Asian girl." Another interviewee described his professor teacher as saying, "This is a bit Asian what you're doing. . . . Asians have technique, play fast, play good but [are] emotionally zero." A violinist who had an Asian teacher said, "My teacher said he will never forgive his Caucasian teacher because he said something like 'Asians can't feel music,' expecting [my teacher] not to understand English or something."

Three interviewees deliberately compensated for the automaton stereotype by playing with larger physical gestures and/or exaggerating facial expressions to telegraph emotion. On some occasions they felt pushed into making choices that did not necessarily come naturally to them, so deeply had the bias been internalized.[10] I remember once playing an unplanned, unconventional fingering at a screenless audition (using a different fingering will cause the music to sound different, however subtly), which upon hindsight I can attribute to my wish to stand out. Yet no amount of "doing more" can make up for constructions of East Asian players as "robotic" and "technical," which are "indicative of a racial hierarchy where 'Western' classical music continues to be associated with whiteness" (Scharff, 2018, p. 97). In summary, these findings (pending further research with a larger, wider sample) show that 25 out of 35 report negative experiences in one or more of the five ways outlined above.[11] Racialized biases manifest in and run all the way through from applications and auditions to backstage, from rehearsals to concerts and tours.

III. East Asian orchestral players in parts of Europe are the new "Yellow Peril"

The Vienna Philharmonic's former chairman recalled in 1974 that the orchestra withheld a vacant position following screened auditions upon discovering that the successful candidate was East Asian.[12] Fifteen years later, the orchestra's managing director was still justifying that foreigners could not be hired because they lacked "specifically Austrian musical colouring" (Fritsch, 1989, p. 70). This echoed comments from leaders of the country's musical institutions such as "the Japanese lack the 'inner glow'" signaling "the fear of a foreigner invasion [*Ausländerinvasion*]"—as music sociologist Elena Ostleitner observed (1995, pp. 46–47). Gerhard Haderer's cartoon caricature of the orchestra in *Profil*, a popular Austrian weekly magazine, is a textbook image of "Yellow Peril"—a term that originally referred to the racist attitude that East Asians posed an existential threat to "Westerners" (Figure 14.1). While the Viennese elite have long been renowned for their conservatism, similar attitudes are also prevalent in other parts of Europe today, as my interviews revealed.

My findings above align with Kolja Blacher's (a former concertmaster of the Berlin Philharmonic) remark, referring to East Asian musicians: "There is the typical saying: 'There is simply something missing.' There is a lot of racism in the orchestras, sometimes even in the universities" (Wiegelmann, 2009). In such a culture, not only could the Festspielhaus Baden-Baden advertise their 2004 performance of Wagner's *Parsifal* with a publicity poster depicting the composer making "slanty eyes" in reference to the Japanese conductor Kent Nagano, the

Figure 14.1 Copyright Gerhard Haderer 1989. Reprinted with kind permission from Margit Haderer.

poster actually won the 2006 "Golden Nail" prize awarded by the Art Directors Club, a Berlin-based media consortium.[13]

My findings also resonate with the racism US-based musicians of Asian descent have long experienced in Europe. Korean violinist Young Uck Kim: "When I play in Europe . . . people still say things like, 'As an Oriental, how can you understand Mozart or Brahms?'" (Jepson, 1991). Korean-American violinist Jennifer Koh: "I think [being a minority] can be difficult when you're in Europe. There, there's a kind of a sense that they have an ownership of ['Western'] music. . . . Actually, people have told me straight to my face, 'I can't believe you're playing Mozart. You're Asian. *I* don't understand Chinese music.' And of course, not all Asians are Chinese. And they say, 'I don't understand *Chinese* music. How can you understand Mozart? It's not in your blood. And you also grew up in America'" (Yoshihara, 2007, p. 90). Korean violist Junah Chung: "A lot of times Europeans think, 'How can Asians relate to Western music? It's not in their culture'" (Yoshihara, 2007, p. 80).

"Western" classical music belongs to these Europeans, in their view. According to the self-conferred logic of cultural ownership (which excludes Kim, Koh, and Chung on the grounds of their Americanness, not just their Asianness), only (white) Europeans can truly understand and therefore give authentic expression to the music of Mozart or Beethoven. Those Europeans believe that only native Western European performers have this "innate capacity" (Wang, 2015, p. 94), that "there is some culturally specific essence to classical music that non-Western people cannot capture" (Yoshihara, 2007, p. 202). White non-Europeans can pass where yellow (and brown and black) faces cannot because of the psychological primacy of the visual, i.e., what listeners see determines their perception of what they hear (Schutz, 2008). The musical performance of a phenotypical outsider will be considered inauthentic before the first note is played. The positioning of all racial minorities as "other" in "Western" classical music keeps every Western European orchestra majority white—without the screenless audition, it seems likely their numbers would swell. However, the use of screened auditions is not enough on its own, without reforming the culture of trials, in which East Asian and other minoritized musicians are still expected to "assimilate." Moreover, it must be said, the idea that some yellow "contamination" in orchestras is tolerable (to a degree) contrasts with what seems to be an almost complete ban on Brown and Black musicians—a point in need of further exploration.

The unequal standing of ethnic minority musicians highlights the myth of "Western" classical music as an international language and its false claims to universality (Yang, 2014; Wang, 2015). The notion that "Western" classical music is a "universal language" yet belongs to white Europeans is hypocritical. As musicologist Mina Yang has written, "The racist attitudes that color the reception of Asian musicians in the 'West' belie classical music's claim to race blindness and universality" (Yang, 2014, pp. 88–89). Koh (2021) has echoed this: "Classical music is often called 'universal,' but what does universality mean when the field was built for white men who still hold much of the power?"

The underlying problem is structural: Eurocentrism, white supremacy, and patriarchy combine to maintain the white male (able-bodied, heterosexual) Western classical musician's normativity and privilege. As Christina Scharff (2018, pp. 106–107) suggested, "Western classical music as a genre is racialized and associated with European descent and whiteness." Musicologist William Cheng's (2019, p. 77) coinage "Vienna Philharmonic So white," a take on #Oscarssowhite, speaks for itself. The judgment that whiteness is a precondition of musicality has been shown in relation to the Sibelius Violin Competition in Finland (Leppänen, 2015). These recent observations echo older studies revealing racist and sexist biases in the evaluation of musical performance in a variety of settings (Elliott, 1995/96; Davidson and Edgar, 2003; Vanweelden and McGee, 2007; Koza, 2008).

By way of conclusion, I recommend that: all European orchestras adopt anonymized applications and standardize screened auditions for all rounds, not just the first round—not because such auditions are ideal or should be permanent, but because they immediately provide much-needed equity in the absence of a level playing field (*pace* Tommasini, 2020); orchestras program more female and diverse composers as a matter of course, not just as tokens, which will entail sacrificing and decentralizing standard fare; orchestral musicians and managers undertake unconscious bias training; conservatoires and universities educate music students to question and reshape the existing canon. Recent initiatives that inspire hope are Chineke!'s European Alliance for Audition Support, which mentors and finances young ethnic minority musicians preparing to enter orchestras, the Lucerne Festival's Diversity Steering Committee, which promotes the programming of non-white and female composers; "Mai Ling," the Austrian advocacy group that mobilizes artists against racism and sexism, and Daniele G. Daude leading the only BAME choir in Germany; others are germinating at time of press. Korean-American concert violinist Jennifer Koh, who actively commissions works from women and minorities, is peerless as a vocal anti-racist activist among a handful of world class classical instrumental soloists of East Asian descent who have to date largely remained silent on the issue.[14] All of her recommendations—to give agency to Asian Americans as performers, composers, administrators, and board members of arts organizations—ought to apply to East Asians settled in Europe, while being mindful of the cultural and historical differences in patterns of immigration and expatriation (Koh, 2021). Ultimately, what East Asian musicians want is equality of opportunity and inclusion which, in my view, can only meaningfully emerge from addressing existing inequality and exclusion, and which can potentially lead to orchestral transformation.

* * *

Acknowledgments: Heartfelt thanks to my courageous anonymous interviewees, to my supportive editors, Anna Bull, Laudan Nooshin, and Christina Scharff, to my fearless research collaborator Shzr Ee Tan, and to the following musicians and researchers for their suggestions and thought-provoking discussions: Dagmar Abfalter, Rasika Ajotikar, Daniela Braun, William Cheng, Abbie Conant, Sadhvi Dar, Daniele G. Daude, Sophie Hennekam, Vijay Iyer, Edward Klorman, Jennifer Koh, Marko Kölbl, Daniel Leech-Wilkinson, Nikki Moran, Daniel Müller, Chi-Chi Nwanoku, William Osborne, Rainer Prokop, Rumya Putcha, Rosa Reitsamer, Grace Wang, Mina Yang, Diana Yeh, and Mari Yoshihara.

Notes

1. By "East Asian," I mean of East Asian ethnicity (Chinese, Japanese, Korean, Taiwanese), whether naturalized elsewhere as citizens or not. The terminology "Asian" (US) includes "East Asian" (UK) and "Asian" (UK), where the latter usually refers to South Asians such as Indians and Pakistanis. The outdated term "oriental" refers to East Asians while the German "orientalisch" usually refers to Arabs or Middle Easterners.
2. By pointing out the greater Asian representation in US orchestras, I do not mean to suggest that issues of race-based power relations do not exist there; certainly the narrative of the "model minority" poses its own set of problems.
3. See also the International Migration Database https://stats.oecd.org, https://www.chathamhouse.org, https://www.newworldencyclopedia.org and https://www.ethnicity-facts-figures.service.gov.uk.
4. Sir Simon Rattle told the *Los Angeles Times*: "'The concertmaster of the Berlin Philharmonic, Tooru Yasunaga, is Japanese, and there are some Asians playing in the Netherlands, but 'the vast majority are in America,'" adding that "it's perhaps because you pay better"'" (Day, 1994, p. 7).
5. No equivalent study to Yoshihara, 2007, has yet been undertaken.
6. Official numbers are difficult to pinpoint. According to Wiegelmann 2009, East-Asians comprised 10% of the Munich Hochschule's student body, 15% of Universität der Künste Berlin, and 26% of the Köln Hochschule.
7. They have the following parentage: one Asian, one Caucasian (6); both Asian (29), of whom 18 were born and raised in Asia, naturalized as Europeans (most commonly by marriage) or resident in Europe with visas; six are descended from Asian immigrants or expatriates, born and raised in Europe, e.g., British-born Chinese; five as previous group but born and/or raised in other countries.
8. Anderson 2006 outlines, for example, methods for researching the homeless by living among them, or self-reflections on hospital care as a patient afflicted with illness—similar to what others describe as "native anthropology" (e.g., Yoshihara, 2007, p. xiv).
9. Research into orchestras in other European countries is pending, as is research into conductors, soloists (including pianists and singers), and chamber musicians. Sociologist Beata Kowalczyk interviewed Japanese orchestral musicians and pianists navigating precarious career paths in France and Poland; in the latter, "Relative ethnic homogeneity of orchestras . . . should be ascribed to low wages . . . rather than to racial exclusiveness in the classical milieu in this country" (Kowalczyk, 2020, p. 20).
10. A psychology study (Peynircioğlu, Bi, and Brent, 2018) has found that East Asian performers *appear* to be less expressive (as measured by the North American university undergraduate participants) than Caucasians because we tend not to physically move around as much.
11. Of these, five were in Britain and 20 in Europe, of whom 14 were in Germany; nine were male, 16 female. Seven had no such experience themselves but had witnessed it.

Two had no such experience themselves nor witnessed it. One had no such experience personally and was unsure if they had witnessed it.
12. He wrote: "An applicant qualified himself as the best, and as the screen was raised, there stood a Japanese before the stunned jury. He was, however, not engaged, because his face did not fit with the "Pizzicato-Polka" of the New Year's Concert" (Strasser, 1974, quoted in Osborne, n.d.).
13. The Festspielhaus declined to comment, except to state that they have changed management and that they now wish to distance themselves from the poster.
14. Yuja Wang's attempts to satirize her exotic/erotic appeal have met with mixed reactions (Barone, 2019).

15
Irreconcilable Senses of Belonging

Transnational Japanese Artists in the Quest for Authenticity in the World of Classical Music

Beata M. Kowalczyk

The entwinement of music and "race" has recently become the subject of much academic and public debate. One major strand of the scholarly investigation explores how racialized discourses fuel the hierarchical segregation of artists in different music fields, starting from blues (Grazian, 2003), through popular music (Haynes, 2013), and up to classical music (Yang, 2007; Scharff, 2018). Ethnomusicologists explain that these practices are undergirded by a rationale according to which variations in music are seen as inherently linked with the racial origins of its creators (Radano and Bohlman, 2000, p. 28). To understand this mechanism, it is important to bear in mind that "race" has long been used to construct people's identities according to "the perceived and phenotypic markers of difference" (Omi and Winant, 2014, p. 111). The very act of mapping musical traditions along the seemingly innate, phenotypical lines of the people who maintain them is itself racializing. According to a racialized discourse in music, racial idiosyncrasies are articulated in distinctive sounds, instrumentations, and musical languages, thereby making it possible to distinguish "our music" from "their music," and to establish a sense of belonging (Haynes, 2013, p. 2). Research from the classical music field provides examples of exclusionary practices against those musicians who are cast as "inauthentic" by the fact of being unencumbered by "Western"[1] tradition and its musical canon (Yang, 2007; El-Ghadban, 2009).

While my findings largely chime with existing studies on the ways in which racially-informed exclusionary mechanisms operate in classical music, I also make several important interventions. Drawing on rich empirical material collected through multi-sited research among Japanese musicians, this chapter investigates how the interviewed artists struggle to gain recognition in the classical music industry, where they are unequally positioned as "inauthentic" on the grounds of their socially constructed ethno-cultural heritage, which is deemed incompatible with the "authentic" classical musicianship. First, I elaborate on the notion of "authenticity" to better understand how my interlocutors are othered in the classical music milieus, both in Japan and in Europe, and how these processes shape their self-perception. Hitherto, the meaning of "authenticity" has been underinvestigated in the literature on classical music and "race," notwithstanding its proliferation in these discussions. By unpacking the senses involved in the social construction of "authenticity" in classical music, and the way these senses surfaced in interviews, the analysis will shed light on the putative conflict that the research participants experienced when raising claims to professional identification with the "authentic" classical musicianship and their Japanese heritage. Second, this chapter demonstrates how "authenticity" fuels the transnational engagements developed by the interviewed musicians, who thereby seek to reconcile their Japanese heritage with classical musicianship.

The chapter begins with the presentation of the research material that informed this analysis. Next, I lay out the theoretical framework and the main concepts that are pertinent for my discussion. This includes the reified notion of "authenticity" in classical music and the racialized sense of ethnic belonging, as well as professional identification and transnational mobility, through which Japanese artists struggle to gain recognition within the global classical music industry. Following that, the core part of the chapter shows how the racialized ideal of "authentic" musicianship influences the working lives of Japanese artists in their homeland. In the closing paragraph, I conclude that the transnational pursuits of the Japanese musicians who participated in this study contribute to further reinforcement of "authenticity" in classical music.

Data and methods

The material presented in this chapter is derived from a larger research project exploring the (trans)national career trajectories of Japanese musicians in Japan, France, and Poland. Specifically, I discuss the data concerning the professional mobility of the interviewed artists. In the period between 2012 and 2019, I conducted 75 semi-structured in-depth interviews with Japanese classical musicians born and educated in Japan, in their native language. All fieldwork was carried out in capital cities, which, being cultural centers, offer artists the widest range of occupational opportunities (Waters and Jiménez, 2005). I interviewed musicians in Tokyo to understand the specificity of the Japanese classical music industry and to trace the origins of professional mobility. Paris and Warsaw were selected as the target destination cities that mainly inform this project due to the disparate migratory routes that bridge music circles between Poland/France and Japan. Networks between Poland and Japan sprouted mostly around the works of one composer—Frédéric Chopin—and the International Chopin Piano Competition, which many Japanese consider to be a trampoline for their professional careers. In France, the connections evolved mainly around the Paris Conservatory (Conservatoire National Supérieur de Musique et de Danse de Paris). Japanese musicians who have completed full-time studies at the Paris Conservatory will have mastered not only the instrument, but also the French language, habits, and traditions, which facilitated their settling in the country. By comparing the professional trajectories of Japanese musicians in these three different socio-cultural and politico-economic contexts, I intended to grasp the potential influence that the idiosyncrasies of a particular environment might have on how individuals deal with the racializing discourse in classical music.

I met 24 musicians in France, 26 in Poland, and 25 in Japan, most of whom were aged between 30 and 45. Women comprised 75% of the group, whereas 25% identified as male. Piano (43%) and violin (32%) were the most common instruments, but I also met a flutist, cellists, orchestra conductors, and opera singers. The demographic makeup of the group reflects historical music practices and socially defined gender roles, the combination of which explains the feminine image of classical music in Japan, and the domination of piano and violin—these being among the most popular instruments taught in Japan. Given the uncertain employment prospects for musicians, the profession has long been an "avocational pursuit" of married women financially dependent on their spouses. The composition of the studied group is also partly an unintentional product of the snowballing method I used in recruiting people for the research. As there are relatively few Japanese musicians in Europe, I interviewed all those who met the basic requirements for my study—Japanese by nationality and heritage, musicians by profession, and having connections with the European classical music milieu.

The very idea of mobility as well as the decision about the country of destination were inspired by colleagues or teachers, and sometimes relatives, from my interlocutors' closest surroundings. Seldom were their choices motivated solely by professional purposes, such as the educational excellence and reputation of the person and place where they were going to study. However, access to informal cross-border networks linking institutions and people played an important role in channeling mobility specifically to France and to Poland rather than elsewhere. Also, the profiles of all the artists whom I interviewed in Japan included a record of overseas education. In most cases, this meant short-term master classes held in one of the European countries, in which they participated while still students in Japan.

The collected data were analyzed manually (Charmaz, 2006). The recurring problems and topics I uncovered comprise the main axis of the argument developed below. I obtained the musicians' informed consent to use and quote from their accounts on condition that any information that might reveal their identities would be anonymized.

"Authenticity" and essentialized sense of belonging as triggers of transnational mobility

In sociological studies on classical music, the term "authenticity" is frequently used in reference to prevailing myths that undergird people's expectations toward ideal music practices, based on which the audience ascribes superior value to some artistic performances and not to others (Yang, 2007; Wang, 2014). But to understand on what grounds the socially constructed notion of "authenticity" in classical music operates as a tool to delegitimize the claims of some artists—here, those of Japanese heritage—to a genuine professional identification with classical musicianship, it is necessary to extend the problem beyond the narrow discussion of stereotypical images projected by the audience onto artists and their works. Charles Lindholm (2008, p. 1) offers a multifaceted discussion of "authenticity," regarding it as a social substance that binds people together "in collectives that are felt to be real, essential, and vital, providing participants with meaning, unity, and surpassing sense of belonging." Persons and communities are deemed "authentic" if they manifest a common, traceable biological and cultural heritage, and if they can act according to that heritage (Lindholm, 2008, p. 2). In other words, to characterize any entity as "authentic," one should consider both its overlapping forms: genealogical or historical (*origin*) and identity or correspondence (*content*). In classical music, these translate first into a musical genealogy (*origin*), which indicates mentoring relationships between music masters and their disciples. Second, it implies the musician's identity, which is expressed on stage through the interpretation of a classical composition that remains true to its roots and properly conveys its essence. The definition of each of the two aspects changes over time and thus is subject to endless debates and contestation. As we shall see, both modes of "authenticity," as set out by Lindholm, overlap, and both are invoked in contexts in which Japanese musicians claim affiliation with their ethno-cultural heritage and classical musicianship. I will demonstrate that one salient reason for which these artists develop transnational mobility is to challenge the Eurocentric, racialized discourse of "authenticity" in classical music, based on which the combination of their ethnic and vocational claims is contested, as discussed below.

Entangled in the history of European expansion, "Western" art music permeated the musical cultures of colonized communities worldwide, thus remodeling Indigenous traditions after its fashion and transforming itself into world music (Cook, 2013, pp. 75–79). Henceforth, African, Chinese, Japanese, and Iranian musicians began to apply "Western" musical language even to the performance of their ethno-cultural identities (Cook, 2013; Nooshin, 2003). Concomitantly, the "authenticity" discourse has been constructed to preserve the hegemonic status of "Western" classical music. "Authenticity" serves as a tool to demarcate hierarchical relations between classical music practitioners along the lines of the geopolitical world order, which in the past contrasted the modern civilization of "Westerners" with that of backward "Others" (Haynes, 2013, p. 32).

The process of constructing artists as "authentic" or "inauthentic" representants of classical music intersects with the mechanisms of their racialization: that is, hierarchically ordering them along allegedly innate, phenotypical lines, which are believed to determine these artists' cultural and moral traits. It is noteworthy that in racializing discourses and practices, biological and cultural characteristics are blurred (Wodak and Reisigl, 1999). Racialized discourse in classical music draws precisely on these ideas, which foreground innate racial phenotypical and cultural predispositions as an essential attribute of an authentic performer. However, the concept of "authenticity" may also serve to delegitimize arguments about racially informed inequalities in classical music by reframing them as the natural outcome of an uneven distribution of knowledge and experience of the European socio-cultural context. As this chapter shows, the interviewed musicians believed that they could align themselves with the ideal of authentic performers only if they maintained professional linkages with the "authentic"—in their opinion, European—classical music milieu.

In this sense, the transnational mobility of my interlocutors fits into the definition of this phenomenon proposed by Glick Schiller, Basch, and Szanton Blanc (1995), who cast transnational mobility as a process driven by economic and political inequalities between the various socio-cultural contexts in which migrants operate. It consists of creating and maintaining social relations by migrants, linking them with the communities in both their home and host countries, in "a response to the fact that in a global economy, contemporary migrants have found full incorporation in the countries within which they resettle either not possible or not desirable" (Glick Schiller, Basch and Szanton Blanc, 1995, p. 52). In this chapter, I bring to the fore specifically this aspect of my interlocutors' transnational mobility, which is an effect of structural inequalities underpinning the asymmetrical positioning of the Japanese classical musical milieu vis-à-vis the "Western" one. I will demonstrate that the interviewed musicians engage in transnational music activities to enact and negotiate professional and ethnic identities by maintaining relations with the "Western" world of classical music (when one lives in Japan) or with Japan (when one is based in Europe) (Kowalczyk, 2021).

On this point, it is worth emphasizing the impermanence of identities and senses of belonging, which the Japanese musicians constantly negotiate through their transnational engagements. Their struggles to be legitimately recognized—in Japan and in Europe—as both Japanese and professional classical instrumentalists do not produce a secure and coherent sense of self or fixed belonging (Beech et al., 2016). The dynamics of mobilities, the fact that music projects are often short-lived, and the precariousness of freelancing creative works are important factors in constantly unsettling the process of musicians' co-construing their identity and sense of belonging through mutual interaction with both the home and the host society as well as its structures (discourses, institutions, and culture) (Negus and Velázquez, 2002, p. 143). Central to this chapter is understanding how the tensions between the two putatively irreconcilable senses of belonging—ethno-cultural and vocational—operate in the transnational working lives of Japanese musicians.

Negotiating irreconcilable senses of belonging in the unequal world of classical music through transnational mobility

I begin my analysis with a discussion of how oppressive, racialized constructs of "authenticity" in classical music affected the ways in which my interlocutors self-identified as classical musicians and Japanese. Next, I demonstrate how they developed transnational music activities in order to reconcile their Japanese heritage with their professional identification.

Irreconcilable senses of belonging: being a classical musician and Japanese

The "authenticity" argument surfaced firstly in this part of the interviews, which concerned reasons for moving to Europe. The majority of my interlocutors relocated to Europe to hone their music skills. They explained that to become a "real" classical musician, one needs to experience the "authentic" sound of classical music in its "European cradle": that is, the socio-cultural setting where it was originally created. Consider the quotation from a female pianist living in France, which illustrates how she self-others as a performer of music belonging to "Europeans," based on internalized essentializing constructions of differences between "Western" art music and Asian music.

> This trip is not indispensable from your career point of view, but you do want to know "authentic classical music," don't you? It's European music, after all. We are Asians . . . and in the end, we are just imitating. We are born in a different culture and we grow up in a different environment. . . . For us, Western music is not our own Asian music and studies abroad give us this rare opportunity to see how music is embodied by people from the original culture.[2]

Another female pianist clarified that in order to grasp the sense of "authenticity" in classical music, it is important not only to master the "authentic" instrument technique at European conservatories. In the opinion of this woman and other musicians, to understand music of a specific European country, it is equally salient to acquire all kinds of experiences and knowledge of cultural practices of that country, from spoken language through social habits and rituals to the rules of interpersonal relationships. All of these elements were considered to nourish classical music and resonate in its melody, instrumentation, and distinctive language:

> If you don't go to study abroad, you wouldn't be able to grasp the real thing.... One will never get to know it unless one lives there. It has to do with the language; it's something you get by living there on a daily basis. There, unlike in Japan, classical music is a part of everyday life. You go to church, for example, and you can listen to it.

The Japanese that I spoke to felt that they fell short of the "European pedigree." Further, they tended to link professional success in classical music with "Western" scholarly genealogy in music. Put differently, they were convinced that to win any major musical competition held in the "Western" music world, for instance, it is necessary to study with "Western" teachers in Europe. These opinions were expressed notwithstanding the intensive exchanges between Japan and the "Western" world of classical music since the introduction of this art to Japan at the end of the nineteenth century and despite the fact that all of my interlocutors had the opportunity to practice their instruments under the tutelage of a French, Polish, German, Italian, or British musician in their homeland (Kowalczyk, 2021).

The genealogy issue surfaced in a story by one violinist about their prize-winning participation in a major European music competition, in spite of their solely Japanese educational background:

> In the 1970s I won a prize in [X] music competition, without previously studying abroad. I remember even today that when I got that prize, they wrote in the newspaper in Japan that this was the "First-ever purely domestic prize." Until then, there were other Japanese who won even second and third prize. Yet, they were all studying somewhere in Europe and went to participate in this competition directly from there.

The interviewed Japanese musicians were constructed as "inauthentic" for the reason of their heritage and scholarly genealogy, which in both the "Western" and the Japanese music world are construed as incompatible with the "authentic tradition." My interlocutors had already been imbued with these oppressive constructions of "inauthentic Asian musicians" in Japan, through the education system, grounded in "Western" instrumental techniques and the "Western" musical canon. In interviews, they often juxtaposed themselves with the ideal of an "authentic musician," which they associated with "Western" heritage. The feeling of not fitting the "authentic model" was enhanced by their experiences— and those of their colleagues—accrued throughout their professional careers within and outside their homeland. I frequently heard opinions that "European musicians" are generally given preference in Japan, as they represent for the Japanese public "the real classical music tradition." This and other similar statements are hardly verifiable, but they can be partly supported by the Japanese literature on the classical music milieu in Japan. One such example of preferential treatment of "Western" musicians is provided by an analysis of events planned in Japan to commemorate the 200th anniversary of Mozart's death in 1991 (Kowalczyk, 2021). A five-page detailed year-round program for the celebration listed uniquely foreign performers and not one single Japanese artist, as if to "confirm that classical music belonged to foreign culture" (Wajima, 2005, p. 183).

I shall add that in Japan, these denigrating constructions of Japanese musicians are additionally coupled with a common-sense portrayal of classical musicians more in terms of the pursuit of a passion or a hobby, rather than as a legitimate profession, due to the precarious working conditions in the Japanese music sector. These unfavorable opinions surfaced in most of the interviews and were echoed in my conversation with this female orchestral musician living in France:

> In Japan ... [t]he social status of orchestral musicians is questionable.... Orchestras [there] must often perform commercial music. I [would] ... have to seek outside jobs in entertainment or recording sectors to support myself [in Japan].

My interlocutors headed to Europe to attain the "authentic sound" through educational and life experience, and thus to self-align with "authentic" musicianship. Most of them were determined to settle in one of the European countries, explaining that "classical musicians are better off" there. Referring to the "authenticity" argument, they constructed the European classical music milieu as a place where "the [spoken] language, culture, habits," interpersonal relations, and way of thinking, "all matches the music" and consequently the quality of performed music is higher there than in Japan. They also believed that the European classical music industry offers more opportunities for permanent posts (e.g., in orchestras) with decent working conditions, including higher salaries, paid holidays, sick leave, and maternity leave. A female violinist playing with a French orchestra explained that she "wouldn't like to go back to Japan," because she "wasn't guaranteed to be able to build a similar career back there." These arguments underpinned their decisions to undertake all endeavors to establish their professional careers in Poland or in France.

However, the racially-informed "authenticity" discourse complicated these endeavors. One violinist recalled how he often witnessed disadvantaged treatment of Asian musicians by European jury members during the auditions of candidates for orchestra posts in which he participated. Another interviewed artist had her compositions negatively evaluated by her French professor as being "too Japanese," due to the fact that they resonated more with the "bodily rhythms" instead of arising from "intellectual reflection." Stereotypes of "inauthentic Asian musicians" were easily mobilized in many professional contexts (e.g., orchestral rehearsals), since, as a female violinist put it: "We're Asians after all and we stand out in Europe. Whatever we play, we're constantly in the spotlight. So . . . it gets even more difficult [to be accepted as a member]."

I encountered musicians who had successfully integrated the French and Polish music milieus after graduation from music universities in France and in Poland. They admitted that studies in Europe facilitated their entrance into the labor market—often upon recommendations of their French and Polish music professors—as they were already well embedded in the local environment. However, some of them revealed that outside their milieu, they were still constructed as "Asian" and thus as "inauthentic musicians." The fact that my interlocutors associated "inauthenticity" with "Asian-ness" already suggests that the problem of asymmetrical positioning expands beyond the narrow group of Japanese musicians and equally concerns artists self-identifying as Koreans, Chinese, or Taiwanese. These findings dovetail with the existing research on professional experiences of musicians from East Asia in Europe, as described by Mai Kawabata in this book and in others (Scharff, 2018), as well as in the United States (Yang, 2007; Wang, 2014).

While strongly wishing to self-align with "authentic Western musicianship," the interviewed artists declared strong allegiances to Japan, where their relatives and friends lived, and where everyday life habits suited them more (i.e., dietary customs). This was apparent in their decision to retain Japanese nationality,[3] even in the face of the many difficulties associated with third country citizenship in the EU.[4] Home country attachments motivated their regular returns to Japan. Some of my interlocutors overtly posited that they were torn between Japan, where "they feel at home," and Europe, which is "the right working environment for a classical musician." These tensions reverberated in the interview with a female pianist, who returned to Japan having spent some time in England: "It's a very basic thing, but in terms of daily life, I wanted to return to Japan because I'm Japanese. . . . When it comes to classical music, there it's better, without a doubt."

She was echoed by another female pianist, who posited that "the ideal would be to stay here and do various things in Japan [participate in music projects] but . . . it's extremely difficult." I argue that the interviewed artists develop transnational music activities to cultivate their Japanese-ness and to achieve professional identification with the "authentic Western musicianship."

Reinstating professional and ethno-cultural identification through transnational mobility

Propelled by the desire to maintain allegiances toward their homeland, many of the interviewed musicians based in Poland and France developed and sustained moderate relations with the Japanese music milieu. They (co-)organized and performed in salon concerts, solo or with colleagues on occasional visits to their home country. A quotation from a young female pianist married to a Pole gives an idea of such enterprises:

> I perform in Japan when I come back to see my family. I have a friend who organizes small music events. Last summer, I played with a friend with whom I used to perform in a duo. Elsewhere, I held a small salon concert of Chopin music. I want to maintain that kind of connection. I'm Japanese, after all, and I want to have a place in Japan where I can always go back to.

Those most actively involved in the classical scene back in Japan were predominantly male orchestral members free from family responsibilities.[5] This was possible owing to their predictable work schedules, which enabled them to combine both working calendars, as well as visits to Japan with the French/Polish orchestras. Touring in Japan, they created opportunities for future artistic cooperation. My interlocutors presumed that their affiliation with a European ensemble facilitated access to such extra jobs (solo recitals or performances with orchestras, chamber music, or masterclasses) back in their home country. By their belonging to the world of "Western" music, they were believed to be capable of enacting "authenticity" through their performance. One musician admitted that "sure, it matters that my quartet consists of members of a famous French orchestra. It is easier for the agency to fill the concert hall." Some of these transitional engagements evolved into more regular collaborations. One of the players described his professional attachments to the Japanese music milieu as follows:

> I come back to Japan every year. I cannot take a long break from work, so I do it mostly during my summer holidays. . . . I perform with a Japanese pianist or solo. . . . With other orchestra members, we formed a chamber music quartet

and went touring in Japan.... Aside from the duo and the quartet, I played part-time as a section leader with orchestras in Tokyo and Osaka. It all started with the manager and my musician friend, and my connections progressively expanded through introductions.

However costly in terms of time and money, cross-border ties with Japan allowed my interlocutors to evidence their successful integration into "authentic" musicianship despite their Japanese heritage. Claiming legitimate linkages to the "Western" music milieu, they attempted to resist denigrating constructions of them within Japanese society and to reposition themselves on Japan's social map.

Similar motivations underpinned the mobilities of musicians who shuttled between the Japanese and European music worlds while living in Japan. One male orchestra conductor ascribed the differences he experienced when working with Japanese and "Western" ensembles to the particularities of Japanese culture, thus reinforcing the essentializing discourse associating classical music with "Western" heritage:

> I conduct in Europe whenever I can.... Japanese orchestras... have improved a lot now, but... they still tend to play music in a very formal... way.... The sense of tempo in classical music... slightly differs depending on the music piece. But in Japan, they don't pay so much attention to these nuances, because it's foreign music and they don't understand it. So, they think that tempo is something constant. It gives the sense of a metronome.... and it's very difficult to come up with diverse expressions.... To me, everything sounds the same. To change this tendency, the Japanese hire foreign conductors.

These transnational mobilities would not have been possible without networks and connections that were forged upon exchanges between the Japanese and the French, Polish, German, Italian, or British artists. These interactions were initiated during the interviewed artists' educational sojourns in Europe. Most of the long-lasting music relationship that binds Poland and Japan revolves around Chopin and the International Chopin Piano Competition, which is popular in Japan. Many of the interviewed pianists who had returned to Japan upon completion of their studies in Poland continued to cherish their relations with the Polish music milieu by performing in the country on various occasions and inviting Polish musicians to Japan, as in the case of this female pianist:

> Musicians in Japan don't get many calls from abroad. It's all about connections.... [A]ll performing opportunities I had in Poland came by the initiative of my former piano professor in Poland.... If one can expand and

sustain connections developed during such a time, then that person may be invited to come and play from time to time. Nothing is guaranteed, though.

To the question of why they continued their endeavors to remain as transnational musicians despite the many hardships related to this sort of lifestyle, the interviewees unanimously highlighted that they were "not doing it for financial reasons, but purely for [their] musical interests," "artistic satisfaction," and to increase "career prospects" in Japan, which in the long run could translate into financial benefits. These elements resonated with the narratives of two musicians who, at the time of the interviews, had been dividing their work schedules between Japan and Europe for more than a decade:

> It doesn't matter where you live, but it matters where you play. Here's a mere imitation, and the *honba* [the birthplace] is out there, in Europe. It's totally different. It's as different as the language. We don't go there for money. Playing a good performance with good musicians becomes our treasure and our asset. We've sacrificed everything to music. If, one day, I'm no longer able to play music anymore, there will be nothing left [in terms of family life or other jobs].

Arguably, by embarking on transnational music activities, these musicians strove to align themselves with the "authentic Western" world of classical music while maintaining their allegiances toward Japan.

Concluding remarks

Identity struggles as the motive fueling transnational mobility have been understudied in the literature on transnationalism, which has focused on the economic, political, and social factors underpinning cross-country movements. The analysis presented in this chapter extends our understanding of how transnational activities shape identities within the group of highly skilled professionals into which classical musicians fall by their education. I demonstrated how the interviewed artists experience racially-informed inequalities whenever they self-identify as Japanese and classical musicians. These inequalities are propelled by the racialized discourse of "authenticity" in classical music, which perpetuates persistent associations between classical music and "Western" heritage. To reconcile what is constructed as putatively irreconcilable, namely their professional and ethno-cultural self-identification, and to gain recognition as Japanese classical musicians, the interviewed artists embarked on transnational music activities. Put differently, their transnational musical pursuits developed as a response to the structural inequalities undergirding the global classical music industry, which tends to exclude them on the grounds of their Japanese heritage. Concomitantly, however, their transnational engagements, while aimed at challenging the racialized oppressive constructions of non-White performers, inadvertently led to further reification and reproduction of racialized representations of authentic musicians (Gans, 2016). This is because the interviewed musicians exploited the essentialized discourse of "authenticity" in classical music to self-identify with its elements and thus to be perceived as legitimate members of the global music milieu.

Notes

1. The notion of the "West" here refers to an essentialized and reified entity that has been constructed in radical opposition to the Orient and that constitutes a "set of interrelated understandings that people have of themselves and of others" (Carrier, 1992, p. 197).
2. Some of the quotes from interviews presented in this chapter have been also included in the monograph (Kowalczyk, 2021).
3. Japan does not permit dual citizenship. Children born to parents of Japanese and non-Japanese nationality are required to select one nationality at the age of 21, when they achieve maturity.
4. Third-country citizens are not eligible to obtain the formal qualifications required to be employed in French academia (Héran, 2012, p. 10).
5. This observation upholds other findings on the cross-country movements of highly-skilled male professionals (Beaverstock, 2002).

16
[Re-]training Classical Musicians Toward Polymusicality and Hybridization

An Interview with Jon Silpayamanant

Jon Silpayamanant

ANNA: Could you start by telling me a bit about your musical training and heritage?

JON: I guess I should start from the beginning. I was born in Thailand and moved here to the States when I was very, very young. I have a lot of memories of listening to and singing along with Thai music even here in the States and my mother even teaching me lyrics, and she's told me stories as well of me singing along in Thailand even as a two-year-old. The first songs I learned how to sing were in Thai. And then growing up in the States, assimilative pressures eventually came in. To adapt, you start to experience the music of the culture, which is, of course, generally pop music or classical music in the US. I started on violin when I was six and then switched to cello when I was seven. After that, I just started going on that classical music track until I went to music school. I went to music school, got a performance degree, and promptly quit playing the cello for eight years. I was very frustrated with the music school experience. One of the reasons is, when I was in music school, I actually started exploring more of my cultural heritage. I'd read anything that they would have in the music library, listen to recordings. That helped me to realize a lot of the things I thought I understood about Thai music weren't true. And then while I was in music school, anytime they would bring in an artist that was from another "non-Western" culture or even "Western" culture, like Native American music, Indigenous music, I would take a workshop or go to the performances. I took some Indian music workshops, African drumming workshops, African dance workshop even once, a Native American drumming workshop, things like that. I was often one of very few music students to do that. After that, I quit playing for eight years. I started exploring a lot of electronic music, a lot of new music and, of course, a lot of music from all around the world. I was still performing a little bit, just not on the cello. And when I came back to the cello, it was in the context of experimental music and I played cello with a lot of electronics. Not long after that I co-founded and played with a group called Il Troubadore based in Indianapolis. The other member was a classically trained vocalist who worked his way through college by playing in bands and doing R&B, heavy metal, pop, whatever, to make enough money. We formed this group and we started playing mostly Italian bel canto music, some pop covers, some Irish jigs, and things like that. And eventually, we started just interacting with other musical communities and cultural communities. We slowly morphed into doing a lot of Middle Eastern music. We started working with belly dancers. Probably outside of Thai music, Middle Eastern music is the type of music I've done the most that wasn't strictly "Western" or classical. Since 2004 I've been playing music from the Middle East and learning as much as I can about that, and then music from Muslim majority countries in general. Ever since then, most of the groups I've joined have been ethnic community musics from different cultures—I don't really like using the word ethnic because it implies that White isn't an ethnicity or the dominant majority isn't an ethnic group.

ANNA: Just to follow up on that. I think for a lot of classically trained musicians, such as myself, the idea of working across different genres in that way or working with different musical communities is a bit terrifying because you don't know the rules. You're back to square one in terms of your own skill. And you're terrified of getting it wrong because, of course, we're socialized to try and get it right. Was that an experience that you had?

JON: I think what I'm finding very interesting is that, because of the classical music training, I had a little bit of that mindset. But I also had a little bit of the mindset that I have the *right* to participate in these cultural groups, in these musical contexts. This is a very colonialist type of mindset. It's like, "I can do this because I have the right to do this. And I have the right to share all this music, I have the right to do whatever I want with this music." But I've slowly learned that there are some musics that I just do not have the right to even touch, even to perform. And there are some musical contexts within which I cannot really be a full participant because I'm just a visitor, if that makes any sense. But as far as the actual feeling of performing, one of the things I didn't talk about in relation to my music school experience, my cello professor had started improvising just a couple years before I got there. He made all his students improvise, and he started a chamber music improv group. Sometimes in recitals, we improvised. That was a training you don't normally get in classical music organizations that I think was very important for helping me to be able to adapt to these other musical contexts. Now obviously, just being able to improvise isn't the same thing as being fluent in the musical languages of other cultures, but it's easier if you have that base skill. I think having that skill is something that may be very important to include in the curriculum, because you can't interact if you're not adaptable in that sense. The other thing was, improvisation also changed the way I use my ears; you have to listen to what's going on because you don't have a visual cue anymore. So, you have to listen to chord changes or you have to listen to the particular type of scale or mode you're in or just understand the stylistic differences to be able to adapt your playing to match that.

ANNA: One of the areas this book is going to explore is ways forward for what you might call "diversity" in classical music. I'm wondering if you could tell me about the ensemble you set up and what diverse music-making, if you want to use that word, looks like in your new ensemble.

JON: The most recent ensemble and, I think the one that I've invested the most time in, is Saw Peep. It was started as a result of the "Muslim ban," the executive order that banned people from a selection of Muslim-majority countries from entering the US (BBC, 2018). At that point, I hadn't been doing a lot of Middle Eastern music, and I wanted to do it again, and so because of that executive order, I decided it was time to start this group because we needed to start talking about the music of Muslim-majority countries. At first I was thinking we would just be playing music from the countries on the Muslim ban. This is where it gets interesting. Of the players that I did draw in, some were classically trained, some were musicians that had done some Middle Eastern music, or were belly dancers that then started to love the music so much, they wanted to play it. The idea was to adapt this music for the group, which is the difficult part because obviously when you have an ensemble that's not a set ensemble, you have to rewrite parts or rearrange them. Or when it's music that's not generally written, then you have to transcribe it, and then train the players on how to play with the appropriate style, or how to learn how to hear the scales or to be comfortable with the types of rhythmic modes. In many cases, those scales have what we sometimes erroneously call microtones in them. And a lot of the rhythmic modes, especially in Middle Eastern music and Balkan music, tend to be asymmetrical and odd-metered rhythms and one of the other difficulties is just getting everyone comfortable with the different types of rhythmic modes. Sometimes we would have to do rhythm exercises just to be able to get through [to] the ensemble as a whole to feel the groove. Of course, the other hurdle working with musicians with diverse musical backgrounds is that some can read music well, others don't read it at all or very little, and others have learned from oral traditions. The way I approach it, I go ahead and write a full score. I write in the basic melodic lines, write in a basic meter. But then we have to adapt each player to working within that context, sometimes with doing rhythmic exercises or just working on tuning because of the scales and modes. And then, of course, trying to get them to work together as an ensemble, which is tricky because then you're talking about a non-standard group, which means balance becomes a very specific issue. With the symphony orchestra, you're used to the forces you have, so it's easy to write for that in a way because you know exactly what forces exist. When you have a malleable ensemble or an ensemble with a non-standard instrumentation, then you've got to adapt parts to work to make sure that you're not losing something. At least here in the States, we have lead sheets that are just basically the melodic line and sometimes we will notate the rhythmic cycle or modes, if that's applicable. Everyone generally knows that, okay, I'm playing this instrument so this is how I would ornament it or I'm playing this instrument so I don't ornament it like this one, I've to ornament it like this. The heterophony that comes out of that is natural. But with players who are classically trained and/or not in those musical contexts, you have to basically either write it all out, which then makes it more difficult to read, or just write the basic melodic lines and then teach them how to actually play some of those ornaments, those stylistic things. That's also time consuming. This goes back to an issue that I've been thinking about lately, which is that I spend probably half my time just training musicians. That's something that you don't have to worry about when you're just working with orchestras. Everyone knows the style, they just play their notes. The director then becomes someone who shapes the phrasing or shapes the music. I have to actually shape how the players play the music. It basically puts a bigger load on me, which also says something about the classical music world; neither my ensemble, nor other BIPOC (Black, Indigenous and People of Color) ensemble directors working with similarly diverse groups, tend to have players who are trained to be able to adapt easily. As a result, I had to spend a lot of extra time doing that, which means I have less time to spend maybe making new arrangements or just making music. I think that's a very, very interesting issue: . . . that training gets offloaded onto basically, "non-Western" trained musicians. And in many cases, those tend to be musicians of color or musicians from other cultural backgrounds.

ANNA: This also brings to mind a point that Kristina Kolbe writes about in her chapter for this book, describing intercultural music-making in an opera company in Germany (Kolbe, chapter 5). The production she describes has a few Turkish musicians and a whole orchestra of classical musicians, and it is the Turkish musicians who have to adapt to the practices of the classical musicians, rather than the other way around. Could you reflect on that example?

JON: Reading her work, it was just amazing to see it from the other side, that is, trying to fit musicians who aren't classically trained into a classical context. Because I sometimes feel like this is an issue with a lot of the intercultural orchestras that exist really all around the world, but especially in the so-called "Western" world. Sometimes when I hear them do their arrangements of music, it almost sounds too "Westernized." When you're talking about bringing together a wide diversity of musicians from China, from Iran, from African countries, and then from the "West" into one group, then what style do you focus on? Even if you're doing a very specific type of piece from a specific region, still, you have to adapt all those players with completely different styles into something. And that sometimes ends up being, at least from my standpoint, very "Westernized," because we lose a lot of that natural heterophony that happens within a very specific cultural context, or we lose some of the sense of the style, the timbres that happen as a result of the instrumentation too, because instrumentation really affects how the style and the playing happen. I think the idea of adapting "non-Western," non-classically trained musicians into any other contexts in general is going to be tricky because you have to make a lot of changes in the way you're playing as well. Which, again, puts more work on generally People of Color that are going to be doing music in those contexts. I think it's very similar to the idea of bringing the Turkish musicians into the "Western" classical context, as Kristina Kolbe describes. Not just the music itself, but rehearsal styles have to be adapted, obviously, because we have a very specific way of rehearsing in the "West." It's even different to the pop music world where I've been in bands and you just get together and you play through songs, basically. If there's something wrong, maybe you'll work on it, but you just basically will play through your songs. Generally a lot more of it is improvised. You'll have solos or you'll do varied things or whatever, then that comes out naturally. You can't really rehearse improv solos. You can rehearse maybe what the ensemble is doing while someone is soloing so that you don't cover them up or whatever. There are so many issues that are involved when you try to have musicians from different backgrounds working together. Depending on the balance of power, someone will ultimately have to adapt more. And that in my experience happens to be the People of Color and musicians from "non-Western" musical contexts.

ANNA: I'm interested to hear that you've had to find your own way of rehearsing. Could you say a bit more about that?

JON: Yes, a lot of the techniques I use are just your standard classical music rehearsal techniques, where you work on a part. If something falls apart, you go back and just drill that one part several times. Or if something's not quite in tune, then you'll slowly work through the tuning, make sure everyone's matching and things like that. Some of the rehearsal things we do are drills on rhythms just so we can get a feel for the groove, and then we'll go back and then play through the song. Other times, it's checking the balance because it's an issue in "Western" music, but the balance is a little bit easier to manage because the instrumentation and ensemble types have developed for a long time. Whereas a lot of the music we play from different cultural contexts, it still has some of its basis on informal jams, I guess, the idea that you would just get a group of musicians together: they all know this tune and they'll all play it. And I think that's something that could help the classical musicians as well, is just being able to be in those types of contexts. I think that improvised chamber music ensemble my cello professor started at school was great.... Someone would take a solo, and so everyone else would pull out of the texture a little bit, but you'd have to know and be able to listen and hear when someone is taking a solo, or you'd have to figure out a way to decide how you're going to acknowledge when someone's taking a solo or when I'm going to take a solo. Things like that require very different types of rehearsal that you have to consider when you're not in a classical music context. If classical musicians want to be able to adapt to other types of playing styles, knowing a lot of these things would be very helpful.

ANNA: This theme of the importance of musicians' adaptability, it's just coming through really strongly. And maybe that's one of the biggest challenges for classical musicians. Another of the questions I wanted to ask is whether and how the genre of classical music needs to change.

JON: I think this is one of the reasons why I keep talking about the background of some of the things I'm thinking about—because the orchestra has never really been a set ensemble. In the "West," especially in Europe and North America, we've said that we have this symphony orchestra, which was something that matured at the last part of the 19th century, early part of the 20th century. And this is the instrumentation, so this is what we use. But the orchestras never stopped evolving in other parts of the world. We have multi-musical educational contexts in countries outside of the "West" in general. Bi-musicality or polymusicality is what I tend to talk about. And a lot of those players are trained in both styles or at least are very familiar with both styles and so can adapt and do that. Whereas in the "West," we have our training, it's classical and so we don't generally have that level of bi-musicality or polymusicality ingrained in us, so we get stuck with just playing in one style. But as far as orchestras, we have all these different types of orchestras all around the world. I'm keeping this Twitter thread, that's got well over 100 ... different types of orchestras, just to show people that other countries, other cultures, have taken this idea of an orchestra—which is a very "Western" one—and built on that and created their own. But this music is not considered classical because it doesn't have that standard orchestration that we have from the turn of the 20th century. But why isn't it? And part of that is because "Western" orchestras can't play a lot of the repertoire because they don't have the instrumentation. For one, they wouldn't even know the first thing about playing those microtones or rhythmic modes or whatever. It becomes a big barrier, I think, in a way that we have what's universal and standard as opposed to what's ethnic and cultural. But really, why can't we reconsider that standard? What would happen if we started training our "Western" musicians to play mugham symphonic works or traditional Chinese orchestra works?

ANNA: Or just to be bi-musical in whatever languages they chose. Thinking about instruments, we're both cellists and I've currently got my cello sitting guiltily on the cupboard. I suppose cello is a pretty quintessential classical instrument, or at least that's how I see it. Can you talk about how you've used a classical instrument in intercultural music-making?

JON: Yes, that's actually an interesting thing. Because I'm in the middle of working on my own set of cello method books, which are going to be focusing on diversity, not just diversity of composers, but also diversity of styles. Because one of the things I've learned through all of my experiences is that the cello has been used in very different ways in different cultural contexts, and for centuries in some cases, which is an amazing thing to think about. I think of the cello—any instrument really, but the cello in particular since that's my main instrument—as more of a prototype that has been used in many different ways across different cultures. Cello-like instruments exist all around the world. In the "West," it's used in a very, very particular way or a small set of ways, for Baroque music or new music or classical music, sometimes in pop music. Due to colonialism, the cello had been imported to many other countries. And then there are other countries that have instruments that are very cello-like that have evolved from their native bowed string instruments. There are cellists all around the world who are playing completely different styles than the way we do in "Western" classical music. That's one of the things I want to focus a little bit on in my method book . . . not necessarily train young cellists to be able to play in any style, but at least to let them know that these exist, that you don't have to be stuck with just doing classical music. There are hundreds, if not thousands, of cellists that could do this classical repertoire. And given the changing demographics of, especially, the US, you may have the opportunity to play in an Arabic orchestra on cello, or in a traditional Chinese orchestra.

ANNA: Yes, I've been socialized into thinking about the instrument as one thing, when it's got all these possibilities that many of us haven't explored. Could we now zoom out and think about classical music more widely? Do you have any more thoughts on the idea the music itself has to change in order for classical music to diversify? I'm guessing you might be on board with me on that one.

JON: Yes, I'm on board with it. I think we have to recognize that it already has changed—going back to the theme of being adapted in different cultural contexts or being hybridized in different cultural contexts. That every country outside of Europe, North America, and other "Westernized" countries, have created their own type of classical music. And, of course, a lot of that is due to the fact that colonialism has imported "Western" classical music culture all around the world. Some of that stuck, and there's this recognition that classical music is a thing. But there's also recognition that we have our own musics. And why do we need to just play Beethoven or Bach? Or why can't we have our own composers write their own things? Why can't we incorporate these instruments into the classical music context? You'll find that all around the world, and I think that's something we have to acknowledge and recognize and include in the discussion, that classical music is much more diverse than we think. And it's just because we've ignored those places outside of the "West" that have developed classical music in their own direction. I think that's a really important distinction. For example, I think the first time I encountered early South American and Baroque music was through a group here in town called Ars Femina, which only played music by women composers. And it's an early music group, so they would look for women composers from that period, Baroque and maybe early classical. But they released a CD that was all Baroque music from Cuba and Mexico (Ars Femina Ensemble, 1996). That was just mind-blowing—it was like, wait, Baroque music from the Global South? And it makes perfect sense because the Spanish and Portuguese influence in South America has been there for centuries—why would they not have music that was being composed during that time? We don't play those composers, but they've been around. And then, of course, in my research into slave orchestras, I discovered that Manila, which had been colonized by the Spanish since the 16th century, has a classical music tradition that has co-evolved with Western European classical music. How many more examples are out there like that? And why don't we discuss that as a part of the classical music history?

ANNA: These are great questions. Perhaps linked to this, I also wanted to ask you what you think are the biggest challenges or barriers to making change in classical music as it's institutionalized in Europe and North America?

JON: I think the biggest issues are infrastructural ones that don't necessarily have to deal specifically with classical music, but with how classical music has been incorporated into the larger cultural contexts, like venues or presenters. Or just the social expectation of what classical music means. I think those are much bigger issues that classical music as a field could do better in addressing. And a part of that just goes back to acknowledging the fact that it's much more diverse than it is. We don't have to necessarily change the core but I think we need to acknowledge that the core is not the only thing. So having groups come and do presentations in classical music organizations [would be helpful], or even having instructors or musicians that work in those contexts in a normal— I don't want to say normal because that makes the assumption that there is a normal classical music—but in a "Western" classical music context. I think here in the States, Berklee in Boston[1] is a model that could possibly be adapted for other universities and schools, where they actually do have musicians from different cultural backgrounds that teach classes. Depending on the student body, they have dozens of different types of ensembles. Everything from the Arabic music ensemble, Indian music ensemble, [to] an Indonesian music ensemble. They also have specific ensembles that deal with specific artists' works, whether they be pop artists or a specific type of genre. They have teachers from different musical backgrounds, and they allow the students to form their own ensembles. This is for the string department. I haven't explored the rest of the school. I think it's a model that would be very difficult for other schools to follow just because it's a completely different way of approaching what it means to teach music. But I also think the other issue is that it would mean the resources of having those types of instructors would be difficult to find. And then with the adjunctification of universities, there's the issue that employment may turn into being more hourly-paid contracts rather than actual faculty positions, which is a separate issue. This wouldn't solve all the problems I have had to deal with but I think in the broader context of things, it may make it easier for people to understand that things aren't as set as they are thinking. The canon isn't set, it's just a thing that's been constructed. The instrumentation isn't set, it's just something that's constructed and been handed down to us. We can make our own ensembles, make our own types of musics. We can hybridize it how we want. Of course, that goes back to the issue, like I said earlier, that I don't feel like I have the right to play all types of music anymore because there are some musics that just don't need to be played by someone outside of that culture, who is not a culture bearer, who isn't a part of that tradition. But there's enough music outside of those very strict core set conditions that can allow us to create hybrid musics, whether it be in the pop music world or even in the classical music world, from each and every country around the world. It's just [that] we have to acknowledge that it even exists in the first place. I think that's the biggest hurdle.

ANNA: I guess the last question I want to explore is, what message would you give to musicians and activists who want to make change in classical music?

JON: I think that's a two-pronged issue because obviously, there need to be a lot of changes made in the wider classical music world, but also locally, you can do some specific things. One of the things I do with my group is, I generally give a context, a background to all the pieces we perform. We perform at the university where I teach, occasionally, and since there are a lot of students that come to that, I will talk about the musical style, the composer, if there was a composer, where it came from, what it's used for, or some of the other interesting stories about that—just to normalize the fact that there are composers of music that isn't "Western" music, because I think there's this mentality where anything that's not "Western" music is anonymous, it's just folk music or traditional music. I think just normalizing the fact that composers exist all around the world already will help to change how we view what classical music means. As far as the larger classical music world goes, like we talked about, we need the recognition that classical music isn't this core, "Western" and European and North American thing, but that it exists well outside of the "West." And to also acknowledge that there are composers living today who are doing things where they hybridize their own musical style backgrounds into their classical music contexts, or they're approaching classical music from a completely different cultural context that isn't specifically European or North American. And then, of course, just like what's happening now, [we need] to push for diverse repertoire, because that diverse repertoire already exists. There's no reason why we shouldn't be performing Florence Price's symphonies regularly now, because they've been around long enough. And it's great that they are now releasing recordings of those because there are so very few of them. Even within Europe and North America, there are composers that have written who are not White and not male, and just acknowledging that as part of our own individual classical music traditions and histories [would be helpful]. Classical music has always been diverse, it's just we've not allowed that diversity to become a part of the official training or the canonical training that we normally get.

Note

1. https://bostonconservatory.berklee.edu/strings [accessed November 22, 2021]

17
Inclusion and Diversity in the Early Music Scene in the US

A Conversation with Patricia Ann Neely

Patricia Ann Neely

CHRISTINA: Could you tell me how you got into working on diversity and early music?
PATRICIA: Well, I started this project way back, before it was a topic of discussion, because I was always wondering why there were very few African Americans involved in early music professionally. When I started, I could maybe name two people, myself and an organist in Boston, James S. Nicolson. And as time grew, and more attention was being paid to diversity in mainstream classical music, I wondered what kind of initiatives we would need to increase the demographic of People of Color in early music. At the time, I was involved in a management development certificate program at Mannes College of Music, one of the three conservatories in New York, and one of the components of that program was looking at diversity in nonprofits and education. My thesis for that program was a study of the Sphinx Organization, an advocacy organization for African American and Latino classically-trained musicians. I chose this as my topic as a result of a meeting at Mannes where the Dean expressed concern that the school was not attracting a more diverse community of students, and this was especially true in the string department. I introduced myself to Aaron Dworkin, founder of Sphinx, and began to work on a partnership, first by learning more about their mission. I learned that Juilliard and Manhattan had established a partnership with Sphinx, and so I created one between Mannes and Sphinx to offer a full tuition scholarship to a Sphinx laureate who met the requirements for admission to Mannes. And that's how I got started, and that was way back in the 90s, late 90s.
CHRISTINA: Leading on from there, my next question is about why and how the IDEA taskforce was set up, the Inclusion, Diversity, Equity and Access Taskforce for Early Music America (EMA). If you like we can talk specifically about this, or more generally about your trajectory, because I imagine

there's a whole trajectory that got you from your work in the late nineties to today, 2021.

PATRICIA: I presented a paper in 2019 at the Historical Performance Conference at Indiana University on the history of African Americans in classical music and how it intertwined with the civil rights movement of the 60s, which in my view failed to thrive and this is why, in my opinion, we are where we are today. I thought about where we were lacking in our own field by looking at history, visual images from the periods, and recent scholarly research about the history of Africans in Europe. A few months later, Karin Brookes, who was at that time the Executive Director of Early Music America (EMA) and an attendee at the conference, called me and asked if we could talk about creating an initiative at EMA to address equity and diversity. In the meantime, radio host of a program entited, Sunday Baroque, Suzanne Bona called me and said that she had been at a music presenter's conference, and became interested in the discussions on equity and diversity in classical music. She was curious as to what was going on in our field. The president of the board of the Amherst Early Music Festival, Richard Pace and I also spoke—all this came at the same time and at the right time, September of 2019. Karin and I decided to send out a survey to canvass the membership of EMA, we analyzed those surveys, and we were able to convince the board in January of 2020 that we needed to have some kind of formal committee. I was asked to be chair, and to also think of people who might be a good fit for that committee, active in the field, and representing as diverse a group as possible. Not just People of Color, but a broader range of people. And then of course things were compromised by the pandemic, and then by the Black Lives Matter movement. And we, by June, had not really been able to meet in person. I don't think we've ever met in person, and all this compromised our plans. So where are we now? We've been able to discuss the need to develop a common language with which to communicate, and that was very important to us, because no matter who you get together, everyone has to feel comfortable, everyone has to be transparent, and everyone has to be respectful, I call it respect and responsibility. A responsibility to make sure that everyone knows how you feel, so that they can understand how to approach you as an individual. We had monthly meetings with anyone who was a member who wanted to join us, to talk about those sensitive issues, how to bring transparency into the discussion, and how to engage and come across as genuine rather than patronizing. So that's where we are today, and we're ready to move forward, hopefully this fall.

CHRISTINA: Thank you, that's fascinating. And my following question potentially leads on from that, the question is whether there is a particular project or aspect of the work of the taskforce on diversity that you are most proud of, and if so, whether you could describe it?

PATRICIA: As a member of the board of the Viola da Gamba Society of America (VDGSA), our approach was more proactive, and what we decided was based on the major activity of the Society—the annual conclave. The definition of conclave means getting together. The VDGSA has always been a very welcoming community where you get together for a week and play consorts coached by distinguished faculty, you talk about the repertoire, and you discover new things from scholars who attend. It is a place where both professionals and amateur players can share ideas, research work and transcriptions of music from the original manuscripts. The Conclave serves everyone: professionals, amateurs, teachers, and scholars. And the society, in my mind, has been a model for equity and diversity throughout its 50+ years. Anyone in the US who enjoys the viola da gamba has most likely attended the Conclave. When I started attending, there was one other African American there, and I knew that I was going to be able to feel comfortable in this environment. The board presently has four members of color on it and is a very different board than my first term on the board in the 80s. At that time I was the only Person of Color. So this was a situation where we had already started our diversity work, and we were managing it. What could we do to increase the number of emerging artists and youth studying music in middle school and high school? At this past summer's conclave we decided to hold a teen beginners' class for free, because we had the instruments, and the technical resources to hold the classes on Zoom at this virtual conclave. We enrolled 20 teens from all different backgrounds. I brought 6 teens in from New York City who are in a choir at a church in NYC where my ensemble, Abendmusik, performs. We had about 11 teens from Washington DC, and several from the West Coast as well as several students from British Columbia. It was an incredible example of what you can do with outreach. And believe it or not, even parents decided to attend. Two of the parents from New York City took the adult beginners' class. This was all free and we did it at a time, if teens were working during the day, that they could then attend these classes early in the evening. And now, because we're getting back positive feedback, we're thinking of extending this program to these regional areas during the year. The great thing about the Viola da Gamba Society is there are regional chapters, and therefore the possibility exists to have more contact with communities in that region that may be marginalized or may not know about the work that we do, and partnerships and relationships are developing. And with EMA, we started talking about reaching out to historically Black colleges and their music programs. The music programs at these colleges for the most part appear to concentrate on the business of music, choral music and organ studies. There is not much study of music before the 19th century at some of the institutions. There has been an initial reach out to that community as well, and I hope to be able to continue that.

CHRISTINA: We've talked about your achievements and my next question is about some of the challenges. What would you say have been the main challenges in doing this work, and to what extent are these challenges specific to working in early music as opposed to the classical music field more widely?

PATRICIA: I think my biggest challenge is convincing other People of Color in early music that this is a positive and genuine initiative, a genuine project. There's a lot of hurt, and there's a lot of anger within my own ethnic group because we're talking about hundreds of years of discrimination toward African-Americans. I continue to analyze why we are back where we are by studying the history of the Civil Rights movement of the 60s, where more People of Color were playing classical music, and how it eventually failed. When we reach a goal we think "Okay, we did it." And then something happens and the project or an initiative fails to thrive. And I think part of that is the fact that the work is very difficult, and no one wants to have the onus of being at the helm because of the criticism. I've been criticized greatly by my own colleagues of color because they don't think that there is a possibility for change and that my approach is benign instead of radical. Well, I understand that, but what is the alternative, I always say. Show me some examples, give me an idea of how you think we should approach the issue to start making changes. And I think we're at that point where we have to work toward a positive outcome, rather than continue accusations. But someone has to take the helm to say "Okay, we all understand about White privilege and White fragility, we now need to act on it, and start to work together for a solution. And understand that we will never reach the goal as racism, just like the COVID virus, can mutate into other forms, but we can keep on top of equity and diversity by managing its care.

CHRISTINA: And leading on from what you just said, these very important issues about, exactly, acknowledging White privilege, White fragility, taking it seriously and putting that at the heart of our work, my next question would be: if you could change one thing about the classical music or the early music world, what would it be?

PATRICIA: Well, for the early music world, it's a small field, and basically you need to network. What I would like to see are auditions, and particularly screened auditions as is customary with classical orchestras. You don't know who you're listening to, but you are listening to what the candidate has to offer musically. If there is no plan to make the playing field equal, then our attempt to address the lack of diversity becomes a study in quotas. But does that really solve the dilemma if a Person of Color has to wonder if they've been contracted because of their musicianship or because of their color.

CHRISTINA: And do you think that diversifying classical music and early music means that the music itself needs to change at all?

PATRICIA: Well, yes. Historically early music is looking back, looking back at history. History is shaped by what scholars want us to hear. And in some cases, some of that history of People of Color has not been explored or, if it has been explored, it hasn't been followed up. For instance, in the Renaissance period, we now know that there were Black musicians, and many were wind players serving a nobleman or serving the Crown. We know that Henry VIII's trumpeter John Blanke was believed to be a Muslim. My interest right now is exploring Alessandro de Medici. He is believed to have been bi-racial, his mother being a servant in the household of the Medicis, and I want to find out if he was an arts patron, and what composers and visual artists he may have supported, so that you get a clearer picture of the contribution of People of Color in all facets of the arts. In the classical music field, we've been doing that. Even Le Chevalier de Saint-George is a crossover between early music and mainstream classical music, but we've discovered other people. George Augustus Polgreen Bridgetower, Florence Price, Frederick Douglass's grandson, Joseph Henry Douglass, was a classical violinist. So it's a lot easier to track the 19th century and beyond, but there is information that may have been buried that we can unearth, and if scholarship can actually focus on that we'll be increasing our knowledge of what happened before the 19th century regarding People of Color.

CHRISTINA: Coming back to the more recent past, because you mentioned that earlier, and because musicians have been so affected by the pandemic, my next question is about the pandemic. Could you talk about how COVID-19 has affected your work and these challenges? You mentioned that briefly earlier, you might also like to talk about Black Lives Matter because you mentioned that as well.

PATRICIA: Yes. The pandemic changed everyone's outlook in terms of music. Here in the United States, the idea of being threatened was very high; this was before Black Lives Matter. Those of us who are freelance musicians, and make our living teaching, were completely caught by surprise by this. And so for several months, the only thing that we could do was wonder what was going to happen in the future—How are we going to make a living? How are we going to be able to sustain ourselves?—as schools shut down for a while, as all concerts were eventually canceled. We didn't know just how long this was going to last, and we still really don't know how this is going to progress. But what we have done, is witness social Darwinism: it's survival of the fittest, it's how can you make what you have work? And so we've all become great technicians in being able to continue our work. And for me as a professional—I have a string ensemble—we gave virtual performances, which were videotaped and put up on YouTube. You can take that medium and you can use it in other ways. And I suggested that these videos should become part of a library at EMA as part of the Task Force, to be utilized by anyone. We are expanding outreach and growing audiences now throughout the entire country and beyond, not just the small local areas. So our committee led by example, and I began to ask other members of the Task Force to send in their videotapes—countertenor Reggie Mobley sent a tape of his recording session out on the West Coast, harpsichordist Joyce Chen offered a video, and I offered one as well. What I hope to accomplish is building a library of performances that include People of Color performing on early instruments and singing the repertoire with the utmost attention to performance practice. In terms of Black Lives Matter, that is a much more global concern. And although we have our own problems within the small field there are people, as I mentioned before, who are making it known in a very vocal way on social media that they are angry about the way we're generally treated. I guess what I want to say is it's a global issue for which I don't have to express anything more. It has taken on a journey of its own, but . . . it has made me feel more connected to my field than I have in the past, because when I was the lone voice, I didn't have a voice. Now there is a status quo, and people have to be cognizant of how sensitive this whole issue is, and they're paying more attention to what we have to say. So for me, I feel as if I am finally being heard as a musician, scholar, as well as a speaker and an advocate for change to a more equitable environment.

CHRISTINA: Thank you. And what you mentioned at the end, that's really interesting, that you said you feel that you are being heard musically, as well as a scholar, as well as a speaker, as well as an advocate for change. Do you think there's a connection between your musical voice, your voice as an activist, [and] your voice as a professional, and if so, how would you describe that?

PATRICIA: Well, I went to a college that was originally all female, Vassar College. It is an institution that has, throughout its history, been known for encouraging women to have a prominent and public voice. Vassar has been successful in increasing the population of outspoken women in politics, in entertainment, in academia, and so forth. I come out of that legacy. I did not think that my professional aspirations would encounter so many pitfalls, and when I said I wanted to explore early music, that was because I was encouraged by my professors to do it. And two of the professors were very well known musicologists, Edward Reilly, who translated the treatise on Quantz, and Janet Knapp, who was a medieval music scholar. When I graduated I knew that historical performance would be my calling. I entered a graduate program in historical performance at Sarah Lawrence College in New York, one of three such programs in the country at that time. The road to becoming a professional was rough for me and the pitfalls started to arise. I wasn't seen as a professional; there were always excuses that didn't make sense to me. So, I had to work this out, because I knew that I had the talent, and when you know that you have it, it's almost as if someone robbed you of part of your life that you've already lived, or that you had already envisioned. And again, survival of the fittest, social Darwinism—I just said I'm going to continue to do it, no matter what. And there have been times when it's been very scary, but I always knew that I would come out of it in some way on top, that I would not fail, because I know who I am as a musician, and I just needed to communicate that, and people needed to be receptive to that.

CHRISTINA: Finally, what message or advice would you give to activists and musicians who want to make change in classical and/or early music?

PATRICIA: For one, I think that we all know how sensitive the issue is, we all know how people are beginning to feel. I think the first thing to do is to make sure that you are an impeccable musician, that you know your field, that you know your music, that you know your scholarship. And if you are confronted by someone who doubts what you do, hold back, count to ten, and then I think the delivery of your answer is going to be much more powerful than the alternative, which may be a defensive remark. Right now, we're at the point, as I said before, where people are continuing to be defensive, and there was place for that but now they may be pushing people away. If you want to be part of the club, then you have to work the system and that means using your voice and communicating and collaborating. And I think that once we can all be on the same page, then I think we'll all be able to move forward.

CHRISTINA: That's a great note to end the interview on, but I do want to ask you whether there's anything else that you'd like to add that you think is important to touch on?

PATRICIA: I think it's incredible, in the past 15 months, that there has been global attention to social justice and equity. The Black Lives Matter movement came by way of public violence and oppression, revealing a major flaw in the concept of US democracy. The past four years politically have been very difficult for us all, and I think we all feel as Americans that we have lost our status as a functioning democratic society. What I am encouraged to think now is that other European arts organizations, by reaching out to us, have opened the doors through dialogue between global entities, and hopefully we are doing our due diligence to present a comprehensive look at our respective histories when it comes to People of Color. In the past

(1940s and 1950s) many People of Color in the arts became expatriates, and moved to Europe; James Baldwin, Paul Robeson, and Josephine Baker, among others. In the 60s, the movement was centered here in the US. I am cautiously optimistic that the work we're doing now in the 21st century is going to be sustainable. We're all firmly committed to researching the history and contributions of People of Color in Europe and the Americas and the longer we continue our work, the more we're going to be able to work together to make this a much more equitable environment.

18
On Leaving Classical Music
An Interview with Anthony Gray

Anthony Gray

ANNA: Could you start off by telling me how you got into classical music in the first place?

ANTHONY: It was just luck, really. I grew up with quite a religious family, both my parents are from the West Indies, so I grew up as a good Catholic boy. I went to the London Oratory, which is linked to a church, the Brompton Oratory. I always liked singing, and I was pretty good at singing. I was in my local church choir and I just auditioned for the London Oratory Choir and jumped into their cathedral choir. I sang most days either in the school chapel or the Brompton Oratory and was really well supported by my music teachers all the way through school. When it came to A-Levels, my teachers sat me and my parents down and they said something like, "Look, Anthony's got a really good chance of going to university to read music." I think that helped, you know, my teacher talking to my parents helped them understand that it was a valid career path. So I went to [a music conservatoire in London]. I remember my first week. All the new students from all disciplines, had to go to this amazing church as part of our induction. All the tutors and professors were wearing gowns. And I remember this Black girl came up to me. You've gotta remember, I'm a London boy through and through, and at school my Blackness was never a thing. In fact, the only thing that made young boys different was whether they were from north, south, east, or west London. But when I got to the conservatoire that all changed. This Black girl came up to me, Chenna, she was two or three years above me, and she was like, "Don't worry, I'm going to look after you." And I just remember being like, what'd you mean? First of all, who are you? And what'd you mean, you're going to look after me? Across those first few weeks I understood what she meant because, you know, I came from quite a posh school, really, but there was such a mad mix of people, we were like the United Colours of Benetton. When I went to [music conservatoire] and I looked around, I was one of three Black people in the whole of the four years. So, suddenly, my Blackness was a thing, straight away. That really weirded me out. That was the first moment when I thought, "Oh, I'm *other* in this world." I'd never really had that before. So that was how I got into classical music.

ANNA: Can you tell me a bit about your experiences as a Black person studying and working in classical music in the UK?

ANTHONY: Yeah. It was difficult because there was always a reaction, no matter what room you walked into. I was always the surprise. And at first I was like, this is quite cool, actually. With my name being Anthony Gray—like most typical West Indian names, they're quite Anglicized—so I know they would have had a name on their sheet and then, you know, if I walked into an audition, you would see a reaction. It would be an eyebrow raised or it would be really minute, but it's a reaction you're taught to look out for. It's been something that happens for your entire life. You walk into a shop, you see a slight reaction, so you know that you have to be careful in that situation. It's those small, small microaggressions that you just become really aware of, and you have to see them because you have to protect yourself at all times. A microaggression is often a precursor to something less "micro." So at first, it felt great. It felt like I was different and therefore I was maybe getting more opportunities. But actually, after a while it just felt quite heavy to always walk into an audition, to see the look and know that a judgment has already been passed, whether they know it or not. And there's nothing you can do about it. So you're almost two steps below the last person who is in and the person after you in that audition, even before you open your mouth to sing. And as a singer, it's a really difficult instrument, because if you have any emotion which you can't control that's heard in your voice straight away. Don't get me wrong, I had some amazing times. I've got one or two very close friends from those days. I got by. I did enough gigging around to, to make a bit of an earning for it. But to be honest, I didn't feel comfortable going out [socially] with people from [the conservatoire]. The only people I met were of a very specific background. It was very rare to meet anyone from my background—someone who was working-class or Black or a Person of Color. The support network and the building of relationships and friendships in the classical music world was something that I never quite got used to. And that's a massive part of that world. You have to be networked. You have to be connected with lots of different people. I got on with loads of people, but at the end of the day, I was always the other, that's how I felt. One moment [when "race" became really apparent to me] was at music college when we did a musical called *Cabaret*. I was given the role of a Nazi officer. It's a bit embarrassing, it's a bit odd—I still couldn't tell you why I just went ahead and did it. I guess I felt I just had to and it was my job. But I felt extremely uncomfortable, and I didn't know who to talk to. So I did something that I regret now, because I was young back then. I just did what I felt I had to do, I walked on in a Nazi uniform and did the best German accent I possibly could.

ANNA: Could you say a bit more about that? How would you have wanted your tutors at music college to deal with this? Sorry to make you do the work here to explain this.

ANTHONY: I think a conversation, first and foremost, should have been had to try and make me understand why that decision had been made. It could have been that they wanted to subvert it and be like "Oh, wouldn't it be really edgy if we had a Black person being a Nazi and being in that position of power?" And then, if that was an issue, to then support me. I guess that conversation would have then opened up a myriad of different choices that could have been made. But because I was just given that role without any explanation. It was almost like a power play, I felt. To be like, well, we can make you do what we want, essentially. Like, we will make you play a Nazi.

ANNA: So to summarize, it's problematic that they're trying to be color-blind, because it's impossible. And then it's uncomfortable because they're putting you in a position of power when you were actually in a position of powerlessness.

ANTHONY: Yeah, totally. And I think what you're saying there is really important and lies at the crux of the problem within the classical music sector. Any example of racism I give, will essentially always be that the institution, that the system in the classical music world, is the be-all and end-all. That is what you're taught from the very beginning, and I think that's why it will always be a problem. Because the system of classical music, be that the form, be that who leads—a conductor or a director, be that the hierarchy in an orchestra or a choir, will always be there. Therefore, you're always shown that the system is more powerful than the individual. And God help you if there is an individual who then is at the head of this system who thinks in any kind of [prejudiced] way. So, if we're talking about stories where [my Blackness] became quite obvious, there was one moment. It was honestly the scariest moment in my ... I thought I was going to get kicked out of college. I got this amazing opportunity, well, what I thought was an amazing opportunity to go to a festival abroad, an amazing classical music festival. Myself and my friend were asked to go and lead some workshops, and also do some singing there. We must have been in our third year [of our studies]. But we slowly began to understand that we weren't being paid, and we had to pay to fly over and the flights were really expensive. I think they were giving us house and food. Both my friend and I were like, we can't afford to do that. If we're going away for two weeks, there's probably a couple of gigs we're going be missing out on so we're doubly losing out.

My friend got told off, I think he got sent an email saying oh, we're disappointed you can't do this. But I got called into [the principal's] office and was told that I had embarrassed him, embarrassed the conservatoire. Even my friend, who is white, was not sure why he didn't get called. I was really, really upset and he was looking after me, as I thought I was going to let down my parents, I was going to get kicked out of college. And, I felt really embarrassed 'cause I genuinely couldn't afford to pay for a flight. If I could, I would have. But I got made to feel so small. Because, you know, there was no way I was going to ask my parents, one who was on a building site and another who was a nurse. So that was kind of the first moment really when I just felt that it wasn't for me. I still had another year, so I just kind of put my head down, got on with it and finished music college as quickly as I could. But then I guess where really it started going a bit pear-shaped was when I went and worked at [an opera company] and then at [a major arts institutions] afterward. I first worked in the learning and development department at [the opera house]. I just felt I had to stop singing. I had fallen out of love with it. I was meeting the same people day in, day out. I didn't feel that I had any connection with anybody. I literally had no one around me who looked anything like me. So very slowly but surely, I just pulled out more and more because I knew that world just wasn't for me. I still was really into classical music, I still loved it as a medium and . . . I guess I wanted to give other people the chance that I felt that I had had. So I worked for the education department to bring people whose voices weren't being heard, to bring them into this sector that they didn't think they belonged to. It was extremely difficult because, again, with the system, you were trying to bring in people who were very skeptical of classical music as a form. They just didn't feel it was for them. And you were bringing them into a space where it had the most talented people in the sector, and of course, when you looked across that there was not much of a breakdown [of People of Color]. I stayed there for eight years. One moment [that stands out to me] happened after I launched something called the Youth Opera Company with my manager. It was really dear to my heart. We worked with young children in Kent and all over London. Every Saturday, you would come to [London] and we would, you know, put them with different opera directors and these kids would learn how to, to look after their voices and sing. We eventually got them to a place where they started singing in some of the productions on the [opera company] stage. There was an old production, *La Bohème*, Puccini—the company don't do this particular production anymore—but this production was with a really famous opera director. In this production [there is] a boy-solo. He comes center stage and belts it out to the audience and it's a massive opportunity. We had to decide who the two soloists were, your main soloist, and a cover. And our main soloist was a stunning singer. White, sandy brown-blond hair, blue eyes, you know, the type of boy you will always see in this kind of role. Our second choice was a Black boy, he was Ghanaian and had a brilliant voice as well. On the first day, we brought both the boys down, and my manager called me over. She was in a really tough discussion with the director. It goes back to that, you know, the system and the hierarchy. So obviously, I was nervous to be in front of this director. He was saying he wasn't happy with the soloists. So we asked him why, and he said I am not happy with your cover person because he's Black and the character, is a really spoilt, rich child, and an audience member will not see that Black boy as a rich, spoilt child. They'll see him as someone who is poor, so I don't want him to be the cover. This is even though the boy would be in a top hat and tails, all the rest of the kids are in rags—it couldn't be more obvious. I guess he was an old director, so I was disappointed, but I wasn't surprised by his reaction. It was the reaction of my manager and of [the] chorus master and other colleagues that annoyed me. They allowed it to happen. They turned to me and they were like, oh, sorry, Anthony, obviously he's old and that's just the way he thinks. And I guess it wasn't good enough for me because those people were my age. For me, if you stay silent or you support a decision like that, then, then you're in that lane. To me, there's no Black and white in that kind of situation. Silence is complicity. So I think that was the moment when I realized, I'm not sure this place is for me anymore, because I wasn't backed by my own manager.

Another moment that stands out was at a different classical music institution, where I was also working for the education department. It's very security-heavy, so you had to have a pass with you at all times. I'm quite an easy-going person and especially with security guards and people like that, I almost feel more affinity with those types of people than the people who were working in the buildings themselves.

So I knew all the security guards. And I remember one day, I went in with my colleague, a really good friend of mine, who is white, and we both clicked through the security pass. We were carrying instruments. We went into the instrument room and this guy roared into the room, he literally stormed into the room and demanded to know who I was and and what was I doing in that room? And, he was talking to me. It was straight at me. It wasn't to my colleague, it wasn't to the security people. He demanded to see my security badge. There was no apology. He just said, we have to be careful, these instruments are really expensive, and things could be stolen. I was definitely someone who had put my foot down at those kind of things, but again, the system kicked in and I knew it wasn't my place to say anything in that moment and I was also really shaken 'cause I hadn't had that happen to me in a really long time, to be accused of something. I went to my boss. I explained what happened. And I broke down. I got really, really upset and I was there crying in his office. All I could say was, you're asking me to bring people who look like me into our spaces. What if that had been someone I had brought in? What if that was a participant on one of our projects who was just helping me out and carrying an instrument in and didn't have a pass? I thought something would be done. I thought that there would be some type of . . . I didn't want retribution, I didn't want revenge. But I just thought that he would be pulled up on it and there would be something that would come as a result of his behavior. I was told, I'll talk to his boss but don't worry about it, we'll look after it. And that was the last I heard of it. Those two incidents in very different buildings, that's essentially what the classical music world is like for me. It's about making sure that the system isn't rocked, that the hierarchy isn't challenged, and that you just fit. If you can fit, then it works. But if you can't, then it's not even like you can make change. It's just not for you.

ANNA: What would you say to people who want to make change in the classical music world?

ANTHONY: In all honesty, I know there are amazing people who are trying to do brilliant things, but I would be very surprised if I were still alive and I saw a monumental shift in the classical music world. I think it's years behind the theater world, and the theater world's not great. I guess, at the end of the day, the classical music audience is a dying audience. And at some point the classical music sector will need to try and reinvent itself. Part of me hopes that it gets a real wake-up call and things really, really have to change. But I'm not sure it will, because the power still lies in the 1%, and that's where a lot of the money is, so I'm not sure there is much of a need to change.

ANNA: Since you've now moved into working in theater, could you reflect a bit on the differences between classical music and theater? In particular, what classical music can learn from theater in terms of becoming more inclusive?

ANTHONY: That's the million-dollar question, really. I think it comes down to communication. And I think there's a communication issue in the classical music world, and again, it comes down to structure and hierarchy and systems. The form is built on that, and so you're forever beholden to that system. Whereas theater, it just revolts all the time. There's always some type of revolution, there's always someone who is pissed off enough to demand change and to be an activist about it. There's a lack of activism in the classical music world. I think that's maybe something that needs to change. There needs to be a hunger and a want for open dialogue and open communication. There's been a step toward that with some of the drama schools [in the UK], openly talking about the institutional racism that has occurred in their buildings and owning that and opening those conversations. I think the lack of those same statements in many music conservatoires across the country speaks volumes. And no one's called them out. The moment a [drama school] didn't do it, there would be a whole load of students demanding, why aren't you saying anything? They literally scared colleges into doing it. So drama schools were scared enough to have to put out some type of statement, and now they're being held to those statements. That didn't happen with any of the conservatoires that I can think of. Then there's always this blame game as well, so the [opera company I worked for] always did this thing where they said, there aren't any Black singers on our stage because we're not getting any Black singers from the conservatoires. But then the conservatoires would turn around and say, well, there aren't any Black singers who are interested, 'cause they don't see themselves on the stage. So no one wants to talk, they just want to shift the blame. What can they learn from theater? It's about having those conversations, being held accountable. There needs to be change from up top as well. There are huge institutions in the theater world where directors only have terms of four or five years and then they have to move on. You don't get that in the music world. You'll have Tony Pappano at the Opera House and he will be there for the rest of his life. And it means there's no movement, there's nothing fresh that comes in and everything that is done to diversify the classical music world, is just a fad. It's a stale environment and people are very happy to be there forever and be very protected. I knew this would come up and I wanted it to be a call to change, but I'm not hopeful, to be honest. I don't think things will change because I don't think there's a need to change it.

ANNA: One of the things I want to explore is whether you think the music itself needs to change, as part of this change?

ANTHONY: I think it needs to be changed in terms of how it's taught in some way. I still listen to classical music every day. I still love classical music. There's nothing about classical music, as in the product, as in, you know, what you listen to at the end of the day. There's nothing that needs to be changed about that. It's the most, it's just the most amazing music, I think, still to this day. It can be taught in such different ways, but there's a canon that [dictates] it will always be this way: this is how classical music is taught. A perfect example is that in the Youth Opera Company, we made sure that anyone who came in didn't need to read music. They were seven, eight years old and they would come in from all walks of life. Some of them read music and some of them didn't, but it wasn't a prerequisite. Since I've left . . . there's been a few changes and you have to read music to join. And that might seem like a really small thing, but honestly, that would probably have taken out three quarters of the people who we brought on in that first iteration of that company. And that's not fair; you've just ousted a whole load of people because they haven't gone to a really well-known school where they have the resources and the money to teach someone how to read music. Or their parents don't have the extra money from working second jobs, to bring in a piano teacher, which is what my parents did. But there's loads of people who are already working two jobs 'cause they wanna put food on someone's plate, and those people will never have the chance to do that. So the music doesn't need to change. It's the teaching and the accessibility and the reasons why you make those decisions [that] need to change.

ANNA: Okay, it's just that you were talking about the hierarchies within the music world. And those are embedded in the musical works as well.

ANTHONY: Yeah. I have never thought that. You're absolutely right. Even when you split that down in terms of being a singer: Was I a Baroque singer, was I an opera singer, was I a church singer, or a choral singer? There's so much hierarchy even in that. That's been something that's different in the theater world. Don't get me wrong, there's load in theater that's still wrong, but they are way, way further down the line than classical music will ever be, I think.

ANNA: I wanted to ask you to reflect on the intersection of being working-class as well as being Black. Do you think things would have been different for you if you were middle-class and Black, or if you were white and working-class?

ANTHONY: One of my really close mates, he passed away a few years ago, but, he was proper working-class, a white lad from Manchester, Mark. And he looked after me more than anyone in that college. And I remember he just knew, "You and me, we're different." I just feel that I might have had a few more opportunities to at least, make a fist of it if I wasn't a Black man. So being working-class and Black was difficult but I think it was the color of my skin that was difficult.

ANNA: That's really interesting 'cause it's hard to pull the two apart sometimes.

ANTHONY: Yeah. And it's really important that those things are said in the same breath, because when people [in the UK] say working-class, they automatically think, a white Northerner. It's the stereotype.

ANNA: Looking back, if you had your time again, would you have made different choices rather than going to conservatoire and working in classical music?

ANTHONY: Yeah, absolutely. I'd have gone and studied English or something. I'd have gone to a normal uni. It's that thing of everyone thinking we're all in the same race, and I'm like, yeah, but there are two different start guns. The start gun goes off for all these people, and then I have to just wait and wait and wait and then the start gun goes. So I'm never going to win that race. And it's not that I want to win it, I just want to be in the same foot race. So that's what it feels like.

same race as Te... rest you picked the race two different ways... short gun event... until the people underhand level the standard... shoot and then there is a gun goes. So I am over going to win the race. We... that I want to come in first. I am not even the same. How much do I need to race...

V
ACTIVISM
Starting with the Self

19
(Dis)orient Yourself!

Disrupting White Ontologies in Classical Music

Eleanor Ryan

My flight from London touches down in Trinidad in the Southern Caribbean, the first of many arrivals I will experience in the decade that follows. Standing in the immigration queue, violin on my back, I look around me and am suddenly hyperconscious of my whiteness.

"Ah, you play the violin?" somebody observes. "That's white people music, eh"?

The classical violinist as an embodiment of whiteness? I am immediately on the defensive:

"No! I mean, I trained as a classical player, but I'm really a musician in a global sense, and classical music isn't only by and for white people! I don't discriminate. It's a universal language!"

Doubt creeps into my mind. I quickly swat it away.

Yet there is something disorienting about my arrival here. I feel my whiteness ambushing me. It performs with both subtle and strident affect. My body fidgets and sighs. It casts impatient glances. And this whiteness expresses a natural expectation of motility, tilting forward slightly, walking that bit faster, queue-hopping, claiming importance (Ahmed, 2007).

"I bet our luggage won't be searched," a white colleague says: "After all, we have the 'white passport'... Gosh, why are these people so slow?"

A sense of shame spreads upward, through my belly, arriving hotly in my face.

I am immorally, stiffly, pinkly, prudishly white (James, 2015).

I observe my whiteness imposing itself upon Trinidad. It extends far beyond me, so that my usually unobtrusive body seems to be writ large and knocks against my surroundings.

Some of my white companions seem to enjoy this impact. Their energy thrusts outward, chests lifted, shoulders squared. I hear their voices louder here, expressing a distain I had never noticed before. They stride purposefully. Our instrument cases are directed forward with a phallic-missile intention, eager to occupy space, a new world to conquer, as if nothing was here before but a cultural void.

(Brathwaite, 2002; Yancy, 2012b)

The violinist meets her white self

In 2009 I relocated from the UK to Trinidad and Tobago at the invitation of the Trinidadian government, ultimately working in the region for nearly a decade. I moved as part of a group of white conservatoire-trained professional orchestral musicians from the UK and USA. We were recruited to establish a professional orchestra and higher music education performance program. This was not the first international move of my musical career. A white New Zealander of Irish-Dutch-British heritage, I had established myself as a professional violinist in the UK by following a well-trodden route into the profession for music students from settler-colonial nations, by entering postgraduate study at a British conservatoire, followed by successful auditions into the British classical music industry. It was through personal relationships within these industry networks that I found myself a member of this hand-selected group of musicians arriving in the Caribbean. The main aim of our recruitment to Trinidad was to utilize our world-class credentials as performers to support Trinidadian musicians to reach similar levels of skill, knowledge, and global recognition.

At the time, the Trinidadian government's recruitment of a sizeable group of white, foreign musicians seemed an entirely reasonable investment, commensurate with a government policy of development, globalization, and economic diversification. That classical music training seemed to be co-constitutive with and symbolic of economic and cultural development was an implicit assumption that, at first, I did not question. After all, my love for this art form had oriented the trajectory of my life from one side of the globe to the other, from the new world to the cultural metropole of the old, and back out to the new again. I saw my classical musicianship as an embodied global cultural passport and was blind to the power implications of this. My belief in the transcendent qualities of classical music—its power to connect communities through performances that I felt expressed emotional truth, emancipated from politics, class, "race," or gender—had been a constellation by which to navigate the intense challenges of my performance training. Furthermore, I subscribed without critique to the dogma that "Western" music theory, instrumental techniques, aesthetic sensibilities, and bodily discipline were a foundational education for all musicians, independent from geographical location or musical genre. That my teaching might offer Trinidadian students' equity of access to pedagogical knowledge that I had had to travel to the UK to fully develop, seemed a compelling and socially just reason to join this expedition.

The (dis)orientation of musical subjectivity

My move to Trinidad was the beginning of a disorientation of the structuring ideas that underpinned the temerity of my musical subjectivity. This relocation revealed what I have since come to recognize as white ontologies (ways of being). I will argue that these ontologies had become naturalized as part of my subjectification and furthermore, as forms of orientation, were acting to position me and give me agency in the world. When thinking with the concept of subjectivity I draw on a definition informed by Foucault and expanded by Butler. These philosophers argue that subjectivity is formed "in relation to a set of codes, prescriptions, or norms" (Butler, 2005, p. 17), the effects of discourse, but also acts of self-making and delimiting (limits placed on the self) that "take place within the context of a set of norms that precede and exceed the subject" (Butler, 2005, p. 19). In other words, my musical subjectivity had been formed through the acquisition of standardized practices over time, infused with specific values and ideas, inherited from the past and maintained by myself and the wider institution in the present and into the future.

Subjectification takes place within a historical scheme or inheritance that appears to have natural and normalized boundaries. This is a key consideration when thinking about classical music as a racialized space. It emphasizes the depth of the challenge of critiquing the whiteness of the institution because of the ways in which whiteness informs performance aesthetics as a historical inheritance. Subject formation emerges from both external forces (imposed via teachers and institutions) and internally as a form of self-making. My classical music practice came into view in Trinidad, not just as something that I did innocently as a profession, but as practice that acted politically to reinforce the positioning of whiteness as a hegemonic and oppressive force in the world, carried as a performance by my musician body.

The *dis*orientation I experienced was a confusing set of revelations and denials, where the glimpses I caught or sensations I felt of an occluded colonial violence embedded in my practice, were initially ignored, or avoided because my subjectivity and way of being felt threatened. These moments emerged *affectively* as bodily sensations of discomfort, confusion, ambivalence, disjointed, and defensiveness. They appeared in response to a dawning realization of the whiteness and Eurocentricity of my *epistemological* grounding (the scope and validity of my knowledge) and a comprehension of the limits this placed on my flexibility and creative imagination as a musician. And my disorientation presented *discursively*, as our insistence on the importance of classical music as the foundation of music education began to emerge as a white supremacist and neocolonial doctrine against the backdrop of Trinidad's musical ecology.

The rich landscape of locally developed musical practices in Trinidad, which include calypso, soca, rapso and steelpan, originate and continue to evolve through and in relation to the yearly Carnival (Dudley, 2007; Elder, 2004; Guilbault, 2007; Lovelace, 1998). As Trinidadian novelist Earl Lovelace has pointed out "the much-vaunted cultural creativity expressed in Trinidad and

Tobago has come principally from the ordinary African-descended people at the bottom of the economic ladder" (Lovelace, 1998, p. 56). This Black diasporic community arrived in the Caribbean via European colonialism and plantation slavery and was later diversified post-emancipation via the arrival of East Indian indentured laborers and waves of immigration from China, Syria, and the South American mainland. Carnival musical praxis is often described as a performative expression of defiance against coloniality through a spirit of resistance and rebellion (Guilbault, 2004; Lovelace, 1998; Rohlehr, 2001). This spirit of resistance is predicated on a continuously reinvented performative creativity, where non-European cultural practices, under continuous threat from (neo)colonial disapprobation, find creative ways to adapt and survive. As Lovelace explains:

> European colonialism was not motivated to create anything since its very rule and mystique rested upon the enlightenment it was introducing to these islands. Its laws, parliament, literature, music, even its brutality: all of it was brought in from the centers of its civilization. Its civilizing mission established a minority that for the purposes of its own advancement and privilege doomed itself to imitation. . . . The remainder, unexposed to the formal colonising education, were forced to draw on their own resources of memory, myth, genius, and the consciousness of their circumstances to construct, from the fragments of their broken culture, a new culture by which to live. (Lovelace, 1998, p. 56)

Trinidad is therefore a location where creative aesthetics are recognized as political, and the aesthetic is utilized as a performative, decolonializing act of resistance. Against this backdrop I could, for the first time, perceive white supremacy within my classical musical practice, appearing in stark relief against the performative defiance of Carnival music.

The epistemic violence of the white and male-dominated curriculum of classical music, and the whiteness of the social sphere of classical music has been well-documented, critiqued, and reported in recent years (Bull, 2019; Ewell, 2021; Gellerstein, 2021; Hess, 2018; Lewis and Wassermann, 2020; Scharff, 2017; Vaugeois, 2014). Epistemic violence is a recognition that knowledge can be utilized and experienced as a form of violence in a (post)colonial setting, through the positioning of certain knowledges (in this case the creative work of white men) as more important, valuable, and worthy of study than the knowledges and voices of others (Spivak, 1988). But beyond a recognition of dominant white knowledges within the institution of classical music, my practice in Trinidad seemed to reveal whiteness and coloniality as an ontology that has been normalized. While it makes sense to tackle the whiteness of an institution by addressing equity of representation (*Music Mark EDI Report April 2021*, n.d.; Griffiths, 2019), this chapter questions to what extent representation alone dismantles the modes by which white supremacy moves through classical music as a form of ontological inheritance. In other words, what sort of subjectivities are we being taught to perform and maintain, and how do these intersect with processes of racialization? How do beliefs and discourse around classical music as a superior and universal art form become performed as *affective* phenomena, shaping and controlling bodily performance, motility, and agency within musical institutions? If whiteness has historically orientated classical music, how might we *dis*orientate, flip, and disrupt whiteness, *re*orientating practice in ways that enable an antiracist openness toward the multiplicity of humanity (Diawara, 2011), to differences in bodies, and in aesthetics? Ultimately, how might we practice a richer creative imaginary in musical practices, as a source of unfolding relation with the world (Diawara, 2011)?

The evidence underpinning the arguments I make in this chapter emerged out of a critical autoethnographic project (Ryan, 2020), which interrogated how whiteness functioned within my experiences of working in Trinidad. This study drew on memories of my time there as *affective* data, which I sensed related to racialization and colonialism, but which I struggled to analyze or name at the time. Critical autoethnography is a research methodology in which a researcher develops critical and reflexive accounts of their life and culture in a relational, collaborative conversation with theory (Ellis et al., 2010; Holman Jones, 2016). To make sense of my experiences in Trinidad I applied critical race theory and decolonial theory as analytical frames through which to interrogate the memory of my experiences.

The violinist's formation in the orchestra of colonial imaginary

Who was this musician who left her professional life behind in the UK and relocated to Trinidad? How had she become the embodiment of the classical musician? How had her practice and her social world shaped her way of being? As I recalled memories of my pre-Trinidad professional life, an image of my arrival in the upper echelons of the British orchestral scene spontaneously emerged as an autoethnographic poem:

> *In the professional orchestra, she is subsumed.*
> *She is the motion shadow of the violinists before her*
> *To trail, with gestures,*
> *to sound the same*
> *"Focus," she whispers to herself*
> *high-strung with conscientiousness,*

paranoid with attention.
The body of string players twitch, wince and shy away from audible errors.
To be a musical alterity,
is to inflict disaster,
too early,
too late
She enfolds herself deep within her body
Tiny extended antennas of hyper-sensitivity stretch, reach, with a fervent, nervous attention
Shoulders ache and sight blurs with intensity
Ears on stalks,
sweeping,
mapping
To carve a sonic space within collective sound
Ecstatic body
In synch
She feels as if nothing matters but this performance,
Which through a mastery of self
Performs an exalted and celebrated humanity
Eyes cling to the music, the canon
As fingers gripping a bare immoveable rock,
To look up, to the maestro
To glance
To God

The daily practice of the orchestra played a large role in the forging of my professional musical subjectivity. *Experiencing of subjectivity* involves an awareness of one's aims, desires, and self-image within a regulatory frame. In my case I desired to belong to what I now call my *orchestra of the colonial imaginary*. I found myself writing the memories of an ambitious violinist, thrilled to symbolically arrive as a musician in the metropole of my white settler-colonial imaginary. My hopes as a young violinist in New Zealand were tied to this imaginary, where belonging to a professional orchestra in the UK appeared as a shining portal to global citizenship via musical mastery. Years of training and struggle led to this arrival, which perhaps increased its value to me, as it represented such a huge investment in the shaping of myself into a body that would be recognizable to the musical institutions of the former empire. My recognition in this social-cultural space increased my perceived value of my musicianship through my identification as a member of the professional orchestra, which had been placed on such a high pedestal by the discourse that surrounds it. I, the orchestra, and the conductor collectively disciplined the practices of my/our body, via often imperceptible gestures, affects, and glances. These regulatory forces required me to shape myself within a white, exclusive, elite, male-dominated and highly policed conception of the musician. I imagined I was performing a bodily transcendence, yet to do so required intense bodily dislocation.

My musical socialization emerges as an uninterrogated *perspective*, which encompassed "I" and the "Other"—myself, the orchestral body, the conductor—and governed my desire to become a body who fits (Butler, 2005). Yet I was blind to this orchestral body's white historical and political inheritances or my own white settler coloniality within it. At no point in my classical music education was the whiteness of our practices named. Instead, they were applauded as universal performances of high moral value fuelled by the "belief that classical music is a pure, autonomous artform" (Bull, 2019, p. 111). The nature of white supremacy is such that it occludes the political power embedded in aesthetic performance and naturalizes as universal a thoroughly European aesthetic philosophy that established a "set of discriminations and distributions by which 'savage' is distinguished from the civil Subject, the partial and particular human from the universal Subject, and the 'pathological' or suffering, needing, desiring human from the ethical human Subject" (Lloyd, 2018, p. 3). Thus, the persona I represent in the orchestra is one that in its discipline, focus, and perfect synchronicity with the orchestra body performs an idea of the civilized human as one who has mastered themselves in their advanced and elite musical development within a white frame. Creative difference or alterity in my performance might have marked me out as unable to be part of this collective body. Yet the wider forces that this was performing—what this was doing in terms of maintaining white supremacy—were opaque to me until I moved to Trinidad and began to realize the extent to which my musicianship was projecting a white supremacist discourse.

The disorientating, disjointing power of the white gaze

I teach a young woman of mixed Trinidadian heritage. We've worked together for several years, since I first arrived on the island.

My student submits herself to me to be crafted. She wills her body toward ways of being that will pass my judgment, which is not just our local institutional judgment, but a judgment that has the weight of decades of European institutional practice pressing onto it. I carry this as a heavy weight. I glance anxiously across the Atlantic, seeking nods of approval for my work. My eyes, my ears, my knowledge, my body oriented always back toward Europe.

I push my student's body toward the west, trade winds at our backs. . . .

> *My student takes on her unruly body as a problem to be solved and I marvel at her courage. She is both a patient with dis-ease and her own nurse, tending daily. I break the motions down again. Her joints disarticulate through the linear logic of my instructions. I hear her sound, which is her unique voice, the voice of a young, Black, Caribbean woman, and it is my ears, and my eyes are ordering them, making her self-conscious, adjusting, fixing, striving. I mould her into me, fold her into me, judging her as I judge myself, as my institution judges me.*
>
> *My student's stance is grounded, almost fused, like a tree with deep roots, rooting in the Trinidadian soil. But she cannot sway freely. She stands as if a statue, frozen, steadfast, going into battle with this canon.*
>
> *Are bodies neutral? A form of "cultural blank slate that belongs nowhere"? (Nooshin, 2011)*
>
> *My white female teaching body presents itself as the universal musician/human site, but whose body is imprinted into me? The somatic gestures of the Western man, reproduced in musical semiotics? (Rose, 2019; Wynter, 2003)*

In Trinidad it was within my one-to-one teaching that the persistence of my white ontology tended to emerge most powerfully, and where I sensed, within my own body and gaze, the power of the institution within which I was formed. In writing autoethnographically a sense of the forceful imprint of white inheritance appeared like a haunting. Derrida's theory of *hauntology* is helpful here, describing a present where "we come to face our past lives and previous historical figures as ghosts, exerting a hauntological influence on the present. We encounter these ghosts of our past in a time 'out of joint,'" (Crockett, 2017, p. 130). I carried within me the embodied haunting gaze of teachers, conductors, juries, all gazing on my Trinidadian student. And this is not a neutral gaze, for in whiteness it carries within it an objectifying *missilic* "destructive ontology" (Yancy, 2012b, p. 84). This is both the memory of a gaze that dehumanizes as it oversees on the plantation, or the gaze that allows the Black body to participate in the white-oriented world but only as an object (James, 2015), reducing the Black body to a "thing among things" (Ahmed, 2006, p. 111).

It is crucial to interrogate the mechanisms by which whiteness maintains its supremacy in classical music if we are ever to disrupt its operation. As a claimed universal we imagine that classical music "transcends" the body, that it is there for anyone to train "into," rather than being "of" the body. Conscientious bodily ordering is part of its daily practice. Yet an aesthetic is an extension of taste. Connected to the senses, it is "of" the body (James, 2009). Dyer has argued that whiteness dislocates white subjectivity from a natural embodiment because to "be contaminated by the corporeal" (Dyer, 1997) is to be associated with reproduction and sexualization (the female body) and "demeaning" physical labor (slavery, working class), both of which have been constructed as less-than-human (Wynter, 2003).

Thus, we observe a rigidity—the privileging of imitation and sameness—as the ontological orientation of white coloniality, and the exclusion and rejection of bodily differences and cultural métissage (mixing and blending). To clarify, I am not suggesting that classical music is and will ever be a white practice as an absolute, but rather that whiteness as a discursive and affective force functions to exclude the unique differences of a truly global humanity because its self-description of the ideal human performance holds whiteness in place.

Words as white weapons

> "Well, we were willing to do the work, even though it hurts," says the white musician. "If they really wanted to do it, they'd find a way."
>
> We are worried. Our students don't put in enough time. Sure, they must travel many miles by maxi taxi to school, they have part-time jobs, it pours with rain, the roads flood and they don't have any practice space at home. We sympathize, but only so much. We are here to raise standards. Our standards.
>
> "I'm from a working-class background," says the white musician from a London orchestra. "I identify with steelpannists—we're all the same, working toward the same world-class ideals."
>
> "The steelpan is so thrilling, but it could be even better! Imagine if they could arrange for symphony orchestra. They would learn so much more. Shall we add more Mahler to the listening list?"
>
> "The problem in this country is they already think they're professional," says the outraged teacher. "So, our opinions about practice and standards are simply ignored."
>
> "Our detractors aren't real people," says another. "Their education level is too low to appreciate us. Their opinions don't count anyway."
>
> "The students must learn proper orchestration. They're hopeless at recognizing different timbres. They can't recognize the oboe! They must know what an oboe is, right?"
>
> "And the local music they perform!" another remarks. "Soca is, frankly, noise. I'm sure it leads to poor intonation. It's banal! Where's the emotional depth?"
>
> "I know she's worked at it all year, but I don't think she should perform the solo. It'll sound much better if one of the faculty play it. We are trying to promote quality."

> "They must present a proper recital. Every string player in the world studies Bach," she says. "She wants to do what? Perform Bach during the interval, while people are socializing? She can't do that; it's inappropriate. How will we grade it?"
>
> "All this dancing about while playing," he complains. "It's a distraction; it disturbs the sound. Maybe it's a ruse, using her body to distract from her poor tone quality."
>
> "Keep going everyone, you're all doing a great job," they write to each other. "We will win this battle—Hearts and Minds—we'll win this argument."

These floating snippets of conversations emerged from my memories of office conversations, phone conversations, emails, and informal exchanges between faculty members at the institution in Trinidad. These snippets reverberate through time, as barely subtle acts of hostility that become "accumulated expressions of bias that reinforce racial hierarchies" (Kraehe et al., 2018b, p. 26). They sound white supremacy as a discursive weapon, a way to sustain and defend the power of white orientations within the institutional space. Yet we would never have recognized these words as racializing micro-aggressions at the time. All this commentary was made under the auspices of normal expectations, believing ourselves to be upholding appropriate curriculum, assessment, and work practices in-line with British conservatoire norms. In this respect aggressive language was framed as tough love, focused on a desire for our students to succeed, and nothing to do with racializing epistemic violence.

Initially, we could see no reason to change our practices. It seems we had imagined that our musical world would simply relocate unchanged, an inter-Atlantic Royal Albert Hall arriving like a spaceship onto the Savannah of Port-of-Spain. Trinidad exposed the privileges and conservatism of UK classical musical life. We discovered that the taken-for-granted conditions of work, such as adequate music stands, access to scores, audiences who knew the usual concert protocols such as when to clap, controlled climates, and easy access to the correct number of players and instruments for repertoire were missing. Anxiety around the maintenance of our world-class status became almost all-consuming. Anna Bull has aptly named the policed maintenance of habitual classical music traditions as "boundary-drawing around the proper" (Bull, 2019, p. 27). I suggest that this boundary-drawing expands beyond class separations to racial-cultural separations, represented by aesthetic rigidity. For example, an argument around musical impropriety arose at a suggestion to add steelpans to an ensemble to fill in missing instrumental parts (something we later did as a matter of course). Those against this notion wielded the concept of *the proper* as a shorthand for protecting the property/properties of the music, casting the steelpan, the national instrument of the country in which we were guests, as an improper aesthetic stranger, unwelcome in our domain.

Ultimately, unexpected political upheaval and policy change in Trinidad caused the setting up of a "world-class" professional orchestra to falter. Loss, grief, and anger exploded among my colleagues as it became clear that our orchestral habits of work could not be sustained. A chasm opened across the white faculty group, separating those who were willing to attempt a creative paradigm shift toward new ways of working and being, including greater integration with Trinidadian colleagues and musical culture, from those who were not. The group was disoriented and ripped apart as seven colleagues permanently left. Ironically, it was destruction that paved a way toward a gradual decentering of whiteness within the faculty. Given that classical music tends to maintain traditions via repetition and reinforcement I had been unprepared to consider destruction as necessary to the process of creation. Yet our vulnerability and grief at the loss a professional orchestra in the European model was, for me, the beginning of a letting go of a white supremacist and colonial mindset, which I can now see was limiting my imagination of what a musical subjectivity might become in unfolding relation to what Martinican poet Édouard Glissant calls métissage—the braiding and revisioning of creative cultural practices that forms part of the defiance against coloniality in the Caribbean.

Decolonizing white musical ontologies: "Flipping scripts"

Embracing disorientation and affective discomfort was the beginning of a disruption of the white ontologies of my musician subjectivity. As the Martinique poet Glissant has observed, writing about the Caribbean as a space of evolving cultures:

> *Culture is the precaution of those who claim to think thought but who steer clear of its chaotic journey. Evolving cultures infer Relation, the overstepping that grounds their unity-diversity. (Glissant, 1997, p. 1)*

Glissant's concept of Relation offers a framework for imagining ways of being in music that, rather than reinscribing whiteness, overstep the (un)naturalized boundaries whiteness constructs. Working for a decade in Trinidad did make ontological shifts in my musician practice as my body began to open out toward a creativity and flexibility in pedagogy and performance in *Relation* with the multiplicity of ways of being in Trinidad, a reminder that all practices, ultimately, are creations and can change. Fundamental to these changes was nurturing creative collaborations with Trinidadian colleagues both within and beyond the music department and the institution. These included experimenting with interdisciplinary creative projects that centered Caribbean cosmologies and language, that embraced improvisation, and that grounded performance projects in environments beyond the institutional buildings and the concert hall. For example, I ventured with a colleague from the theater department into the central and southern parts of Trinidad to explore belief systems around Black Madonna statues, engaging in experiments of free improvisation as forms of intuitive response to Caribbean religious cosmologies. In another example that troubled the boundaries of classical practice, a steelpan orchestra invited me to perform a Vivaldi violin concerto with the steelpan taking over the string ripieno parts—an example of the *unity-diversity* that can emerge when the standardization of canonical practice is disrupted. Another colleague and I took multiple trips to Tobago to learn from Tobagonian folk fiddle players about the situating of their musical practice within the manifestation of African spirituality on the island. I also worked closely with Trinidadian-British poet-musician Anthony Joseph, to include string performance on an album of spoken word and music, synching my aesthetic sensibilities with his unique rapso-jazz-funk aesthetic (Joseph, 2018). These experiences ultimately led to a deeper critique and interrogation of my classical pedagogical practices, which in turn informed the imperative to engage in critical autoethnographic research.

There is no decolonial arrival point in this storytelling, but rather glimpses of strategies toward the dismantling of the whiteness of classical music institutions. Gayatri Spivak reminds us that "what I cannot imagine stands guard over everything that I must/can do, think, live" (Spivak, 2012, p. 25). Critical autoethnography, carried out with perspectives that challenge whiteness, is one way to see occluded power structures and imagine new ways of being. It can be difficult to imagine what a decolonized higher music education space might be, due to its colonial foundations, and yet we must strive to construct it if institutional white supremacy is to be undone. One point of entry is for white people to take on white ontologies as fundamentally problematic, a move that "flips the script," a script that has often focused on the non-white body as "less-than-human" (Yancy, 2012a). We therefore need to develop a robust critical attention to the discourse that surrounds classical music and shapes its boundary-drawing behaviors for traces of an ideology that places the music of white Europeans as the apex of human musical development, thereby devaluing other musics and ways of being in music. A recent example is a quote from violinist Nicola Benedetti's speech to the Philharmonic Society in 2019, where she describes classical music as indicative of an "evolution of humankind: it is a grand and beautiful dialogue between instinct and intelligence," an inheritance from "the most enlightened areas of our past," expressing the "profound intelligence of our intuition" (Benedetti, 2019). Benedetti's commentary is a commonly heard discourse around classical music and humanness, evolution, and development, which is in essence a white origin story in music. We need to continuously explore the affective impacts of such statements, to consider how they resonate and shape ontology beyond the rooms in which they are spoken.

The rich intellectual and creative work of Caribbean writers and artists offer particularly astute "flips" in view and examples of experiential, liberatory, and disruptive methodologies. To "flip" is a bodily action as well as a theoretical concept. Beyond reading and thinking with alternative cosmologies, we need to develop pedagogies that embody, aurally and physically, other ways of listening and being in performance. For example, the Trinidadian playwright Tony Hall has spoken of Jouvay (the opening night-to-dawn act of Trinidad Carnival) as a pedagogy of transformation that reveals, through free improvised play and a masking with mud and paint, that the world, as we live it, is a creation and a serious act of performance into which we invest (Dk Rostant, 2017). He suggests that through Jouvay pedagogies we can glimpse the modern world as a (hegemonic) invention and find freedom to dismantle this world and create anew. Rupturing the boundaries of aesthetic containment through welcoming embodied immersion in cultural performance literally *outside* the controls of the concert hall, engaging in improvised performance with musicians outside of classical traditions and working *across* arts disciplines can all contribute to onto-epistemological ruptures of whiteness.

Applying anticolonial and antiracist theoretical lenses to the white classical musician via critical autoethnography enables a view of whiteness and containment *haunted* by the discourse of coloniality, while *being* in a present and indeterminate cultural future, a (post)coloniality as determining, and yet not fully determining of "being" (Ahmed, 2000, p. 11). Reflexivity is a mere starting point. Beyond reflexivity lies pedagogical and ideological shifts toward critical, creative, diverse, and hospitable musical practice open to and for all bodies. This will be achieved by engaging in a process of interference and even, at times, destruction of imitative practices. I argue that both music higher education and the wider classical industry can tackle white ontologies by experimenting with pedagogical and creative processes that engage with critical theories and research methodologies. What might classical music and musicians become if our purpose was less an induction into tradition and more an embrace of critical and creative acts of *becoming* that reimagine musical practices for a multiplicity of human life in music? We must urgently reassess who and what we represent in our performance institutions if we are to dismantle white ontologies in classical music.

20
Everyday Bridges
A View from the Field

Cayenna Ponchione-Bailey

I am an orchestral conductor committed to promoting social justice and environmental sustainability through and within mainstream orchestral performance. For me, this means working with and within existing orchestral institutions to shift orchestral practices, routines, and conventions toward those that are more equitable, and using orchestral music-making activities to promote social justice within the local, regional, and global communities in which orchestras are embedded. In this chapter I discuss some the challenges I have faced and ways I have met those challenges in the development and production of social justice work within the orchestral sector. These thoughts are organized chronologically in the way in which this work usually unfolds and includes a specific example of a project from 2017. For those of you reading this who already do this kind of work, all of this may be quite familiar to you, but for those who have not yet dipped their toe in, it offers a behind-the-scenes peek into what is often required to try to make change in the sector, concert by concert.

Pushing boundaries and building bridges

Nearly every concert I conduct aims to push a boundary or a limit in some way, in an effort to explore what opportunities each performance might provide. Fundamental to my work in this area are the concerns with "whose voices" are being platformed in an orchestra concert (e.g., performers, composers, and other contributors); the "aboutness" of the musical program (what topics does it address?); who has access or indeed is invited to those concerts; and how and where audiences are able to experience them.

However, producing concerts that veer even slightly away from the mainstream conventions of orchestral music-making—conventions that make it possible for 100 otherwise strangers to perform a 90-minute concert on fewer than three hours of rehearsal—invariably takes substantially more time, patience, skills, and resources. The time-money practicalities of the orchestral music industry are particularly constraining in professional settings where the cost of one minute of rehearsal time can easily range from £25 to £100+. In student and amateur settings where the personnel costs may not be as substantial, overall resources including rehearsal time are often quite limited and administrative work is often already carried out on a voluntary basis. In short, to do anything that departs from the everyday routine is costly and requires a great deal of extra off-platform preparation in order to bring it into the orchestral arena without unfruitfully disrupting the everyday flow of orchestral work.

I often find myself acting as a bridge between the conventions and expectations within mainstream orchestral practice and the people and ideas that are not yet part of these everyday routines—bridging the distance between spheres of knowledge and sets of values, obtaining or providing for additional financial needs, and plugging the gaps in the mundane practicalities of bringing people and equipment together into spaces to make things happen. Most of this work is largely unpaid, and my willingness to do it contributes in its own way to perpetuating some of the inequities within the classical music profession, including fair compensation and gender equality. When this type of work benefits organizations by enhancing their real or perceived commitment to social justice within the sector, routinely filling in these gaps with unpaid labor can lead to patterns of exploitation.

Is it a good idea?

I am constantly interrogating my own privileges, positions, and performance opportunities to see what angles can be developed and leveraged to promote social justice values within orchestral music. Sometimes this is as simple as insisting at the time of a conducting engagement that the orchestra program a performer or a piece of music by a composer from an underrepresented demographic. It might entail developing a multi-year collaboration with artists or a community group in order to help break down barriers to participation in orchestral music-making and raise awareness about social justice and environmental issues. Or, depending on my role within an organization, I may even be in a position to work to shape the organization's policies and practices over the long term.

Ideas occur to me, or arise from conversations with colleagues and potential collaborators, and are then interrogated: We could do this—but is it a good idea? What are the values or ideas that are being promoted in this work? Who are the beneficiaries and how do they benefit? What role have they had in developing this idea? What power relationships will be brought into being and how will they be negotiated? Have we maximized the opportunities here? Distilling grand visions into discrete, actionable initiatives is a difficult editorial process that invariably results in exclusions, as decisions are made about who and what will be prioritized, with many excellent and worthy ideas ending up on the cutting room floor. Frustratingly, this process is often driven by available resources—time, money, and personnel—rather than exclusively by needs or opportunities. Work that incorporates creative artists or other participants who are not familiar with orchestras' everyday practices—and who may have even been invited in to creatively disrupt those routines to some degree—requires building and maintaining bridges of trust in multiple directions. Determining the best course of action is never straightforward and no doubt I have got it wrong on occasion—it is the inevitable consequence of engaging imperfectly in an imperfect world.

If it is decided that the answer to "Is it a good idea?" is "Yes," then the next step is to convince other stakeholders of the same. This usually requires bridging sometimes quite radically differing world views—providing insights into issues that stakeholders may not have considered in depth before, and being flexible enough to hear and respect the views of others, which may be ideologically opposed to my own. Sometimes the latter involves substantial emotional labor, particularly when people in power-holding positions are unwilling to acknowledge the very inequities within the classical music industry (or wider society for that matter) that such initiatives are trying to address. Conversations can require doing emotional gymnastics and may include being gaslighted yourself while working to promote greater equity for others. But keeping a place at the table and in the room is essential if the work is to get done. I've been successful in my negotiations if the result is "There's no harm in letting her try so long as it doesn't cost us anything."

Paying for it: time, money, and skills

If anything turns orchestral social justice work into a "project," it is the process of trying to fund it. In order to get the necessary resources, the "need" must be demonstrated, and the work needs to be defined and bounded, and have clear-cut objectives and deliverables so that it can be proposed, funded, evaluated, and reported on. Writing grant applications, speaking with individual donors, and running fundraising campaigns has been, for me, largely unpaid. I was once successful in obtaining a grant that then paid me (part-time) for two years to write more grants for orchestral social justice projects and produce them. Grants such as these are difficult to get and involved months of unpaid labor to obtain. For large initiatives requiring substantial resources, there is no alternative to grant-writing or donor development. However, at every turn there are smaller things that can be done—need to be done—that are more efficiently plugged with one's own skills, time, and money.

If it takes more time to write a grant application for an amount less than what I am able to earn through hourly employment doing just about anything else, I'm likely just to pay out of pocket. This is not because I have extra cash lying around— quite the opposite—but because I spend the money I do have on things that are of value to me. I have spent thousands on commissions, player fees, and production costs over the years—money earned from waiting tables or my own artist fees. There are many situations in which money can't be raised because there isn't time or it isn't practical (or possible) to hire someone with the specialist skills to do the work that needs to be done. Take for example a project I produced as part of my five-year commissioning series *Sounding2020: Commissioning Music for Humanity and the Environment*, which resulted in a new work for orchestra and narrator titled *Borderline Plummet* (https://www.youtube.com/watch?v=ReLGotKOs9A).

Example: *Borderline Plummet*

This project arose when a member of an orchestra I conduct, who has lived experience of mental health issues, approached me and wanted to use the commissioning series to raise awareness about mental health in our small Upstate New York community. We had approximately six months between conception and when we'd need to deliver a performance. We agreed that she would speak with people she knew who also had lived experience of mental health issues at a local agency and invite them to write a statement in response to the prompt: *If you could tell the world anything about your experience, what would it be?* (No one was paid for this part of the project.)

A handful of individuals agreed to respond anonymously and these texts were given to a young and creative local composer, Josh Oxford, who had never written for a full orchestra before and who, a few years earlier, had been in a severe car accident resulting in long-term physical impairments. A local well-respected and well-loved actor, Camilla Schade, passionate about the issue, was engaged to do the narration. In this instance I took the decision to pay the composer and the narrator fees myself rather than take the time to seek additional funding.

The performance took place on an outdoor stage at a large regional music and dance festival on a concert program including Schumann, Smyth, Brahms, and Beethoven. With a short lead time for the project, a composer writing outside of their usual musical milieu and with assistive technology, an actor who could not read musical notation, and limited rehearsal time with a semi-pro orchestra, there were a number of practicalities that needed to be bridged. Someone has to do that bridging, and perhaps naturally it comes down to me, as the conductor and producer.

A creative and unusual score delivered a month in advance of the first rehearsal required quite a bit of negotiation, rescoring, and re-notations to make it effectively sight-readable for the ensemble. With limited rehearsal time, adhering to orchestral conventions in notation is critical. Formatting, extracting, and printing parts for a piece that pushed notational boundaries also took significant time, tools, specialist skills, and money. I endeavor to support the musical imaginations of all of the composers I commission to the best of my abilities, but this can often involve negotiating compromises or finding solutions to bridge the gap between notational ideals and the practical realities of being able to perform the work on little rehearsal time (sometimes only twice the length of the piece itself). In this case we had less than 90 minutes' rehearsal in total for the 12-minute work.

The composition included a highly rhythmic rap-inspired section for the narrator, which was not an idiom in which Camilla was previously versed. Combined with a lack of familiarity with musical notation and no aural reference, this passage ended up being exceedingly difficult for her to learn. There was no other practical solution but for the narrator and I to spend hours together so that the extended passage could be learned by rote. Here I found myself bridging the space between aural and notational practices as well as being an emotional bridge when anxieties about being able to adequately perform the part with the orchestra nearly caused her to withdraw.

This pre-production work was essential to bridge the space between orchestral conventions and creatives who operate on the outside of day-to-day orchestra practices. However, it was in the crucible of time-pressured rehearsals that a great many more bridging skills were required: the psychological and emotional bridging needed to bring the orchestra onboard with a challenging and unusual score; the skills and experience needed to efficiently and effectively translate the composer's ideas into instructions and find split-second solutions to errors in parts or musical ideas that just didn't work within the practical constraints; the ability to bridge communication between the composer and the orchestra to ensure ideas were communicated clearly and efficiently; as well as the emotional labor required to help the narrator feel at ease in this entirely new performance setting. Finally, in the concert it was my role to be the bridge between the piece/project and the audience—introducing and framing the work and providing the emotional and organizational focus needed in performance to effectively convey the content of the work and facilitate the musicians' and narrator's performance.

While my own experience of the process and the feedback I received from the composer, narrator, and emotionally moved audience and orchestra members was overwhelmingly positive, there was not an audience survey or a series of follow-up interviews with the participants that can verify success of this initiative or that of my bridge-building efforts. Indeed, someone in my position as producer and conductor may be the last one to hear of the criticisms, or be informed by others of their failings. Now, whenever possible, I add a budget within grant applications for independent research strands and evaluations, in order to provide a critical perspective on the process and impact of such projects including my own involvement.

Final thoughts

Some of the above is just part of the everyday work of producing new music as an orchestral conductor. Critically, however, when engaging in social justice work within and through orchestral practices, there is the added responsibility of ensuring that the process for *everyone* is constructive and respectful—that issues are represented thoughtfully and appropriately and driven by the communities for whom they are central. In my roles as producer and conductor, interpersonal relationships, marketing, and communications require much greater attention and energy than needed for routine orchestral concerts produced within the existing framework of orchestral conventions.

Of all of the examples I could have drawn on from my time doing this kind of work, *Borderline Plummet* is actually one of the more straightforward collaborations. In some sense, it is very much representative of my "everyday" approach to bringing new voices to the orchestra platform while raising awareness around pressing social and environmental issues. A reflection on the larger and more socially and politically complex projects I have produced would reveal significant additional challenges and sensitivities involving many more stakeholders.

While often challenging and nearly always time and energy consuming, being these everyday bridges is extremely rewarding with every concert, initiative, or project, and an opportunity to obtain new perspectives, stretch my own imagination, and develop my skill sets in new ways. It is an artistic practice in and of itself. Long-term change seems to be slow in this sector, but there is a growing community of like-minded individuals engaged in this everyday behind-the-scenes work who, like me, are in it for the long haul, changing the way the orchestral world works—one concert at a time.

21

Illuminating Women's Music

Exploring the Canonic Ethos behind the Illuminate Women's Music Concert Series

Angela Elizabeth Slater

Canonization and notions of "canonic status" have long acted as structures through which classical music is understood, both historically and today. Indeed, the extent to which canon formation is determined by powerful structures has been prominently debated (cf. Everist, 1999; Gates, 1994; Shreffler, 2011; Pace, 2021), particularly as a result of greater importance attached to diversity and inclusivity in contemporary discourse. Exclusionary canonic structures are problematic when considering the place of women composers in the wider classical music landscape (Citron, 1993). In my recent work, I have explored the idea of "Invisible canons," whereby individuals have their own personal canons which, when combined, can play a key part in making overlooked composers more visible. As I have shown elsewhere, the powerful cycle of omitting women composers from what has been termed the "pedagogical canon" (inter alia Legg, 2021) enables continued ignorance of a vast body of repertoire (Slater, 2022). The exclusionary practices of the pedagogical canon serve as a catalyst for further exclusion of women composers, and those from other underrepresented groups, in the performance repertoire and recording canon.

The present chapter delves deeper into what we mean by the canon and explores practical ways in which we can use concepts of canonization to make meaningful change. I will discuss the ethos behind Illuminate Women's Music, the theoretical impetus underpinning the work it has achieved so far, and what it can tell us about audience knowledge of, and attitudes toward, women composers. This will demonstrate how much Illuminate is reaching new audiences, and how introducing new composers can maintain interest in classical and contemporary-classical music broadly going forward and, importantly, diversify our concert audiences.

Framing Illuminate Women's Music

I founded Illuminate Women's Music in 2017, and it now continues with the support of fellow composers Illuminate co-directors Dr. Blair Boyd and Sarah Westwood. It is a touring concert series that seeks to highlight the creativity of women both as performers and composers working today, as well as promoting the rich legacy of composition works written by women composers historically.

Before Illuminate came into being the idea of it had been forming in my mind for several years. There were a number of things that I had started to notice and become increasingly agitated about, which ultimately led me to form Illuminate. During my composition PhD, whenever I was at a composition course or development scheme, I was usually the only woman or, if I was lucky, one of two. These moments where I was so clearly the "other" made me realize how I could not see "myself" in other working composers or composers of the past. There was a sense of not belonging in both my gender and state school educational background. I reflected on my education—both at school and university—and could not recall women composers being introduced to me. When I did some research into this, I found my recollection to be worryingly accurate, a more expansive discussion of which can be found in Slater (2022).

Fielding my music education

My music education in the East Midlands British state-school system in the 2000s centered on a generalized approach to a range of genres. Male composers and songwriters were the musical creators. None of the materials provided by the exam board for both my GCSE (2004–2006) and A-level music (2006–2008) courses made reference to women composers; women composers were completely absent for students who were engaged with these specifications. Unless fortunate enough to have a forward-thinking teacher, who was knowledgeable about women composers, students would have little chance of developing this knowledge through mainstream curricula in the early 2000s.

I was fortunate enough to have my school-based music education supplemented with private instrumental lessons. Throughout my musical development, graded exams from the Associated Board of the Royal Schools of Music (ABRSM) were the main and consistent influence on my musical education. All of my instrumental teachers used these qualifications to guide their pedagogical practice. These exams, undoubtedly, had a significant impact on my view of the musical world and compositional landscape.

Surveying the historic syllabuses, it came as little surprise to me that my own musical education through ABRSM's piano exams (1999–2008) did not include women composers. During this time period there were just 23 works by women out of 784 in total available to me. These were not necessarily on the examination grade I was taking that year, meaning that I could not have chosen these pieces. While studying piano, the highest percentage of works by women across grades 1–8 only reached 4% (Slater, 2022; Bull, 2018).

My university music course was typical of a traditional music qualification at an elite British university. Modules covered a range of topics, but focused mostly on surveying and establishing the accepted cultural figures, alongside a number of highly-specialized modules aligned closely to staff research specialisms. Such an approach facilitated a cycle of cultural reproduction as described by Bourdieu, discussed in relation to A-levels by Robert Legg (2012), and debated internationally in higher music education (inter alia Heile et al., 2017; Robin, 2017). Women composers were notably absent, even in the modules on 20th- and 21st-century composers.

The realization that I had not been introduced to women composers through the pedagogical canon I was exposed to, and to only recognize this so late in my music training, was quite shocking. Why it hadn't occurred to me earlier perhaps speaks to how much we are all predisposed to accept the patriarchal structures that surround us as the norm.

While studying for my PhD in composition, I was looking at how I could musically map concepts from the natural world and embed these into the fabric of the music through various parameters of composition: the architecture of the work, the gestural material, or the harmony, timbre, and rhythmic language. I was asking, how can these phenomena or existing structures in the natural world be used to create something musically meaningful? This research took me to many different composers and repertoire, but it also led (perhaps with the feeling of being one of very few women composers) to start searching for women composers.

Moving toward my personal canon

I began with a list of women composers and works I had started to engage with. This list made me begin to consider what a collection of works can be to an individual and how it might relate to the "Western" art canon. A canon can be defined as a set or ever-shifting body of works that embodies values and aesthetics of the people who make and experience the music, as Ellen Koskoff has laid out (1999, p. 547). The continued existence of a canon is sustained through a cycle of cultural reproduction, with new works being subsumed over time into this conceptual and collective archive. This seemingly cyclic nature allows for new works to enter the canon or for existing works to become more established, but whether a work has longevity in the canon is down to several factors, as laid out by Shreffler (2011, pp. 1–18): frequency of performance and academic engagement, both of which show a presumption of longevity and staying power; frequent programming well after initial honeymoon period; and historical significance, realized in retrospect.

A canon is therefore maintained through the shared values of multiple agents determining a dominant discourse. As Citron perceptively notes in her work exploring why women composers are absent from the canon, "Canon formation is not controlled by any one individual or organisation" (1993, p. 19). As such, several offshoot or parallel canons may exist and overlap, creating canonic discourse with each other (inter alia Everist, 1999, pp. 378–402). A prime example of this is the pedagogical canon, which serves to demonstrate the power of officially sanctioned knowledge structures that filter through and exert an influence on what we value in society beyond educational spheres. It demonstrates the knowledge that has been deemed of suitable "quality" to be incorporated into the educational syllabi and informs the next generation of musicians.[1] Indeed, Citron describes the canon as a "narrative of the past and a template for the future" (1993, p. 1). This shows that if better representation of women composers in the cultural fabric of the classical music industry is going to be achieved, then we need to actively change what the canon (and its underlying concepts) represents as a template for the future. This means considering pedagogy, performance repertoire, and the recording industry, among many other aspects.

The hegemonic power of canonic structures in music educational syllabuses has been discussed extensively in recent educational research and policy (cf. Whittaker, 2020; Legg, 2012; Slater, 2022; Kinsella et al., 2019; Department for Education, 2021). The cumulative effect of these education spheres has contributed to the pedagogical canon that our society is exposed to and in turn influences our repertoire canon and concert programming. As Green notes, "The music curriculum tends to reiterate the canon," further serving to perpetuate a cycle of cultural reproduction (Green 1997, p. 237). Arguably, the educational sphere is so intertwined with the performance canon that they essentially have a symbiotic relationship.

As this brief exploration of the pedagogical canon has shown, there are a number of systemic factors that tilt the balance against composers outside of the dominant discourse. In this context, it is plain to see that women composers are excluded and, in all probability, will not be included in the future if the status quo remains. The implications of this are important as the links to overlapping canons, and the processes through which they are filtered and maintained, are apparent. As noted above, canons are both created and sustained through shared values. We might see the formation of an established societal canon as emerging from a number of influential individual canons coalescing around a common body of works. Though we may wish to throw out the whole idea of a canon, its structural influence is deep-rooted. As such, a productive first step may be to engage constructively with the concept. Perhaps due to my educational background being so bound up with "Western" art-music canons, I came to conceptualize the collection of works of significant women composers I had become aware of as part of my doctoral research as my *personal canon* of women composers.

Through my exploration of works by women, I found something different from the confines of a male-dominated construct of musical worth. These formed a parallel canon for me. The wealth of repertoire by these women composers offered new modes of engagement, new role models, something that had been lacking before and whose omission made it hard to see how I fitted into being a "composer." Broadening my view of music history opened up new creative possibilities. The confidence that discovering women composers brought to me changed my outlook on my career prospects. I felt passionately that this was extremely important and ought to be far more widely known by other women striving to be composers; there is both a historical legacy and a community of women composers forging careers as composers today.

Illuminate Women's Music—putting theory into practice

Beyond the educational sphere, the classical music industry is notoriously unbalanced in its representation of women musicians. There are many unfortunate statistics and metrics that highlight the underrepresentation of women composers, and despite some changes, there is still a long way to go before reaching more equal representation. This point has been highlighted annually by the BBC Proms Survey undertaken by Women in Music each year. For example, the 2017 BBC Proms survey showed that the overall programming of women composers accounted for 7.5% of all composers performed at the Proms, 22% of living composers programmed, and 30.8% of new commissions. These figures have improved over the last few years, with the 2019 survey showing women composers overall accounted for 18% of all works performed, 33% of living composers programmed, and 33% of new commissions (Women in Music, 2017 and 2019). While this direction of travel is encouraging, there is still a long way to go before women have the same musical opportunities and prominence in major festivals as their male counterparts.

Indeed, reading about these inequalities led me to ask questions about the classical music world: how are classical musicians and audiences meant to become aware and appreciate the music of women composers if they are never given the opportunity to explore the music in their education or through mainstream media? How do we expect aspiring women composers to have the confidence to go forward with their music if they do not have role models in their education?

It was with these questions in mind that I established the Illuminate Women's Music project [from now on "Illuminate"] in 2017, as described above. Illuminate aims to highlight and celebrate the work and creativity of women as composers from the past and present, as well as performers working today. Illuminate provides a concert space where women composers are the norm, highlighting the rich historical legacy of women composers alongside the exciting new work of women composers working today. The pervasive sense that women composers were absent from musical history, though explained through societal and historical factors in relation to canon formation, is an extremely damaging message that serves to further perpetuate the myth. If I could go through the majority of my formal education in music being unaware of women composers from the past, or those working today, then it is safe to assume that this could be the case for many performers and other composers working today, as well as the general concert audience.

The influence of this cannot be understated, presenting conscious and subconscious hurdles for women forging careers as composers, and for all artists in marginalized groups. If aspiring artists cannot see themselves in the composers who are taught and programmed in the classical concert scene, they also cannot see a lineage of women composers, or composers who break from the "White male genius" mold; it can feel as though they alone are doing this for the first time. Of course, it is not the case that women composers are doing this alone. We need composers, musicians, and our audiences to realize this. These historical women composers can become inspirational figures and demonstrate that there is an historical lineage and legacy to build upon.

Building networks for collaboration

I started gathering contacts initially from my professional networks, asking women composers and performers if they would be interested in organizing a few concerts where the entire programs consisted of works by women composers. This would create a space in which the status quo was turned on its head: a musical space where women were the norm for once. As I started booking concerts, I began to feel that this was really important work and necessary to create real change. I realized I needed a name for the project that could encapsulate my aims. I wanted to highlight the creativity of women as both performers and composers, and demonstrate the rich legacy of historical works by women that exist—which I was still learning about for myself. The project has always been from the premise of highlighting and celebrating women's work, not about excluding men. An exclusively female space wouldn't be needed if the structures that govern our society and canon had not created a situation where all-male concerts were a daily occurrence. There were many draft names for the concert series and various logos before I eventually settled on Illuminate with the tag line "Shining a light on the work of women composers and performers," which I have since updated to Illuminate Women's Music.

The Illuminate concert series draws upon some of the key principles of what a work needs to enter into the canon as laid out by Shreffler (2011), "Frequency of performance and academic engagement." As such, Illuminate aims to offer five to seven performances of newly commissioned works for each season in a number of geographical locations across the UK. This is set up alongside a blog series, hosted on our website, where commissioned composers write about their new works and their compositional practices. Invited academics and other industry experts also write blog articles on historical women composers. These blogs constitute a valuable resource in their own right, allowing industry experts and our audiences to learn more about music by women from both past and present. One of the other aspects is frequency of programming well after the initial honeymoon period (Shreffler, 2011). Although Illuminate does not necessarily provide this through its live in-person concert seasons, we support ongoing programming through both our digital legacy and the incorporation of these works into the repertoire banks of the performers we work with. We know, for example, that works that were new to the musicians in our concerts have then gone on to become regular pieces in other programs. This demonstrates how building partnerships between composers and performers can help to facilitate changes as an investment in the next generation of professional musicians.

Our work so far

Through programming women composers, Illuminate aims to provide some of the conditions for these pieces to enter the personal canons of audience members and, eventually, be considered alongside those canonic works whose place in concert programs seems safe. In 2018, Illuminate's inaugural series, along with the help of my fellow Illuminate composers-in-residence Sarah Westwood and Blair Boyd, we staged ten concerts, supported four performers, seven different living composers, 11 new commissions and programmed several works by seven historical composers (Morfydd Owen, Lili Boulanger, Grazyna Bacewicz, Hilda Jerea, Claude Arrieu [aka Louise Marie Simon], Clara Schumann, and Amy Beach). The living composers we supported were Gemma McGregor, Blair Boyd, Sarah Westwood, Carol J. Jones, and myself. These composers were commissioned to write new works to draw on the instrumental forces of performers Késia Decoté (piano), Cassie Matthews (classical guitar), Sabina Virtosu (violin), and Gemma McGregor (shakuhachi and flute). The new works were premiered and given repeat performances across the UK. This concert series launched in London at Goldsmiths University on International Women's Day (March 8, 2018) and continued across 2018, visiting Oxford, Stafford, Birmingham, Cardiff, Brighton, Liverpool, and Nottingham, before returning to London.

In 2019 Illuminate built on the success of our first season and organized 12 concerts spread across further two seasons. We supported 13 performers, eight living composers, commissioned 11 new works and programmed pieces by nine historical composers (Morfydd Owen, Grazyna Bacewicz, Ruth Crawford Seeger, Lili Boulanger, Ethel Smyth, Barbara Strozzi, Vivian Fine, Rebecca Clarke, and Elizabeth Lutyens) with performances in both the US and UK.

In our first season of 2019 we had two sets of performers-in-residence, the Boston-based Prism trio with pianist Anna Arazi, violinist Subaiou Zhang, and cellist Tim Paek, and the UK-based Ethel Smyth Trio with pianist Jelena Makarova, violinist Emma Purslow, and cellist Daryl Giuliano. For our second season, Illuminate formed a new string quartet who performed alongside soprano Patricia Auchterlonie. Across these two seasons in 2019 we supported new commissions from composers Kerensa Briggs, Laura Shipsey, Angela Elizabeth Slater, Sarah Westwood, Blair Boyd, Joanna Ward, Caroline Bordignon, and Yfat Soul Zisso.

Overcoming hidden barriers to progress

One of the challenges with producing Illuminate concerts is researching and finding the sheet music for historical women composers. When Illuminate started out, this was more difficult, but now there does seem to be more repertoire on IMSLP, on publishers' websites, and more databases with resources of where and how to resource music.[2] However, when I first started and was expanding my own knowledge, I found Bangor University's First International Conference on Women's Work in Music (and its subsequent iterations) to be a hugely significant resource containing the contacts of musicologists, performers, and composers. This conference gave me a wealth of ideas and suggestions of composers to explore for programming purposes for the inaugural year of the concert series. It also helped me to build professional networks with other activists.

A significant figure for me has been musicologist Dr. Rhian Davies, who is an expert on the Welsh composer Morfydd Owen (1891–1918), a composer whom I have gone on to program several times throughout Illuminate seasons so far. Even with a composer such as Owen, who has been the subject of considerable research and whose works have been catalogued, there were still barriers in accessing some of her works for performance. For example, in 2019, I programmed Owen's piano trio work. To make this happen, I used my contact of Dr. Davies to liaise with the National Library of Wales to be given digital access to a copy of the original manuscript and obtain permission to typeset this. Thanks to work by Dr. Blair Boyd, we now have a typeset version of this piece, making this work available for future performances.

For works that are unpublished, out-of-print, or otherwise unavailable on web-based repositories like International Music Score Library Project (IMSLP), I have drawn upon my network of performers and musicologists to help source the music. On some occasions (and through several contacts) I would reach a distant relative of the composer who is now the holder of collections of manuscripts and would ask if it were possible to perform the work. I have undertaken similar work for other groups that I support with programming. Across the board, there needs to be more editorial leg work to bring this music into performance-ready editions, publishers willing to expand their catalogues, and musicological scholarship to better understand the value of a largely unknown body of repertoire. Without ready access to good editions, it is much more difficult to share this music.

Another challenge in planning concerts for Illuminate is knowing how the piece will fit in a program, in terms of its character and practical things like its length. Such information is not always immediately clear from a score and, without recordings, it can be challenging to make these decisions. For most repertoire a musician would listen to a recording of the work to find some of these things out, but the recorded repertory for women composers—though growing—is still relatively limited.

Securing funds, raising our profile, and developing audiences

Since founding Illuminate five years ago, we have received prestigious arts funding in the UK, including multiple grants from Arts Council England, Ambache Charitable Foundation, PRS Open Fund, Hinrichsen Foundation, RVW Trust, and Gemma Classical Music Trust. Illuminate relies on these grants and support from our audiences to continue our work in commissioning and engaging our performers and composers.

Performances from these seasons were included on BBC Radio 3 International Women's Day programming in 2019, and on the New Music Show in 2020. My own supporting research on the representation of women composers in ABRSM exams between 1999–2020 was featured in two UK national newspapers, *The Sunday Times* and *Daily Telegraph*, helping to draw attention to the debate around our pedagogical canons and their subsequent impacts on the performance canon.

Over the course of the 2018 season, we gathered audience feedback to help us develop our programs and understand the experiences of our audiences. Our ethos was to expand audiences' knowledge of women composers and consequently have an effect on their personal canons. 63.4% of our audience surveyed had not previously heard of the composers programmed, and 58.8% of respondents said they would be very likely to recommend this concert. This demonstrates that, despite a large proportion of the audience not previously being aware of the composers or repertoire, they were convinced of the music and its quality enough to recommend an Illuminate concert going forward.

In 2020, Illuminate had plans for another 12 concerts with two sets of performers in residence and 11 newly commissioned works. These were unfortunately delayed, canceled, and postponed due to the COVID-19 pandemic. At the time of writing, we are planning for these concerts to take place during the autumn of 2021. Though our original plans were derailed by the pandemic, I felt it was important to continue Illuminate's work in highlighting the creativity of women. This resulted in Illuminate launching a monthly digital concert series that started in September 2020. For this series, Illuminate featured solo instrumentalists and vocalists from across the world. Our digital concerts included recitals from classical guitarist Eleanor Kelly, mezzo soprano Patricia Hammond with pianist Andrea Kmecova, double bassist Maggie Cox, violinist Sofia Yatsyuk with pianist Suren Barry, pianist and composer Ania Vu, oboist Nicola Hands, and soprano Rose Hegele with Julia Scott-Carey.

Shifting across to an exclusively online platform of concert presentation for the pandemic period threw up a set of questions for me. Were we actually having a wider reach, both in terms of geography and in the make-up of our audiences? Were we retaining some of the in-person audience members? If we were reaching a wider international base, were these audience members already convinced of the cause, or looking for new music? In what ways might a digital concert help to expand personal canons?

I surveyed those who attended the digital concerts to see if I could shed some light on some of the questions above. We received 33 responses. The overwhelming majority of respondents indicated making concerts available digitally had enabled them to engage with far more of our events than they could otherwise attend. Twenty-three respondents said that they were attending an Illuminate concert for the first time. Based on web traffic numbers, it seems likely that there were also significant numbers of new audience members who engaged with our digital concerts, with one of our digital concerts reaching 1,000 views over a period of six months. These points emphasize the potential for digital concerts to facilitate access to events and programs.

It was encouraging to see that our digital concert programs had expanded the range of composers our audience was aware of, with 31 respondents indicating that they had been introduced to composers they didn't know about before. Three quarters of our respondents would look to attend future concerts if they knew pieces by the same composers were going to be on the program.

Our audiences were passionate about composer diversity in the concerts they chose to attend. Respondents were asked to indicate the importance of this issue on a scale of 1 (not important at all) to 10 (very important); they responded with a mean average response of 8.4. Despite this relative importance of composer diversity, our respondents still told us that less than half of the other concerts they attended included works by women. For all the widespread discussion of promoting diversity, most concerts still seem to be beholden to patriarchal programming structures.

Our approach was bringing new music to audiences in an accessible manner that was tapping into something that other concert series were not. On reflection, the digital concert series has been a hugely positive aspect of our work, enabling further reach to international audiences as well as UK concert goers. We have been able to provide more opportunities and exposure to a larger range of performers over this time frame. However, the digital series in its current form does not support the creation of new works but has promoted early career women composers working today. We hope to retain some of these digital elements post-pandemic as there is clearly an appetite for these and the wider international scope is important to reach audiences from different cultures and backgrounds.

Concluding comments

Over the course of this chapter, I have outlined how canonic conceptualizations were foundational to the work Illuminate Women's Music does, and that I believe that such structures can be used constructively, not least if we come to think of canons in plural terms, rather than as *the* canon. I hope to have demonstrated how the theoretical framework of canons, and the ways these are sustained, has had a direct impact on the active work undertaken by Illuminate Women's Music. After all, canons need not be fixed museum pieces; Citron describes canons as "*ad hoc* conceptualisations of paradigmatic repertoire" (Citron, 1993, p. 25).

There are some steps we can take; we should program music by women regularly, commit to teaching these works on an equal footing to those by male counterparts, and adopt a historically critical lens of the canon. Illuminate Women's Music will continue to try to address these points to make change and, we hope, expand the knowledge concert audiences have about works by women, both past and present. By influencing personal canons, these changes will gradually feed into a broader societal understanding of the musical canon.

Recalling Citron, we must remember, "Canons simultaneously reflect, instigate, and perpetuate value systems" (1993, p. 19). If we can begin to change what is valued in musical society, we can begin to restructure the canon and rightly add women's repertoire to it instead of allowing an endless cycle of reproduction. Through discussing pre-existent canonic structures, the ways they have been sustained and challenged, and the formation of my own personal canon, I believe we can take important steps toward meaningful change in the promotion of women's music.

Illuminate tries to lift barriers on getting commissions and concert performances and—vitally—repeated performances for women composers from the past and present. However, the reach of our work can only go so far. For this problem to be resolved fully, larger classical music institutions need to start actively finding, programming, and valuing music by women from all eras and educating their audiences about this lesser-known repertoire. Illuminate will contribute to the incremental cultural shifts that will eventually reach a point, we hope, where it is no longer acceptable to program male composers exclusively.

Notes

1. On the English music education landscape and its influence on access, definitions of quality, and on inclusion, see Spruce (2013). For a perspective on slightly earlier policy decision-making see Wright and Davies (2010).
2. See, for example, Kassia database https://www.kassiadatabase.com/; Diversify the Stand https://www.diversifythestand.org/; Composer Diversity Project https://www.composerdiversity.com; Donne Women in Music https://donne-uk.org; Music Theory examples by Women Composers https://web.archive.org/web/20220124070212/https://musictheoryexamplesbywomen.com/; Archiv Frau und Musik https://www.archiv-frau-musik.de/en/; Boulanger Initiative https://www.boulangerinitiative.org; A Modern Reveal https://www.amodernreveal.com/; Clarinet Music by Women https://clarinetmusicbywomen.com/?fbclid=IwAR1-9ap9QY73OxSQ4_U9tv58OH9p1RTX21ii2kAnPQUncI_kt5bUPohRUUc; Women in Music Theory https://womeninmusictheory.wordpress.com/contact-us/; Expanding the Music Theory Canon https://www.expandingthemusictheorycanon.com/?page_id=313; Hildegard Music Publishing https://www.hildegard.com.

22
Changing Classical Music from the Inside
An Interview with Chi-chi Nwanoku

Chi-chi Nwanoku

ANNA: Could you start off by telling me why you initially decided to set up the Chineke! Orchestra?

CHI-CHI: I'd had a very active and fulfilling 35-year career on the international concert platform, and I was always the only Person of Color. I'd been brainwashed into thinking that was the norm and I should be lucky that I was included. But of course I know that's not good enough. And the more I thought about it, the more I knew I didn't have a say or a voice. I'm from the generation where we were taught to assimilate and be grateful. We didn't ask the questions that young people ask today. And when we did ask a question, as when I was a school child, the answer from teachers would often be, "Because I told you so." That was a very common answer. I was one of those little girls who always wanted to get things right, to get the brownie points, and to get the stars in my homework books. You try and toe the line as much as you can. I was always the only Black child in my year and usually in my school. And so, I learned how to make the system work for me, which was possible because I'm very creative, I'm versatile, I'm flexible, I can see opportunities and want to make the most of them.

ANNA: Would you say that's the case for a lot of People of Color in classical music, that you have to be versatile, you have to assimilate, you have to find these creative ways to get to be included?

CHI-CHI: I didn't know anyone of color for all those years. Where were they? Why were they not next to me in orchestras? I literally didn't see anybody. So, I don't know what the vibe was in their minds because they were not operating in the same circles as me. And that's why, when Ed Vaizey (the Culture Secretary in the UK government at the time), called me into his office in Westminster, asking why he only saw me regularly on the international concert platform, I didn't know what the answer was. I had to find out. When I had decided what I was going to do, plenty of people said, "Oh, you'll never be able to do that, Chi-chi. There aren't any People of Color in classical music. It's not really for people like you, is it? You're just a one-off. And even people who do play, the standard's just not good enough, is it?" I was thinking, do they already know this? Because I didn't know that. I didn't know why I didn't see People of Color. Part of me questioned whether they were more knowledgeable about this, seeing as they professed that People of Color were not interested in classical music. But it was when they said, "But it's not really your sort of music, is it, Chi-chi?" And I'm thinking, hang on a minute, you've been playing with me for 30 years, and you're now telling me it's not really my sort of music? What kind of a comment is that? So have you just been putting up with me all these years? You're just tolerating me? That's the kind of thing that is dished out to us, and people didn't even blink an eye before they said things like that to me six years ago when I was creating Chineke! I doubt they would dream of saying it now. So I thought, okay, if that's what you think; I tell you what, I'm going to try and do it anyway. And the more I looked, the more I found. The well of talent runs deep.

ANNA: So, to ask perhaps an obvious question, why is it important to have an orchestra that's primarily for and with Black and ethnically diverse classical musicians?

CHI-CHI: Because of representation. For all those young people who are already playing instruments. One of the problems is that access points, starting points for all young musicians are not the same. Kids in economically-challenged boroughs in state schools, where their economic resources are less, their social status is lower, those are the areas that are less likely to have music education in the schools. It's for those kids who do manage to get their hands on an instrument, and fall passionately in love with it. By the time they get to midteens when they're beginning to think about subject choices for their school exams, that'll be the time when they're beginning to get a bit conscious about what they might do as a professional, and whether or not to go to university.

And as a young Person of Color, if you start looking a bit further into the area that you might be heading into, and you watch the BBC Proms or any other rare appearance of classical music on the TV, you might not see a single face that looks like yours. That's the reason why people drop out. That's the reason why it's so important that we, Chineke!, are there: for that one child with an affinity and an ability. That music for that child is putting them on a road to a beautiful, fulfilled life where they're going to succeed and flourish and be part of something they dream of. And why should it only be a dream? Why can't they realize it like every other white kid around them? It's also a loss to the music industry if we lose that one child. And we can't just think of it as the other way around—it's the music industry's loss as well. And it's not just the children who think this. It's their parents who think, I don't want my child going into an industry that does not look as if it's going to welcome them because there's no one else from the same background or that looks like my child there. That's the critical time where people drop out of music. And even if you do go to tertiary education and go to one of the music colleges, even if you graduate with a very good degree, there is no guarantee that you're going to get work, because the orchestras pick and choose who they want with them. It doesn't matter how good you are, you have to "fit in."

ANNA: I think one of the really interesting things that Chineke!'s doing is changing the music itself, both the repertoire and the canon, and the performance norms, and the ways of experiencing and playing classical music. You're changing the rules, as far as I can tell. Can you talk a bit about that?

CHI-CHI: Six and a half years ago, after our first concert, the rule book went out the window the minute we walked onstage. I looked at a sold-out Queen Elizabeth Hall audience and for the first time in my 35-year career, the audience looked like London. It looked like the community in which I live and serve. Not just culturally, but age as well. You'll see a range of four generations. At our London Royal Festival Hall concert on recently, there were seven-year-olds, six-year-olds, five-year-olds, and 95-year-olds. And the age range in our orchestra covers five decades as well.

ANNA: Wow. And could you expand on what you're trying to change about the music?

CHI-CHI: I want to change how people listen to it. I think it's so important. The BBC Proms got me to write a response to all those people complaining about people clapping in-between movements. Three years ago, at the BBC Proms opening night, the BBC Symphony Orchestra played Gustav Holst's *The Planets*. And as we know, the BBC Proms is one of those music festivals where loads of people go who don't normally go to concerts the rest of the year. Even if you don't know any single other piece of classical music, you will recognize some of *The Planets*. And so, when a piece of music that you recognize stops, you clap—that's normal. And then people complained about the audience members who were clapping in between the movements of Holst's *The Planets* and started writing messages in public places saying that those who were clapping were uneducated, that they need to learn the traditional ways of behaving in concerts. The *Guardian* called me and said, "Chi-chi, we need you to write a piece about this." The World Cup was going on at the same time. I just thought about it for a second, and started to write, "It's the World Cup final, the ball has just smashed into the back of the net, the crowd rises to cheer, the ref blows his whistle and says, 'Sit down and wait till the end of the match before you make a noise.' Sounds ridiculous? Welcome to the world of classical music (Nwanoku, 2018)." Or words to that effect. As soon I wrote my first sentence, I laughed my head off because

I just knew I was going to have fun writing this, and I did. There were hundreds of comments. Some people were really angry, some people completely empathized with my point of view. At the end, I was entertained and cool with the variety of responses. Another thing I wrote was, "Chineke!'s purpose is to bring about greater diversity and inclusion in classical music by showcasing players and music that are currently underrepresented. This will inevitably include more diverse forms of appreciation, and may well serve to 'educate' the traditionalists (Nwanoku, 2018)." Not only are we diversifying who you see on stage, it's also about what you hear on stage. But our audience's responses are also diverse. We're not going to try and script them into clapping when we think they should clap.

ANNA: It seems like you're trying to make classical music more fun. Would that be part of your mission?

CHI-CHI: No, I think that's too simple. I just want to make it accessible. I just want it to be clear that it's for everyone. For example, we walk onto the stage together. We tune up and warm up offstage. This idea came to me when we'd just finished the final rehearsal for the first concert. I realized we hadn't discussed how we made our entrance. Most orchestras shuffle on in dribs and drabs, warm up a bit, scrape their reeds if they're oboists, and work on a passage. There's many a time, when I've observed audiences, who might be sitting in the auditorium a little bit early; they're so focused on the stage, and as soon as someone walks onto the stage they spontaneously start clapping because they rightly think the concert is about to start. This applause is usually met with absolutely no acknowledgment from those walking onto the stage (as they know they're going on early to tune or warm up). As far as I'm concerned, that is when the barrier has gone up already—before the concert has even started. But people are supposed to be performers. That's not performance. And so, at the end of our final rehearsal at Queen Elizabeth Hall, before the first concert, I suggested we all came on as one, including the conductor. We remain standing in front of our seats, greeting the audience by visually engaging with them, acknowledging their applause, and we take a bow together with the conductor before we sit down and begin the concert. By making this united gesture at the start of our concerts it also symbolizes our shared philosophy of inclusion.

ANNA: Disrupting the hierarchy?

CHI-CHI: Yes, the first presentation of us to the audience, we come as one. This demonstrates our philosophy of togetherness—unity in diversity—which is what our Ghanaian Adinkra symbol stands for. Our philosophy is that we want to see a more diverse industry in classical music. We want to see change in the industry and that's why we present ourselves together. The first thing the audience hears is music, not tuning up. We tune up backstage. We come on and we perform, that's it.

ANNA: Part of the aim of this book is to inspire other classical musicians to become activists, so could you say something about what the biggest challenges have been for you in doing this work?

CHI-CHI: To begin with, I'd never fundraised before in my life, and I had to fundraise to pay the musicians. I had to persuade people to believe in the idea. Well, actually it didn't take much. I'm quite good at persuading people. People say to me, "Chi-chi, you're so convincing because it's coming from your heart. And because you believe in it so much, I'm completely pulled into your way of thinking." To start with, we managed to raise enough money to just about get us through the first concert. I didn't know if that would be our last concert. And then as soon as our first concert happened, the vibe in the industry seemed to wake up with quite a positive response. Everyone wanted to suddenly be friends with Chineke! and help find ways to support us and our mission. As soon as the first charities, trusts, and foundations started to give to us, it seemed to have an immediate knock-on effect. I think other charities did not want to appear to not be supporting us where they could. I'm so glad I created Chineke! when I did because if I had just created it now, it would have been a bit of a zeitgeist because of Black Lives Matter and George Floyd. I'm so glad that we already existed. People can see more clearly now how important it is, that we should be given as many opportunities as any other musician regardless of skin color or background. And if we're not given adequate training, why is that? Why do some of our students of color graduate from the esteemed Music Colleges not as qualified as their white counterparts? . . . Why are some of them not at the same level? I've been made aware of how many of the Black students at music college are not being given the same orchestra experiences during their time at college. Why is that? How are they being prepared, and how will they possibly stand a chance at auditions for jobs if they've not been given all the experience needed at college?

ANNA: In relation to Black Lives Matter, has anything changed since then in terms of the environment and the support for your work?

CHI-CHI: I've been very interested and pleased that more orchestras in the UK are now wanting to play the music we're playing: Samuel Coleridge-Taylor, Florence B. Price, George Walker. In the summer of 2020 after George Floyd's death we had meetings with all the South Bank orchestras—I asked them what their plans were to demonstrate their support of composers of ethnicity. I asked whether they thought it was only our responsibility to play music written by Black composers. I asked whether they thought that because we were playing it, then they did not need to. I reminded them that we also play white composers' music. I was so happy to see that most of the South Bank orchestras responded positively to the idea and have begun their journey into diversifying some of their programming. We've started it; the door has been cracked open. That's a marvelous feeling for me. We've lent some orchestras the music, and they liked what they found. And now they're choosing other pieces of their own.

ANNA: And so, what messages would you give to musicians and activists who want to make change in the classical music world?

CHI-CHI: Don't just accept everything that's put on a plate in front of you; question it. For example, when you see yet another symphony by Brahms, always look for a counterpart by a composer of color. Always look for a desk partner who might not look like you when you look in the mirror. White people, please, don't just assume that because somebody doesn't look like you, or dress like you, or speak like you, that they are any lesser than you. If you're truly wanting to be proactive about inclusion and demonstrate that you are actively anti-racist, then you have to take action. When you're putting together a group of players for a project, go and actively ask somebody who doesn't look like you, sound like you, speak like you, or walk like you. Invite them to join your group. Invite more than one to join your group. Make them feel not only that you're including them for this project, but that they belong as well. You've got to work a little bit harder for that.

ANNA: You've set up this flagship organization that is now internationally renowned. What advice would you give to somebody who's wanting to set up an organization, a campaign group, or a project?

CHI-CHI: Always look outside the box. Think, what makes you uncomfortable? Then try it out. I thought by going to the Royal Academy of Music and all these places, that I was learning everything I needed to know about music. Can you believe that I'd never played a piece of music by a female composer until halfway through my career! I never knew they existed! I never knew a piece of music by a Black composer until the first concert with Chineke! in 2015. 62 of us walked onto the stage, including the conductor, and none of us had played a piece of music by this composer, Samuel Coleridge-Taylor. It was deeply shocking to us all that this wonderful music of such high quality was unknown to us before this moment. We were all very moved by it, and many of the players began to question why none of us had ever heard of or been taught about Samuel Coleridge-Taylor as part of our music education. It wasn't just because Coleridge-Taylor was of African heritage, but because this was such good music! By playing his music, a true sense of belonging was felt by everyone on that stage; that there was a true piece of themselves in the music, written by a composer of mixed-ethnicity, African heritage—played alongside Beethoven in the same concert program, as it should be. Yes, we belong right in there. We inspire this music. We are the purveyors of this music. It belongs to us as much as everybody else.

VI

ACTIVISM

Building Networks for Change

23

(Un)Silencing Blacktivism in Opera

An Interview with Quodesia Johnson about the *Letter to the Opera Field from Black Administrators*

Antonio C. Cuyler

In June 2020, an unidentified group used Instagram, @operaisracist, to share anonymous stories about their experiences with racism in opera (Chang, 2020). Also in June of 2020, the Black Opera Alliance (BOA) emerged to "empower Black classical artists and administrators by exposing systems of racial inequity and underrepresentation of the African diaspora in all facets of the industry and challenging institutions to implement drastic reform" (Black Opera Alliance, 2021). This international group comprised hundreds of Black opera professionals throughout the world. On September 14, 2020, BOA released *A Pledge for Racial Equity and Systemic Change in Opera* (Black Opera Alliance, 2020). The pledge asked the opera industry to acknowledge the artistic and financial contributions of Black artists and administrators and pledge a commitment to a number of items to manifest racial equity for opera's Black cultural workers. It gained a relatively high level of traction in the US; as of August 24, 2021, 48% of US opera companies had replied *yes* to the pledge, and only 1% replied *no* (Black Opera Alliance & TRG Arts, 2021).

Despite these responses, concerns still remained. On October 29, 2020, the Black Administrators of Opera (BAO) released a *Letter to the Opera Field from Black Administrators* (Black Administrators of Opera, 2020). This letter, addressed to "Colleagues in the Opera Art Form," read: "We, the Black Administrators of Opera, call upon each of you to help make the necessary changes for greater equity in our field." It argued that:

> While this letter comes in the wake of the recent deepening in commitment to bringing about change in the field, it is the industry's long-standing, cyclical and destructive approach to change that serves as a catalyst for this letter. The industry continues to call on our stories and experiences, our creativity, our communities, our expertise, and our networks without ceding power, demonstrating a reluctance to progress beyond a White-centered approach to opera.

The letter presented a "list of actionable solutions for racial equity for arts administrators in the opera field." These five solutions aim to have companies commit to equity in salaries, wages, and promotion opportunities; company-wide racial equity education and professional development; equitable hiring and recruitment practices; company-wide intentional inclusion in the execution of mission and programs; and to adequately fund company Diversity, Equity, and Inclusion initiatives and working groups.

In closing, the letter stated, "Certain members of the Black Administrators of Opera elected to remain anonymous for fear of retaliation." Initially, the letter cited 25 Black professionals from a cross-section of opera companies, working in "diversity, education, community and civic engagement, artistic, production, operations, development, and company culture." However, only 14 signed the letter while 11 "elected to remain anonymous for fear of retaliation."

This action from the Black Administrators of Opera demonstrates some of the shortcomings of the type of diversity work signaled by the Black Opera Alliance's pledge. While it may initially seem successful due to having nearly half of US opera companies sign the pledge, important critiques remain that obscure this story. In the conversation that follows, the founder of *Black Administrators of Opera*, Quodesia (Quo) Johnson, discusses "Blacktivism" in opera with Antonio C. Cuyler, an academic and access, diversity, equity, and inclusion consultant.

Blacktivism in opera

ANTONIO: Artistically, I pursued a career in opera as a singer and manager, which has given me a highly nuanced understanding of the art form, its conventions, and its racialized history. Yet, I consider myself an outsider within the art form because my professional identities as an administrator, consultant, and scholar position me at opera's margins. I had hoped that the summer of 2020's "Great Racial Awakening" would become an opportunity to seismically address long-suffered anti-Black racism in all aspects of US life. Although I am not hopeful that the US will truly atone for its longitudinal abominable treatment of Black people, the way that the reckoning has compelled change in opera makes me optimistic. Observing the phenomenon of Blacktivism in opera has prompted me to contemplate a series of questions. First, where are we now? What has changed? What still needs to change? What will remain the same in the emerging normal? Is the curse of unearned White privilege and power maddening fear? Lastly, is operatic White supremacy culture so retaliatory that it would cause some Black people to only advocate for themselves under the cloak of anonymity? But perhaps to start with, I should ask, given that the Pledge had already been taken up, why was the *Letter* from Black administrators necessary?

QUO: Because we knew that there would be pushback for the BOA *Pledge*. We also knew that the industry needed to hear directly from its administrators because there is a habit of dismissing the artists who do not often see all of the moving pieces outside of what happens onstage. The administrative voice was necessary because we're in the space, doing the work. We knew that there would be an excuse of "We don't know what to do, tell us what to do, give us instructions" in a desire to check the racial equity box. Simply saying, "Move out of the way so I can do it" is not always beneficial because White supremacy culture characteristics include the right to comfort, being the only one, individualism, and power-hoarding. So we wanted to provide a supplemental document from the administrative perspective that said, "Do this, start here, do these things" so that it can align with what Black Opera Alliance presented with little space for excuses. Building on the work that Black Opera Alliance did, because we share some of the members and definitely similar goals, we wanted to present what accountability and change looks like from an administrative focused space because we know the reasons behind the budget, hiring, and casting decisions. We're the ones doing the work to administer this art form to others and could further break down the steps for change by speaking the language of administrators.

ANTONIO: I want to link these ideas to Blacktivism, to show why Blacktivism is necessary. Blacktivism is Black peoples' use of advocacy, personal agency, and political action to actualize racial equity and justice (Cuyler, forthcoming; Hines, 2020; Lorde, 1984). White opera professionals respond differently to Black artists practicing Blacktivism than they do to Black administrators practicing Blacktivism. BAO's letter stated that "the industry calls on our stories and experiences, creativity, communities, expertise, and networks without ceding power, demonstrating a reluctance to progress beyond a White-centered approach to opera." This statement signals that its authors believe that opera is not ready for change. In my observations, too many cultural organizations have become comfortable asking historically oppressed people to help them to become anti-oppression organizations without compensating them appropriately for or making budgetary investments in said work. One can find evidence of this socially irresponsible practice articulated in both the *Pledge for Racial Equity and Systemic Change in Opera* and the *Letter to the Opera Field from Black Administrators*. Yet, these same organizations reap the benefits of Black peoples' emotional and intellectual labor. As I have argued before (Cuyler, 2021), too often cultural organizations initiate access, diversity, equity, and inclusion (ADEI) work without honestly acknowledging the necessity for change. If opera truly acknowledged and apologized for the ways in which it perpetuated and profited from anti-Black racism, perhaps then it would open itself up to the kinds of transformations that BAO and BOA seeks to manifest. This, to my mind, is why opera needs Blacktivism. Effective Blacktivism begins with Black people gathering to discuss priorities and strategies for achieving them. Blacktivism also has healing properties because by standing up for themselves, Black people internalize that they, indeed, matter.

QUO: The way that I approach healing looks at the internal and then external state, allowing the external to benefit from internal growth. Black Administrators of Opera is a unique space because it has the intent and impact of us gathering as well as the experience of what it means for us to truly be in a space where we can thrive, heal, correct, address things, share resources, and do work as a community. Those who know about the space are rejuvenated and supported as they go back into their respective workspaces. They start to thrive in a way that does not continuously break them down as they face dehumanizing experiences due to White supremacy culture knowing that they are fully supported and nurtured in the Black Administrators space.

ANTONIO: And after the emergence of BOA and BAO, so, too, did the LatinX Artists Society in Opera and the Asian Opera Alliance. The groups have connected, but there's a wider question about the conditions by which BIPOC can collectively wield power for racial equity and justice in opera.

QUO: Much of the social and racial progress within the United States of America has come at the expense of Black lives and bodies. The world watched a Black man die as if it were [broadcast] on Animal Planet, and then started to move. This has been a practice of our society and the world for generations, looking to the suffering, determination, and courage of Black people while denying our humanity. Uniting is beautiful and must be done as long as we address the rampant anti-Blackness inherent to this system. That includes Black spaces. So as long as we commit to disrupting and erasing that hierarchy as we unite and as long as we acknowledge that we benefit from an economy that's on stolen land, built by stolen people, with stolen labor, we can go from there.

ANTONIO: At the same time, BOA, BAO, the LatinX Artists Society in Opera, and the Asian Opera Alliance must hold opera companies accountable for the decisions they make that suppress, thwart, and undermine racial equity and justice. A collective of BIPOC may galvanize the most power to achieve this critical goal in opera. For me, Blactivism and power remain inextricably linked. At the same time, power is also neutral and democratic. It has no investment in right or wrong, or bad or good. Anyone, at any time can access power to advocate for themselves (Alleyne, 2021).

QUO: Power's definitely neutral. It moves as we actively create opportunities to not just wield power, but to direct, shape, and share it in ways that achieve what we want to do. It's when power is consistently hoarded by groups of people, by individuals, that it becomes a weapon for dehumanization and destruction. If we look at the ways that even the OPERA America conference attempted to respond to the racial wave of awakening of last year, many leaders were trying to learn what to do, not to bring about change, but to maintain power. So we faced these opportunities for people to try to get it right but within their own comfort. That comfort came at the expense of Black people to all these White leaders, coworkers, and colleagues who were freaking out and going to their Black staff for assistance and absolution. I believe that there's this fear of us gathering because people suddenly realize how much they depend on their Black staff. The system says that those who are racialized as White are supposed to have power, even if it is not earned, even if it is placed in the hands of someone who does not truly know the meaning of equity and justice. The system supports them and mandates a space in which others, particularly Black people, should yield to their authority. If you remove the false competence that seeks to maintain power by creating barriers that say, I need to watch you; I need to "understand" what you're doing without a desire to change; you need to come to me for approval even though you are the best voice for this, people begin to see the truth. This awakening took away their feeling of authority on this subject, and suddenly people started to see the ways in which their roles don't matter, or that they're not as effective in their roles as they thought they were.

White supremacy culture

ANTONIO: Okun (2021) has defined White supremacy culture as internalized attitudes and behaviors that do not serve humans because they target and violate Black, Indigenous, and People of Color (BIPOC) and communities with the intent to destroy them directly. In addition to targeting and violating BIPOC with the intent to destroy them directly, it also targets and violates White people with a persistent invitation to collude that will inevitably destroy their humanity. In relation to White supremacy, do you think the opera industry is ready to change?

QUO: The opera industry is just as prepared as everybody else in that nobody's ready until we're actually in the work, but that's okay. If we were ready to do it, it would have been done by now. We've taken the very compliant approach, which is normal in White supremacy culture of: "Let's name all the things that have happened. Let's attribute it to the art form as opposed to our nation, individual selves, or lack of accountability within organizations. Let's look at the systemic things, as opposed to the intentional, systematic exclusion of Black people in the nation and in the field." We even saw examples of this last year in the black squares on social media, the sudden statements for Black Lives Matter. Suddenly, everybody cares and wants to eradicate racism, and that care and desire for change lasted all of three months. The industry, like much of the world, continues to benefit from our suffering, propelling itself forward with performative promises of "We'll do better." A lot of organizations put out statements without truly doing the work or understanding that there is still work to do. They most likely went to the one or two Black individuals, if they did that, to make a statement, or tuned to White leadership for a statement, those types of things. Once we start to understand that this work is continuous and radical and must take place in a way that challenges what we are used to doing as individuals and as organizations, then we'll be ready to get to that next step of change.

ANTONIO: Some White people have a lot of fear about racial equity and justice: the fear that racial equity and justice will force them to grapple with the lie of their supremacy. I wonder, who are White people without Whiteness? White supremacy culture always seeks to obstruct Blacktivism. What barriers does White supremacy culture pose to racial equity in opera?

QUO: The false belief that to focus on Black people harms other identities, when we know that in this nation, equity has moved at the sacrifice of Black individuals and bodies. That idea that to focus on one means that we are dismissing others, or the idea that you cannot focus on more than one thing at the same time, that either/or thinking of White supremacy culture gets in the way. White supremacy culture is present in every facet of the nation. Dismantling it is creating a ripple effect that is shaking a lot of sectors. The ways in which the philanthropic field has to catch up and commit to equitable funding is an example. Many of our opera companies rely on philanthropic support, and as philanthropy is being called into the conversation of racial equity, the knowledge and commitment to know what to look for in grant-making requires a type of truth-telling and vulnerability that inherently challenges White supremacy culture. We see a lot of funders now saying, "Okay, tell us about your EDI work," as a blanket solution to all organizations but do not understand or recognize the ways this adds to the inequities of those already facing systemic racism while inadvertently benefitting those with greater resources to check the EDIA statement and action plan boxes. Much of opera in the US moves on funding and the whims of donors—add that we are in a White supremacist society with dehumanizing structures, and there is no way the opera field can develop solutions without looking at the deep roots of this system. We have to see and experience what companies are doing with their communities and have the education and humility to seek truth necessary for equitable conditions. This prioritizes the voices of the people facing barriers as the experts of their own experiences and as those who measure change, not White leadership, not funders. I believe the concept of what community means for the opera field is also a barrier because it inherently contradicts White supremacy. I believe the exclusionary practices and lack of awareness within the organizations are also barriers. I've spoken to a lot of general directors. They're like, "Oh, we're great. This is wonderful. We implemented this and that and have this statement, so we don't really need that much work in order to bring about change." Then you talk to Black people on the staff, and they're miserable. They're ready to quit the field or [they] face health issues because of their work environment. But many companies dismiss the harm racism causes their Black staff, artists, and communities as if art cannot cause harm. That's also one of the barriers, the difference in lived experience; how we perceive what is happening based on our own lived experience; and who has the power to dismiss and prioritize experiences and narratives.

ANTONIO: Indeed, BAO asked opera companies to "develop a Code of Conduct for managing discriminatory or racist rhetoric/action from board members, patrons, donors, artists, or guests." Given the heinous stories shared on @ operaisracist, this request makes perfect sense. The letter went on to state, "It is demeaning, unfair, and inappropriate to create a working group to address systemic oppression without allocating the financial resources and agency necessary to fund activities, programs, and training."

QUO: Understanding those who do not live this experience cannot speak to it. We can collaborate, but you don't speak for your Black staff. I would also say the ways in which we value repertoire. As we look at what it means for opera in the United States, if the rep and the voices do not include the Black community, then which works and which nation are we talking about? We have so many different stories we can tell as we live the full human experience, as all human beings do. It's the racism laced in the language of "skill, excellence, and fitting the role," those kinds of covert White supremacy culture norms of meritocracy, bootstrap theory, of you just have to work harder, those concepts that continue to feed into the fallacy of White supremacy. There are quite a few barriers. And then the barriers that exist outside of your organization in the assumption of what it means to sing Black, what it means for you to compose, conduct, lead, guide, as we look at our current White-majority leaders, right? And how people are still trying to find their way in this field, and the silencing that takes place to keep the status quo or maintain traditions rooted in the exclusion of Black people.

ANTONIO: The letter also asked opera companies to "commit to engaging Black communities in an honest and mutually beneficial manner without the intention of solely profiting from their networks, donations, and ticket sales." BAO also commented that "current business practices in the opera field are built on structures of exclusion and cannot play a productive role in addressing the issues that plague our organizations." But that does not mean that the industry should not aspire to the principle of engaging Black communities in an honest and mutually beneficial manner, especially because it advances antiracism and creative justice in opera.

QUO: Leaders and colleagues will go to their Black staff, to absorb, pull, take, and demand superficial guidance just to inform their decisions so that they can continue to feel like they are competent enough to do the job. The act of colonizing and silencing stems from White supremacy culture for our nation. Which is what we ran into so heavily in summer 2020. "Explain your pain and struggle to me. Educate me so I can feel better at the expense of your trauma, so I can help." Where so many people were literally asking questions, "How do we talk to communities?" That's a very simple thing to do depending on your space and experiences. You've been sending your Black staff to go talk to the community and using that to present the art that ultimately is still hurting the community because it's showing false depictions of those communities, or these harmful depictions of identities. And not just the Black communities, but all communities. White supremacy culture does not know community because it upholds individualism and a false hierarchy of human value. You cannot profess what you do not know, and it is painstakingly clear that the opera field is trying to find a path for equity through a lens of White supremacy, which is not possible.

(Un)Silencing Blacktivism

ANTONIO: So why did you feel comfortable signing the letter, and why do you think others didn't feel comfortable signing?

QUO: I will say my recent experience in building relationships with people and the honest communication with different individuals and entities in the field, it would not have been the first time they heard me say these things. People know where I stand and why I do this work. It was necessary, and what we shared is the truth. And what are you going to do? I personally cannot operate from a space of self-preservation, not when I know what it means to truly connect with others in meaningful ways. I also had the support of my family, and general director, Ian Derrer, at *The Dallas Opera* because of the work that we've been doing on company culture. We did not put our organization's names on there because we could not speak for our organizations and knew there would be a greater wave of resistance from those seeking to find a reason, and excuse to not engage in this work. We went back and forth about the conversation as a community. Should we sign the letter? Should we list our organizations? We can't speak for organizations. We can speak as ourselves. I will not speak directly for the members, but as the founder and the space moderator for Black Administrators of Opera, we wanted to first lead with those individuals who did not feel comfortable enough to sign the letter. It is profound and speaks volumes to the ways that shallow statements and false claims of committing to racial equity create dangerous spaces for Black people. People did not feel comfortable signing the letter because they were and still are working in extremely hostile environments that tokenize, dehumanize, use, dismiss, and abuse Black employees. They were not in safe spaces to put their names on the letter because they knew that there would be repercussions that would require a lot of sacrifices that would have been inequitable and unfair. It was not safe for them to do so because of that angry and violent Whiteness that would have come back toward them. For some of our members, they may have been one of few Black employees or Black artists within the space, as it is not uncommon for Black administrators to also be artists. They wanted to ensure, and we wanted to ensure, that we're not creating progress at the expense of their lives, livelihoods, and careers in the field. The issue lies with the system. The issue is with the angry leader who is going to be upset that you signed this letter of truth. We did not want to punish or isolate them. We wanted to support them in the community. We have some members who signed and faced repercussions, microaggressions, violence, assumptions, and accusations because of the shedding of false narratives and bringing such conditions to the light.

ANTONIO: (Un)silencing Blacktivism relies on community protecting and uplifting. But at the same time, this requires understanding that throughout US history White supremacy culture has suppressed, thwarted, and undermined Blacktivism while attacking Black peoples' psyche making it untenable to continue by negatively impacting their quality of life.

QUO: Black Administrators of Opera is a shared space for all, including the power structure in that the priority is to center truth and connection. It's one of our group agreements. And what it means to center truth for us is revolutionary. Truth is everybody does not feel safe, is not safe, will not be safe if they sign it. Truth is everyone will be uplifted and affirmed in their decision because it is a system that is against us. We can dismantle it and move forward together. By centering connection, we take care of us as a people because no one else will in a way that is truly meaningful without disrupting the system. People will benefit from what we do, appreciate what we do, but will not take care of us as Black people in the same way. We want to center truth, and then connection. People do not feel safe signing this letter, that is evidence as to why systems of White supremacy culture, dehumanization, and oppression need to be eradicated in this field.

The future of Blacktivism in classical music

ANTONIO: Blacktivism simultaneously pushes opera and all of classical music toward antiracism and creative justice while threatening White supremacy culture's power, even as it silences Blacktivism. As you're dismantling and re-imaging, how will the BAO ensure that they do not hoard power and wield it in the same ways as White administrators have historically?

QUO: I won't say that that's not possible because, as human beings, it is very much possible. I will say it's not truly possible in this system because, as we looked at the antiracist organization continuum, it requires that we have to be in a transformed society for us to have enough power to wield it the same way. Which we're not a transformed society. We won't be able to impact White people's lives the way that we are impacted. That's just what racism is and what it means. But the ways in which we move as community is what allows us to keep one another aligned, and to correct, guide, and disrupt through community. It is very difficult to hoard power when you're in community with someone because you start to share space, you start to be accountable, you start to witness the narratives of others, and you're forever changed when that happens, when you connect on a human level. Which is what Black Administrators of Opera is all about, that very real connection between individuals and the family and the community that comes out of it. It's very difficult for hoarding to take place in a dedicated, shared space. We engage in a community that is about shared experience; that is about uplifting who we are and accepting who we are and inviting everybody into this space in that way.

ANTONIO: In terms of organizational structure, BAO does not formally function as a nonprofit organization. Black cultural organizations have a number of models from which to choose when formally structuring themselves. Culturally responsive management suggest that Black organizations might use the principles of an African tribe, the Black church, Historically Black Colleges and Universities (HBCUs), National Association for the Advancement of Colored People (NAACP), Urban League, Black Panther Party, Black Lives Matter, or the Black Futures Lab when formalizing themselves organizationally

(Prieto & Phipps, 2019). But the cultural specificity of the principles these organizations enshrine may find themselves at odds with the characteristics of the White supremacy culture within the nonprofit business entity. But with a purpose as compelling, forward-thinking, and impactful as BAO's, I wonder if institutionalizing as a nonprofit makes BAO vulnerable to co-opting by White supremacy culture, even when it comes from those who consider themselves "liberal (Brooks, 2021)?" Do you think BAO will formally establish itself as a nonprofit, or will organizing itself as a nonprofit undermine the shared governance and communal space that BAO has carefully curated?

QUO: As long as we are committed to the community, no matter how we institutionalize, it won't undermine the space that we're in because we know how we want to operate. If we have to present ourselves a certain way to provide an access point for others to be able to see and support, then we can do so while clearly defying White supremacy culture and defining our own space. Openly doing so allows us to transparently say we decided to organize this way because White supremacy culture requires it, but we are actively demonstrating how to remain committed to our unique space by redefining what it means to be this type of institution. We're creating something new. You can call it whatever allows you to connect in truth, understand that it is not like the average space for opera professionals. It is and will remain a place for us, by us.

24
Reflecting on the Work of Gender Relations in New Music
Institutional Critique and Activist Strategies

Brandon Farnsworth and Rosanna Lovell

Gender Relations in New Music (GRiNM) is a heterogeneous collective advocating for increased gender equality, inclusivity, and further diversification of people and practices in the new music community.[1] Since its foundation it has been a priority to include queer, LGBTQ+, and intersectional perspectives in our work and in relation to our concept of gender. Active mainly in Germany but also across Europe, GRiNM has generated statistics about gender representation at new music festivals, organized workshops and talks at various international festivals and conferences, used artistic interventions and protest tactics, exercised critique through digital social media platforms, and in November 2019 organized its own international conference on gender and diversity issues in new music. The group's approach across all these activities is to create space for these issues, connect practitioners interested in change from across the music ecosystem, and apply pressure to those who defend the status quo.

This chapter will give an overview of the group's actions and explain some of the strategies behind them. We argue that GRiNM's method of critiquing new music and its institutions is unique in its focus on building coalitions of people, rather than establishing yet another institution to achieve its goals. We want to emphasize however that this is just one interpretation by two members of GRiNM of complex and multifaceted actions worked on by many people, and that different interpretations are as welcome as they are probable.

Before delving into details, it is important to say that we view contemporary classical music (CCM) as inextricably linked to classical music, as a "high art subculture" (Emerson 2020) that is dependent on much of the same training and institutions as classical music, such as conservatories. Though the genre understands itself as being about breaking traditions rather than continuing them like classical music, Anna Bull has argued convincingly that CCM has inherited classical music's problematic class and gender biases (2019, p. 14), something we have also seen first-hand in our own activism. This means new music's understanding of its own "newness" is understood as a succession of works by individual geniuses, as in classical music. Focusing too much on music as the creation of one singular individual comes at the cost of thinking about it as the product of a specific set of social, historical, institutional, even technological circumstances. Because these conditions have been ignored while universalizing its appeal and accessibility, the CCM scene has ignored the fact that it strongly favors the music of White, "Western," bourgeois male subjects.

GRiNM's earliest actions thus focused on producing statistics that challenged these universalist claims. Its first action took place in 2016 (as Gender Research in Darmstadt, GRiD), "digesting" the statistics produced by Ashley Fure about the Darmstadt Summer Course. The summer course is a biennial composition academy and music festival in Germany and perhaps one of the most influential CCM institutions, cultivating links to young composers around the world since its founding in 1946. Fure's research showed for example that until 2014, only 7% of compositions performed at the summer course were by female composers. The statistics unleashed a fury of informal meetings and debates among the course's students, leading to guerrilla protest interventions, and to the formation of the group that would later come to be known as GRiNM.

After that summer course, GRiNM went on to organize several more actions to generate statistics on gender representation at CCM festivals in Germany. We for instance found that at the MaerzMusik festival in Berlin, from 2010 to 2018, just 28% of pieces were by women,[2] trans-masculine, or non-binary people, while at the Donaueschingen Musiktage, an important CCM festival in Southern Germany, between 2011 and 2017 it was only 18% (Gender Relations in New Music, 2020a). GRiNM also continued to use guerrilla actions to get these messages across: At the Donaueschinger Musiktage for instance, the statistics we generated were presented as an advertisement in the festival program (see Figure 24.1) as well as on flyers and stickers we handed out at the festival. Doing these actions led to us engaging in informal discussions with organizers and festival-goers about why this was important.

GRiNM produced these statistics through crowdsourcing them via "data-harvesting workshops" appended to various festivals, where attendees would be invited to sit together with their laptops and go through physical or digital festival archives, entering the statistics on a shared Google Sheet. The significance of these statistics is twofold. First, while these findings do not come as a surprise to any experienced observer, they serve the purpose of making the very blatant inequalities in this field visible and sayable. They provide quantifiable evidence that can be used in discussion and to further activist goals (see also Scharff, 2018, p. 42). Second, the crowdsourcing activities, as well as the initial GRiD

Donaueschinger Musiktage

92.44%

of pieces made by men

since 1921

Gender Relations in New Music
GRINM.ORG

Figure 24.1 Statistics on the gender balance in Donaueschingen Musiktage's program in 2018. Reproduced with permission from Gender Relations in New Music.

debates spurred by Fure's statistics, functioned to connect like-minded people together who were interested in this topic. The data-harvesting activities gave a straightforward, informal, monotonous goal that led to people chatting and getting to know each other. We found this particularly effective because many participants were interested in these topics, but felt unqualified to discuss them. Inevitable questions of categorization like assuming gender based on names, or how to deal with composer/performers or other non-standard categories led to equally productive discussions about the challenges of categorization, and the nuance and complexity associated with achieving equal representation in real-world conditions. In many cases, we were able to rely on the community's collective pool of knowledge about festival artists' self identification (in terms of both gender identity and the spectrum between composing and performing) to fill in data. In others, we used the close collaborative situation to decide collectively on the best ways to categorize information, and apply the same rules of thumb consistently across the dataset. The first point of the exercise was always to emphasize that when looking at the data itself, the inequalities were so blatantly clear as to leave no question about the lack of representation of women and non-binary people in festival programs, irrespective of how any one particular composer/performer was categorized. The second point was then to show that strict or rigorous categorization, as is often emphasized throughout music training programs, inevitably fails to capture the complexity of lived experience.

GRiNM grew and began to expand the kind of events it participated in beyond the festivals in Germany that had invited us to take part in their program. Members led workshops and talks at various international symposiums, conferences, and festivals more widely in Europe with the aim of creating dedicated spaces for presenting and discussing these important issues around gender and diversity and allowing a broad range of practitioners, from academics to musicians, to speak and exchange on these issues. We found that these sessions resonated deeply with those attending and in each context there was a tangible need to speak about these issues. Through this, GRiNM's collective knowledge, first developed through moments of activism and generating statistics, became part of academic discourse, with different members connecting their own research to the experiences and knowledges of the group, enriching and broadening the scope of the network. While at these events certain individuals would represent GRiNM, the collective nature of the group was always emphasized in event programs. As will become apparent later, the possibility to act under an anonymous collective name is also a crucial function of GRiNM.

As the group's activities continued, its network of artists, researchers, organizers, educators, and academics gradually expanded. This strengthened the important role GRiNM serves as a network of like-minded individuals crossing over national borders and fields of practice. The aim is to connect people together who are working on different aspects of these issues, in various settings and with different approaches. However, since these issues are systemic, it is important to acknowledge how different parts interconnect and influence each other, forming the CCM music world that we know and engage with. For example, people working at cultural institutions or festivals could have similar issues to those working in higher education regarding diversifying the composers that are part of their programs. Exchanging experiences and strategies regarding how to deal with such issues across institutional and often national boundaries can be empowering and productive for those involved. Similarly, providing a platform for researchers to share their work with practitioners can help the latter better contextualize and articulate their own personal observations.

Marking two years since GRiNM's inception, the group returned to Darmstadt in 2018. Running parallel to the summer courses was a conference entitled *Defragmentation—Convention on Curating Contemporary Music*, held partly in response to the actions by GRiD in 2016. In our view, it did not go far enough in addressing the issues that we see as ingrained in CCM and the decision to hold the conference at a location separate to that of the summer courses reinforced the idea that these difficult discussions were taking place without practitioners from the field, who themselves must be part of any meaningful change. Following the opening speech, members of GRiNM stood up and read in unison a statement criticizing it as tokenistic and merely paying lip service to this slew of crucial issues. We invited delegates to join the group in a "parainstitutional" discussion space in the form of a temporary marquee set up in the front yard of the school building where the summer courses take place. Over the next week GRiNM held a series of open discussions in the marquee on various topics with participants from both the summer courses (students and teachers) and the conference, creating ourselves a necessary "off" or "para" space, which we thought was necessary in order to have meaningful discussions on these issues as well as crossing the divide between discourse and practice.

GRiNM also engaged in other forms of creative activism at Darmstadt. We began an Instagram account where we would post memes that were both making fun and being critical of the Darmstadt Summer Courses (see Figures 24.2 and 24.3). We would tag these with official hashtags, thus inserting ourselves into the online presence of the summer courses and conference. It also provided a way for those not attending in person, but part of the CCM world and aware of the role Darmstadt plays in it, to engage with and follow what GRiNM was doing there. We also performed interventions, raining down flyers (see Figure 24.4) onto the

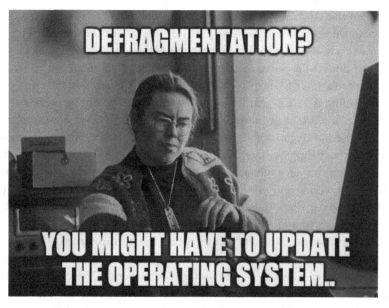

Figure 24.2 An image macro posted to GRiNM's Instagram channel protesting the conference *Defragmentation: Curating Contemporary Music* at the 2018 Darmstadt Summer Course. Reproduced with permission from Gender Relations in New Music.

Figure 24.3 An image macro posted to GRiNM's Instagram channel. Reproduced with permission from Gender Relations in New Music.

audience at the end of the premier of Lisa Lim's opera *Atlas of the Sky*, provoking thoughts around what the Darmstadt Summer Courses are, and more interestingly, what they could be.

GRiNM paid for these various actions by using the speakers' fees, which two members of the group received for running a workshop at the *Defragmentation* conference. This exemplifies the position GRiNM often has in relation to these big festivals; invited yet not fully included to be part of fundamental discussions around what is necessary or possible for such an event. We often have intimate insider knowledge of these events through our members and network, yet through acting collectively as GRiNM we are able to engage both as individuals (composers, academics, etc.) and as a group. As GRiNM it is possible to exercise a critical position that would be a challenging undertaking for any individual, as well as potentially having a negative effect on their career. The collective voice of GRiNM is one of its strengths, and the open structure of the group allows for people to become involved or join an action for a short period of time, as well as to do their own actions under this moniker.

Rather than continuing to be invited as a pressure release valve for festivals who felt obligated to discuss their lack of diversity, GRiNM decided to initiate its own event. In November 2019, the group organized the *GRiNM Network Conference 2019: Experiences with Gender and Diversity in New Music* at the

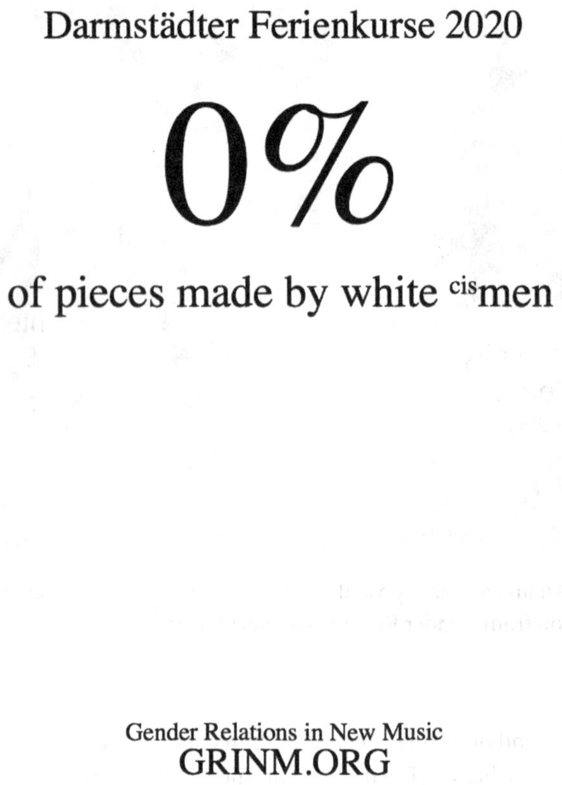

Darmstädter Ferienkurse 2020

0%

of pieces made by white ᶜⁱˢmen

Gender Relations in New Music
GRINM.ORG

Figure 24.4 A flyer shared by GRiNM after a concert at the 2018 Darmstadt Summer Course. Reproduced with permission from Gender Relations in New Music.

Zurich University of the Arts. The idea was to bring together a wide range of people working in the fields of research, education, programming, and administration, to share their experiences on the topic from different perspectives. The resulting conference thus activated the network that GRiNM had been gradually growing, bringing them together as a peer group, and thus demonstrating that the issues that GRiNM had been advocating for were important for the larger CCM community to take seriously. We extended this gesture also via a special issue of *OnCurating Journal* that included the academic papers and reports from the field presented at the conference, solidifying the existence and importance of these positions within the growing debate in CCM and sharing them with an audience beyond those who attended the conference.

During 2020 and 2021 GRiNM turned to mostly text-based interventions, due to the pandemic sweeping the world and dramatically impacting the performing arts and our own careers. At the beginning of 2020 we began a collaboration with the new music magazine *Positionen*, where over four issues GRiNM directly addressed its readership through a series of full-page spreads. We returned to working with statistics, taking a playful approach, calling the series *Checking Boxes with GRiNM*. "Chapter 1: Composition Professors" focused on the gender of those holding professorship positions (not teaching contracts or lectureships) at major universities and music schools in German speaking Europe (Germany, Austria, Switzerland). For this we adopted a tick-the-box approach that had three options, taken from what has now become standard for all job advertisements in German: Male (M), Female (F), Divers (D).[3] This highlighted the fact that the vast majority of professors were male. "Chapter 2: Curators of some New Music Festivals," in the next edition, left the boxes unchecked as an open invitation to readers to tick the boxes themselves, and as a gesture back toward our desire to crowdsource statistics as itself a form of activism. Here we included more categories such as class/socio-economic background and "race"/ethnicity/migratory background.[4] We wanted to move away from solely gender-based categorization and make visible the many ways in which discrimination manifests itself. This is based on our intersectional approach, which is core to our understanding of these issues. "Chapter 3: Selected Juries" looked at the people making the decisions about composition awards and prizes. In our final letter to readers, "Out of the Box with GRiNM," we wrote about the limitations of statistics in understanding the complexity of privileges and exclusions that exist, but also their necessity in illuminating the reality of institutions and power structures in the European new music scene. It was an invitation to reflect critically, and a demand to develop solutions and enact change.[5]

In September 2020, GRiNM was invited to be part of a symposium by the Creative Europe project *Sounds Now* entitled "Curating Diversity in Europe—Decolonizing Contemporary Music." We decided to contribute to the symposium by publishing an online questionnaire in advance of the event. As we explain at the beginning of the document,

> A danger of symposia on such fundamental issues is to spend too much time establishing definitions and problems. Our goal is rather to jumpstart this process so that we can spend more time committing to meaningful exchange and enacting prompt, lasting, and tangible changes. (Gender Relations in New Music, 2020b)

The action tried to highlight the danger of "diversity talk" becoming an end in itself among those concerned about a lack of diversity in CCM. Responses to the survey confirmed this danger, while also revealing a large amount of what Ahmed (2004) has called "declarations of Whiteness," where declarations of bad practices such as racist attitudes (saying you are racist) are implied to be the same as good practices (not being racist), when they are not. This suggested that there were complicated dynamics at work in the group around the perceived role of the symposium that could have been further explored during the event.

In 2021 GRiNM united with *Archiv Frau und Musik* and the female: pressure network in a spontaneous protest action against the all White male event *Einklang freier Wesen* at the ZKM Centre for Art and Media Karlsruhe. Open letters were written to the organizers and pressure was applied online through social media posts and memes on the GRiNM Instagram account. This resulted in the postponement of the event and a new program, as well as us being invited to a discussion with the organizers to address these issues. This exemplifies how the (increasingly online) network we have built over time can effect change. Regarding these various text-based interventions it is important to tailor the form and language to the relevant context and audience to maximize their impact.

The importance of addressing gender and diversity has become increasingly acknowledged in new music, which has led to an increase in the number of large and small organizations focusing on them. While many concentrate on discrete projects or goals, what we think still sets GRiNM's approach apart is our process of becoming-together, calling out, and exerting various forms of pressure in situations where gender and diversity concerns are not being taken seriously enough. Because much communication in our field is either processed via PR people, or otherwise happens in small late-night conversations at the bar, we believe there is a power in speaking out plainly and publicly about the realities of the field, not least because neither conservatories, festivals, or established venues make significant space for the sort of critical questioning that is currently required in Western European new music.

In this article we have given an overview of some of GRiNM's actions and explained how they relate to our larger activist goal. While certain mainstays like statistics and texts reoccur across our actions, we always try to consider what form of action would produce the intended effect and best achieve our goals in a particular setting. Additionally, the networks and personal relationships we build provide access to a pool of information and resources that we can work with to realize our intended effects. In this way, the group is not a funded organization that works to fulfill quotas or cultural policy, but takes a more fluid form, a collective voice that dares to speak and act on issues we consider crucial and relevant. Its most fundamental activism is thus its continued existence, which provides a banner that can be made useful by all activists in new music to help achieve their goals.

Notes

1. We will use the terms "new music" and "contemporary classical music" (CCM) interchangeably here, drawing attention to the terms' current instability as well as their relative prevalence in the German and UK contexts respectively.
2. This work is based on intersectional feminism, and as part of that, references to women include "all those who travel under the sign women" (Ahmed, 2017, p. 14).
3. In Germany, this third gender option "divers" (literally the word diverse) has become widespread in many official documents as well as job advertisements since it was introduced in 2018. It was established to provide an alternative legal gender classification for intersex people, but is also commonly understood to include gender diverse or non-binary people.
4. "Migratory background" is used here as the English translation of the German *Migrationshintergrund*.
5. The interventions appeared in the German magazine *Positionen: Texte zur aktuellen Musik* (tr. "Positions: Texts on contemporary music"), between issues 123 and 126.

25
Addressing Inequalities in the Music Industry before, during, and after COVID-19

The Campaigning Work of the UK's Independent Society of Musicians

Deborah Annetts, Vick Bain, Chris Collins, Vinota Karunasaagarar, and Dr. Kathryn Williams

The Independent Society of Musicians (ISM—http://www.ism.org) is the UK's professional association for musicians, with a membership of over 11,000, encompassing composers, performers, teachers, and many other music professionals, working across all genres. Founded in 1882 to support and promote the interests of musicians, it was early in its history that it admitted women as full members, something that other music membership bodies did not so readily embrace, and at a time when women had not yet been given the right to vote.

Even today, the ISM is unusual in that it has not just a majority female membership, but also an equal representation in terms of gender at board level and a largely female-led senior leadership team. It strives to be the authoritative voice of music professionals and is very aware of the inequalities within the profession, whether it is in classical music or the wider profession, ranging from underrepresentation to pay inequalities to racialized, gendered, and classed constructions of who counts as an "ideal" musician (Scharff, 2017).

Existing inequalities in classical music are well documented, not least in the work of Scharff, which highlights inconsistencies between the numbers of White, Black, and minority ethnic musicians in conservatoire education and in performing careers. The Counting the Music Industry report (Bain, 2019) shows gender disparity in both recruitment and remuneration—13.71% of signed classical composers and 30.16% of all signed classical musicians to UK labels are female. And data analysis by Drama Musica revealed that of 1,445 classical concerts performed throughout the world in 2018–2019, only 76 included works by female composers (Donne Women in Music, 2018). In this chapter we will focus on the ISM's campaigning and lobbying work to address equality and diversity, to demonstrate how a professional association can make a difference not only for its members but for all musicians.

Gathering data on discrimination within the music sector

In 2017, the revelations in connection with Harvey Weinstein slowly pervaded other art sectors including music and the ISM began to receive phone calls from women who wanted to share their experiences in the work environment. To discover exactly what was going on within the music industry, the ISM launched its Dignity at Work campaign, beginning with a comprehensive survey, which was promoted across the whole of the music sector.

The survey and subsequent report (ISM, 2018a) revealed that the music industry was being undermined by a high level of discriminatory practices and behaviors, including sexual harassment. Nearly half of 600 respondents stated that they had experienced some form of discrimination with reference to the nine "protected characteristics" under the UK's Equality Act 2010 (age, disability, gender reassignment, marriage and civil partnership, pregnancy and maternity, "race," religion or belief, sex, and sexual orientation). Of these, 71% were female and 72% were self-employed.

The ISM then investigated higher education institutions, including universities and specialist music, drama, and dance colleges. Researched collaboratively with Equity, the trade union known for representing the acting profession, and the Musicians' Union, the results (ISM, 2018b) echoed the findings of the workplace survey. About 57% reported experiencing inappropriate behavior, and those who did not report their concerns to their institution cited their main reasons for this as the risk of not being believed or taken seriously, the risk of damaging their reputation, the risk that the complaint would not be handled appropriately, and that the behavior seemed to be culturally acceptable in the higher education institution where it happened.[1]

Four years later, the ISM undertook similar research to determine whether there had been any change in the profession (Bain and Williams, 2022). The survey received 660 responses from people who work across the UK music sector, including educators, performers, composers, producers, studio workers, venue staff, and so on. In 2018, we reported that 47% of respondents had experienced discrimination at work (defined as direct or indirect discrimination, harassment, and victimisation). In 2022, the result was 66%, suggesting that the situation has become worse for the music workforce. Other key findings include: 78% of discrimination was committed against women; 72% was committed by people with seniority or influence; 58% was identified as sexual harassment, and 88% of self-employed people did not report their experiences.[2]

In both the 2018 and 2022 reports, over 75% of respondents did not report their experiences and the main reason for this was that they were frightened of losing work. The nature of the music world is often informal; people are recommended for jobs by word of mouth and there is a general feeling that complaints and concerns could bring retribution. The two other most common reasons for not reporting were the fear of not being taken seriously and the acceptance that this behaviour is part of the culture. It is hardly surprising that discrimination is not reported, as many workers do not have the normal protections found in more traditional workplaces such as a human resources (HR) function.

In response to feedback from the respondents in the 2018 survey, the ISM developed a Code of Practice with the Musicians' Union that, at time of writing, has been endorsed by over 120 music organizations (see also the interview with John Shortell, this volume). In the 2022 survey, 94% of respondents were supportive of all music sector organizations endorsing and promoting the Code of Practice. The ISM also developed training webinars for all those working in the music sector on the rights and obligations under the UK's Equality Act.

Campaigning for better legal protections against harassment

Legal protections against harassment and discrimination vary across national contexts. Here we focus on the legal framework in the UK, the Equality Act (2010), although the challenges outlined may be similar elsewhere in the world. One of the main barriers to musicians enforcing their rights under the Equality Act is the limited scope of the legislation and its inability to offer effective protection to those in non-standard employment. There is also the fear that if someone brings a case in the Employment Tribunal they will be victimized and lose out on work. A particular difficulty for musicians is that the flexible nature by which work is both offered and accepted means that it is often difficult to identify an underlying "contract personally to do work," as the legislation requires, to qualify for protection. One very common practice in the music sector highlights these issues clearly—a musician could be offered work, then discover that they are unavailable to perform and find someone who is available to deputize for them (known as "depping"). These types of practices do not fit comfortably into our current equalities legislation and in these circumstances, the musician who performs the work may fall foul of a strict interpretation of the Equality Act, leaving this vulnerable workforce without an effective safety net.

Until October 1, 2013, workers were able to bring claims for third party harassment such as from audience members or the public under the Equality Act. That provision was repealed by the Enterprise and Regulatory Reform Act 2013 and this means that a person who seeks to bring a claim of harassment against their employer will have to rely on nebulous provisions involving vicarious liability to bring a claim. Musicians often find themselves in public places such as concert halls, clubs, large venues, weddings, theaters, and so on. Performances often take place at night and in licensed premises where alcohol is served. ISM's research shows that while sexual harassment, inappropriate behavior, and discrimination is most often perpetrated by a complainant's peer, victims are also at risk from third parties.

The ISM met with the UK Government Equalities Office in 2019 while it was carrying out its consultation on how to ensure that we have safer workplaces and explained to them the importance of putting in place a legislative framework that will protect vulnerable freelance workers such as musicians. The ISM also responded to the government's consultation on sexual harassment in the workplace. The consultation aimed to gather evidence on whether the current laws for protecting people from sexual harassment in the workplace are effective, including how best to strengthen and clarify the laws in relation to third-party harassment. The ISM's submission included suggestions for amending the Equality Act to provide clear protection for all freelance musicians, including those who suffer discrimination while "depping," reintroducing rights around third party harassment, and asking for an extension to the time limit for bringing discrimination cases under the Equality Act.

Nearly two years after its launch in July 2019, the UK government has published its response to the consultation on sexual harassment in the workplace in July 2021. It is a wide-ranging response, considering everything from sexual harassment in the workplace to the length of time to bring claims in the tribunal. However, throughout the response the language is about employers and employees. There is no recognition that in many workplaces today there is no employer and indeed no HR department workers can go to if they feel that they have been badly treated. The response is very much written from the perspective of a 20th-century workplace, not a 21st-century workplace—leaving us to wonder if the government really understand how the modern workplace has changed.

In their consultation on sexual harassment in the workplace, the UK government has committed itself to bringing forward legislation that will "introduce a duty requiring employers to prevent sexual harassment . . . to make the workplace safer for everyone." It outlines a number of steps linked to preventing sexual harassment in the workplace such as the Equality and Human Rights Commission (a public body that challenges discrimination and protects and promotes human rights) developing a statutory code of practice and accessible guidance being produced for employers. The commitment to introduce a preventative duty on employers preventing sexual harassment will only be introduced "as soon as parliamentary time allows" so we wait to see what the time scale is on this proposal. The ISM will be asking the government to extend all these measures so that they clearly cover freelancers, an ever-increasing part of the UK workforce.

While the response reiterates the government's commitment to legislate on third party harassment when parliamentary time allows, again the language focuses on employers and their staff, even though reference is made to the hospitality industry, which has a high number of freelancers. We note that the government states that they will look "closely" at extending the time limit for bringing cases under the Equality Act, but this is an issue that requires immediate action. And we would ask that more is done to protect those who are brave enough to avail themselves of the legislation to ensure that they are not victimized or backlisted as a result.

Though the government explicitly acknowledges the ISM's concerns that many musicians may fall outside of the scope of the Equality Act's current protections, and confirms that broader issues around which groups are covered by the act will be an aspect of any wider future review of the legislation, there is no commitment to such a review, so freelancers will continue to be left materially unprotected by the current legislation. We are disappointed by the lack of urgency of a review around the scope of the Equality Act, particularly since the numbers working in the so-called gig economy are growing.

Exposing inequalities during the COVID-19 pandemic

In 2020 and 2021, the COVID-19 pandemic in the UK shone a spotlight on the inequalities faced by those working in the arts including music, many of whom are self-employed. During this period, the ISM's campaigning work evolved to campaigning for improved support during the pandemic, beginning in early 2020, before the first lockdown. While acknowledging the importance to public health of the various government lockdowns or local restrictions, the music profession suffered disproportionally as a result of lockdown measures. Musicians not only experienced a significant drop in earnings to, in many cases, zero income, but also struggled psychologically as they were prevented from doing what they are trained to do. It is an industry with little or no job security, unstable earnings, a constant fear of injury, and fear of being unsuccessful in getting the next piece of work. Most musicians are self-employed (Office for National Statistics, 2021a).[3] In 2019, median earnings were below £20,000.[4] They do not have access to holiday or sick pay, have no employment rights and no HR department to call on if something goes wrong. They are truly on their own. Those who are employed are likely to be on zero-hour contracts or undertaking casual work.

Musicians work as arrangers, composers, songwriters, performers, in sound engineering, and in all kinds of settings including orchestras, churches, choirs, musical theater, and all kinds of bands—folk, world, rock, pop, techno, wedding, jazz, and many other genres. All these sectors were affected by the various government lockdowns or local restrictions, leaving many musicians with no income and nothing to fall back on except general government schemes such as Universal Credit and Income Support. Even for those in employment the situation was not straightforward, as some employers refused to furlough those on zero-hour contracts, of which there are many within peripatetic and academic teaching staff. For any profession to be inclusive of all, and to encourage those from diverse socio-economic backgrounds, the ability to make income from your work is a basic requirement. Both before the first lockdown and throughout the continuing pandemic the ISM campaigned for support for the self-employed and then for an extension of the Self-employment Income Support Scheme (SEISS)—a temporary scheme introduced by the government, offering grants to self-employed people to help them get through the pandemic; at the time this chapter was written (August 2021) the scheme was on its fifth grant.

Almost a year after SEISS was announced, a report released by the Institute for Fiscal Studies (2021) found that 1.8 million self-employed people were not eligible for support. Musicians were not just falling through the cracks of the SEISS, but they also found themselves ineligible for support from the Culture Recovery Fund (CRF) announced by the Department for Digital Culture Media and Sport. A report to the Public Accounts Committee on June 23, 2021, questioned whether freelancers and supply chains essential to the culture sector were able to access support via the CRF (House of Commons, 2021). The report notes that of the £830 million awarded to the sector only £495 million has been actually paid out and in its implementation the CRF has presented risks of fraud, error, duplication, and overpayment.[5] Some musicians had to rely on benevolent funding, such as that offered by Help Musicians (2021), Creative Scotland (2021), and the ISM (2021a).

The gradual easing of restrictions in spring 2021 did not result in a quick return to normality for performing musicians and they faced limited performance opportunities. As a consequence, the ISM lobbied strenuously for the UK government to provide insurance solutions so that festivals and venues could go ahead without fear of huge losses that could destroy them financially, as well as calling for the publication of crucial data such as the results of the Events Research

Programme (Gov.uk, 2021); this examines the risk of transmission of COVID-19 from attendance at events and explores ways to safely allow attendance. The failure of the commercial insurance market to offer policies including coverage against COVID-related cancellation, and the lack of a suitable government backed scheme, saw the cancellation of many festivals (Thomas, 2021). Cancellations in the world of classical music in 2021 included the Aldeburgh Festival (Fairman, 2021) and the Harrogate Music Festival (Harrogate International Festivals, 2022). Similar insurance policies were already widespread across Europe and by comparison the German federal government pledged €2.5 billion to insure events for the second half of 2021 (Hickley, 2021), while Austria, Sweden, and the Netherlands invested in similar schemes (IQ Magazine, 2020; Costello, 2021; IQ Magazine, 2021). In August 2021, after several months of campaigning by the ISM, the government announced a £750 million government-backed insurance scheme. While this is a step forward in the right direction, the scheme does not cover all scenarios, for example, the scheme does not cover the situation of a sold-out show having to reduce audience numbers due to the reintroduction of social distancing and being unable to go ahead as it is no longer financially viable to do so. There is still more work to be done in this area and the ISM will encourage the government to extend the scheme where needed.

The ISM is also calling for the creation of a new tax relief for live music, touring, and new compositions, following the regulatory elements of the Theatre Tax Relief, which helped delayed productions obtain insurance. The proposed cover would include production costs of musical performances, including commission fees for new music, production costs for a new presentation of existing works, music hire and copyright licenses, and as part of the campaign, the ISM has provided template letters for members to adapt when writing to their members of Parliament.

Some musicians were able to perform digitally, as shown by research from Haferkorn, Kavanagh, and Leak (2021), but this was not without complications; the main issue was not being able to monetize a digital performance, as it has long been the case that established acts make more income from touring than from CD sales (Delfino, 2018). Musicians were able to teach digitally, and the annual ISM Teachers Fees survey showed that those who did charged similar rates to face-to-face teaching (ISM, 2021b). However, the feasibility of such teaching depends on whether students have access to technology, instruments, and suitable Wi-Fi connections.

Then of course there are the many challenges facing musicians as a result of Brexit (the UK's withdrawal from the European Union [EU]—a political and economic union between 27 European countries). The EU is one of the most important marketplaces for UK-based touring musicians and since the UK's departure from the EU, musicians who wish to tour there are subject to a whole set of provisions that did not apply to them previously. International travel restrictions during the pandemic masked the impact of Brexit, but the ongoing effects on musicians' careers and incomes are going to be extremely significant as shown by the case studies contained in ISM's report *Professionally paralysed* (ISM, 2021c). The ISM has proposed to the UK government a mechanism called a bespoke visa waiver agreement with the EU specifically for the creative and cultural sector, which would solve one aspect of mobility namely visas and add a greater level of certainty for the future. Other aspects also need to be addressed, such as bilateral agreements with individual EU member states on work permits for creative workers such as touring musicians. The ISM will continue to lobby government for solutions to enable musicians to tour in the EU without encountering mountains of costly red tape, which not only undermines our previously thriving creative industries but also inhibits cultural exchange and collaboration.

For many musicians much of 2020 and 2021 was a period of little or no income, and there is evidence of musicians leaving the profession. In 2019, 53,700 people worked as musicians as their primary occupation; this fell by 16% to 45,300 in 2020 (Office for National Statistics, 2021b). This disappearance of talent will undoubtedly have a long-term effect on the industry. Our suspicion is that those who were able to work during much of 2020 were already established and were impacted least by other demands on their time during the pandemic. Early research by Parents & Carers in Performing Arts (2021) revealed that 90% of those that took on parenting responsibility during school closures were women and three quarters of them were considering leaving the profession; this research also found that under-25s, and particularly women, lost their jobs in greater numbers. However, this statistic is built on the back of a previously existing inequality that the COVID-19 restrictions has exacerbated—that of the motherhood penalty. This is one of the key causes of the gender pay gap, with the gap rising from 5% for women in their 20s to 33% in the 12 years after a woman has had her first child. Freelance women receive a maternity allowance and although the right to share parental leave was introduced in the UK in 2015 to try and promote a level playing field for child care, it does not apply to people who are self-employed, and while self-employed mothers get maternity allowance, self-employed fathers cannot claim paid leave (PiPA, 2019). Earlier research by PiPA (2019) revealed 80% of respondents who worked across a variety of roles in performing arts had turned down work opportunities. Some 70% had been unable to attend an audition, interview, meeting, or rehearsal because of problems with child care, and for nearly a quarter of respondents this happened at least once a month. Of the 2,551 respondents to PiPA's survey, 551 worked in music. These statistics again show how inequality already existed in the world of self-employed people working within the music sector and how restrictions to prevent the spread of COVID-19 widened existing inequalities.

Building back better

There has been much talk in the music community about building back better. The pandemic has exposed grave inequalities and vulnerabilities and the question is: Can these be solved? This chapter has shown how professional associations such as the ISM can campaign to improve musicians' lives across a wide variety of issues. The ISM will continue to campaign on behalf of musicians, whether it be for short-term solutions—such as an extension to the newly introduced government-backed reinsurance scheme that would cost very little to implement but would make a huge impact on the cultural life of the country and the income of so many businesses and musicians—or on long-term issues such as tackling the practices that allow discrimination to exist within the music sector; but we also need proper joined up thinking across different branches of government when it comes to music. At present, there is little to suggest that the UK government recognizes the value of artistic professions—a situation evidenced by redirecting subsidies in English higher education institutions from creative arts courses to "provision that supports key industries and the delivery of vital public services" (Williamson, 2021), and the circulation of an advertisement from a government campaign encouraging ballet dancers to retrain for careers in cyber security (Duffield, 2020).

The industry itself needs to look at how it works if we are to build back better. The inequalities around all legally protected characteristics (such as "race," sex, and disability) mapped out in this chapter must cease. And musicians need a more robust set of terms of condition to work to—they must not be left to the vagaries of the welfare state if disaster strikes. If we do not sort out these basic contractual issues, then the profession will increasingly be attractive to only those who can afford to work in such financially fragile circumstances. And that just does not make for good art or good music.

Notes

1. Other findings include: 42% experienced bullying, 36% experienced gender discrimination and 27% experienced sexual harassment.
2. Other findings include: 80% disabled female respondents and 94% of Black, Black British, Caribbean or African respondents experienced discrimination.

3. According to the latest ONS statistics 83.44% of all musicians were self-employed during 2020, while the average across all other sectors is 16%.
4. ISM research in 2019 found that 55% of ISM members who all worked in the music sector earned less than £20,000; 79% of musicians earned less than £30,000.
5. Including by January 2021, when three reports of fraud relating to two grants administered by Arts Council England (ACE) had been received through the COVID Fraud Hotline. The grants, totalling £473,000 were withheld by ACE and no funds were paid out. See House of Commons, 2021.

26

"A Community of 30,000 Musicians behind You"

An interview with John Shortell from the UK Musicians' Union

John Shortell

ANNA: To start with perhaps an obvious question, why is it important for a union to work on EDI [equality, diversity, and inclusion] issues?

JOHN: It's important because the MU are very familiar with the issues members face when reporting discrimination or sexual harassment. Often, people won't report incidents because sticking their heads above the parapet means that they may lose work or be blacklisted. At the MU, we can do things on a collective level, and are able to have conversations that individuals may not be comfortable having. We're able to be challenging, in ways that an individual probably wouldn't want to be, especially if you were a self-employed musician or even an employed musician. Some of the conversations about equality, diversity, and inclusion [EDI] are really challenging and we have to be robust and sometimes refuse ideas that employers or the industry put to us if they're not good for musicians. The collective action that we can take means that you don't have to stand alone, you've got the weight of a community of 30,000+ musicians behind you.

ANNA: That's a large membership, and so how does the MU make sure that it is representative of all the diverse experiences of all of those 30,000 members?

JOHN: That's important in relation to my role as Head of Equality, Diversity, and Inclusion, because sometimes, people will ask me, why is a white guy talking about "race," or women's rights, when you haven't got the lived experience? And I should be asked those questions, but I think they come from a lack of understanding of how our trade union works. So, I thought that might be a good place to start. Any work that we undertake on EDI needs people with lived experience feeding in those experiences and shaping that work. That's essential. However, having lived experience shouldn't mean you also then have the responsibility of solving the issue. For example, I'm gay; because of what I do I have ideas on how to tackle homophobia, but if I weren't

John Shortell, *"A Community of 30,000 Musicians behind You"* In: *Voices for Change in the Classical Music Profession.* Edited by: Anna Bull and Christina Scharff with Associate Editor Laudan Nooshin, Oxford University Press.
© Oxford University Press 2023. DOI: 10.1093/oso/9780197601211.003.0027

doing my job, I might not. Although I'd be able to tell you how it feels to experience homophobia and how homophobia manifests in everyday life, I wouldn't necessarily have, or should have all the answers on how to solve that problem. To tackle EDI issues, the voices of people with lived experience are essential and must be centered and evident in the final strategy or project, but it cannot be the only thing we rely on. EDI work needs resources, a budget, a strategy, and buy-in from all sections of an organization to be successful. If you haven't got lived experience of an issue, you should still be actively involved in those conversations. Your voice shouldn't be the loudest, but you are definitely part of the solution. I work via an EDI committee and on that committee, I have representation from Black, Asian, and minority ethnic members, disabled members, LGBT+ members, and women members. As an offshoot of that committee, we have member networks that represent each of those strands. We speak to these networks every couple of months, and then I meet with the EDI committee four times a year. This is where we discuss musicians' lived experiences. The networks and the committee will tell me the issues they are experiencing, what barriers they are facing, and so on. Then we'll discuss potential solutions and that forms the basis of the work that the committee asks me to do. Overall, I see my job in two parts: the work I do to make the MU more diverse in terms of members and committees, and then EDI work on the industry side. In terms of internal diversity within the MU, most of our committees are well on their way to being representative of society or the way the music industry looks at the moment. We've introduced a "reserved seat" structure on our industrial committees, which is a quota, so that all industrial committees are working toward a minimum of a 50/50 gender balance, 20% representation of Black, Asian, and minority ethnic members, 10% disabled members and 5% LGBT+ members. It was really important to implement this structure, so that when we're considering industry issues, we've got diverse voices on our committees, giving their perspectives. Then there's the inclusion part of the work, where I'm ensuring that we aren't just improving representation on committees, but that we are also making sure that there's space for those members to be heard in a supportive and psychologically safe environment. This is happening through regular EDI training sessions that raise awareness of different lived experiences, combat stigma, and promote inclusivity. Members can also access panel discussions and resources that focus on EDI issues. Through this educational work, I'm hoping that members will go into their workplaces and instill the MU EDI values in those workplaces and advocate for themselves and each other. That's the big picture of what I'm trying to do!

ANNA: It's really inspiring to hear about the MU doing the work to get your own house in order as well as advocating for the change in the wider industry, and I think that's really important when you do EDI work.

JOHN: It would be really embarrassing if someone asked, "What's the MU doing on this?" and I have to say, "Actually, our committee is all men or all white people," and even worse, "We're not doing anything about it"! I think now that work is mostly all in place, we're going to see a more proactive role from the MU in terms of industry issues.

ANNA: Could you just give us an overview of the areas you're working on at present in the music industry in the UK?

JOHN: We've got Safe Space, which focuses on sexual harassment. That is a big part of my work at the moment. Safe Space includes support for people who've experienced sexual harassment, work to prevent it happening, and then lobbying government for legislative change that we think will make routes to justice more accessible to people who've experienced it. We're also working on diversity in music education, and this last year's been transformative for that work because I've been able to have conversations with people I haven't been able to before or who haven't been engaged in this work before. "Blackout Tuesday" that took place in 2020, where people working in the music industry posted a black square on their social media channels to protest racism and police brutality, was a really useful tool to be able to do that. I'm generally skeptical about social media actions like that, because I think, what are people going to do to follow through on it so it doesn't become just some performative action? But it was useful leverage to be able to say to people who posted the black square, "Okay, so now you're engaged with this issue, let's have a conversation about what you're going to do after the black square and how we can support that." Another issue we work on with orchestras is increasing the representation of Black, Asian, and minority ethnic players. That's been one of our long-term projects. We're currently working on a standardized, inclusive auditions process, so we can support orchestras looking to increase the diversity of players but might not know how to begin that process, and I think the MU are in a good position to offer guidance on that. As part of this work the MU are founder partners of Chi-chi Nwanoku's Chineke! Alliance for Audition Support and partners with organizations Black Lives in Music and Power Up. Another campaign, "Fix Streaming" is a call to regulate the streaming industry so that performers and musicians get paid a fair amount for their work when it's streamed because at the moment they're definitely not. Fix Streaming has a really specific focus on what the MU wants to achieve, but part of that campaign would also help tackle some of the equalities issues we see in that sector, such as the exploitation of marginalized musicians, issues such as Black female vocalists who'll be used on recording for tracks, but they won't necessarily be paid appropriately or be credited appropriately so it really does nothing for their career or finances. Another important piece of work is the MU Equality Action Plan that we have recently published. That sets out our EDI aims over the next four years, with targets for recruitment of new diverse members. This will be the first time the MU has targeted underrepresented groups of musicians via a recruitment campaign, and we have set ourselves aspirational targets so we can be really focused about that piece of work. Another current project is our work on accessibility riders. We've created an access rider document with our disabled members. This is a document where members can communicate their access requirements really clearly and use that when booking work. That project was set up to encourage people to proactively ask about access.

ANNA: Can we hear in a bit more detail on a couple of these campaigns? For example, in relation to disability, you were saying earlier that disability is an area that still needs to have its "moment."

JOHN: Disability discrimination, and the disabled community, in my opinion, are not considered in the same way or level as other types of discrimination or communities by the music industry or wider society. It's something I've really been conscious of and wanted to make sure that the MU are not perpetuating that. The project has enabled the MU to have conversations about implementing the access rider as part of a standardized booking process, and three festivals have adopted it so far. So rather than singling out disabled musicians, the access rider will be sent to everyone, and whoever has access needs sends it back. We've also introduced our disabled musicians' reduced membership rate, that takes into account the extra costs that come with being disabled and also the lack of work that some disabled musicians experience specifically because they're disabled. We wanted to make sure those groups of disabled musicians have access to our membership benefits and support. I'm working much harder to make sure that we're having conversations with the industry about what it's like to be a disabled musician, or disabled musicians are supported to have those conversations with the industry and highlight what barriers they experience and what can be done to remove them. A lot of those barriers are attitudinal, which is generally the hardest to remove, unfortunately. I'm not trying to minimize other barriers but there are a lot of instances where throwing money at the problem would be a solution. Changing attitudes is not that simple. For example, we have had reports of musicians being asked to perform and then when the booker is told that musician is disabled, they're dropped from the gig, because assumptions are made about what that musician can and can't do or that it might be too much trouble to meet their access needs.

One of our members who is a wheelchair user wanted to take part in a competition, and they were told that the building was inaccessible because it had stairs and that they wouldn't be able to attend. The member can also use sticks for short distances, but they were never asked or given the opportunity to tell the organizer of the competition this. No one ever thought to say to them, "The building has 10 stairs and isn't wheelchair accessible; is there another way we can do this so you can participate?" Obviously, I'm talking about a dignified way of solving the issue, not like carrying someone upstairs, but those conversations just don't happen, and that member was automatically excluded. We need to get to a point of always asking, not assuming. I think there's an expectation that disabled musicians are going to be too difficult to engage and have really complex access requirements. Some might be! but unless people are asking and having those conversations, disabled musicians are automatically excluded because of assumptions. Some disabled musicians will have really straightforward access needs, like extra time setting up, or need someone to meet with them early to walk them through the venue for example. Others will be more complex, but these musicians will be able to tell you what they need and how to solve any access related issues if they are asked. They are experts in what they need to do their jobs. There is tons of work to do there, but we are making positive progress!

ANNA: Are there any specific disability issues that relate to classical music that you have come across?

JOHN: Physical access may be more of an issue because of some of the venues that classical musicians work in, but again, that's about having a conversation, and about being open to doing things differently. The demands on players in standard rehearsal structures is another thing that can be prohibitive for some disabled musicians, and also for some aging musicians as well. So, for instance, if you've got a player on the autism spectrum, does the way you rehearse work for that player, or is there a different way to rehearse that allows them to participate more fully? That's something COVID's been super useful for—one of the only things—that we have had to find different ways to do things. That's been transformative for some disabled musicians, for example, they don't have to go to physical rehearsals, rehearsals can be spread over different times, and so on. There are new ways of doing things. I think some of the problems we have in the classical music sector are because it's so rooted in tradition in every single aspect. And now COVID has forced us to think, well, actually this isn't the best way to do things; this doesn't work for everyone.

ANNA: Moving on to another of your campaigns, which I'm particularly interested in, around sexual harassment. The Musicians' Union's been really proactive in making positive change in the UK in this area. Can you talk us through how you've responded to the MeToo movement, what's going on at the moment and what the challenges are?

JOHN: When the MeToo movement started we knew this was going to blow up for the music industry because there's certain aspects of the industry that mean sexual harassment is more likely to happen: the informal way we work; alcohol and drugs, late-night working; and massive power imbalances. So, we created Safe Space, as a forum for anyone working in the music industry to share instances of sexism, sexual harassment, and sexual abuse and to get advice on their rights, links to support services, and in some instances, support in making a complaint. We have had some successes for example, if someone's experienced sexual harassment and they can no longer work with the person who has harassed them, we can make sure that they're paid for the work they can no longer do, and make sure that it's really clear that the person who's reporting isn't the issue, which we so often see. It's important for the MU to be transparent about how we use Safe Space and to manage expectations about what Safe Space is and what the MU can do. Sometimes, people just want to share their experience and say, "This happened to me" and they don't want it to go any further, but other times there are issues that the person reporting wants us to challenge organizations and perpetrators on. We've recently launched the Safe Space app, which will make it easier for people to report, and that is going to help the MU collect data. For example, anonymous reports can tell us whether there are specific parts of the industry where sexual harassment is more likely to happen or if there is a certain venue where this is happening all the time. If the data is telling us this, we can then we can go and have a conversation with that venue or organization without revealing who the person reporting is and let them know incidents are happening on a regular basis. We can then support and advise them on their policies, or with accessing training, whatever the solution to the issue may be. We've also been developing a resources package, to help people create policy, or highlight support services. A lot of the venues and organizations that we speak to won't have the resources or won't have a Human Resources department to do this work. We completely understand that, so part of that work is taking the work out of it for them, and then we know it's best practice advice because we designed it with our members and with advice from our legal team. Then finally there's the lobbying side and our campaign, "Protect Freelancers Too." This focuses on legislative changes to the Equality Act to better protect our members who predominantly work freelance or are self-employed. We're not saying sexual harassment doesn't happen to employed people, but freelancers have got no HR, they're not often included in policy, and some of that group of members will fall outside the protections of the Equality Act because of the way they work or how they've been engaged. Other changes that we're lobbying for include: an extension to the time limits for reporting sexual harassment, as well as protection from third-party harassment, for example from audience members, which is a massive issue for our members. I'm not saying these legislative changes will solve the problem, but it's a step in the right direction. Training is another area that the MU are really going to focus on; for example, bystander training is something we want to provide for our members so that people who witness sexual harassment or know sexual harassment is taking place know how they can safely respond. One thing we are very conscious of with this work is to not put this issue back on the people who experience it, who are women—women disproportionately experience sexual harassment—but it's not their issue to solve. I know we always get people saying, "But men experience sexual harassment too," and yes, they do, but not on the scale that women experience it. It's overwhelmingly women who experience sexual harassment and its overwhelmingly men who are the perpetrators.

ANNA: So if somebody came to you and said, "I've experienced sexual harassment at work and I want support with this," what kind of things would you be able to do?

JOHN: We're always led by the person reporting. The first thing we would do is acknowledge what has happened to them and signpost them to support services. Then we'd have a frank conversation about what they would like to happen and what a good result looks like for that person. There are so many different outcomes that a person could be happy with; success is kaleidoscopic. Success could be that person sharing information with the MU and saying, "I don't want to go any further, I just wanted you to know that happened to me," and for them, that might be enough. Or it might be, "Someone engaged me and acted inappropriately toward me, and I can't work with them any longer." In that situation, if the person reporting wanted us to, we would work to get them out of the engagement but ensure they are still paid and make sure that the company know why they can't continue to work with that person. We could then put pressure on the company to ensure that the situation is handled appropriately whether that be through training, policy change, whatever is needed. The person's (who reported the incidents) career hasn't suffered, they have still been paid, and they haven't been "blacklisted." That's success. This is something that's actually happened. One of the things we struggle with, is that some organizations who we contact about reports of sexual harassment will not tackle higher-profile people that they employ; they just don't want to hear it and the problem isn't dealt with. There are no real consequences, because a lot of the people who operate at that level can move from job to job and it's an open secret that this person is a sexual harasser. There are currently issues in the UK and Europe around ways that data protection legislation stops us communicating company-to-company that someone is a known sexual harasser. The MU are in a good position to take action against these types of people, with the consent of the person reporting, but we can't always deliver full legal justice because of the reasons I've already explained.

ANNA: What kinds of advice are you giving to classical music organizations about making change in this area?

JOHN: Education. I think that is always a great place to start. For example, what is sexual harassment, what is consent, what behaviors could make people feel uncomfortable, those types of topics. I must be honest, sometimes I do roll my eyes and think, surely you must know this? it's obvious! But it isn't always obvious to everyone. This is something the MU wants to see all the way through the industry, starting at conservatoires, music colleges, and universities. We talk about encouraging a culture of reporting, so we make sure that there's a clear policy specifically dealing with sexual harassment, that everyone knows about, and everyone knows how to report, what the process will be and, more important than anything, knows that they will be supported and treated fairly. In addition, have multiple reporting mechanisms, including anonymous methods. A massive barrier to reporting is being identified as someone who's experienced sexual harassment or someone who's making a complaint about sexual harassment; anonymous methods would help encourage a culture of reporting. Transparency is another issue; reporting needs to be a transparent and open process. People who report need to be able to see what steps have been taken to deal with the perpetrator. What are the consequences for this person who has sexually harassed someone and what's been done to prevent it happening again? And finally, more gender-balanced staff, particularly, boards and people in decision-making positions, would really be transformative in terms of dealing with sexual harassment.

ANNA: These are great points, and some of the ways that music conservatoires in Europe are tackling this issue are covered in David-Emil Wickström's chapter in this volume, and of course they are familiar issues from my own research and activism on sexual harassment in higher education (Bull et al., 2019; Bull and Page, 2021; 2022; Bull, 2022). Moving on to thinking about your work more generally, what messages or advice would you give to activists and musicians who are trying to make change in the classical music sector?

JOHN: Obviously, join the Musicians' Union and get involved with our networks! Connect with people doing this work. One problem is that there's lots of fantastic work going on but we're not connected. People aren't talking to each other because they've just got their heads down, doing the work. So, think about that wider network, find out who's doing this work, and connect with them. It stops replicating work and gives us opportunities to support each other. There'll be different issues for different sectors, but I do think a community, holistic approach is the way that we're going to achieve things. I'd also say that it's important to understand that this work takes time. This comes up with new activists who are saying "We need to change this; we need to change it now," and I love that passion, so keep that, but just understand that there's a process, and that sometimes you've got to play the long game to get the result that you want. I think it's also about learning how to have these conversations with people in a way that doesn't make them feel threatened and helps them feel supported, so taking time to make sure someone fully understands the issue, they understand what they are being asked to do, and that you're there to help them take those steps. It's a skill that I've definitely had to learn! And I'm still learning. Another piece of advice is to talk outside of your communities. We've got a tendency in the EDI world to talk to people who agree with us and are already on board. That's great, but we need to be having these conversations outside of our communities, with men, or with white people, or with straight people or with non-disabled people. Again, that's a skill, to be able to do that, and to get people to listen and to engage with what you're saying. That's a massive part of my job, because a lot of our members will be white men who are non-disabled, who are heterosexual; so how do we get those groups to engage with an issue of sexual harassment or discrimination when they may think, "It's nothing to do with me, I don't sexually harass people and I don't discriminate," which most of them don't. It comes back to what I said at the very beginning, about how we encourage members to advocate for themselves and each other and instill these MU EDI values in their workplaces and raise awareness about people's lived experiences.

ANNA: That's really inspiring! A final point I wanted to discuss was, you mentioned how COVID has affected your work, but is there anything more you wanted to say about that?

JOHN: There have been positive changes as I've mentioned, for some disabled musicians. Disabled musicians have been saying for years, "If we do things this way, it'll be more accessible," and now people are doing things that way, so it's great to see. I've also been able to engage a lot more people as the way most people work has become much more flexible. The MU are going to be pushing to preserve that flexibility when we're back to normal, whenever that is. I have definitely been able to engage people that I haven't been able to engage before, not just because of COVID, also because of world events like the BLM protests, but COVID has definitely made people more aware of inequality. It's made explicit the inequalities that exist in society and why they exist; most of the reasons we can draw back to discrimination. I am worried about what members are willing to put up with to get back to work; some members probably won't be reporting if they experience discrimination or they are being treated unfairly, because they just want to get back to work. I also think that we'll lose some progress on the work we've done to increase diversity because of COVID. The MU are ensuring that the conversations we're having about getting the industry back on its feet always have an EDI focus and that we're considering issues specific groups of people who share a protected characteristic may have. The MU's role is to make sure we're having really robust conversations on behalf of those groups of members with the industry and being really clear that if any plans to reopen disproportionately impact groups of members with protected characteristics, then that is discriminatory, and we will challenge it.

ANNA: Is there anything else you wanted to mention?

JOHN: I need to touch on bad practice. The focus on recruiting a more diverse workforce is fantastic, but there's a real lack of focus on inclusion. Organizations are recruiting more diverse workforces, but haven't done any work on inclusion, no work with their existing workforce to make sure that the workplace is an inclusive environment or making sure that the existing workforce understand and support their EDI agenda. Ultimately if you haven't done the work to cultivate an inclusive environment, the diverse staff you've spent all that time recruiting aren't going to stay. Inclusion is an essential part of any EDI strategy, if you haven't done that work, you're setting yourself up to fail. Some organizations and employers are not speaking to their existing workforce about their EDI plans and when existing staff are asking them why they've made a decision to hire someone new, they're saying things like, "We hired that musician because we need to be more diverse." No! That musician was hired because they're fantastic at what they do and are the best person for the job. They were not hired because they are Black, or a woman, or gay, but if you're telling your existing workforce someone was hired because of the need to be more diverse, how are they going to treat that musician when potentially that could mean one of their friends, who was also an excellent player, didn't get that job? Now you've created this myth that you're just hiring people because of their sexuality, their ethnicity, their gender, and they're being elevated to these roles that they're not qualified to do, when that's not the case at all. These more diverse musicians that you're recruiting may not have applied before because until you've started to do the work to be more diverse, they may never have felt welcome or may not have wanted to work for your organization. Existing workforces have concerns about EDI agendas, and I understand that. Questions like: What does it mean for my job? What does it mean for my future here? Will I be able to progress? All these are valid concerns that are easily addressed, if you're clear and transparent about what you're trying to achieve and how, but those conversations aren't happening in some sections of the industry. The other thing I've experienced is I'm having a conversation about how an organization can recruit more diverse staff, and I'm giving the organization advice on how they can achieve that. Then the organization tells me that they plan to put these new, more diverse staff on much shorter contracts that inevitably lead to worse terms and conditions. They plan to do this because that's good for diversity, because staff turnover will be quicker, which means they can offer vacancies to more people. That is not good practice. That's just numbers. The problem here is that let's say in this case the more diverse staff are women, and you are putting them on shorter contracts and worse terms and conditions than your existing staff who are mostly men. By doing that, your organization is perpetuating the cycle of women being in insecure work, earning less than men, not being able to plan for the future because they're in insecure or short-term work, and all those negative things that come with worse terms and conditions and you've taken these steps, to improve diversity?! By trying to improve diversity your reinforcing existing inequalities. There's no long-term thinking around this strategy and it'll end up costing your organization more, long term. It's bad practice.

ANNA: So we have a long way to go in terms of just actually understanding the fundamental issues around inequalities.

JOHN: We do, but I have to say we've moved on so much in the classical sector, we really have. From having conversations five years ago to now, it's leaps and bounds. Just look at the organizations and projects that have popped up in the last 12 to 18 months to help diversify the classical music sector specifically, such as Black Lives in Music and Chineke! Alliance for Audition Support. But organizations really need to think about the way they approach this work. Talk to the communities that are underrepresented in your workforce, talk to your existing workforce, come and speak to me, don't just do things in silos and think it might be a good idea. Engage with people! That's a positive message to end on, isn't it?

Afterword

Gillian Moore

That this book is called *Voices for Change in the Classical Music Profession* suggests that change needs to happen. The chapters in this book, written by scholars, artists, and curators, show us many different facets of a piece of our cultural life, which does not appear to be at ease with itself. The chapters identify areas in which classical music has been found wanting and, in many cases, the writers propose ideas and inspirational examples of positive change.

Right since the start of my working life in classical music in the UK nearly four decades ago, I have written and read many articles, attended conferences, given and listened to speeches, and read academic papers that propose that classical music needs to change—needs to become more relevant, more urgent, more diverse, and more reflective of our society, more porous and more engaged in people's lives, less formal, less forbidding, less elite, less White, less rich, less male. Although I've spent much of my professional energy trying, with varying degrees of success, to address The Problem, I sometimes reflect on the idea that this corner of our cultural life, which I've loved with a passion since I was a small child, spends so much energy on self-flagellation.

Classical music is, after all, a product of historic imbalances of power, just like so many aspects of life, is it not? Is it any worse than theater or film, where the creative voices of women, of People of Color, of working-class writers, were largely absent until recent generations? Or rock and pop music, where the only women were, with notable exceptions, singers out at the front? Or visual art where exhibitions of artists of color have, until recently, been extremely rare? And, when it comes to audiences, it's still the case that a higher percentage of people who attend all art forms, not just classical music, are from higher socio-economic groups: the upper middle classes.

But what we inadequately call classical music has some particular problems all of its own. One issue that contributes to a sense of "unreachability" for many people is that the core activity of classical music, the orchestral concert, is a rather extraordinary ritual, a rather dimly and inaccurately remembered version of a performance that has been frozen in time since somewhere around the middle of the 19th century, when big public concerts were still a novelty. The starkly hierarchical ritual of the orchestral concert, based on the high-status individual of the conductor, his (yes, his) lieutenant the concert-master or first violin, the soloist, the orchestral principals, and then the "rank and file" players are each acknowledged according to their place in the hierarchy. The hierarchy is military—or perhaps industrial, since the rise of big public concerts coincided with the industrial revolution—and the ritual is strange to many. "Why does the conductor keep pretending to leave the stage and then immediately come back on, and then off again?" asked a well-educated but classical novice friend of mine at the end of a concert recently. In the 19th century, when public concerts became established, the repertoire would have been mainly new music. Now, the majority of the music played is from the 19th and early 20th centuries (Marín, 2018); the orchestral musicians are playing on instruments whose technology has barely developed since the 19th century—think how fast it was developing up until then; and the musicians in the orchestra are, in the majority of cases, wearing 19th-century evening dress. In the 19th century, performers and audiences would have been wearing the same clothes. The audience has changed with the times; the orchestra remains in costume.

I love orchestral concerts and feel comfortable watching this costume drama, because I've grown up with it and am used to its rules and rituals—although even I, as a professional concertgoer, am dismayed to witness and sometimes fall foul myself of the self-appointed behavior police who seem to notice and berate every movement or sound or clap in the wrong place. I'm writing this in the autumn of 2021, shortly after public concerts have resumed after COVID lockdowns, and the joy of audiences and performers coming back together is palpable. The orchestral concert is one of our great human achievements but, because the listener is committed to a period of time sitting in silence in a seat following a piece of art with, often, no conventional narrative, its rituals can be intimidating to the uninitiated.

In his essay "Performance as an Extreme Occasion," Edward Said suggests that another factor that creates distance between classical music and its audience is the separation that happened in the 20th century of the roles of performer and composer, and the "almost total ascendancy of the former over the latter" (Said, 1991). Beethoven, Mozart, Haydn, Chopin, and Liszt were all composing their music, performing it, connecting directly with their audience. Said suggests that the fetishization of the performer, marketed for perfect performances of music from a bygone age, has

> widened the distance between the artists in evening dress or tails and, in a lesser, lower, far more secondary space, the listener who buys records, frequents concert halls and is routinely made to feel the impossibility of attaining the packaged virtuosity of a professional performer. Whether we focus on the repeatable mechanically reproduced performance available on disc, or on the

alienating social ritual of the concert itself—the listener is in a relatively weak and not entirely admirable position. (Said, 1991)

In the latter half of the 20th century, some composers broke away from reliance on musical institutions and the need for recognition and commissions from orchestras and opera houses, formed their own bands, and reached large audiences by being responsible for their own musical performance and production, communicating their music directly to their listeners; Steve Reich, Philip Glass, Pauline Oliveros, Gavin Bryars, and Meredith Monk rebuilt the bridge between composer, performer, and audience. And, from my standpoint writing in 2021, huge inventiveness and energy is going into providing alternatives to the ritual of the orchestral concert. Aurora Orchestra has joyfully reimagined it as a theatrical performance with lighting, staging, and in some cases, performing whole symphonies from memory. With the musicians liberated from the printed page and music stands, the connection between performers and audience is extraordinarily direct—almost as if they are making the music up in front of us. Or, in Peckham South London, Bold Tendencies is presenting orchestral performances and chamber music in an open-sided 1970s concrete car-park right beside a railway line. As the noise of trains and street life wafts into the performance space, it's hard to imagine people turning to their neighbor to berate them for clapping in the wrong place or moving in time to the music (both of which have happened to me recently in concert halls). Despite the far from "ideal" concert conditions, the sense of concentration and focus from performers and audience is electric.

Edward Said's discussion of extreme specialization as a problem for classical music also extends to the notion of the valuing of professionalism over wider participation in music-making. In the 19th century when, say, a new Brahms symphony was given its first performance, people in the audience may well have got hold of a piano duet arrangement of the work in advance and got to know it first by actually playing it themselves; the audience were active listeners. The idea of an active, participating audience is, for me, an exciting one and vital for the health of music-making. Focusing on the UK context, which I am most familiar with: although the great majority of public funding of the arts goes to support professional arts, the origin of Arts Council England (which distributes state funding for the arts in the UK) was in funding amateur music-making. The Council for the Encouragement of Music and the Arts (CEMA), the precursor to Arts Council England, was set up during World War II to encourage amateur activity as well as funding professional musicians to perform to servicemen and -women and to encourage music, dance, and drama in communities. It would be perverse to argue against funding professional artists; it's vital that we can experience the thrill of performances by people who spend their lives dedicated to music and it's also vital that people can see the possibility of making a living in the arts—but it's also vital that everybody has the opportunity to join in music-making for their own enjoyment and fulfilment at whatever their level, and to be those active listeners for our professional musicians. In the recently published 10-year strategy to cover the years 2020–2030, *Let's Create*, Arts Council England appears to have reached back for inspiration to its wartime roots, encouraging active, creative participation in the arts by everyone alongside supporting arts professionals (Arts Council England, 2020). The first desired outcome of the strategy is entitled "Creative People" and suggests that "everyone can develop and express creativity throughout their life" (Arts Council England, 2020, p. 28). The second is "Cultural Communities," with the intention that "villages, towns and cities thrive through a collaborative approach to culture" (Arts Council England, 2020, p. 28). This approach can only be a good thing for the encouragement of a vibrant and healthy musical life.

But, as the writers of the chapters in this book describe, there are still huge—and in some cases widening—inequalities that create barriers, making classical music vulnerable to criticism of being irrelevant, remote from people's lives and concerns. These barriers are socio-economic; they pertain to gender, to disability, and to "race." In the week that I'm completing this chapter, Arts Council England (ACE) has published another set of reports, called "Creating a Fairer and More Inclusive Classical Music Sector for England" (Arts Council England, 2021; Cox 2021a; 2021b; Cox and Kilshaw, 2021; ICM Unlimited 2021). These reports identify that there are still chasms of opportunity for people becoming involved in classical music, either during their school years, as an adult amateur participant, or as a professional performer, composer, manager, or board member.

The Arts Council reports starkly identify how participation in specialist music training is disproportionately available to young people from higher socio-economic groups, who go to private schools, and whose parents have university degrees. They describe how opportunities narrow and decrease for young people from less advantaged socio-economic groups as they get older and progress through school; and how National Youth Ensembles have a far higher proportion of young people from independent schools than is the case nationally. Informal tactics such as booking consultation lessons before auditioning for a conservatoire are unavailable to young people and their families who do not have the confidence and networks to understand the system. The reports also suggest that the precarious nature of a freelance career in music, coupled with the high costs of training and buying instruments and equipment, discourages participation from people from lower socio-economic groups.

Though women make up a substantial portion of the classical workforce, the reports confirm that they are increasingly absent the further up the professional ladder you look. Like many people, my own memories are predominantly of women as music teachers and school or church choir leaders, but women are, the ACE reports confirm, woefully underrepresented in professional activities like recording, theater work and composing. Women are in the majority among non-musicians working in classical music organizations, including in management roles, but in the minority in board/trustee positions. Although women musicians are now present in UK orchestras in almost equal proportion to men, that proportion rapidly decreases when it comes to named, principal positions in the orchestras, and to soloists. And, as for conductors, the numbers are still eye-wateringly unequal. The Royal Philharmonic Society's recent count of women conductors found that there were only two British orchestras that had a female principal conductor and only six women conductors had titled roles amid the several hundred conductors on the staff of professional British orchestras. Furthermore, only 22 of the 371 conductors represented by British agents were female (Royal Philharmonic Society, 2019).

The same pattern of diminishing opportunity and visibility in classical music is identified in the reports for people from Black, Asian, and ethnically diverse backgrounds in the UK. Although the evidence suggests that Black, Asian, and ethnically diverse children take part in early musical training opportunities in reasonable numbers, their representation becomes smaller the more advanced and elite musical training becomes until, in the UK's professional orchestras, the report suggests that between 3% and 6% of the musicians in England's professional orchestras are musicians of color, against a national figure of 16.1% (Cox and Kilshaw, 2021, p. 12).

It is the responsibility of people in my position, the decision-makers in music, to take personal responsibility for changing things, and for making our musical life as great and broad, as surprising and as ambitious as it can be. It is simply not good enough to say, as is still said to me often, "I'm only interested in good music" or "Quality will always rise to the top." But often, as programmers and curators, we simply have to spend a moment longer thinking about our choices, about what artists we are going to present, whose stories we are going to tell, who we want to be in the audience. Before we automatically reach for what we have been told all our lives, throughout our training, is "great," we must pause to think about what other voices there might be, who is missing. It is also, of course, our responsibility to ensure that we are open to, and ultimately making way for, the decision-makers who will replace us, actively opening up opportunities for as diverse a pool of talent as possible.

A great deal of energy and inventiveness is going into tackling these inequalities. Bassist Chi-chi Nwanoku's determination that she should no longer be the only musician of color on the platform drove her to found Chineke!, Europe's first majority Black and ethnically diverse orchestra (see Chapter 22, this volume). In the six short years since Chineke! gave their first concert in the

Queen Elizabeth Hall at Southbank Centre, they have shown, quite simply, that it is possible for the orchestral stage to look very different, and they have uncovered many previously unheard or forgotten voices. For example, Chineke! has been responsible for reviving the music of the once very popular Black British composer Samuel Coleridge-Taylor, as well as commissioning contemporary talent. And when what's on the stage is different, the audience is different. When Chineke! played the reopening concert of the Queen Elizabeth Hall in April 2018, the Radio 3 presenter said delightedly on air: "The audience looks like London!" In relation to another underrepresented group, disabled musicians, initiatives such as Bournemouth Symphony Orchestra's Resound project and the British Paraorchestra have shown, with flair and style, that we ignore disabled musicians to our great artistic loss.

The Royal Philharmonic Society has acted on the stark statistics they uncovered about lack of women conductors and has, with conductor Alice Farnham, instigated a Women Conductors' Programme which, rather brilliantly, starts with teenage musicians who, like my teenage self, see so few women on the podium and assume that this, the highest status job in music, could never be for them. The PRS Foundation's Key Change program has thrown down the gauntlet to music festivals—classical *and* contemporary—to achieve a 50/50 gender balance in artists and staff by 2022. At the Southbank Centre, we strive for gender balance in our own promotions and also program a range of other activities including the kind of informal networking opportunities that women still feel are largely unavailable to them. For example, during one of our Women in Music breakfasts, a conductor pointed out that she missed out on the kind of "soft training" of going for a drink or hanging out in a maestro's dressing room for some post-rehearsal tips because it might be misconstrued as "hitting on them."

The initiatives described tackle inequalities in what is presented on our stages. But what about the audience? I'm writing this in London which, on any given night, has a huge amount of choice available for anyone who knows that they love classical music. The way that the industry is set up, the way that institutions compete with one another, strengthens the view that there is one "proper" way to serve up classical music and that is in a formal concert at 7:30pm. Large and reasonably diverse audiences behave in the ways required by this set-up, and the vast majority of money, resources, and press attention is still focused on this "core" way of delivering music. But what would happen if we changed what is core? What would happen if we had, say, as many concerts for children—family concerts, school concerts, learning projects—as for adults? What would happen if we had more short, relaxed concerts for people who have never attended before? What would happen if we had more late-night, cutting-edge, contemporary performances for people who really want new, cutting-edge music? What would happen if a large proportion of our program was free and in open spaces? These are areas of our work which, while important, have always been on the edges in terms of funding, recognition, status. It's time to bring them into the center.

Lastly, it's the responsibility of the decision-makers, people like me, to ensure that we're not only concerned with presenting brilliant professional performances to audiences. The arts will thrive if people are actively involved themselves and we must create opportunities for this to happen. In 2018 in the Royal Festival Hall, Marin Alsop conducted a performance of *Mass* by Leonard Bernstein—surely one of the most socially committed artists of the 20th century. Of the 470 people on stage, only seven, including Marin Alsop, were professionals. The rest were students, schoolchildren, a diverse range of amateur choirs, and refugee and other community groups. A teenage girl from a secondary school near the Southbank was asked, on film, what she thought of Bernstein's *Mass*, after her experience. "It makes me feel that I should be in this world—that I shouldn't be left out," she said. That's what music can do; that's how important it is; and that's why it's crucial that we get this right.

Discussion questions for teachers, students, reading groups, and industry leaders

General discussion questions

- How important is it to name and describe inequalities and exclusions (in addition to challenging them)?
- Does it make sense to think of classical music as a "genre"? What are the advantages and disadvantages of this approach when thinking about diversity and inclusion? (Introduction)
- What role have higher music education institutions played, historically and today, in reproducing or challenging social inequalities in classical music? (Chapters 1–4)
- In this book some authors have capitalized the terms Black, White, Asian, and other racialized identities to indicate that these are socially constructed categories. This can help to make visible issues with the language we use to discuss "race," such as talking about "Black" and "White" people or musics. Does the language we use to discuss "race" play a role in addressing or reproducing inequalities?
- How do we understand the relationship between different kinds of exclusion based on "race," class, gender, sexuality, ethnicity, religion, health, maternity, citizenship status, and education, among other inequalities? Are there particular intersections that result in greater chances of exclusion or underrepresentation? (Chapters 1, 10, 18)
- Some people have argued that without systemic change, nothing will fundamentally change in the relationships of power in the classical music industry. To what extent do local and small-scale changes have the capacity to lead to wider systemic change? (Chapters 5, 6, 7; Chapters 23–26)
- Is there a connection between classical music and "Whiteness"? More broadly, what are the implications of essentialized ideas about connections between particular kinds of music and "race" or cultural heritage? (Chapters 12, 19, 23)

Inclusion across different forms of difference

- Some authors in this book describe schemes whereby underrepresented groups in classical music, such as Black people, are offered fellowships or pathways into classical music. What are the strengths and weaknesses of such schemes?
- What differences between the experiences of racially minoritized classical musicians exist internationally? How does this vary for different racially marginalized/minoritized groups, such as East Asian musicians, and Black musicians? (Chapters 12, 14, 15, 18, 22, 23). Which racialized groups of musicians are not represented in this volume?
- Do you agree with the statement "If we were ready to [make change], it would have been done by now"? (Introduction; Chapter 23)
- Why do you think we don't often hear accounts of people leaving classical music? (Chapter 18)
- What does the classical music industry need to do to work toward better representation and inclusion of disabled people? (Chapters 9, 11)
- What are some of the different ways in which gender inequalities affect women in classical music? (Chapters 1, 8, 10, 21).
- Which forms of difference are not covered in this book? How might you find out more about the experiences of people in those groups?

Rehearsal and performance practices

- How could rehearsals work in a more inclusive way for musicians across diverse musical and social backgrounds? (Chapters 5, 16)
- Who gets to be seen as "authentic" when playing classical music? (Chapters 12, 13, 14, 15)
- To what extent does the music itself need to change in order to work toward inclusion and equality for people who have historically been marginalized or excluded from it? (Introduction, Chapters 5, 11, 16, 21, 22)

Activism and making change

- What kinds of activist strategies are described in the book? Which of these do you think are likely to be most effective in the contexts you are familiar with, and why? (Chapters 19–26 and Afterword)

- To what extent are larger-scale collectives such as unions or professional societies needed to make change in classical music? (Chapters 25 and 26)
- What is neoliberal philanthropy, as described by Mina Yang (Chapter 6)? What problems do Mina Yang (Chapter 6) and Marianna Ritchey (Chapter 7) identify with trying to make classical music more inclusive within a neoliberal context?

References

Introduction

Ahmed, S. (2007) "The language of diversity," Ethnic and Racial Studies, *30*(2), pp. 235–256. Available at doi: 10.1080/01419870601143927

André, Naomi, and Von Glahn, Denise (Convenors), Brown, G.K., Carter, M.G., Kernodle, T.L., Maxile Jr., H.J., Smith, A., Turner, K.M., and Wright, J.R.B. (2020) "Colloquy: shadow culture narratives: race, gender, and Am'rican music historiography," Journal of the American Musicological Society, *73*, pp. 711–784. Available at https://doi.org/10.1525/jams.2020.73.3.711

Andre, N. (2018) Black opera: history, power, engagement. Illustrated edition. Urbana: University of Illinois Press.

Baker, G. (2014) El Sistema: orchestrating Venezuela's youth. Oxford: Oxford University Press.

Baker, G. (2020) "Rethinking social action through music: the search for coexistence and citizenship in Medellín's music schools," Open Book. Available at https://doi.org/10.11647/OBP.0243

Boghossian, P., and Beckerman, M. (eds.) (2021) "Classical music: contemporary perspectives and challenges," Open Book. Available at https://doi.org/10.11647/OBP.0242

Bell, J. M., and Hartmann, D. (2007) "Diversity in everyday discourse: the cultural ambiguities and consequences of 'happy talk.'" American Sociological Review, *72*(6), pp. 895–914.

Benedict, C., Schmidt, P., Spruce, G., and Woodford, P. (2015) The Oxford handbook of social justice in music education. New York: Oxford University Press.

Bennett, D.E. (2008) Understanding the classical music profession: the past, the present and strategies for the future. Aldershot: Ashgate.

Born, G. (2011) "Music and the materialization of identities," Journal of Material Culture, *16*, pp. 376–388. https://doi.org/10.1177/1359183511424196

Brackett, D. (2016) Categorizing sound: genre and twentieth-century popular music. Oakland: University of California Press.

Browning, J. (2019) "Remaking classical music: cultures of creativity in *Pleasure Garden*," Twentieth-Century Music, pp. 1–39. Available at https://doi.org/10.1017/S1478572219000355

Bull, A. (2016a) "Gendering the middle classes: the construction of conductors' authority in youth classical music groups," Sociological Review, *64*, pp. 855–871. Available at https://doi.org/10.1111/1467-954X.12426

Bull, A. (2016b) "El Sistema as a bourgeois social project: class, gender, and Victorian values," Action, Criticism & Theory for Music Education, *15*, pp. 120–153.

Bull, A. (2016c) "Safeguarding and youth voice in music education," Dr. Anna Bull *(blog)*. Available at https://annabullresearch.wordpress.com/2016/11/28/safeguarding-and-youth-voice-in-music-education/ (Accessed December 21, 2016).

Bull, A. (2018) "Uncertain capital: class, gender, and the 'imagined futures' of young classical musicians," in Dromey, C., Haferkorn, J. (eds.), The Classical Music Industry. London: Routledge, pp. 79–95.
Bull, A. (2019) Class, control and classical music. New York: Oxford University Press.
Bull, A. (2022) "Getting it right: why classical music's 'pedagogy of correction' is a barrier to equity," Music Educators Journal, 108(3), pp. 65–66. Available at: https://doi.org/10.1177/00274321221085132
Bull, A. (2022) "Catalysts and rationales for reporting staff sexual misconduct to UK higher education institutions," Journal of Gender-Based Violence, 6(1), pp. 45–60. Available at: https://doi.org/10.1332/239868021X16270572218631
Bull, A. (Forthcoming) "Classical music after #MeToo: tackling sexual harassment and misconduct in music higher education institutions," in Reitsamer, R., Prokop, R. (eds.), Higher Music Education and Employability in a Neoliberal World. Bloomsbury.
Bull, A., Page, T., and Bullough, J. (2019) "What would a survivor-centred higher education sector look like?" in Gamsu, S. (ed.), A new vision for further and higher education. London: Centre for Labour and Social Studies, pp. 73–82. Available at: http://classonline.org.uk/docs/A_New_Vision_For_Further_and_Higher_Education_220519_1647_forwebv1.pdf (Accessed May 29, 2019).
Bull, A., and Page, T. (2021) "Students' accounts of grooming and boundary-blurring behaviours by academic staff in UK higher education," Gender and Education, 33(8), pp. 1057–1072. Available at: https://doi.org/10.1080/09540253.2021.1884199
Bull, A., and Page, T. (2022) "The governance of complaints in UK higher education: critically examining 'remedies' for staff sexual misconduct," Social & Legal Studies, 31(1), pp. 27–49. Available at: https://doi.org/10.1177/09646639211002243
Bull, A., and Scharff, C. (2021) "Classical music as genre: hierarchies of value within freelance classical musicians' discourses," European Journal of Cultural Studies, 24 (3), pp. 673–689. Available at: https://doi.org/10.1177/13675494211006094
Bull, A., and Scharff, C. (2017) "'McDonald's music' versus 'serious music': How production and consumption practices help to reproduce class inequality in the classical music profession," Cultural Sociology, 11, pp. 283–301. Available at: https://doi.org/10.1177/1749975517711045
Burnard, P., Trulsson, Y.H., and Soderman, J. (eds.) (2015) Bourdieu and the sociology of music education. Aldershot: Ashgate.
Cox, T. (2021) Creating a more inclusive classical music: a study of the English orchestral workforce and the current routes to joining it. DHA.
Curtin, A., and Whittaker, A. (eds.) (2021) "Representing classical music in the twenty-first century," Open Library of the Humanities, 7(1).
Dados, N., and Connell, R. (2012) "The Global South," Contexts, 11, pp. 12–13. Available at: https://doi.org/10.1177/1536504212436479
De Benedictis, S., Allen, K., and Jensen, T. (2017) "Portraying poverty: the economics and ethics of factual welfare television," Cultural Sociology, 11(3), pp. 337–358. https://doi.org/10.1177/1749975517712132
Dromey, C., and Haferkorn, J. (2018) The classical music industry. New York: Routledge.
Ewell, P.A. 2020. "Music theory and the white racial frame," Music Theory Online, 26(2).
Feder, S., and McGill, A. (2021) "Diversity, equity, inclusion, and racial injustice in the classical music professions: A call to action," in Boghossian, P., Beckerman, M. (eds.), Classical music: Contemporary perspectives and challenges. Open Book. Available at https://doi.org/10.11647/OBP.0242

Frierson-Campbell, C., Hall, C., Powell, S.R., and Rosabal-Coto, G. (eds.) (2022) *Sociological* thinking in music education: international intersections. New York: Oxford University Press.

Fuller, S. (1998) *Women* composers *during the British* musical renaissance, *1880–1918*. King's College, University of London.

Goehr, L. (1992) *The* imaginary museum of musical wor*ks: An* essay in the philosophy of music. Oxford: Clarendon Press.

Green, L. (1997) *Music,* gender, education. Cambridge: Cambridge University Press.

Green, L. (2003) "Why "ideology" is still relevant for critical thinking in music education," Action, Criticism, and Theory for Music Education, *2*, pp. 1–24.

Hastie, B., and Rimmington, D. (2014) "'200 years of white affirmative action': white privilege discourse in discussions of racial inequality," Discourse & Society, *25*(2): pp. 186–204.

Hines, C. (2020) "Cosplaying while black: the transgressive pleasure of blacktivism," Journal of Cultural Research in Art Education, *37*, pp. 219–230.

Johnson-Hill, E. (2015) *Re-examining the* academy: music institutions and empire in nineteenth-century *London*. PhD dissertation. New Haven, CT: Yale University.

Johnson-Williams, E. (2020) "The examiner and the evangelist: Authorities of music and empire, c.1894," Journal of the Royal Musical Association, *145*, pp. 317–350. Available at https://doi.org/10.1017/rma.2020.16

Kajikawa, L. (2019) "The possessive investment in classical music," in Crenshaw, K. (ed.), Seeing race again: countering colorblindness across the disciplines. Berkeley: University of California Press.

Kok, R.-M. (2006) "Music for a postcolonial child: theorizing Malaysian memories," in S. Boynton, S., Kok, R.-M. (eds.), Musical childhoods and the cultures of youth. Connecticut: Wesleyan University Press, pp. 89–104.

Kok, R.-M. (2011) "Music for a postcolonial child: theorizing Malaysian memories," in Green, L. (ed.), Learning, teaching, and musical identity: voices across cultures. Bloomington: Indiana University Press, pp. 73–90.

Leech-Wilkinson, D. (2020) *Challenging* performance: classical music performance norms and how to escape them, version 2.04 (30.iv.21). ed. Available at https://challen gingperformance.com/the-book/ (Accessed December 16, 2022).

Leppänen, T. (2015) "The West and the rest of classical music: Asian musicians in the Finnish media coverage of the 1995 Jean Sibelius Violin Competition," European Journal of Cultural Studies, *18*, pp. 19–34. https://doi.org/10.1177/1367549414557804

Lochhead, Judith, Moore, A., Ritchey, M., Lochhead, Judy, Pippen, J.R., and Shreffler, A.C. (2019) "Boundaries of the new: American classical music at the turn of the millennium," Twentieth-Century Music, *16*, pp. 373–455. Available at https://doi.org/10.1017/S1478572219000288

Mayne, I., Bull, A., and Raven, J. (2022) *Embedding youth voice in classical music pedagogy. Sound Connections.* Available at https://issuu.com/soundconnections/docs/the_mus ic_lab_-_toolkit

Maxile, H.J. (2008) "Signs, symphonies, signifyin(G): African-American cultural topics as analytical approach to the music of Black composers," Black Music Research Journal, *28*, pp. 123–138.

Mellinger, G. (2003) "Counting color: ambivalence and contradiction in the American Society of Newspaper Editors' discourse of diversity," Journal of Communication Inquiry, *27*(2), pp. 129–151.

Moore, A. (2016) "Neoliberalism and the musical entrepreneur," Journal of the Society for American Music, 10, pp. 33–53. Available at https://doi.org/10.1017/S175219631 500053X

Neale, S. (1980) Genre. British Film Institute.

Negus, K. (1999) Music genres and corporate cultures. London: Routledge.

Nooshin, L. (2011) "Introduction to the special issue: the ethnomusicology of Western art music," Ethnomusicology Forum, 20, pp. 285–300. Available at https://doi.org/10.1080/17411912.2011.659439

Peerbaye, S., and Attariwala, P. (2019) Re-sounding the orchestra: Relationships between Canadian orchestras, Indigenous peoples, and people of colour. Orchestres Canada.

Pullinger, A. (2020) Facilitating the empowerment of transgender voices through singing. Sound Connections.

Ritchey, M. (2019) Composing capital: Classical music in the neoliberal era. University of Chicago: Chicago Press.

Saha, A. (2018) Race and the cultural industries. Cambridge: Polity.

Scott, A. (2014) Romanticizing Brahms: Early recordings and the reconstruction of Brahmsian identity. PhD dissertation. Leiden University.

Scharff, C. (2015) Equality and diversity in the classical music profession: a research report. Available at https://www.impulse-music.co.uk/wp-content/uploads/2017/05/Equality-and-Diversity-in-Classical-Music-Report.pdf (Accessed December 2021).

Scharff, C. (2016) "The psychic life of neoliberalism: mapping the contours of entrepreneurial subjectivity," Theory, Culture & Society, 33(6), pp. 107–122. Available at doi:10.1177/0263276415590164

Scharff, C. (2018a) Gender, subjectivity, and cultural work: the classical music profession. London: Routledge.

Scharff, C. (2018b) "Inequalities in the classical music industry: The role of subjectivity in constructions of the 'ideal classical musician,'" in Dromey, C., Haferkorn, J. (eds.), The classical music industry. London: Routledge, pp. 96–111.

Scharff, C. (2020) "From 'Not Me' to 'Me Too': exploring the trickle-down effects of neoliberal feminism," Rassegna Italiana di Sociologia, 60(4), pp. 667–669. Available at https://doi.org/10.1423/96111

Scharff, C. (2021) "From unspeakability to inequality talk: why conversations about inequalities may not pave the way for change," Open Library of Humanities, 7(2), DOI: https://doi.org/10.16995/olh.4674

Shim, J. (2021) "Token fatigue: tolls of marginalization in white male spaces," Ethnic and Racial Studies, 44(7), pp. 1115–1134. Available at doi: 10.1080/01419870.2020.1779947

Shreffler, A.C. (2019) "Afterword in Boundaries of the new: American classical music at the turn of the millennium," Twentieth-Century Music, 16, pp. 373–455. Available at https://doi.org/10.1017/S1478572219000288

Stirling, C. (2019) Orbital transmissions: affect and musical public-making in London. PhD dissertation. Oxford: University of Oxford.

Toynbee, J. (2000) Making popular music: musicians, creativity and institutions. London: Arnold.

Wang, G. (2009) "Interlopers in the realm of high culture: 'music moms' and the performance of Asian and Asian American identities," American Quarterly, 61(4), pp. 881–903.

Wang, G. (2015) Soundtracks of Asian America: navigating race through musical performance. Illustrated edition. Durham, NC: Duke University Press.

Wright, R., Johansen, G., Kanellopoulos, P.A., and Schmidt, P. (eds.) (2021) The Routledge handbook to sociology of music education. Abingdon: Routledge.

Yang, M. (2007) "East meets West in the concert hall: Asians and classical music in the century of imperialism, post-colonialism, and multiculturalism," Asian Music, 38(1), pp. 1–30.

Yoshihara, M. (2007) *Musicians from a different shore: Asians and Asian Americans in classical music*. Philadelphia: Temple University Press.

Chapter 1

Abbott, A. (1988) The system of professions. an essay on the division of expert labor. Chicago: Chicago University Press.

Bataille, P., Bertolini, S., Casula, C., and Perrenoud, M. (2020) "From atypical to paradigmatic? the relevance of the study of artistic work for the sociology of work," Sociologia del Lavoro, 157(3), pp. 59–83. Available at doi: 10.3280/SL2020-157004.

Becker, H.S. (1982) Art worlds. Berkeley: University of California Press.

Bourdieu, P. (1992) Les règles de l'art: Genèse et structure du champ littéraire. Paris: Seuil.

Brinkmann, S., and Kvale, S. (2015) InterViews: learning the craft of qualitative research interviewing. Los Angeles: SAGE.

Bull, A. (2019) Class, control, and classical music. Oxford: Oxford University Press.

Buscatto, M. (2010) "Professional music in light of gender: toward a sociological understanding," Labrys, 18, special issue. "Women and Music."

Casula, C. (2021) "Boosting gender equality through music production: a case study on two Italian female brass bands," Tafter Journal, 117. *Available at* (https://www.tafter journal.it/).

Casula, C. (2019) "Gender and the classical music world: the unaccomplished professionalization of women in Italy," Per Musi Journal, 39(July), pp. 1–24. Available at: https://doi.org/10.35699/2317-6377.2019.5270.

Casula, C. (2018a) Diventare musicista: indagine sociologica sui conservatori di musica in Italia. Mantua: Universitas Studiorum.

Casula, C. (2018b) "Torn between neoliberal and postmodern trends, corporatist defence and creative age prospects: the ongoing reshaping of the classical music profession in Italy," Cambio: Rivista sulle Trasformazioni Sociali, 8(16), pp. 71–82. Available at doi: 10.13128/cambio-23296.

Coulangeon, P. (2004) Les musiciens inteprètes en France: portrait d'une profession. Paris: La Documentation française.

Delfrati, C. (2017) Storia critica dell'insegnamento della musica in Italia. E-book, Antonio Tombolini.

DeNora, T. (1995) Beethoven and the construction of genius: musical politics in Vienna, 1792–1803. Berkeley: University of California Press.

Frederickson, J., and Rooney, J.F. (1990) "How the music occupation failed to become a profession," International Review of the Aesthetics and Sociology of Music, 21(2), pp. 189–206. Available at doi: 10.2307/837023.

Fresu, P. (2009) Musica dentro. Milan: Feltrinelli.

Green, L. (1997) Music, gender, education. Cambridge: Cambridge University Press.

Grimaldi, E., and Serpieri, R. (2012) "The transformation of the education state in Italy: a critical policy historiography from 1944 to 2011," Italian Journal of Sociology of Education, 1, pp. 146–180.

Kingsbury, H. (1988) Music, talent and performance: a conservatoire cultural system. Philadelphia: Temple University Press.

Laillier, J. (2017) Entrer dans la danse: L'envers du Ballet de l'Opéra de Paris. Paris: CNRS.

Loesser, A. (1954) Men, women and pianos: a social history. New York: Simon & Schuster.
Maione, O. (2005) I Conservatori di musica durante il fascismo: La riforma del 1930: storia e documenti. Turin: EDT.
Pegourdie, A. (2015) "L'«instrumentalisation» des carrières musicales. Division sociale du travail. Inégalités d'accès a l'emploi et renversement de la hiérarchie musicale dans le Conservatoires de musique," Sociologie, 4(6), pp. 321–338.
Powell, W.W., and DiMaggio, P. (eds.) (1991) The new institutionalism in organizational analysis. Chicago: University of Chicago Press.
Scharff, C. (2018) Gender, subjectivity, and cultural work: the classical music profession. London: Routledge.
Thomassen, B. (2010) "'Second generation immigrants' or 'Italians with immigrant parents'? Italian and European perspectives on immigrants and their children," Bulletin of Italian Politics, 2(1), pp. 21–44.
Wagner, I. (2015) Producing excellence: the making of virtuosos. New Brunswick, NJ: Rutgers University Press.
Wajcman, J. (1991) Feminism confronts technology. University Park: Pennsylvania State University Press.
Weber, W. (1992) The rise of musical classics: a study in canon, ritual and ideology. Oxford: Oxford University Press.

Chapter 2

Allen, K., Quinn, J., Hollingworth, S., and Rose, A. (2012) "Becoming employable students and 'ideal' creative workers: exclusion and inequality in higher education work placements," British Journal of Sociology of Education, 34(3), pp. 431–452.
Beljean, S., Chong, P., and Lamont, M. (2015) "A post-Bourdieusian sociology of valuation and evaluation for the field of cultural production," in Hanquinet, L., and Savage, M. (eds.) Routledge international handbook of the sociology of art and culture. New York: Routledge, pp. 38–48.
Bourdieu P. (1993) The field of cultural production. New York: Columbia University Press.
Bradley, D. (2016) "Hidden in plain sight: race and racism in music education," in Benedict, C., Schmidt, P. K., Spruce, G., and Woodford, P. (eds.) The Oxford handbook of social justice in music education. New York: Oxford University Press, pp. 190–203.
Bull, A. (2019) Class, control and classical music. New York: Oxford University Press.
Bull, A., and Scharff, C. (2017) "'McDonald's music' versus 'serious music': how production and consumption practices help to reproduce class inequality in the classical music profession," Cultural Sociology, 11(3), pp. 283–301.
Burke, P.J., and McManus, J. (2011) "Art for a few: exclusions and misrecognition in higher education admission practices," Discourse: Studies in the Cultural Politics of Education, 32(5), pp. 699–712.
Born, G. (2005) "On musical mediation: ontology, technology and creativity," Twentieth-Century Music, 2(1), pp. 7–36.
Casula, C. (2019) "Gender and the classical music world: the unaccomplished professionalization of women in Italy," Per Musi, 39, pp. 1–24.
DeLorenzo, L.C. (2012) "Missing faces in the orchestra: an issue of social justice?," Journal of Music Education, 98(4), pp. 39–46.

Elpus, K., and Abril, C.R. (2011) "High school music ensemble students in the United States: a demographic profile," Journal of Research in Music Education, 59(2), pp. 129–145.

Frankenberg, R. (1993) White women, race matters: the social construction of Whiteness. Minneapolis: University of Minnesota Press.

Green, L. (1997) Music, gender, education. Cambridge: Cambridge University Press.

Gustafson, R.I. (2009) Race and curriculum. Music in childhood education. New York: Palgrave Macmillan.

Hennion, A. (2005) "Pragmatics of taste," in Jacobs, M.D. and Hanrahan, N.W. (eds.) The Blackwell companion to the sociology of culture. Malden, MA: Blackwell, pp. 131–144.

Hess, J. (2021) "Music education and the colonial project: Stumbling toward anti-colonial music education," in Wright, R., Johansen, G., Kanellopoulus, P.A., and Schmidt, P. (eds.) The Routledge handbook of sociology of music education. New York: Routledge, pp. 23–39.

Yang, M. (2007) "East meets West in the concert hall: Asians and classical music in the century of imperialism, post-colonialism, and multiculturalism," Asian Music, 38(1), pp. 1–30.

Lareau, A. (2011) Unequal childhood: class, race, and family life. Berkeley: University of California Press.

Lamont, M. (2009) How professors think: inside the curious world of academic judgment. Cambridge, MA: Harvard University Press.

Leppänen, T. (2015) "The West and the rest of classical music: Asian musicians in the Finnish media coverage of the 1995 Jean Sibelius Violin Competition," European Journal of Cultural Studies, 18(1), pp. 19–34.

Nylander, E. (2014) "Mastering the jazz standard: Sayings and doings of artistic valuation," American Journal of Cultural Sociology, 2(1), pp. 66–96.

McCormick, L. (2015) Performing civility: international competitions in classical music. Cambridge: Cambridge University Press.

Puwar, N. (2004) Space invaders: race, gender and bodies out of place. Oxford: Berg.

Saner, P., Vögele, S., and Vessely, P. (2016) Art.School.Differences: researching inequalities and normativities in the field of higher art education. Final report. Zürich: Institute for Art Education, Zürcher Hochschule der Künste.

Scharff, C. (2015) Equality and diversity in the classical music profession: a research report. King's College London.

Scharff, C. (2018a) Gender, subjectivity, and cultural work: The classical music profession. London: Routledge.

Scharff, C. (2018b) "Inequalities in the classical music industry," in Dromey, C. and Haferkorn, J. (eds.) The classical music industry. New York: Routledge, pp. 79–95.

Wagner, I. (2015) Producing excellence: the making of virtuosos. New Brunswick, NJ: Rutgers University Press.

Chapter 3

Bourdieu, P. (1979) Distinction: a social critique of the judgement of taste. English translated version published 1984. Translated by R. Nice. London: Routledge & Kegan Paul.

Bull, A. (2018) "Uncertain capital: class, gender, and the 'imagined futures' of young classical musicians," in Dromey, C. and Haferkorn, J. (eds.) The classical music industry. New York: Routledge, pp. 79–95.

Bull, A. (2019) Class, control, and classical music. Oxford: Oxford University Press.

Bull, A., and Scharff, C. (2017) "'McDonald's' music' versus 'serious music': how production and consumption practices help to reproduce class inequality in the classical music profession," Cultural Sociology, 11(3), pp. 283–301

Cottrell, S. (2004) Professional music-making in London: ethnography and experience. Aldershot: Ashgate.

Davies, A. (2002) Conceptions of "talent" in official and student discourses within a music conservatoire: a critical discourse analysis. PhD Thesis. University of Central England in Birmingham.

Davies, A. (2004) "Preparing professional performers: music students' perceptions and experiences of the learning process at Birmingham Conservatoire," International Journal of Qualitative Studies in Education, 17(6), pp. 803–821.

Hall, S. (1990) "Cultural identity and diaspora," in Rutherford, J. (ed.) Identity, community, culture, difference. London: Lawrence and Wishart, pp. 222–237.

Hall, S. (1997) "Old and new identities, old and new ethnicities," in King, A.D. (ed.) Culture, globalization, and the world-system: contemporary conditions for the representation of identity. Minnesota: University of Minnesota Press, pp. 42–68.

London School of Economics (2012) The impact of three London conservatoires on the UK and London economies: a project for the Royal Academy of Music, the Guildhall School of Music & Drama and the Royal College of Music, with universities UK. Available at: http://www.lse.ac.uk/geographyAndEnvironment/research/london/pdf/LSE-London-Conservatoires-Report-FINAL-July-2012.pdf (Accessed November 2012).

Perkins, R. (2011) The construction of "learning cultures": an ethnographically-informed case study of a UK Conservatoire. PhD Thesis. University of Cambridge.

Perkins, R. (2013) "Hierarchies and learning in the conservatoire: exploring what students learn through the lens of Bourdieu," Research Studies in Music Education 35(2), pp. 197–212.

Porton, J. (2020) Contemporary British conservatoires and their practices: experiences from alumni perspectives. PhD Thesis. Royal Holloway University, University of London.

Scharff, C. (2018) Gender, subjectivity, and cultural work: the classical music profession. Oxford: Routledge.

Chapter 4

AEC Council. (2013) AEC guidelines on establishing institutional codes of good practice for professional teaching conduct in conservatoires. Available at https://www.aec-music.eu/userfiles/File/Policy%20Papers/Issues%20within%20the%20Higher%20Music%20Education%20sector/aec-guidelines-on-professional-teaching-conduct%20(1).pdf (Accessed March 8, 2021).

Barbera, C. (2021) Engaging female students at Berklee College of Music–Valencia. Available at https://sms.aec-music.eu/diversity-identity-inclusiveness/engaging-female-students-at-berklee-college-of-music-valencia/ (Accessed March 8, 2021).

Barbera, C., Dickson, J., Grandgirard, B., Guerra, A., Heckel, S., Piskor, M. Thomson, K., and Wickström, D.-E. (eds.) (2021) Artistic Plurality and Inclusive Institutional Culture in HME. *Association Européenne des Conservatoires, Académies de Musique et Musikhochschulen (AEC)*, Brussels. Available at https://aec-music.eu/publication/artistic-plurality-and-inclusive-institutional-culture-in-hme/ (Accessed December 17, 2021).

Bartsch, M., Knobbe, M., and Möller, J.-P. (2019) "#MeToo-Vorwürfe gegen Professoren in Hamburg und Düsseldorf—Seine Erwartungen—'reden, trinken, vögeln.'" Spiegel Online, 26(4). Available at https://www.spiegel.de/plus/metoo-vorwuerfe-gegen-professoren-in-hamburg-und-duesseldorf-a-00000000-0002-0001-0000-000163612070 (Accessed May 20, 2019).

Bull, A., and Rye, R. (2018) Silencing students: institutional responses to staff sexual misconduct in UK higher education. Portsmouth: 1752 Group and University of Portsmouth.

Carlsen, M. (2019) "Maestro or mentor? On cultural differences in performance education," in Gies, S. and Sætre, J.H. (eds.) Becoming musicians—student involvement and teacher collaboration in higher music education. Oslo: Norges musikkhøgskole, pp. 91–106.

Creech, A., and Gaunt, H. (2012) "The changing face of individual instrumental tuition: value, purpose and potential," in McPherson, G.E. and Welch, G.F. (eds.) The Oxford handbook of music education, Vol. 1. New York: Oxford University Press, pp. 694–711.

Criado-Perez, C. (2019) Invisible women: data bias in a world designed for men. New York: Abrams Press.

Daniel, R. (2004) "Innovations in piano teaching: a small-group model for the tertiary level," Music Education Research, 6(1), pp. 23–43.

Encarnacao, J., and Blom, D. (2020) "Teaching and evaluating music performance at university: a twenty-first century landscape," *in* Encarnacao, J. and Blom, D. (eds.) Teaching and evaluating music performance at university—beyond the conservatory model. New York: Routledge, pp. 1–6.

Fasang, A. (2006) "Recruitment in symphony orchestras: testing a gender neutral recruitment process," Work, Employment and Society, 20(4), pp. 801–809.

Feltes, T., et al. (2012) Gender-based violence, stalking and fear of crime. Bochum: Ruhr-Universität Bochum.

Fetters, A., Chan, J.C., and Wu, N. (2020) "Classical music has a 'God status' problem," Atlantic, January 31. Available at https://www.theatlantic.com/education/archive/2020/01/conservatories-sexual-harassment-abuse/604351 (Accessed February 21, 2020).

Gaunt, H. (2008) "One-to-one tuition in a conservatoire: the perceptions of instrumental and vocal teachers," Psychology of Music, 36(2), pp. 215–245.

Gaunt, H., López-Íñiguez, G., and Creech, A. (2021) "Musical engagement in one-to-one contexts," *in* Creech, A., Hodges, D.A., and Hallam, S. (eds.) Handbook of music psychology in education and the community. New York: Routledge, pp. 335–350.

Gilbert, P. (2021) "Elevate! Empowering, promoting and supporting women across Leeds Conservatoire." Available at https://sms.aec-music.eu/diversity-identity-inclusiveness/elevate-empowering-promoting-and-supporting-women-across-leeds-college-of-music/ (Accessed March 8, 2021).

Gluckman, N. (2017) "How one college has set out to fix 'a culture of blatant sexual harassment,'" Chronicle of Higher Education, November 29. Available at https://www.chronicle.com/article/How-One-College-Has-Set-Out-to/241927/ (Accessed May 24, 2019).

Goldin, C., and Rouse, C. (2000) "Orchestrating impartiality: the impact of 'blind' auditions on female musicians," American Economic Review, 90(4), pp. 715–741.

Green, L. (2002) How popular musicians learn: a way ahead for music education. Burlington: Ashgate.

Guerra, A., et al. (2021) "Decentering curricula: questions for re-evaluating diversity and inclusiveness in HMEIs." Available at https://sms.aec-music.eu/diversity-identity-inclusiveness/decentering-curricula-questions-for-re-evaluating-diversity-and-inclusiveness-in-hmeis/ (Accessed April 30, 2021).

Herold, A. (2006a) "Sexuelle Übergriffe gegen Studierende. Ergebnisse einer Umfrage an Musikhochschulen," in Hoffmann, F. (ed.) Panische Gefühle—Sexuelle Übergriffe im Instrumentalunterricht. Mainz: Schott, pp. 57–64.

Herold, A. (2006b) "Zwischen Nähe und Distanz—Beziehungen im Instrumental—und Gesangsunterricht," in Hoffmann, F. (ed.) Panische Gefühle—Sexuelle Übergriffe im Instrumentalunterricht. Mainz: Schott, pp. 101–116.

Josefson, C. (2016) "Svart pedagogik," Fokus, May 27–June 2. Available at https://www.fokus.se/2016/05/svart-pedagogik/ (Accessed April 18, 2019).

Jørgensen, H. (2000) "Student learning in higher instrumental education: who is responsible," British Journal of Music Education, 17(1), pp. 67–77.

Kelly, L. (1988) Surviving sexual violence. Cambridge: Polity Press.

Knobbe, M., and Möller, J.-P. (2018) "Sex im Präsidentenbüro—Skandal an der Musikhochschule München," Spiegel Online, May 11. Available at http://www.spiegel.de/spiegel/sex-skandal-an-der-musikhochschule-muenchen-a-1207253.html (Accessed July 11, 2018).

Lazar, K. (2017) "Berklee let teachers quietly leave after alleged sex abuse, and pushed students for silence," Boston Globe, November 8. Available at https://www.bostonglobe.com/metro/2017/11/08/berklee-college-lets-teachers-quietly-leave-after-alleged-sexual-abuse-students-least-one-found-another-teaching-job/yfCkCCmdJzxkiEgrQK4cWM/story.html (Accessed May 24, 2019).

Lebler, D. (2006) "The master-less studio: an autonomous education community," Journal of Learning Design, 1(3), pp. 41–50.

Lebler, D. (2007) "Student-as-master? Reflections on a learning innovation in popular music pedagogy," International Journal of Music Education, 25(3), pp. 205–221.

Liertz, C. (2007) New frameworks for tertiary music education: a holistic educational approach for many pyramids of excellence. Proceedings of the 8th Australasian Piano Pedagogy Conference. Available at http://citeseerx.ist.psu.edu/viewdoc/download?doi=10.1.1.498.778&rep=rep1&type=pdf (Accessed May 12, 2021).

Midgette, A., and McGlone, P. (2018) "Assaults in dressing rooms. Groping during lessons. Classical musicians reveal a profession rife with harassment," Washington Post, July 26. Available at https://www.washingtonpost.com/entertainment/music/assaults-in-dressing-rooms-groping-during-lessons-classical-musicians-reveal-a-profession-rife-with-harassment/2018/07/25/f47617d0-36c8-11e8-acd5-35eac230e514_story.html (Accessed May 26, 2021).

Mills, J., and Smith, J. (2003) "Teachers' beliefs about effective instrumental teaching in schools and higher education," British Journal of Music Education, 20(1), 5–27.

Mitchell, A. (2020a) "A professional development program to facilitate group music performance teaching," *in* Encarnacao, J. and Blom, D. (eds.) Teaching and evaluating music performance at university: beyond the conservatory model. London: Routledge, pp. 101–115.

Mitchell, A. (2020b) "Implementing group teaching in music performance," *in* Encarnacao, J. and Blom, D. (eds.) Teaching and evaluating music performance at university: beyond the conservatory model. London: Routledge, pp. 119–131.

N.N. (2018) "AEC on Power Relations and #MeToo." Available at https://www.aec-music.eu/about-aec/news/aec-on-power-relations-and-metoo (Accessed March 3, 2021).

National Union of Students and the 1752 Group. (2018) Power in the academy: staff sexual misconduct in UK higher education. National Union of Students, London.

Nerland, M. (2019) "Beyond policy: conceptualising student-centred learning environments in higher (music) education," in Gies, S. and Sætre, J.H. (eds.) Becoming musicians: student involvement and teacher collaboration in higher music education. Oslo: Norges musikkhøgskole, pp. 53–66.

Payne, C., Annetts, D., and Pohl, N. (2018) Dignity in study: a survey of higher education institutions. Available at https://www.ism.org/images/images/Equity-ISM-MU-Dignity-in-Study-report.pdf (Accessed July 25, 2018).

RKM—AG "Sexualisierte Diskriminierung." (2017) Handlungsempfehlungen der RKM—Arbeitsgruppe "sexualisierte Diskriminierung" für die Winterkonferenz der Rektorinnen und Rektoren der Musikhochschulen am 22.01.2017. Available at http://www.hfm-nuernberg.de/fileadmin/user_upload/Text-Pool/Sonstiges/AG_sexualisierte_Diskriminierung_Handlungsempfehlungen.pdf (Accessed February 4, 2020).

Sætre, J.H., et al. (2019) "The music performance student as researching artist? Perspectives on student-centredness in higher music education," in Gies, S. and Sætre, J.H. (eds.) Becoming musicians: student involvement and teacher collaboration in higher music education. Oslo: Norges musikkhøgskole, pp. 17–29.

Wickström, D.-E. (2021) "Dealing with (institutionalized) forms of power abuse." Available at https://sms.aec-music.eu/diversity-identity-inclusiveness/dealing-with-institutionalized-forms-of-power-abuse/ (Accessed April 30, 2021).

Chapter 5

Ahmed, S. (2007) "The language of diversity," Ethnic and Racial Studies, 30(2), pp. 235–256.

Banks, Patricia (2019) Diversity and philanthropy at African American museums. New York: Routledge.

Bhattacharyya, Gargi (2018) Rethinking racial capitalism: questions of reproduction and survival. London: Rowman and Littlefield International.

Born, Georgina (2010) "The social and the aesthetic: for a post-Bourdieusian theory of cultural production," Cultural Sociology, 4(2), pp. 171–208.

Born, Georgina, and Hesmondhalgh, David (2000) Western music and its others. Berkeley: University of California Press.

Bull, Anna (2019) Class, control, and classical music. Oxford: Oxford University Press.

El-Tayeb, Fatima (2016) Undeutsch: Die Konstruktion des Anderen in der postmigrantischen Gesellschaft. Bielefeld: Verlag.

Erigha, Maryann (2018) "On the margins: Black directors and the persistence of racial inequality in twenty-first century Hollywood," Ethnic and Racial Studies, 41(7), 1217–1234.
Gray, Herman (2016) "Precarious diversity: representation and demography," in Curtin, M. and Sanson, K. (eds.) Precarious creativity: global media, local labor. Berkeley: University of California Press, pp. 241–253.
Hall, Stuart (1992) "What is this "Black" in Black popular culture?" in Dent, G. (ed.) Black popular culture. Seattle: Bay, pp. 21–36.
Hall, Stuart (1996) "New ethnicities," in Morley, D. and Chen, K. (eds.) Stuart Hall: critical dialogues in cultural studies. London: Routledge, pp. 442–451.
Kosnick, Kira (2008) "Conflicting mobilities," in Donald, S., Kevin, C., Kofman, E. (eds.) Branding Cities. New York: Routledge, pp. 28–41.
Lentin, Alana (2020) Why race still matters. Hoboken, NJ: Wiley.
Leong, Nancy (2013) "Racial capitalism," Harvard Law Review, 126(8), pp. 2151–2226.
Nooshin, Laudan (2003) "Improvisation as 'other,'" Journal of the Royal Musical Association, 128(2), pp. 242–296.
Nwonka, Clive J. (2015) "Diversity pie: rethinking social exclusion and quota in shaping diversity policy in the film industry," Journal of Media Practice, 16(1), pp. 73–90.
Piketty, Thomas (2014) Capital in the twenty-first century. Cambridge, MA: Harvard University Press.
Puwar, Nirmal (2004) Space invaders: race, gender and bodies out of place. New York: Berg.
Reay, Diane, Crozier, Gill, and James, David (2011) White middle class identities and urban schooling. New York: Palgrave Macmillan.
Saha, Anamik (2018) Race and the cultural industries. London: Polity Press.
Said, Edward (1978) Orientalism. New York: Vintage Books.
Stokes, Martin (2004) "Music and the global order," Annual Review of Anthropology, 33, pp. 47–72.
Titley, Gavan (2014) "After the end of multiculturalism: public service media and integrationist imaginaries for the governance of difference," Global Media and Communication, 10(3), pp. 247–260.
Yılmaz, Ferruh (2015) "From immigrant worker to Muslim immigrant," European Journal of Women's Studies, 22(1), pp. 37–52.

Chapter 6

Austin, P. (2019) "More than a quarter of LA County kids live in poverty," Patch. Available at https://patch.com/california/northridge/more-quarter-la-county-kids-live-poverty (Accessed May 4, 2021).
Baker, G. (2014) El Sistema: Orchestrating Venezuela's Youth. Oxford: Oxford University Press.
Baker, G. (2017) "'Producing musicians like sausages': new perspectives on the history and historiography of Venezuela's El Sistema," Music Education Research, 20(4), pp. 502–516. Available at https://doi.org/10.1080/14613808.2018.1433151 (Accessed May 3, 2021).
Baker, G. (N.D.) "'Playing for their lives': sins of mission and omission," Geoff Baker Music. Available at https://geoffbakermusic.wordpress.com/el-sistema-older-posts/playing-for-their-lives-sins-of-mission-and-omission/ (Accessed May 4, 2021).

Boyles Heights Beats (2020) "Group to Protest Mariachi Plaza Development." Available at https://boyleheightsbeat.com/group-to-protest-mariachi-plaza-development/ (Accessed May 4, 2021).

Callahan, D. (2017) The givers. Kindle Edition. New York: Knopf Doubleday Publishing Group.

Carter, B.W. (2018) "L.A. Philharmonic Brings Youth Orchestra Center to Inglewood," Los Angeles Sentinel. Available at https://lasentinel.net/l-a-philharmonic-brings-youth-orchestra-center-to-inglewood.html (Accessed May 3, 2021).

Edwards, R. (2016) "Being Black at work: a guest post," Medium. Available at https://medium.com/@kellywickham/rachael-marissa-edwards-is-an-art-activist-and-college-student-who-also-works-at-university-of-d1cc6ab30b51#.b6u4xlsxo (Accessed May 4, 2021).

El Sistema: Music to change life (2009) [DVD] Germany: Euroarts.

El Sistema USA (2021) Member directory. Available at https://elsistemausa.org/membership-account/directory/ (Accessed May 4, 2021).

Kajikawa, L. (2019) "The possessive investment in classical music: confronting legacies of White supremacy in U.S. schools," in Crenshaw, K. et al. (eds.) Seeing race again: countering colorblindness across the disciplines. Oakland: University of California Press, pp. 155–74.

Kaplan, E. (2014) "Brann-ded in Inglewood," KCET. Available at https://www.kcet.org/history-society/brann-ded-in-inglewood (Accessed May 4, 2021).

LA Phil (2020) "Breaking ground on the Judith and Thomas L. Beckman YOLA Center at Inglewood." [video]. Available at https://www.youtube.com/watch?v=YVCF6oiYMqw (Accessed May 4, 2021).

LAist (2021) "A very brief history of South Central Jazz." [video] Available at https://www.facebook.com/watch/?v=737509653569319 (Accessed May 4, 2021).

Levine, L. (1988) Highbrow/lowbrow: the emergence of cultural hierarchy in America. Cambridge, MA: Harvard University Press.

Los Angeles Philharmonic (2018) Donor impact report. Available at https://www.laphil.com/support/corporate-governance/donocr-impact-report-2018 (Accessed May 4, 2021).

Los Angeles Philharmonic (2021) "YOLA (Youth Orchestra Los Angeles)." Available at https://www.laphil.com/learn/yola/youth-orchestra-los-angeles (Accessed May 4, 2021).

Poser, R. (2021) "He wants to save classics from Whiteness. Can the field survive?," New York Times Magazine. Available at https://www.nytimes.com/2021/02/02/magazine/classics-greece-rome-whiteness.html (Accessed May 4, 2021).

Public Policy Institute of California (2017) "Geography of child poverty in California." Available at https://www.ppic.org/publication/geography-of-child-poverty-in-california/#:~:text=For%20example%2C%20in%20Los%20Angeles,and%20highest%20rates%20in%20California (Accessed May 4, 2021).

Saifer, A. (2020) "Racial neoliberal philanthropy and arts for social change," Organization, pp. 1–21. Available at https://doi.org/10.1177/1350508420973327 (Accessed May 3, 2021).

Sammon, A. (2019) "The billionaire class created their own wealth tax. It failed," American Prospect. Available at https://prospect.org/power/billionaire-class-created-failed-wealth-tax-giving-pledge/ (Accessed May 3, 2021).

Schnyder, D. (2012) "Criminals, Planters, and corporate capitalists: the case of public education in Los Angeles," in Woods, C. (ed.) Black California dreamin': the crises of California's African-American communities. Santa Barbara, CA: Center for Black Studies Research, pp. 107–126. Available at https://escholarship.org/uc/item/63g6128j (Accessed May 3, 2021).

Swed, M. (2020) "Black music matters, and classical companies are misfiring on diversity," Los Angeles Times. Available at https://www.latimes.com/entertainment-arts/story/2020-12-10/black-music-matters-classical-diversity (Accessed May 3, 2021).

The promise of music (2008) [DVD] Germany: Deutsche Grammophon.

Tocar y luchar (2006) [DVD] Venezuela: Fesnojiv.

Turnstall, T. (2012) Changing lives: Gustavo Dudamel, El Sistema, and the transformative power of music. New York: Norton.

Vasquez, R. (2019) "There's Something in the Water in Watts, Where Music is Alive and Well," LA Canvas. Available at https://www.lacanvas.com/theres-something-in-the-water-in-watts-where-music-is-alive-and-well/ (Accessed May 4, 2021).

Vu (2021) "White Supremacy and the Problem with Centering Donors' Interests and Emotions." Nonprofit AF, March 22. Available at https://nonprofitaf.com/2021/03/white-supremacy-and-the-problem-with-centering-donors-interests-and-emotions/?fbclid=IwAR1FxteEjCoOVpfpgzLMAO1kprlzFKmNYFHsmP7LlYdT8YEoWTg3v-UyI4A (Accessed May 4, 2021).

Woolfe, Z. (2017) "Los Angeles has America's most important orchestra. Period," New York Times. Available at https://www.nytimes.com/2017/04/18/arts/music/los-angeles-has-americas-most-important-orchestra-period.html (Accessed May 3, 2021).

Yang, M. (2014) Planet Beethoven: classical music at the turn of the millennium. Middletown, CT: Wesleyan University Press.

Zanfagna, C. (2017) Holy Hip Hop in the City of Angels. Berkeley: University of California Press.

Chapter 7

Ahmed, Sara (2012) On being included: racism and diversity in institutional life. Durham: Duke University Press.

Appiah, Kwame Anthony (2001) "Liberalism, individuality, and identity," Critical Inquiry 27(2).

Aspan, Maria (2021) "Women accounted for 100% of the 140,000 jobs shed by the U.S. economy in December," Fortune Magazine, Jan. 8. Available at https://fortune.com/2021/01/08/covid-job-losses-women-december-us-unemployment-rate/.

Attas, Robin, and Margaret E. Walker (2019) "Exploring decolonization, music, and pedagogy," Decolonizing Music Pedagogies 39(1), pp. 3–20.

Baltimore Sun (2016) "Diversifying the classical music world," June 9.

Barone, Joshua (2020) "Opera can no longer ignore its race problem," New York Times, July 16.

Boltanski, Luc, and Eve Chiapello (2005) The new spirit of capitalism. Translated by Gregory Elliott. London: Verso.

Brown, Wendy (2005) Edgework: critical essays on knowledge and politics. Princeton: Princeton University Press.

Bull, Anna (2019) Class, control, and classical music. Oxford: Oxford University Press.
Crenshaw, Kimberlé (1989) "Demarginalizing the intersection of race and sex: a Black Feminist critique of antidiscrimination doctrine, feminist theory and antiracist politics," University of Chicago Legal Forum *1989*(1), 139–167.
Crispin, Jessa (2017) Why I am not a feminist: a feminist manifesto. Carlton: Black In.
Currie, James (2011) "Music and politics," in Theodore Gracyk and Andrew Kania (eds.) The routledge companion to philosophy and music. New York: Routledge, pp. 546–556.
Davis, Angela (2017) "Revolution today," Centre de Cultura Contemporània de Barcelona, Oct. 9. https://www.cccb.org/en/multimedia/videos/angela-davis/227656.
Davis, Angela (1996) "Rethinking 'race' politics," in Avery F. Gordon and Christopher Newfield (eds.) Mapping multiculturalism. Minneapolis: University of Minnesota Press, pp. 40–48.
Dean, Jodi (2019) Comrade: an essay on political belonging. London: Verso.
Drennan, William A. (2017) "Conspicuous philanthropy: reconciling contract and tax laws," American University Law Review *66*(6).
DuBois, W.E.B. (1903) The souls of black folk. New York: Penguin Vitae.
Ewell, Philip A. (2020) "Music theory and the White racial frame." Music Theory Online *26*(2).
Federici, Silvia (2004) Caliban and the witch: women, the body, and primitive accumulation. New York: Autonomedia.
Gilbert, Jeremy (2014) Common ground: democracy and collectivity in an age of individualism. New York: Pluto Press.
Goldman, Emma (1911) Anarchism and other essays. London: Active Distribution.
Head, Lesley (2016) Hope and grief in the anthropocene: re-conceptualising human-nature relations. New York: Routledge.
hooks, bell (1984) Feminist theory: from margin to center. Boston: South End Press.
Horning, Rob (2019) "The Shed's fetish for immediate experience ignores the reality of contemporary ritual," Art in America, June. https://www.artnews.com/art-in-america/features/issues-commentary-tool-space-63635/
INCITE! Eds. The revolution will not be funded: beyond the non-profit industrial complex. Cambridge: South End Press, 2007.
Jaffe, Sarah (2013) "Trickle-down feminism," Dissent (Winter). Available at https://www.dissentmagazine.org/article/trickle-down-feminism.
Kajikawa, Loren (2019) "The possessive investment in classical music: confronting legacies of White supremacy in U.S. schools," in Crenshaw, K.W., Harris, L.C., HoSang, D.M., and Lipsitz, G. (eds.) Seeing race again: countering colorblindness across the disciplines. Berkeley: University of California Press, pp. 155–174.
King, Martin Luther, Jr. (1967) "Report to the SCLC staff."
Lewis, George (1996) "Improvised music after 1950: Afrological and Eurological perspectives," Black Music Research Journal *16*(1), pp. 91–122.
Lewis, Holly (2016) The politics of everybody: feminism, queer theory, and Marxism at the intersection. London: Zed Books.
Luxemburg, Rosa (1913) The accumulation of capital. New York: Routledge.
Marx, Karl (1867) Capital, Vol. 1. Translated by Ben Fowkes. London: Penguin Press.
Maysaud, Nebal (2019) "It's time to let classical music die," New Music Box, June 24. https://nmbx.newmusicusa.org/its-time-to-let-classical-music-die/.
McRobbie, Angela (2009) The aftermath of feminism: gender, culture, and social change. London: SAGE.

Melamed, Jodi (2011) Represent and destroy: rationalizing violence in the new racial capitalism. Minneapolis: University of Minnesota Press.
Montpelier, Rachel (2018) "The Met is finally commissioning operas by women," Women and Hollywood, Sept. 24. Available at https://womenandhollywood.com/the-met-is-finally-commissioning-operas-by-women/.
Moore (2016) "Neoliberalism and the musical entrepreneur," Journal of the Society for American Music, 10(1), pp. 33–53.
Mouffe, Chantal (2005) The democratic paradox. London: Verson.
Rhodes, James (2014) "Sexism is rife in classical music," Guardian, Feb. 4.
Robinson, Cedric (1983) Black marxism: the making of the black radical tradition. Chapel Hill: University of North Carolina Press, 2000.
Robinson, Dylan (2020) Hungry listening: resonant theory for Indigenous sound studies. Minneapolis: University of Minnesota Press.
Taíwò, Olúfémi (2020) "Being-in-the-Room-Privilege: Elite Capture and Epistemic Deference," Philosopher, 108(4). Available at https://www.thephilosopher1923.org/essay-taiwo.
Taylor, Timothy (2007) Beyond exoticism: western music and the world. Durham: Duke University Press.
Tomlinson, Barbara (2019) "Powerblind intersectionality: feminism and inclusion as a one-way street," in Crenshaw, K.W., Harris, L.C., HoSang, D.M., and Lipsitz, G. (eds.) Seeing race again: countering colorblindness across the disciplines. Berkeley: University of California Press, pp. 175–199.
Warner, Sarah (2012) Acts of gaiety: LGBT performance and the politics of pleasure. Ann Arbor: University of Michigan Press.

Chapter 8

Abbate, C. (2001) In search of opera. Princeton, NJ: Princeton University Press.
Against Modern Opera Productions (2021) About. Available at: https://www.facebook.com/Against-Modern-Opera-Productions-146292958770872/ (Accessed March 15, 2021).
André, N. (2016) Black opera: history, power, engagement. Urbana: University of Illinois Press.
André, N., Bryan, K.M., and Saylor, E. (eds.) (2012) Blackness in opera. Urbana: University of Illinois Press.
Boland, M., and Lloyd, M. (2019) "*West Side Story* on Sydney Harbour reignites debate on racial casting," ABC News, March 22. Available at https://www.abc.net.au/news/2019-03-22/west-side-story-revamped-at-opera-house/10924814 (Accessed March 15, 2021).
Caves, R.E. (2000) Creative industries: contracts between art and commerce. Cambridge, MA: Harvard University Press.
Chan, P. (2020) Final bow for yellowface: dancing between intention and impact. New York: Yellow Peril Press.
Cooper, M. (2016) "Can David McVicar bring peace to the opera wars?" New York Times, March 20. Available at https://www.nytimes.com/2016/03/20/arts/music/hollywood-nope-the-met-will-do-for-david-mcvicar.html (Accessed March 16, 2021).

Elliott, R. (2016) "Blacks and blackface at the opera," in Ingraham, M., So, J., and Moodley, R. (eds.) Opera in a Multicultural World: Coloniality, Culture, Performance. London: Taylor & Francis, pp. 34–49.

Gentile, D. (2018) "Legendary opera says 'enough' to violence against women, flips gender roles," SBS Italian, January 17. Available at https://www.sbs.com.au/language/engl ish/legendary-opera-says-enough-to-violence-against-women-flips-gender-roles (Accessed March 21, 2021).

Giovetti, O. (2019) "Color blind: Anna Netrebko and blackface," VAN Magazine, May 13. Available at https://van-us.atavist.com/color-blind (Accessed March 5, 2021).

Holton, K. (2020) "Inside and outside the operatic canon, on stage and in the boardroom," in Cormac, N., and Weber, W. (eds.) The Oxford Handbook of the Operatic Canon. Oxford: Oxford University Press, pp. 535–546.

Hopkins, K.B. (2018) "*There's No Business Like Show Business*: abandoning color-blind casting and embracing color-conscious casting in American theatre," Journal of Sports & Entertainment Law, 9(2), pp. 131–155. Available at https://harvardjsel.com/wp-cont ent/uploads/sites/9/2018/06/HLS201.pdf (Accessed April 21, 2021).

Karras, C. (2018) "Seattle Opera's "Aida" spurs discussion of ways Black people are misrepresented—or not represented—in opera," Seattle Times, April 26. Available at https://www.seattletimes.com/entertainment/classical-music/seattle-operas-aida-spurs-discussion-of-ways-black-people-are-misrepresented-or-not-represented-in-opera/ (Accessed April 1, 2021).

Latza Nadeau, B. (2018) "Bizarre Bizet: A #MeToo Carmen doesn't die, and the audience shouts 'Kill her!'," Daily Beast, January 20. Available at https://www.thedailybe ast.com/bizarre-bizet-a-metoo-carmen-doesnt-die-and-the-audience-shouts-kill-her (Accessed April 1, 2021).

Littlejohn, D. (1994) The ultimate art: essays around and about opera. Berkeley: University of California Press.

Lunny, O. (2019) "Blackface scandal divides the world of opera," Forbes, August 17. Available at https://www.forbes.com/sites/oisinlunny/2019/08/17/blackface-scandal-divides-the-world-of-opera/?sh=68748b3d56fa (Accessed March 5, 2021).

Midgette, A. (2017) "In theater and film, we demand that Asian roles be played by Asian actors. Why is opera different?" Washington Post, April 29. Available at https://www.washingtonpost.com/entertainment/music/opera-wants-more-realistic-portrayals-but-in-casting-its-all-about-the-voice/2017/04/27/3a5a46e0-29f0-11e7-b605-3343 13c691853_story.html (Accessed April 25, 2021).

Moon, K.R. (2005) Yellowface: creating the Chinese in American popular music and performance, 1850s–1920s. New Brunswick, NJ: Rutgers University Press.

Morrison, M.D. (2020) "Race, blacksound, and the (re)making of musicological discourse," Journal of the American Musicological Society, 72(3), pp. 781–823. Available at doi: 10.1525/jams.2019.72.3.781.

Operabase. (2021) Statistics. Available at https://www.operabase.com/statistics/en. (Accessed March 1, 2021).

Opera Canada. (2018) "Review: *The Abduction from the Seraglio* reinvented at Canadian Opera Company, Feb. 7, 2018," Opera Canada, February 8. Available at https://oper acanada.ca/review-coc-abduction-canadian-opera/ (Accessed March 15, 2021).

Politi, J. (2018) "A happy opera ending sparks a #MeToo debate in Italy," Financial Times, January 16. Available at https://www.ft.com/content/64e4c704-faac-11e7-a492-2c9be 7f3120a (Accessed March 15, 2021).

Ridout, N. (2012) "Opera and the technologies of theatrical performance," in Till, N. (ed.) The Cambridge Companion to Opera Studies. Cambridge: Cambridge University Press, pp. 159–178.

Rosen, D. (2001) "On staging that matters," in Latham, A., and Parker, R. (eds.) Verdi in Performance. Oxford: Oxford University Press, pp. 28–33.

Salazar, F. (2019a) "Tamara Wilson to make Arena di Verona history," OperaWire, July 24. Available at https://operawire.com/tamara-wilson-to-make-arena-di-verona-history/ (Accessed March 10, 2021).

Salazar, F. (2019b) "Tamara Wilson cancels final Aida," OperaWire, July 28. Available at https://operawire.com/tamara-wilson-cancels-final-aida/ (Accessed March 10, 2021).

Seattle Opera. (2017) Community conversations: cultural appropriation and Madame Butterfly. Available at https://www.seattleopera.org/classes-camps-clubs/for-adults/community-conversations/cultural-appropriation-madame-butterfly/ (Accessed March 10, 2021).

Sgourev, S.V. (2013) "The dynamics of risk in innovation: a premiere or an encore?" Industrial and Corporate Change, 22(2), pp. 549–575. Available at doi: 10.1093/icc/dts021.

Terauds, J. (2018) "Updated opera *Abduction from the Seraglio* a mess in all but the music," Toronto Star, February 8. Available at https://www.thestar.com/entertainment/stage/review/2018/02/08/canadian-opera-companys-updated-abduction-from-the-seraglio-a-mess-in-all-but-the-music.html?rf (Accessed March 21, 2021).

Till, N. (2012) "The operatic work: texts, performances, receptions and repertories," in Till, N. (ed.) The Cambridge companion to opera studies. Cambridge: Cambridge University Press, pp. 225–256.

Weber, S. (1994) "Taking place: toward a theater of dislocation," in Levin, D.J. (ed.) Opera through other eyes. Stanford, CA: Stanford University Press, pp. 107–146.

Chapter 9

André, N. (2018) Black opera: history, power, engagement. Urbana: University of Illinois Press.

Brigolin, L. (2017) "'Embrace what makes you unique': Weston hurt lives by example," Seattle Opera Blog. Available at http://www.seattleoperablog.com/2017/08/embrace-what-makes-you-unique-weston.html (Accessed December 1, 2021).

Bull, A. (2019) "'Instead of destroying my body I have a reason for maintaining it': young women's re-imagining of the body through singing opera," in Class, control, and classical music. New York: Oxford University Press, pp. 132–54.

Church, D. (2011) "Freakery, cult films, and the problem of ambivalence," Journal of Film and Video, 63(1), pp. 3–17.

Deutsche Oper Berlin (2020) Alexander von Zemlinsky: DER ZWERG (Introduction) [YouTube video]. Available at https://www.youtube.com/watch?v=Zbn3gOTlI8U (Accessed March 12, 2021).

Disability Arts International (2017) "The aesthetics of access," February 28. Available at https://www.disabilityartsinternational.org/resources/the-aesthetics-of-access/ (Accessed September 23, 2021).

Fox, A.M., and Sandahl, C. (2018) "Beyond 'cripping up,'" Journal of Literary & Cultural Disability Studies, 12(2), pp. 121–127.

Garland Thomson, R. (ed.) (1996) Freakery: cultural spectacles of the extraordinary body. New York: New York University Press.

Garland Thomson, R. (2017) Extraordinary bodies: figuring physical disability in American culture and literature. New York: Columbia University Press.

Garland Thomson, R. (2009) Staring: how we look. New York: Oxford University Press.

Graeae (2021) Our artistic vision. Available at https://graeae.org/about/our-artistic-vision/ (Accessed September 13, 2021).

Harvey, D. (2019) "SXSW film review: "Come as You Are," Variety, March 19. Available at https://variety.com/2019/film/reviews/come-as-you-are-review-1203164706/ (Accessed September 22, 2021).

Hijinx (2018). Available at https://www.hijinx.org.uk/new-standards-for-casting-neurodivergent-actors/ (Accessed September 25, 2021).

Holmes, M.S. (2009) Fictions of affliction: physical disability in Victorian culture. Ann Arbor: University of Michigan Press.

Howe, B., and Armstrong, C. (2021) Musical representations of disability. Available at https://www.lsu.edu/faculty/bhowe/disability-representation.html (Accessed November 26, 2021).

Howe, B.,` et al. (eds.) (2015) The Oxford handbook of music and disability studies. Oxford: Oxford University Press.

Hurt, W. (2018) "THANK GOD we don't all look and sound the same!," Opera and Disability, April 23. Available at https://www.operaanddisability.com/blog/weston-hurt (Accessed September 20, 2021).

Ide, W. (2020) "*Come As You Are* review: a briskly unsentimental journey," Guardian, July 18.

Johnston, K. (2016) "Critical embodiment and casting," in Disability theatre and modern drama: recasting modernism. New York: Bloomsbury, pp. 37–58.

Kriegel, Leonard (1988) "Disability as metaphor in literature," Kaleidoscope: International Magazine of Literature, Fine Arts and Disability, 17, pp. 6–14.

Little, C. (2020) "Disability & sexuality: nothing about us without us," Flipscreen, July 19. Available at https://flipscreened.com/2020/07/19/disability-sexuality-nothing-about-us-without-us/ (Accessed November 22, 2021) .

Lopez, K. (2020) "The invitation *Come As You Are* gives to disability," Forbes, February 13. Available at https://www.forbes.com/sites/kristenlopez/2020/02/13/the-invitation-come-as-you-are-gives-to-disability/?sh=306152c75d7c (Accessed September 22, 2021).

McClary, Susan (2002) "Excess and frame: the musical representation of madwomen," Feminine endings: music, gender, and sexuality. Minneapolis: University of Minnesota Press, pp. 80–111.

Mitchell, D.T., and Snyder, S.L. (2001) Narrative prosthesis: disability and the dependencies of discourse. Ann Arbor: University of Michigan Press.

Operabase (2021) Available at https://www.operabase.com/en (Accessed November 26, 2021).

Parrott, J.M. (2019) Rolling the boards: the interplay of representation and recruitment in disability casting in UK theatre and television. PhD Thesis. University of Warwick. Available at http://webcat.warwick.ac.uk/record=b3520087~S15 (Accessed October 12, 2021).

Poore, C. (2007) "Disability in the Culture of the Weimar Republic," in Disability in Twentieth-century German culture. Ann Arbor: University of Michigan Press, pp. 1–66.

Quasthoff, T. (2008) The voice: a memoir. Translated by K.S. Wittenborn. New York: Pantheon.

Rosand, E. (1991) "Madness," in Opera in seventeenth-century Venice: the creation of a genre. Berkeley: University of California Press, pp. 346–359.

Sandahl, C. (2005) "The tyranny of neutral: disability and actor training," in Sandahl, C. and Auslander, P. (eds.) Bodies in commotion: disability and performance. Ann Arbor: University of Michigan Press, pp. 255–268.

Sandahl, C. (2018) "Using our words: exploring representational conundrums in disability drama and performance," Journal of literary & cultural disability studies, 12(2), pp. 129–144.

Siebers, T. (2010) Disability aesthetics. Ann Arbor: University of Michigan Press.

Straus, J.N. (2011) Extraordinary measures: disability in music. Oxford: Oxford University Press.

Straus, J.N. (2018) Broken beauty: musical modernism and the representation of disability. New York: Oxford University Press.

Young, S. (2014) *I'm not your inspiration, thank you very much* [YouTube video]. Available at https://www.youtube.com/watch?v=8K9Ggl64Bsw (Accessed February 11, 2019).

Youth Music (2020) Reshape music: *a report exploring the lived experience of disabled musicians in education and beyond*. Available at https://youthmusic.org.uk/reshape-music (Accessed December 1, 2021).

Chapter 10

ISM (2021) "Dignity at work: discrimination in the music sector." Available at https://www.ism.org/campaigns/dignityatwork (Accessed August 31, 2021).

PiPA (2021) *PiPA Covid Research Report 2021*. Pipacampaign.org. Available at https://pipacampaign.org/uploads/ckeditor/PiPA_COVID_REPORT.pdf (Accessed May 4, 2021).

Venvell, J. (2020) *64% musicians considering leaving the music profession [Survey Results]*. Encore Blog. Available at https://encoremusicians.com/blog/musicians-leaving-music-industry/ (Accessed August 27, 2020).

Chapter 12

Brown, B.K. (2020) "Take it from a Black conductor: classical music has a real problem." Available at https://level.medium.com/black-concert-trauma-5fa0459e5b3 (Accessed July 12, 2021).\

Gustafson, R. (2009) Race and curriculum: music in childhood education. New York: Palgrave MacMillan.

Lamont, M., Silva, G.M., Welburn, J., Guetzkow, J., Mizrachi, N., Herzog, H., and Reis, E. (2016) *Getting* respect: responding to stigma and discrimination in the *United States, Brazil, and Israel*, Princeton, NJ: Princeton University Press.

Meghji, A. (2017) "Encoding and decoding Black and White cultural capitals: Black middle-class experiences," Cultural Sociology. Available at https://doi.org/10.1177/1749975517741999

Chapter 14

Anderson, Leon (2006) "Analytic autoethnography," Journal of Contemporary Ethnography, 35, pp. 373–395.
Barone, Joshua (2019) "Was Yuja Wang's concert satirical or offensive? It's complicated," New York Times, February 15.
Cheng, William (2019) Loving music till it hurts. New York: Oxford University Press.
Davidson, Jane W., and Edgar, Richard (2003) "Gender and race bias in the judgement of Western art music performance," Music Education Research, 5, pp. 169–181.
Day, Anthony (1994) "A shift in composition: Asian and Asian American musicians increasingly can be found playing in US symphony orchestras. 'This is a manifestation of a normal cycle in American musical life,' says Joseph Polisi, president of Juilliard," Los Angeles Times, April 3.
Doeser, James (2016) "Racial/ethnic and gender diversity in the orchestra field," League of American Orchestras. Available at americanorchestras.org/images/stories/diversity/Racial-Ethnic-and-Gender-Diversity-in-the-Orchestra-Field-Final-92116.pdf
Elliott, Charles A. (1995–1996) "Race and gender as factors in judgments of musical performance," Bulletin of the Council for Research in Music Education, 12(7), 50–56.
Fritsch, Sibylle (1989) "No Future. Von der 'Kleinen Nachtmusik' bis zum 'Donauwalzer'— Musik ist Österreichs wichtigster Werbeträger. Nicht mehr lange: Die Berufsorchester leiden an Nachwuchsmangel," Profil, 4 (January 23), pp. 70–71.
Hess, Juliet (2019) Music education for social change: constructing an activist music education. London: Routledge.
Ito, Hiroyuki (2021) "Violinist apologizes for 'culturally insensitive' remarks about Asians," New York Times, June 28.
Jepson, Barbara (1991) "Asian Americans struggle for acceptance in the classical music world," Wall Street Journal, January 2.
Kajikawa, Loren (2019) "The possessive investment in classical music: confronting legacies of White supremacy in U.S. schools and departments of music," in Crenshaw, K.W., Harris, L.C., HoSang, D.M., and Lipsitz, G. (eds.) Seeing race again: countering colorblindness across the disciplines. Oakland: University of California Press.
Kang, Sonia K., DeCelles, K.A., Tilcsik, András, and Jun, Sora (2016) "Whitened résumés: race and self-presentation in the labor market," Administrative Science Quarterly, 61(3), pp. 469–502.
Kawabata, Maiko, and Tan, Shzr Ee (2019) "'Cultural Imperialism and the New "Yellow Peril" in Western Classical Music' Study Day Report for Asian-European Music Research," Asian-European Journal of Music Research, 4, pp. 87–98.
Koh, Jennifer (2018) "League Luncheon," speech at the League of American Orchestras: https://www.youtube.com/watch?v=6a95KVFCJzw (Accessed May 22, 2021).
Koh, Jennifer (2021) "A violinist on how to empower Asian musicians," New York Times, July 21. Available at https://www.nytimes.com/2021/07/21/arts/music/jenni

fer-koh-asians-classical-music.html?fbclid=IwAR0OjrPhlrXJbyWzo9kPtC5HJ_Ru DYz8hJ32QIN-_kPBYg5MMzylOXnNPvk (Accessed July 29, 2021).

Kowalczyk, Beata M. (2020) Transnational musicians: precariousness, ethnicity and gender in the creative industry. London: Routledge.

Koza, Julia Eklund (2008) "Listening for Whiteness: hearing racial politics in undergraduate school music," Philosophy of Music Education Review, 16(2), pp. 145–155.

Latham, Kevin, and Wu, Bin (2013) "Chinese immigration into the EU: new trends, dynamics and implications." Europe China Research and Advice Network.

Leech-Wilkinson, Daniel (2016) "Classical music as enforced utopia," Arts and Humanities in Higher Education, 15(3–4), pp. 325–336. doi: 10.1177/1474022216647706.

Leech-Wilkinson, Daniel (2020) Challenging performance: classical music performance norms and how to escape them. https://challengingperformance.com/the-book.

Leppänen, Taru (2015) "The West and the rest of classical music: Asian Musicians in the Finnish media coverage of the 1995 Jean Sibelius Violin Competition," European Journal of Cultural Studies, 18(1), pp. 19–34.

Mehl, Margaret (2014) Not by love alone: the violin in Japan, 1850—2010. Sound Book Press.

Morlang, Eva (2021) "International ist nicht automatisch divers. Hat der klassische Orchesterbetrieb ein Rassismusproblem?" Neue Musik Zeitung, February. Available at https://www.nmz.de/artikel/international-ist-nicht-automatisch-divers.

Osborne, William (n.d.) "Blind auditions and moral myopia." http://www.osborne-conant.org/posts/blind.htm.

Ostleitner, Elena (1995) "Liebe, Lust, Last und Leid: Eine Studie zur Situation des Orchesternachwuchses in Österreich," im Auftrag des Budesministeriums für Unterricht und Kunst. Unpublished manuscript, Vienna.

Peynircioğlu, Zehra F., Bi, Wenyan, and Brent, William (2018) "The 'Asian bias' illusion in musical performance: influence of visual information," American Journal of Psychology, 131(3), pp. 295–305.

Phalnikar, Sonia (2005) "Anti-racism groups slam German ads," DW-WORLD.DE, July 15. Available at https://p.dw.com/p/6v17.

Rosenberg, Donald (2019) "Cleveland Orchestra tuba player finds a home in northeast Ohio—by way of Japan and Austria," Plain Dealer, May 24, 2008; updated March 28, 2019. Available at https://www.cleveland.com/arts/2008/05/orchestra_tuba_player_finds_a.html

Scharff, Christina (2018) "Inequalities in the classical music industry: the role of subjectivity in constructions of the ideal classical musician," in Dromey, C. and Haferkorn, J. (eds.) The classical music industry. New York: Routledge, pp. 96–111.

Schutz, Michael (2008) "Seeing music? What musicians need to know about vision," Empirical Musicology Review, 3.

Strasser, Otto (1974) Und dafuer wird man noch bezahlt: Mein Leben mit den Wiener Phiharmonikern. Wien: Paul Neff Verlag.

Tommasini, Anthony (2020) "To make orchestras more diverse, end blind auditions," New York Times, July 16.

Vanweelden, Kimberly, and McGee, Isaiah R. (2007) "The influence of music style and conductor race on perceptions of ensemble and conductor performance," International Journal of Music Education, 25, pp. 7–17.

Wakin, Daniel J. (2007) "Pilgrim with an oboe, citizen of the world," New York Times, April 8.

Wang, Grace (2015) Soundtracks of Asian America: navigating race through musical performance. Durham, NC: Duke University Press.
Wiegelmann, Lucas (2009) "Deutsche Orchester und ihr Rassismus-Problem" ["German orchestras and their racism problem"], Die Welt, August 11.
Wood, Martin, Hales, Jon, Purdon, Susan, Sejersen, Tanja, and Hayllar, Oliver (2009) A test for racial discrimination in recruitment practice in British cities. National Centre for Social Research.
Wu, Frank H. (2002) Yellow: Race in America beyond Black and White. New York: Basic Books.
Wynter, Sylvia (2003) "Unsettling the coloniality of being/power/truth/freedom: towards the human, after man, its overrepresentation—an argument," New Centennial Review, 3(3), pp. 257–337.
Yang, Mina (2007) "East meets West in the concert hall: Asians and classical music in the century of imperialism, post-colonialism, and multiculturalism," Asian Music, 38(1), pp. 1–30. Available at https://doi.org/10.1353/amu.2007.0025
Yang, Mina (2014) Planet Beethoven: classical music at the turn of the millennium. Middletown, CT: Wesleyan University Press.
Yoshihara, Mari (2007) Musicians from a different shore: Asians and Asian Americans in classical music. Philadelphia: Temple University Press.

Chapter 15

Beech, N., Gilmore, C., Hibbert, P., and Ybema, S. (2016) "Identity-in-the-work and musicians' struggles: the production of self-questioning identity work," Work, Employment and Society, 30(3), pp. 506–522.
Beaverstock, J.V. (2002) "Transnational elites in global cities: British expatriates in Singapore's financial district," Geoforum, 33(4), pp. 525–538.
Carrier, J.G. (1992) "Occidentalism: the world turned upside-down," American Ethnologist, 19(2), pp. 195–212.
Charmaz, K. (2006) Constructing grounded theory: a practical guide through qualitative analysis. London: Sage.
Cook, N. (2013) "Western music as world music," in Bohlman, P. (ed.) The Cambridge History of World Music. Cambridge: Cambridge University Press, pp. 75–100.
El-Ghadban, Y. (2009) "Facing the music: rituals of belonging and recognition in contemporary Western art music," American Ethnologist, 36(1), pp. 140–160.
Gans, H.J. (2016) "Racialization and racialization research," Ethnic and Racial Studies, 40(3), pp. 341–352.
Glick Schiller, N., Basch, L., and Szanton Blanc, C. (1995) "From immigrant to transmigrant: theorizing transnational migration," Anthropological Quarterly, 68(1), pp. 48–63.
Grazian, D. (2003) Blue Chicago: the search for authenticity in urban blues clubs. Chicago: University of Chicago Press.
Haynes, J. (2013) Music, difference, and the residue of race. Abington: Routledge.
Héran, F. (2012) Parlons immigration en 30 questions. Paris: La Documentation Française.
Kowalczyk, B.M. (2021) Transnational musicians: precariousness, ethnicity and gender in the creative industry. Abington: Routledge.

Lindholm, C. (2008) Culture and authenticity. Malden, MA: Blackwell Publishing.

Negus, K., and Velázquez, P.R. (2002) "Belonging and detachment: musical experience and the limits of identity," Poetics, 30, pp. 133–145.

Nooshin, L. (2003) "Improvisation as 'other': creativity, knowledge and power: the case of Iranian classical music," Journal of the Royal Musical Association, 128(2), pp. 242–296.

Omi, M., and Winant, H. (2014) Racial formation in the United States: From the 1960s to the 1990s. 3rd ed. New York: Routledge.

Radano, R.M., and Bohlman, P. (2000) "Introduction: music and race, their past, their presence," in Radano, R.M., and Bohlman, P. (eds.) Music and the Racial Imagination. Chicago, IL: University of Chicago Press, pp. 1–53.

Scharff, C. (2018) "Inequalities in the classical music industry: the role of subjectivity in constructions of the "ideal" classical musician," in Dromey, C., and Haferkorn, J. (eds.) The classical music industry. London: Routledge, pp. 96–111.

Wajima, Y. (2005) "Kurashikku ongaku no katararekata" in Watanabe, H., and Masuda, S. (eds.) Kurashikku ongaku no seijigaku. Tokyo: Seikyusha, pp. 176–211.

Wang, G. (2014) Soundtracks of Asian America: navigating race through musical performance. Durham, NC: Duke University Press.

Waters, M.C., and Jiménez, R.T. (2005) "Assessing immigrant assimilation: new empirical and theoretical challenges," Annual Review of Sociology, 31, pp. 105–125.

Wodak, R., and Reisigl, M. (1999) "Discourse and racism: European perspectives," Annual Review of Anthropology, 28, pp. 175–199.

Yang, M. (2007) "East meets West in the concert hall: Asians and classical music in the century of imperialism, post-colonialism, and multiculturalism," Asian Music, 38(1), pp. 1–30.

Chapter 16

Ars Femina Ensemble (1996) Musica de la puebla de Los Angeles:music by women of Baroque Mexico, Cuba & Europe. Nannerl Recordings.

BBC News (2018) "Trump travel ban: What does this ruling mean?," June 26. Available at: https://www.bbc.com/news/world-us-canada-39044403 (Accessed November 22, 2021).

Chapter 19

Ahmed, S. (2000) Strange encounters: embodied others in post-coloniality. London: Routledge.

Ahmed, S. (2006) Queer phenomenology: orientations, objects, others. Durham, NC: Duke University Press. Available at https://www.dawsonera.com:443/abstract/9780822388074

Benedetti, N. (2019) "Nicola Benedetti: 'Music is the art of all the things we can't see or touch. We need it in our lives.'" Guardian, November 8. Available at https://www.theguardian.com/music/2019/nov/08/nicola-benedetti-violin-rps-speechwe-need-music-in-our-lives

Brathwaite, K. (2002) Magical realism. Jamaica: Savacou Publications.

Bull, A. (2019) Class, control, and classical music. Oxford: Oxford University Press.

Butler, J. (2005) Giving an account of oneself. New York: Fordham University Press.

Crockett, C. (2017) Derrida after the end of writing: Political theology and new materialism. New York: Fordham University Press.

Diawara, M. (2011) "One world in relation: Édouard Glissant in conversation with Manthia Diawara," Nka Journal of Contemporary African Art, 2011(28), pp. 4–19. Available at https://doi.org/10.1215/10757163-1266639

Dk Rostant (2017) A Jouvay experience: the Tony Hall perspective, March 24. Available at https://www.youtube.com/watch?v=Gga1Wv0Y8IE

Dudley, S. (2007) Music from behind the bridge: steelband aesthetics and politics in Trinidad and Tobago. Oxford: Oxford University Press.

Dyer, R. (1997) White. New York: Routledge.

Elder, J.D. (2004) "Cannes Brûlées," in Riggio, M.C. (ed.), Carnival: culture in action—the Trinidad experience. Abingdon: Routledge.

Ellis, C., Adams, T.E., and Bochner, A.P. (2010) "Autoethnography: an overview," Forum: Qualitative Social Research, 12(1), Article 1. Available at https://doi.org/10.17169/fqs-12.1.1589

Ewell, P. (2021) "Music theory's white racial frame," Music Theory Online 26(2).

Gellerstein, B.A. (2021) Daring to see: White supremacy and gatekeeping in music education. Ph.D., University of Massachusetts–Boston. Available at https://www.proquest.com/docview/2525691107/abstract/7E4EB0E9BAEE41E7PQ/1

Glissant, Édouard (1997) Poetics of relation; translated by Betsy Wing. Ann Arbor: University of Michigan Press.

Griffiths, A. (2019) "Playing the White man's tune: inclusion in elite classical music education," British Journal of Music Education, 37(1), pp. 55–70.

Guilbault, J. (2004) "On redefining the nation through party music," in Riggio, M.C. (ed.), Carnival: culture in action—the Trinidad experience. Abingdon: Routledge.

Guilbault, J. (2007) Governing sound: the cultural politics of Trinidad's carnival musics. Chicago: University of Chicago Press.

Hess, J. (2018) "Troubling Whiteness: music education and the 'messiness' of equity work," International Journal of Music Education, 36(2), pp. 128–144. Available at https://doi.org/10.1177/0255761417703781

Holman Jones, S. (2016) "Living bodies of thought: the 'critical' in critical autoethnography," Qualitative Inquiry, 22(4), pp. 228–237. Available at https://doi.org/10.1177/1077800415622509

James, R. (2009) "In but not of, of but not in: on taste, hipness, and White embodiment," Contemporary Aesthetics, spec (2). Available at http://hdl.handle.net/2027/spo.7523 862.spec.209

James, R. (2015) "Contort yourself: music, Whiteness, and the politics of disorientation," in Yates, G. (ed.), White self-criticality beyond anti-racism: how does it feel to be a White problem? Lanham, MD: Lexington Books, 2015.

Joseph, A. (2018) People of the sun. Villard-de-Lons: Heavenly Sweetness.

Kraehe, A. M., Gaztambide-Fernandez, R. A., and Carpenter, B. S. (2018) The Palgrave handbook of race and the arts in education. London: Palgrave Macmillan.

Lewis, F.A., and Wassermann, J. (2020) "Ebony and ivory in imperfect harmony— reexperiencing music education at the University of Cape Town," African Identities, pp. 1–18. Available at https://doi.org/10.1080/14725843.2020.1813545

Lloyd, D. (2018) Under Representation. New York: Fordham University Press. Available at https://www.degruyter.com/document/doi/10.1515/9780823282401/html

Lovelace, E. (1998) "The Emancipation-Jouvay tradition and the almost loss of Pan," TDR (1988–), 42(3), pp. 54–60.

Music Mark EDI Report April 2021. (2021) Music Mark. Available at: https://www.musicmark.org.uk/wp-content/uploads/Music-Mark-EDI_Report.pdf

Nooshin, L. (2011) "Introduction to the special issue: the ethnomusicology of Western art music," Ethnomusicology Forum, 20(3), pp. 285–300. Available at https://doi.org/10.1080/17411912.2011.659439

Rohlehr, G. (2001) "Calypso and Caribbean identity," Bucknell Review, 44(2), p. 55.

Rose, E. (2019) Neocolonial mind snatching: Sylvia Wynter and the curriculum of man. Curriculum Inquiry, 49(1), pp. 25–43. https://doi.org/10.1080/03626784.2018.1554950

Ryan, E. (2020) Mapping locations of "Whiteness" in a higher music education faculty in Trinidad and Tobago: a critical autoethnography. Master's thesis. Cambridge: University of Cambridge.

Scharff, C. (2017) Gender, subjectivity, and cultural work: the classical music profession. London: Routledge. Available at https://doi.org/10.4324/9781315673080

Spivak, G.C. (2003) "Can the subaltern speak?," Die Philosophin, 14(27), pp. 42–58. https://doi.org/10.5840/philosophin200314275

Spivak, G.C. (2012) "In a word: interview," in Spivak, G.C., Outside in the teaching machine. Routledge, pp. 17–42. Available at https://doi.org/10.4324/9780203440872-6

Vaugeois, L. (2014) Colonization and the institutionalization of hierarchies of the human through music education: studies in the education of feeling [Thesis]. Available at https://tspace.library.utoronto.ca/handle/1807/43747

Wynter, S. (2003) "Unsettling the coloniality of being/power/truth/freedom: towards the human, after man, its overrepresentation—an argument," CR: The New Centennial Review, 3(3), pp. 257–337.

Yancy, G. (2012a) "Introduction: flipping the script," in Yancy, G., Look, a White! philosophical essays on Whiteness. Philadelphia: Temple University Press.

Yancy, G. (2012b) "Looking at Whiteness: The colonial semiotics in Kamau Brathwaite's reading of *The tempest*," in Yancy, G., Look, a White! Philosophical Essays on Whiteness. Philadelphia: Temple University Press.

Chapter 21

Adams, R., Kräussl, R., Navone, M., and Verwijmeren, P. (2017) "Is gender in the eye of the beholder? Identifying cultural attitudes with art auction prices," SSRN Electronic Journal, January. Available at https://papers.ssrn.com/sol3/papers.cfm?abstract_id=3083500.

Atterbury, B.W. (1992) "Old prejudices, new perceptions," Music Educators Journal, 78(7), pp. 25–27.

Bull, A. (2018) "Classical music education for the 21st century," ArtsProfessional, March 22. Available at https://www.artsprofessional.co.uk/magazine/article/classical-music-education-21st-century (accessed October 16, 2021).

Citron, M.J. (1990) "Gender, Professionalism and the Musical Canon," Journal of Musicology, 8(1), pp. 102–117.

Citron, M.J. (1993) Gender and the musical canon. Urbana: University of Illinois Press.

Department for Education (2021) "New music curriculum to help schools deliver world-class teaching." Available at https://www.gov.uk/government/news/new-music-curriculum-to-help-schools-deliver-world-class-teaching (Accessed June 28, 2021).

Donne Women in Music (2021) "2019–2020 | Donne research." Available at https://donne-uk.org/2019-2020/ (Accessed June 30, 2021).

Everist, M. (1999) "Reception theories, canonic discourses, and musical value," in Cook, N and Everist, M. (ed.), Rethinking music. Oxford: Oxford University Press, pp. 378–402.

Gates, E. (1994) "Why have there been no great women composers?" Journal of Aesthetic Education, 28(2), pp. 27–34.

Green, L. (1997) Music, gender, education. Cambridge: Cambridge University Press.

Green, L. (2012) "Gender identity, musical experience and schooling," in Wright, R. (ed.), Sociology and music education. Aldershot: Ashgate, pp. 139–154.

Heile, B., Rodriguez, E.M., and Stanley, J. (2017) Higher education in music in the twenty-first *century*. New York: Routledge.

Kinsella, V., Fautley, M., and Whittaker, A. (2019) Exchanging notes: research report. Youth Music and Birmingham City University. Available at https://www.bcu.ac.uk/Download/Asset/af9f693c-b68d-e911-abc4-0003ff39cbaf (Accessed September 4, 2021).

Legg, R. (2012) "Bach, Beethoven, Bourdieu: 'cultural capital' and the scholastic canon in England's A-level examinations," British Journal of Music Education, 23(2), pp. 157–172.

Legg, R. (2021) "Women and music education in schools: pedagogues, curricula, and role models," in Hamer, L. (ed.), The Cambridge companion to women in music since 1900 (Cambridge Companions to Music). Cambridge: Cambridge University Press, pp. 235–290.

Lindeman, C.A. (1992) "Teaching about women musicians: elementary classroom strategies," Music Educators Journal, 78, pp. 56–59.

Pace, I. (2021) "How the culture wars are killing Western classical music," Spectator, October. Available at https://www.spectator.co.uk/article/how-the-culture-wars-are-killing-western-classical-music (Accessed October 16, 2021).

Robin, W. (2017) "What controversial changes at Harvard mean for music in the university," Log Journal. Available at https://nationalsawdust.org/thelog/2017/04/25/what-controversial-changes-at-harvard-means-for-music-in-the-university/ (Accessed October 16, 2021).

Shreffler, A.C. (2011) "Musical canonization and decanonization in the twentieth century," in Wald-Fuhrmann, K.P.M. (ed.), Der Kanon der Musik: Theorie und Geschichte. Ein Handbuch. Munich: Hanser, pp. 1–18.

Slater, A. (2022) Invisible canons: a reflective commentary on the formation of my personal canon of women composers. London: Routledge.

Spruce, G. (2013) "Participation, inclusion, diversity, and the policy of English music education," in Harrison, C. (ed.), Reaching out: music education with "hard to reach" children and young people. London: UK Association for Music Education, pp. 23–31.

Whittaker, A. (2020), "Investigating the canon in A-Level music: musical prescription in A-level music syllabi (for first examination in 2018)," British Journal of Music Education, 37(1), pp. 17–27.

Women in Music (2017) "Women in music—programming survey." Available at http://www.womeninmusic.org.uk/proms17.htm (Accessed June 30, 2021).

Women in Music (2019), "Women in music—programming survey." Available at http://www.womeninmusic.org.uk/proms-survey.htm (Accessed June 27, 2021).

Wright, R., and Davies, B. (2010) "Class, power, culture and the music curriculum," in Wright, R. (ed.), Sociology and music education. Aldershot: Ashgate Publishing, pp. 35–50.

Chapter 22

Nwanoku, C. (2018) "For a 21st-century Proms, we must let the people clap when they want," *Guardian*, July 20.

Chapter 23

Alleyne, S. (2021) "Examining the Black British Arts Management Experience through the Lens of Power," in A. Cuyler (ed.), Arts management, cultural policy, and the African diaspora. London: Palgrave Macmillan.

Banks, M. (2017) Creative justice: cultural industries, work and inequality. London: Rowman & Littlefield.

Black Administrators of Opera (2020) Letter to the Field from Black Administrators, October 29. Available at https://blackadmofopera.medium.com/letter-to-the-opera-field-from-black-administrators-240977b355e5

Black Opera Alliance and TRG Arts (2021) US opera company responses to "Pledge for Racial Equity and Systemic Change in Opera" Insight Report—August 2021. https://trgarts.com/blog/boa-trg-insight-report-aug-2021

Black Opera Alliance (2021) Mission. https://www.blackoperaalliance.org/mission

Black Opera Alliance (2020) Pledge for racial equity and systemic change in opera. September 14. Available at https://www.blackoperaalliance.org/pledge

Brooks, D. (2021) "How the bobos broke America," Atlantic, August 2. Available at https://www.theatlantic.com/magazine/archive/2021/09/blame-the-bobos-creative-class/619492/?mc_cid=9963cfb71a&mc_eid=4254e9122a

Chang, B. (2020) "No more whispers: opera's reckoning with racism." https://www.ludwig-van.com/toronto/2020/06/24/feature-no-more-whispers-operas-reckoning-with-racism/

Cuyler, A.C. (forthcoming) "Moving beyond @operaisracist: exploring Black activism as a pathway to antiracism and creative justice in opera," in Music as labour: inequalities and activism in the past and present.

Cuyler, A.C. (2021) Access, diversity, equity, and inclusion in cultural organizations: insights from the careers of executive opera managers of color in the U.S. Milton Park, UK: Routledge.

Hines, C. (2020) Cosplaying while black: the transgressive pleasure of blacktivism. Journal of cultural research in art education, 37(1), pp. 219–230.

Lorde, A. (1984) "The master's tools will never dismantle the master's house," in Sister outsider: essays and speeches. Berkeley, CA: Crossing Press.

Okun, T. (2021) "White supremacy culture characteristics." Available at https://www.whitesupremacyculture.info/characteristics.html

Prieto, L., and Phipps, S. (2019) African American management history: insights on gaining a cooperative advantage. WA, UK: Emerald Publishing Limited.

Chapter 24

Ahmed, S. (2004) "Declarations of Whiteness: the non-performativity of anti-racism," borderlands e-journal, 3(2), pp. 1–19.
Ahmed, S. (2017) Living a feminist life. Durham, NC: Duke University Press.
Bull, A. (2019) Class, Control, and Classical Music. Oxford: Oxford University Press.
Emerson, G. (2020) Between the "experimental" and the "accessible": investigating the audience experience of contemporary classical music. Available from: ediss.SUB. Hamburg at https://ediss.sub.uni-hamburg.de/handle/ediss/8963 (Accessed May 21, 2021).
Gender Relations in New Music (2020a) Gender statistics at the Donaueschinger Musiktage. Available at http://grinm.org/20171020%20-%20Donaueschinger%20Musiktage%20Statistics%20GRiNM.pdf
Gender Relations in New Music (2020b) GRiNM x sounds now. Available at http://grinm.org/GRiNM%20x%20Sounds%20Now%28finished%29.pdf
Scharff, C. (2018) Gender, subjectivity, and cultural work: the classical music profession. London: Routledge.

Chapter 25

Bain, V. (2019) Counting the music industry. Available at https://vbain.co.uk/research (Accessed August 16, 2021).
Consultation on sexual harassment in the workplace: government response. Available at https://www.gov.uk/government/consultations/consultation-on-sexual-harassment-in-the-workplace/outcome/consultation-on-sexual-harassment-in-the-workplace-government-response (Accessed September 22, 2021).
Costello, A. (2021) "Sweden joins list of countries with proposed event cancellation fund," We Rave You, April 14. Available at https://weraveyou.com/2021/04/event-cancellation-fund-sweden/ (Accessed August 16, 2021).
Creative Scotland (2021) "Open fund: sustaining creative development." Available at https://www.creativescotland.com/funding/funding-programmes/open-fund-sustaining-creative-development (Accessed August 16, 2021).
Delfino, D. (2018) "How musicians really make their money—and it has nothing to do with how many times people listen to their songs." Business Insider, October 19, 2019. Available at https://www.businessinsider.com/how-do-musicians-make-money-2018-10 (Accessed August 16, 2021).
Donne Women in Music (2018) "Inequality in music: women composers by numbers 2018–19." Available at https://donne-uk.org/2018-2019/ (Accessed August 16, 2021).
Duffield, C. (2020) Rethink. Reskill. Reboot: Why government retraining campaign advert from 2019 was pulled after backlash. i, October 14, 2020. Available at https://inews.co.uk/news/uk/rethink-rekill-reboot-government-rertaining-campaign-advert-2019-quiz-backlash-pulled-714159 (Accessed August 16, 2021).

Enterprise and Regulatory Reform Act 2013. Available at https://www.legislation.gov.uk/ukpga/2013/24/contents/enacted (Accessed August 16, 2021).

Equality Act 2010. Available at https://www.legislation.gov.uk/ukpga/2010/15/contents (Accessed August 16, 2021).

Fairman, R. (2021) "Aldeburgh Festival forges ahead with a Tavener premiere—and a tepee," Financial Times, June 29, 2021. Available at https://www.ft.com/content/d29cf91f-9d08-4822-aad8-78664b76a212 (Accessed August 16, 2021).

Gov.uk (2021) Information on the Events Research Programme. Available at https://www.gov.uk/government/publications/information-on-the-events-research-programme/information-on-the-events-research-programme (Accessed August 16, 2021).

Haferkorn, J., Brian, K., and Leak, S. (2021) Livestreaming music in the UK: a report for musicians. Available at https://livestreamingmusic.uk/ (Accessed August 16, 2021).

"Harrogate Music Festival". (2022) Available at: https://harrogateinternationalfestivals.com/harrogate-music-festival/.

Help Musicians (2021) Make a donation. Available at https://www.helpmusicians.org.uk/support-our-work/make-a-donation (Accessed August 16, 2021).

Hickley, C. (2021) "Germany pledges €2.5bn in aid for cultural events." Art Newspaper, May 27. Available at https://www.theartnewspaper.com/news/germany-pledges-eur2-5-billion-in-aid-for-cultural-events (Accessed August 16, 2021).

HM Government (2021) Tackling violence against women & girls. https://assets.publishing.service.gov.uk/government/uploads/system/uploads/attachment_data/file/1005630/Tackling_Violence_Against_Women_and_Girls_Strategy-July_2021-FINAL.pdf (Accessed August 16, 2021).

House of Commons (2021) COVID 19: Culture Recovery Fund: eighth report of session 2021–22. Available at https://committees.parliament.uk/publications/6383/documents/70055/default/ (Accessed August 16, 2021).

Institute for Fiscal Studies (2021) "Who is excluded from the government's Self Employment Income Support Scheme and what could the government do about it?" Available at https://ifs.org.uk/uploads/BN316-Who-is-excluded-from-SEISS.pdf (Accessed August 16, 2021).

IQ Magazine (2020) "€300M 'umbrella' for Austrian promoters," October 27. Available at https://www.iq-mag.net/2020/10/e300m-umbrella-for-austrian-promoters/ (Accessed August 16, 2021).

IQ Magazine (2021) "Dutch gov announces €300M event cancellation fund," January 22. Available at https://www.iq-mag.net/2021/01/dutch-government-300m-event-cancellation-fund/ (Accessed August 16, 2021).

ISM (2018a) Dignity at work: a survey of discrimination in the music sector. Available at https://www.ism.org/images/images/ISM_Dignity-at-work-April-2018.pdf (Accessed August 16, 2021).

ISM (2018b) Dignity in study: a survey of higher education institutions. Available at https://www.ism.org/images/images/Equity-ISM-MU-Dignity-in-Study-report.pdf (Accessed August 16, 2021).

ISM (2021a) "COVID-19 hardship fund." Available at https://www.ism.org/advice/covid-hardship-fund (Accessed August 16, 2021).

ISM (2021b) The ISM's annual survey of teaching, examining and accompanying rates: Results 2021. Available at https://www.ism.org/advice/the-isms-annual-survey-of-teaching-examining-and-accompanying-rates-survey-results-2021 (Accessed August 16, 2021).

ISM (2021c) "'Professionally paralysed': new report reveals the impact of Brexit on musicians." Available at https://www.ism.org/news/professionally-paralysed-brexit-report (Accessed August 16, 2021).

Office for National Statistics (2021a) [Custom report]. Available at https://www.nomisweb.co.uk/datasets/aps210/reports/employment-by-status-and-occupation?compare=K02000001 (Accessed August 16, 2021).

Office for National Statistics (2021b) [Custom report]. Available at https://www.nomisweb.co.uk/datasets/aps168/reports/employment-by-occupation?compare=K02000001 (Accessed August 16, 2021).

PiPA (2019) "Balancing Act": PiPA's survey into the impact of caring responsibilities on career progression in the performing arts. Available at https://pipacampaign.org/uploads/ckeditor/BA-Final.pdf (Accessed August 16, 2021)

PiPA (2021) PiPA Covid Report. Available at https://pipacampaign.org/uploads/ckeditor/PiPA_COVID_REPORT.pdf (Accessed August 16, 2021).

Scharff, C. (2017) Gender, subjectivity, and cultural work: the classical music profession. London: Routledge.

Thomas, T. (2021) "More than a quarter of UK music festivals cancelled over insurance fears." Guardian, May 4. Available at https://www.theguardian.com/culture/2021/may/04/more-than-a-quarter-of-uk-music-festivals-cancelled-over-insurance-fears (Accessed August 16, 2021).

Williamson, G. (2021) "Letter to the Office for Students, 19 July 2021." Available at https://www.officeforstudents.org.uk/media/0e833c6f-c355-4743-8953-071bbe9b1518/ts-and-cs-on-recurrent-funding-19-july.pdf (Accessed August 16, 2021).

Afterword

Arts Council England (2020) *Let's Create! strategy 2020–2030*. Manchester.

Arts Council England (2021) *Creating a fairer and more inclusive classical music sector for England*.

Cox, T. (2021a) *Creating a more inclusive classical music: a study of the English orchestral workforce and the current routes to joining it: literature review*. Arts Council England; DHA Communications.

Cox, T. (2021b) *Creating a more inclusive classical music. a study of the English orchestral workforce and the current routes to joining it*. DHA Communications.

Cox, T. and Kilshaw, H. (2021) *Creating a more inclusive classical music: executive summary*. DHA and ICM.

ICM Unlimited (2021) *Creating a more inclusive classical music: a study of the English orchestral workforce and the current routes to joining it*. Arts Council England.

Marín, M.Á. (2018) "Challenging the listener: how to change trends in classical music programming," *Resonancias* 22, pp. 115–130. https://doi.org/10.7764/res.2018.42.6

Royal Philharmonic Society (2019) "Women conductors." https://royalphilharmonicsociety.org.uk/performers/women_conductors

Said, E.W. (1991) *Musical elaborations*. New York: Columbia University Press.

Index

For the benefit of digital users, indexed terms that span two pages (e.g., 52–53) may, on occasion, appear on only one of those pages.

Abbate, Carolyn, 103, 104
Abreu, José Antonio, 81–82
Abril, Carlos R., 31–32
ABRSM. *See* Associated Board of the Royal Schools of Music
abuse. *See* misconduct; sexual harassment
access, 134, 249
   accessibility riders, 288–89
   "aesthetics of access," 122
   changing attitudes towards, 289
   and class, 26, 37, 127–30, 247, 298–99
   disability, 119, 138, 288–90, 294
   financial, 153
   and gender, 28
   and requirement to read music, 209
accountability, 208, 257
activism, 7–8, 132–34, 250–51. *See also* Blacktivism; campaigning; diversity
   Black, Indigenous, and People of Color (BIPOC) collective power, 258
   coalition-building, 99–100, 266, 269
   costs and risks associated with, 130–31, 133–34, 262–63
   feminist, 266–75
   importance of support networks for activists, 154
   online activism, 270–71, 274, 288
   parainstitutional organizing, 269–70
   power of collective action, 286, 294
   relationship with academia, 9
   social justice work as bridge-building, 228–29, 230, 231–33
   strategies, 267–69, 270–71, 272–74
   student activism, 55, 63, 208
   use of statistics, 267–69, 272–73
   and whiteness, 147
adaptability, 186, 187, 188, 189–90, 191
Adinkra symbol, 249
administration. *See* Black Administrators of Opera

advocacy. *See* activism; campaigning
aesthetics, 71–72, 218–19, 220–21, 222–23, 224–25, 227
   "aesthetics of access," 122
   "disability aesthetic," 115
   and genre, 13–14
   and inequality, 2–3
affect, 39, 217, 218–19, 226–27
African American classical musicians, 85–86, 195, 198. *See also* Black classical musicians
Against Modern Opera Productions, 104
age, 6
Ahmed, Sara, 70–71, 273–74
Aida, 102, 108–9, 117–18
Allen, Kim, 7, 33–34
All the Black Dots, 143
Alsop, Marin, 303
amateur music-making, 299–300, 303
American Dream, An, 108
Anderson, Leon, 170n.8
André, Naomi, 106, 109–10, 111, 121–22
anticapitalism, 98, 99–100
Arazi, Anna, 241
architecture. *See* starchitecture
Archiv Frau und Musik, 274
Arena di Verona, 102
Armstrong, Charlotte, 6
Ars Femina, 191
artistic personality, constructions of, 38–40
Arts Council England, 1, 299–300
Asian Opera Alliance, 258
assimilation, 12–13, 78–79, 163, 246
Associated Board of the Royal Schools of Music (ABRSM), 235, 242
Association Européenne des Conservatoires, Académies de Musique et Musikhochschulen (AEC), 54–55, 56–57, 58, 61, 64
Atlas of the Sky, 270–71
Auchterlonie, Patricia, 241

audiences
　as active participants, 299–300
　audience development, 242–44
　diverse, 248, 301–2
　experiences of, 11–12
　increasing diversity of, 302–3
　opera audiences, 105, 106–7, 108
　policing behavior of, 248, 298
　relationship between artists and, 298–99
　traditional versus progressive, 105, 106–7, 108
　whiteness of, 145
　and women composers, 234, 242–44
auditions, 288. *See also* conservatoires
　microaggressions at, 204
　screened versus screenless, 159, 162–64, 169, 198
Aurora Orchestra, 299
Austrian conservatoires, 31–41
authenticity
　and casting, 117, 118–19, 121
　racialized discourses of, 168, 172–84
autism, access for musicians with, 290
autoethnography, 160–61
　critical, 219, 222, 226–27

Baker, Geoff, 82
Baltimore (US), 144
Banks, Toria, 122
BAO. *See* Black Administrators of Opera
Baroque music, 114–15, 191
barriers. *See* access; class inequalities
Barry, Suren, 243
Basch, Linda, 176
Basquiat, Jean-Michel, 149, 150
BBC Proms, 238, 247, 248
Beckman, Thomas, 82–83
Beckman YOLA Center, 82–83, 87–89
belonging, 142, 147, 172–84, 235, 251
Benedetti, Nicola, 226–27
Berklee College of Music, 62–63, 192
Bernstein, Leonard, 303
bi-musicality, 190–91
Blacher, Kolja, 166–67
Black Administrators of Opera (BAO), 8, 255–65
Black classical musicians. *See also* African American classical musicians
　experiences in orchestras, 142, 143
　importance of representation of, 247
　in the Renaissance period, 199
Black composers, 143, 250, 251
Black conductors, 141–47

blackface, 102, 106
Black Lives in Music, 288
Black Lives Matter, impact of, 6–7, 146, 199, 250, 259
Black Opera Alliance (BOA), 255, 256, 257, 258
Black organizations, 264–65
"Blackout Tuesday," 288
Blacktivism, 8, 256–59, 262–65
　anonymity within, 256
　community within, 263, 264
　definition of, 257
　as healing, 257–58
　risks for activists, 262–63
Blanke, John, 199
Blues, the, 149
BOA. *See* Black Opera Alliance
body, disciplining the, 2–3, 19–20
body positivity, 6
Bohème, La, 206
Bold Tendencies, 299
Bona, Suzanne, 196
Borderline Plummet, 231–33
Bordignon, Caroline, 241
Born, Georgina, 72–73
Boston Symphony Orchestra, 97–98
boundary-drawing, 2–3, 14, 71–72, 94, 224–25, 226–27
Bourdieu, Pierre, 32–33, 45, 236
Boyd, Blair, 235, 240–42
Bradley, Deborah, 31
Brann, Don, 85
Brexit, 282–83
Briggs, Kerensa, 241
British Paraorchestra, 301–2
Brookes, Karin, 196
Brown, Brandon Keith, 7–8
Bryan, Karen M., 106
Bryars, Gavin, 299
Bull, Anna, 31–32, 46, 56, 72, 94, 224–25, 266–67
Burke, Penny Jane, 33–34
Butler, Judith, 216–17
Butt Philip, David, 118–19
bystander training, 291

Callahan, David, 83
campaigning, 276–85, 286–96. *See also* activism
Canadian Opera Company, 107
canon, the, 11–12
　canonization, 234, 236–38, 244
　disrupting, 225–26
　exclusion of Black composers from, 251

exclusion of women composers, 234, 235–36, 237–38, 239
  the operatic canon, 102–11
  the pedagogical canon, 234, 235–36, 237–38, 242
  personal canons, 234, 236–38, 243, 244–45
  strategies to challenge racism in the operatic canon, 107–10
capitalism, 71, 92, 97–99. *See also* neoliberalism
Caribbean cosmologies, 225–26
Carlsen, Morten, 59
Carmen, 107–8, 110–11
Carnival (Trinidad and Tobago), 217–18, 227
Casula, Clementina, 5–6
CCM. *See* contemporary classical music
cello, the, 191
Chen, Joyce, 199
Cheng, William, 168–69
Chevalier de Saint-George, Le, 199
Chiarot, Cristiano, 107
child care, 283–84
Chineke! Foundation, 1, 169, 246–51, 288, 301–2
Chung, Junah, 167
Church, David, 119–20
Citron, Marcia J., 237, 244–45
classical music, definitions of, 13–15
classical music studies, 13–16
class inequalities, 2–3, 5–6, 94–95, 96, 127–30. *See also* access; boundary-drawing; conservatoires; cultural capital; diversity; elitism; freelance work; middle-class culture; music education, primary and secondary (K–12); social capital; symbolic capital; whiteness
  barriers to classical music, 300
  definitions of class, 46
  and gender equality initiatives, 96–97
  and graduate labor market (UK), 33–34
  and the "ideal" classical musician, 3
  and instruments, 25
  and the media, 7
  and privilege, 36, 94–96
Coleridge-Taylor, Samuel, 251, 301–2
colonialism, 15, 31, 175–76, 191, 217–18
coloniality, 217, 218–21, 227. *See also* whiteness; white supremacy
Come As You Are, 116–17
community engagement. *See* outreach
competitions, music, 33, 178
composition, 78, 148–51, 231–32, 298–99. *See also* Black composers; disabled composers; South American composers; women composers

concert programming, 228, 229–30, 231–33, 236–37, 238, 239–41, 242, 245
concerts. *See also* digital events
  concert halls and belonging, 143, 151
  diversifying delivery of, 302–3
  racism at, 147
  rituals of the orchestral concert, 297–99
conducting, 78, 141–43, 146–47. *See also* Black conductors; women conductors
consent, 62
conservatoires
  admissions and recruitment processes, 22–26, 27–28, 31–41, 300
  and class, 22–26, 28–29, 36–38, 42, 47–53, 205
  definition of, 43
  discrimination against disabled people, 135
  financial pressure for working class students, 50–51
  first generation students, 47–48
  and gender, 26–28
  and the "ideal" classical music student, 36–40
  lack of racial diversity in, 203, 204
  and parents, 128
  practices of valuation within, 36–41
  racism in, 204–6, 250
  and student culture, 130–31
  teachers' self-concepts, 34–36, 37–38, 40–41
contemporary classical music (CCM), 12, 266–75
Cooper, Michael, 104
Cottrell, Stephen, 43
Council for the Encouragement of Music and the Arts, 299–300
COVID-19 pandemic
  expanding access to classical music, 154, 199, 290
  impact on musicians, 127
  and inequalities, 145, 280–84, 294
Cox, Maggie, 243
creativity
  constructions of, 32, 38–40
  and participation, 299–300
Creech, Andrea, 58
creolization, 12–13, 149, 151
CRF. *See* Culture Recovery Fund
cultural appropriation, 109–10, 186
cultural capital, 32–33, 45, 48–49
cultural difference, constructions of, 163, 166–69
cultural repertoires, 142
cultural reproduction, 236–37

cultural supremacy, 86–87. *See also* whiteness; white supremacy
Culture Recovery Fund (CRF) (UK), 281
cultures, evolving, 225
Cuyler, Antonio, 8, 9

Daniel, Ryan, 58
Darmstadt Summer Course, 267, 269–71
data-harvesting, 267–69
data protection legislation, 292
Daude, Daniele G., 169
Davies, Alison, 52
Davies, Rhian, 241–42
de Benedictis, Sara, 7
decoloniality, 217–18, 225–27
Decoté, Késia, 241
defensiveness, responding to, 201
Defragmentation—Convention on Curating Contemporary Music, 269–70
dehumanization, 222, 259
Delta Frauen, 62–63
Derrida, Jacques, 222
Der Zwerg, 118–19
Deutsche Oper Berlin, 118–19
Die Entführung aus dem Serail, 107–8
Die Frau ohne Schatten, 116
digital events, 243–44, 282
digital technologies, 291. *See also* social media
disability, 11–12, 289. *See also* access
  and composition, 135–40
  "disability aesthetic," 115
  discrimination against disabled musicians, 119, 135, 138, 289
  expectations of disabled musicians, 136, 140
  and identity, 136, 138
  "inspiration porn," 120
  mimicry, 116–18
  representation in arts, 112–13
  representation in opera, 6, 112–23
  social model of, 136
disabled composers, 135–40
disabled-led opera companies, 122
discourse, 45, 216–17, 224
discrimination. *See* class inequalities; disability; gender inequalities; racism; sexual harassment; working conditions in the music industry
disorientation, 216–19, 221–23, 225
diversity
  additional labor of diversity work, 187, 188
  and class, 95
  as a contested discourse, 73–76
  critiques of, 7, 69–72, 93, 198, 273–74
  diversity work and communication, 196, 201, 294
  exploitation of marginalized people's labor in diversity work, 9, 78–80, 151–52, 153, 257, 259, 261, 262
  initiatives, 7, 69–71, 74–80
  and lived experience, 286
  and marketing, 97–98
  prioritizing marginalized voices in diversity work, 260, 261
  and programming, 92
  unpaid labor of diversity work, 6–7, 228–29, 230–31
  and white middle-class identity formation, 75
  and workplace culture, 295
Donaueschinger Musiktage, 267
donors. *See* funding; philanthropy
Drama Musica, 276–77
drums, 136. *See also* percussion
Dudamel, Gustavo, 81–82, 84, 85
Dworkin, Aaron, 195
Dyer, Richard, 222–23
dyslexia, 136

early music, 195–202
Early Music America (EMA), 195–96
  Inclusion, Diversity, Equity and Access (IDEA) Taskforce, 195–97, 199
East Asian musicians, 39–40, 159–71
education. *See* conservatoires; music education, extracurricular; music education, higher; music education, primary and secondary (K–12)
Edwards, Rachael Marissa, 87
Elevate (Leeds Conservatoire), 62–63
elitism, 94–95, 98–99. *See also* class
Elpus, Kenneth, 31–32
El Sistema, 81–82, 96
emotional expression, "Western" norms of, 165–66
emotional labor, 9, 230, 232, 257
employment. *See* freelance work; working conditions in the music industry
entrepreneurship, 99
epistemic violence, 218–19, 223–24
Equalities and Human Rights Commission, 279
Equality Act (UK), 278–79, 291
equality, diversity and inclusion (EDI). *See* diversity
Equity, 277

essentialism, 175–77. *See also* authenticity; cultural difference, constructions of
Ethel Smyth Trio, 241
ethnicity. *See* "race"
ethnomusicology, 172
EU. *See* European Union
Eurocentrism, 78–79, 168–69. *See also* whiteness; white supremacy
European symphony orchestras, 159–71
European Union (EU), 282–83
evaluating ideas, 229–30

families, 75–76. *See also* class
  musical versus non-musical, 23, 25, 36, 37, 47–48, 49, 127–30
Farnham, Alice, 302
Farnsworth, Brandon, 12
female:pressure, 274
feminism. *See* liberal feminism
feminist activism, 266–75
festivals
  and COVID-19, 281–82
  feminist activism at, 267–69, 271
Festspielhaus Baden-Baden, 166–67
fetishization of the performer, 298–99
Floyd, George (police killing of), 150, 250
Foucault, Michel, 33–34, 216–17
Fox, Ann M., 120–21
France, Japanese musicians in, 173–74
freelance work. *See also* working conditions in the music industry
  challenging isolation of, 132
  as class barrier, 300
  and COVID-19, 199, 280–82
  and disparities in parental leave, 283–84
  and relationship to music industry, 130–31, 133, 134
  and sexual harassment, 277–78, 279–80, 291
  and status, 131
Fuchs, Wenzel, 164
funding, 242, 250. *See also* philanthropy
  for evaluating projects, 232–33
  financial investment in conductors, 143
  financial support for artists, 153
  of orchestras, 144
  public funding in England, 299–300
  of social justice work, 230–31
Fure, Ashley, 267

Gainor, Gabrielle Kazuko Nomura, 109
Gaunt, Helena, 58, 60
Gehry, Frank, 82–83, 87, 88–89
gender identity, 6

gender inequalities, 2–3. *See also* canon, the; misconduct; sexual harassment
  bias against female students in conservatoires, 26–28
  and class, 96–97
  in the classical percussion environment, 130–32
  and contemporary classical music, 266–75
  depictions of sexual violence in opera, 105, 107–8
  equality initiatives, 62–63
  and instruments, 26–28, 132–33
  recruitment and pay disparities in UK music industry, 276–77, 283–84
  sexism and racism against East Asian women, 163, 165
  students challenging sexism in conservatoires, 131
  underrepresentation of women in percussion, 131–32
  underrepresentation of women in senior positions in UK music industry, 300–1
Gender and the Large and Shiny Instruments, 132–33
Gender Relations in New Music (gRiNM), 12, 266–75
Gender Research in Darmstadt, 267
genius, notions of, 266–67
Genoveva, 114–15
genre theory, 14
Gentile, Giovanni, 20–21
Germany, 72–73
  conservatoires in, 31–41
  contemporary classical music in, 266–75
  discussions of racism in, 146
  diversity initiatives in German opera, 74–80
  events insurance following COVID-19, 281–82
  racialized hierarchies in higher music education, 55
  racism in orchestras, 141, 161–62, 164–65
  gig economy. *See* freelance work
Giuliano, Daryl, 241
Glass, Philip, 299
Glick Schiller, Nina, 176
Glissant, Édouard, 225
globalization, 216
Global South. *See also* "West"/"Western"
  classical music from, 191, 193
  marginalization in classical music literature, 4
Graeae Theatre Company, 122
grants. *See* funding, philanthropy

Gray, Anthony, 8–9
Gray, Herman, 71
Green, Lucy, 237
GRiD. *See* Gender Research in Darmstadt
GRiNM. *See* Gender Relations in New Music
Gustafson, Ruth, 31, 143

habitus, 32–33, 45, 46–47
    educational, 48–50
    familial, 47–48
Haderer, Gerhard, 166
Haferkorn, Julia, 282
Hall, Stuart, 45–46, 70–71, 78–79
Hall, Tony, 227
Hammond, Patricia, 243
Hands, Nicola, 243
Hanusa, Sebastian, 118–19
harmonica, the, 149
hauntology, 222, 227
Hegele, Rose, 243
Hennion, Antoine, 33
Hess, Juliet, 31
heterophony, 187
Higham-Edwards, Beth, 8
higher music education. *See* music education, higher
hooks, bell, 101n.2
Hungarian State Opera, 117–18
Hurt, Weston, 119, 120–21
hybridization, 12–13, 15, 185–94. *See also* creolization

identity
    as a classical musician, 175, 176–83
    formation of, 47–48, 49
    politics, 93, 94, 95–97
    problems with categorizing, 267–69
    theorizing, 45–46
Il Troubadore, 185
Illuminate Women's Music, 11–12, 234, 235, 238–45
improvisation, 186, 188, 225–26, 227
IMSLP. *See* International Music Score Library Project
inclusion. *See* diversity
inclusive practices, 121–22, 140, 249, 286, 295
Independent Society of Musicians (ISM), 8–9, 276–85
    Dignity at Work campaign, 277–78
individualism, 36, 92, 96, 266–67
Inglewood (US), 85–86, 87
Institute for Fiscal Studies, 281
institutions. *See also* conservatoires; diversity; music education, higher

    doing social justice work within, 228–33
    and institutional critique, 266, 269–71, 274
    institutional culture, 61–63, 265
    institutional power, 34, 40–41
    power relations in, 54–65
    racism in, 260, 262
    resistance to change within, 257, 259, 260
instruments
    and class, 25
    cost of, 50–51
    development of, 297–98
    and disability, 136
    and gender, 26–28, 132–33
intercultural ensembles, 187–90
International Music Score Library Project (IMSLP), 241–42
intersectionality, 74–75, 95–96, 210, 266, 272–73
Inuit throat singing, 93
involvement. *See* participation
Iolanta, 116
ISM. *See* Independent Society of Musicians
Italian conservatoires, 19–30
Ivors Academy, 138

Japan, classical music sector in, 178–79
Japanese musicians, 172–84
Jensen, Tracey, 7
Jenůfa, 116
Johnson, Quodesia, 8, 9–10, 255–65
Jones, Carol J., 240–41
Joseph, Anthony, 225–26
Jouvay, 227

Kajikawa, Loren, 86–87
Kavanagh, Brian, 282
Kawabata, Maiko, 7–8, 39, 180
Kelly, Eleanor, 243
Kelly, Liz, 56
Kendall, Hannah, 12–13
Keychange campaign, 1
Kim, Young Uck, 167
Kmecova, Andrea, 243
Knife of Dawn, The, 148, 151
Koh, Jennifer, 167, 169
Kolbe, Kristina, 11–12, 188
Koskoff, Ellen, 236–37
Kowalczyk, Beata, 7–8, 170n.9

labor. *See* diversity; freelance work; working conditions in the music industry
lad culture, 130–31
Lamont, Michele, 34, 144
LA Phil. *See* Los Angeles Philharmonic

Latino classical musicians, 195
LatinX Artists Society in Opera, 258
Leak, Samuel, 282
L'éclair, 113–14
Legg, Robert, 236
legislative change, campaigning for, 278–80, 291
Leong, Nancy, 70–71
Leppänen, Taru, 39
Letter to the Opera Field from Black Administrators, A, 255–57, 261, 262
Levine, Lawrence, 86–87
Lewis, George, 149
liberal feminism, 95, 96–97
liberalism, 92, 95–96, 99
Lim, Lisa, 270–71
Lindholm, Charles, 175
listeners. *See* audiences
Little, Charlotte, 117
Littlejohn, David, 104
lobbying. *See* activism; campaigning
London Oratory School, 203
London School of Economics, 43
Los Angeles Philharmonic (LA Phil), 81–82, 84, 85–86, 87–89
Lovelace, Earl, 217–18
Lovell, Rosanna, 12
Lucerne Festival, 169
luck, trope of, 35–36
Luna Composition Lab, 93–94, 96

Madama Butterfly, 108, 109–10
Maggio Musicale Fiorentino, 107, 110–11
Mai Ling, 169
Makarova, Jelena, 241
Manila (the Philippines), classical music tradition in, 191
Mannes College of Music, 195
Mariachi musicians, 85–86
Märzmusik Festival, 267
Mass, 303
Matthews, Cassie, 240–41
Mauser, Siegfried, 55
Maysaud, Nebal, 99–100, 101
Mazzoli, Missy, 93–94
McCormick, Lisa, 33
McGregor, Gemma, 240–41
McManus, Jackie, 33–34
McMonagle, Louise, 151
Medici, Alessandro de, 199
Meghji, Ali, 144
Mehnert, Mick Morris, 118–19
Mehta, Zubin, 159
memes, 270–71, 274

mental health, 48, 231
representation in opera, 113–14, 115
meritocracy, fallacy of, 2–3, 28–29, 96–97, 99, 135
métissage, 225
MeToo, 54, 63, 290–91
Metropolitan Opera, 91, 92, 96–97, 106
microaggressions, 164, 204, 223–24
middle-class culture, 2–3
Black middle-class experiences, 144
and parenting, 35, 75
and whiteness, 31–32, 75
Middle Eastern music, 187
Midgette, Anne, 110
migration. *See* transnational mobility
misconduct. *See also* sexual harassment
definition of, 56–57
and higher music education, 56–57, 61–63
strategies to combat, 57–63
Mitchell, Annie, 59–60
Mitchell, David, 112–13
Mobley, Reggie, 196
Monk, Meredith, 299
Moore, Gillian, 15–16
Morales, Liliana, 87
Mouawad, Wajdi, 107–8
Murphy Moo, Jessica, 108
Muscato, Leo, 107–8
Musical Representations of Disability Database, 112–16
music box, the, 149
Music BW Women, 62–63
music education, extracurricular, 23, 34–36, 235
music education, higher. *See also* conservatoires; misconduct; pedagogies
admission practices (England), 33–34
decolonizing, 226–27
different national funding models, 55
at historically Black colleges (US), 197
institutional culture, 61–63
power relations between staff and students, 54–65
and professional development, 60, 64
university music degrees (UK), 236
widening participation, 62–63
music education, primary and secondary (K–12). *See also* conservatoires
and class inequalities, 2–3, 300
impact of Black high school music teachers in Los Angeles (US), 85–86
and opportunities for racially minoritized young people, 31–32, 301
and state (public) education, 84–85, 89, 128, 235, 247

musicians of color, historical, 199
Musicians' Union, the, 8–9, 277, 278, 286–96
  access for disabled members, 289
  diversity and inclusion on committees, 286–88
  diversity of membership, 288
  Safe Space app, 288, 291
"Muslim ban" (US executive order), 187
mutual aid, 100

"narrative prosthesis," 112–16
National Youth Ensembles (UK), 300
Neely, Patricia Ann, 11–12
neoliberalism, 3, 83–85, 88, 89, 95, 97–98
Netrebko, Anna, 102, 117–18
networks. *See also* transnational mobility
  building, 8, 62–63, 239–40, 269
  elite, 129–30, 131
  importance of, 154, 274, 294
  and "race," 204
new music. *See* contemporary classical music
Nicolson, James S., 195
nonprofit organizations, 82, 89, 264
Nooshin, Laudan, 15, 71–72
Norwegian Academy of Music, 59
Nos, 116
notation, 78, 231–32
Nwanoku, Chi-chi, 1, 11–12, 288, 301–2
Nylander, Erik, 32–33

Okun, Tema, 259
Oliveros, Pauline, 299
OnCurating Journal, 271–72
ontology. *See* whiteness
opera
  audiences, 105, 106–7, 108
  canon, 105–7
  children's choirs, 74–76
  "color-blind" versus "color-conscious" casting, 109–10
  disability representation in, 112–23
  intercultural opera productions, 72–73, 76–79
  lack of change in, 208
  production, 102–11
  racism in, 206, 255–65
  racism in canonical works, 105, 106–7, 108–9
  revision and reinterpretation of canonical work, 107–8
  the score versus stage interpretation, 103–5
  sexism in canonical works, 105
  women composers in, 91, 92, 93–94

OPERA America conference, 259
Opera Australia, 109
@operaisracist, 255, 261
orchestras, 246–51. *See also* auditions, concerts
  changing performance norms, 249
  cost of rehearsals, 228–29
  doing social justice work in the orchestra industry, 228–33
  evolution of orchestras outside the "West," 190
  formal hierarchy within, 297–98
  increasing representation of musicians of color within, 288
  intercultural, 188
  and the need to build trust with local communities, 144
  racism in recruitment practices, 161–64
  salaries in, 159
  underrepresentation of musicians of color, 301
  underrepresentation of women in principal positions and as soloists, 300–1
OrchKids, 87
organizations. *See* institutions
organizing. *See* activism; Blacktivism; campaigning
Ostleitner, Elena, 166
Otello, 106
othering, 76–79, 168
outreach
  to challenge racism in opera, 108–9
  challenges of doing, 229–30
  community engagement, 262
  community youth music programs, 81–83, 85–87
  as dominant narrative of disability and music, 138, 140
  impact of, 197, 199
  and racism, 206
  as reproducing class power, 94
Owen, Morfydd, 241–42
Oxford, Josh, 231

Padilla Peralta, Dan-el, 86
Paek, Tim, 241
Paradis, Maria Theresia von, 122
Paradis Files, The, 122–23
parenthood/maternity, 6
Parents & Carers in Performing Arts (PiPA), 283–84
participation, 138, 299–300, 303
pay. *See* working conditions in the music industry

pedagogies
    accessible teaching, 209
    decolonizing, 225–26, 227
    and disability, 139, 140
    group tuition, 58, 59–60
    master-apprentice teaching model, 57, 58, 59, 60
    student-centered learning, 58–59
    and whiteness, 222
percussion, 136
    and gender, 127–34
performance, changing norms of, 249, 297–300. *See also* concerts
performer, fetishization of the, 298–99
Perkins, Rosie, 43, 48–49
Perla, Jack, 108
personality. *See* artistic personality, constructions of
philanthropy, 7, 82–84, 88, 89. *See also* funding
    and arts for social change programs, 83–84, 87
    and racial equity, 260
Philpot, Asta, 117
PiPA. *See* Parents & Carers in Performing Arts
Planets, The, 248
Pledge for Racial Equity and Systemic Change in Opera, A, 255, 257
Poland, Japanese musicians in, 173–74, 182–83
policies, cultural, 71, 72
polymusicality, 190
Ponchione-Bailey, Cayenna, 7–8
Popakademie Baden-Württemberg, 59, 60
Porgy and Bess, 108–9, 117–18
Porton, Jennie Joy, 5–6
Poser, Rachel, 86
Positionen: Texte zur Aktuellen Musik, 272–73
power, 45, 258–59. *See also* institutions; music education, higher
    and emotional labor, 230
    hoarding of, 259, 264
    powerblindness, 93–97
    power play, 205
Power Up, 288
pregnancy, 6
Price, Florence, 193, 250
PRIhME. *See* Stakeholder Assembly on Power Relations in Higher Music Education
Prism trio, 241
professional associations, 276–85
professional identification, 177–83
programming. *See* concert programming
Prokop, Rainer, 5–6
PRS Foundation, 302

Purslow, Emma, 241
Puwar, Nirmal, 38

Quasthoff, Thomas, 119–20

"race," 10. *See also* coloniality; racism; whiteness; white supremacy
    constructions of, 172
    and opera casting, 109–10
    "race"-making, 71, 76–79
    racial categories and terminology, 4
    racial equity, 255, 256, 260
racial capitalism, 70–71
racism, 203–11. *See also* coloniality; conservatoires; microaggressions; opera; orchestras; whiteness; white supremacy
    in academia, 141
    against Black conductors, 141
    against East Asian musicians, 161–69, 180
    anti-Black racism, 141–42, 146, 147, 222, 256, 257, 258, 259, 260, 262
    blackface, 102, 106
    and class position, 95–96
    in community youth music programs, 87
    complicity in, 206
    discussions of, 146, 152–53, 208
    in music education, 204–6
    police brutality, 146, 150
    racialized discourses of authenticity, 172–84
    and sexism against East Asian women, 163, 165
    yellowface, 106, 108
    "Yellow Peril," 7–8, 166–69
radical politics, 99–101
Rauch, Dudley, 88
Reay, Diane, 75
rehearsals, 143, 188–89
    racism in, 164–65
    time available for, 228–29, 232
Reich, Steve, 299
Reitsamer, Rosa, 5–6
representation
    importance of, 247
    politics of, 93
Resound (Bournemouth Symphony Orchestra), 1, 301–2
Re-Sounding the Orchestra, 1
resource constraints, 228–32
rhythmic modes, 187
Ritchey, Marianna, 7, 70–71
Robinson, Dylan, 93, 94
role models, 238–39. *See also* representation
Rosen, David, 103–4

Rosenmeyer, Grant, 116–17, 118–19
Royal Opera House, 105, 151
Royal Philharmonic Society, 300–1, 302
Ryan, Eleanor, 7–8
Rye, Rachel, 56

Saha, Anamik, 70–71, 72–73, 77–78
Said, Edward, 298–300
Saifer, Adam, 83–84
Sandahl, Carrie, 119–21
Sandberg, Sheryl, 96–97
Saner, Philippe, 32–33
Saw Peep, 187
Saylor, Eric, 106
Schade, Camilla, 231, 232
Scharff, Christina, 31–32, 39, 43, 46, 168–69, 276–77
Schreffler, Anne, 14
scores, 103–5
  notions of "fidelity" to, 10–11
  score preparation, 232
Scott-Carey, Julia, 243
Sealey, Jenny, 122
Seattle Opera, 108–9
SEISS. *See* Self-employment Income Support Scheme
self-employment. *See* freelance work
Self-employment Income Support Scheme (SEISS), 281
sexism. *See* gender inequalities; misconduct; sexual harassment
sexual harassment, 54, 131, 165, 277–80. *See also* misconduct
  fear of reporting, 277, 278
  and freelance work, 277–78, 279–80, 291
  lack of accountability for high profile perpetrators, 292
  legal protections against (UK), 278–80
  organizing against, 288, 290–93
  policies and reporting processes, 293
  risks of reporting, 286
  support for victims, 291–92
sexuality, 6
Shipsey, Laura, 241
Shortell, John, 8–9
Shreffler, Anne C., 236–37, 240
Siebers, Tobin, 115
Silpayamanant, Jon, 12–13
Silvana, 114–15
Skuse, Amble, 122
Slater, Angela, 11–12
Snyder, Sharon, 112–13

social capital, 45
social class. *See* class
"social cloning," 38
socialization of classical musicians, 19–20, 34–36, 221
social justice work. *See* activism; Blacktivism; campaigning; diversity
social media, 270–71, 274, 288
socio-economic class. *See* class
Sounds Now, 273
South American composers, 191
Southbank orchestras, 250
Southbank Sinfonia, 129–30
Southeast Symphony Orchestra, 85–86
Sphinx Organization, 1, 195
Spivak, Gayatri, 226–27
Stakeholder Assembly on Power Relations in Higher Music Education (PRIhME), 55
Stamatakis-Brown, Andy, 135
starchitecture, 87–89
steelpan, the, 224–26
Stokes, Martin, 70–71
streaming industry, 288
subjectivity, 3, 33–34, 39
  musical, 216–19, 220–21, 225
Supporting Women and Parents in Opera (SWAP'ra), 132, 133
SWAP'ra. *See* Supporting Women and Parents in Opera
Swed, Mark, 81
symbolic capital, 32–33, 47–49, 50
Szanton Blanc, Cristina, 176

Taíwò, Olúfémi, 95–96
taste, 33
teaching. *See* pedagogies
Terauds, John, 107–8
Terracini, Lyndon, 109
theater, 208
Titley, Gavan, 70–71
tokenism, 142
Tomlinson, Barbara, 95
trade unions, 286–96
transnational mobility, 174, 175–77, 181–84
Trinidad and Tobago, 216, 217–18, 225–26, 227
Trinity Laban, 128
truth-telling, 260, 263
Turkish music, 77–78
Tuxedo series, the, 149–50

UK. *See* United Kingdom
UK Government Equalities Office, 279

UK Music Masters, 148
unconscious bias training, 62
United Kingdom (UK), 127–34, 246–51, 276–85, 286–96
  conservatoires in England and Wales, 42–53
  discussions of racism in, 152–53
  racism in classical music industry in, 203–11
United States (US), 141–47, 255–65
  classical music discourse in, 91–101
  discussions of racism in, 152
  early music scene in, 195–202
universalism, 168, 221
US. See United States

Vaizey, Ed, 246
valuation practices, 32, 33, 34, 36–41
Vassar College, 200
VDGSA. See Viola da Gamba Society of America
Venezuela, 81–82
Vibrans, Oliver, 11–12
Vienna Philharmonic, 166
Vincent, Caitlin, 11–12
Viola da Gamba Society of America (VDGSA), 197
violin, the, 149
Virtosu, Sabina, 240–41
visual impairment, 135. See also disability
  representation in opera, 113–14
vocational education. See conservatoires
Vu, Ania, 243

Walker, George, 250
Wallen, Errollyn, 122
Wang, Yuja, 171n.14
Ward, Joanna, 241
We Ask These Questions of Everybody, 122–23
Weber, Samuel, 104
West Side Story, 109–10
"West"/"Western"
  complexifying understandings of "Western" classical music, 15
  terminology of, 4
  "Western" constructions of "non-Western" music, 71–72
  "Western" depictions of "non-Western" cultures, 105
Westwood, Sarah, 235, 240–41
whiteness, 7–8, 147, 168–69. See also
  coloniality; racism; white supremacy
  and class, 210
  "declarations of whiteness," 273–74
  and the development of "Western" music education, 31
  and diversity initiatives, 7, 69–80
  and embodiment, 220–23
  and epistemology, 217 (*see also* epistemic violence)
  and the "ideal" classical music student, 38–40
  and ideas of European culture, 167–69
  and middle-class culture, 31–32, 75
  white gaze, the, 221–23
  white middle-class identity, 75
  white ontologies, 216–17, 218–19, 222–23, 225–27
  white people's fear of racial justice, 259, 260
  white saviorism, 83–84, 85–87
white supremacy, 143, 221, 259. See also
  coloniality; racism; whiteness
white supremacy culture, 256–57, 259–62, 263, 264–65
white supremacist patriarchy, 91–92
Wickström, David-Emil, 5–6
Wilson, Tamara, 102
women composers. See also canon, the
  audiences' knowledge of, 243
  challenges of finding sheet music for historical composers, 241–42
  First International Conference on Women's Work in Music (Bangor University), 241
  in opera, 91, 92, 93–94
  as role models, 238, 239
  underrepresentation of, 238
women conductors, 300–1, 302
women instrumentalists, 127–34
working conditions in the music industry, 8–9.
  See also freelance work
  campaigns for legal protections, 278–80
  discrimination in UK music industry, 277–78
  fair wages for musicians, 288
  gendered disparities in UK music industry, 276–77, 283–84
  importance of workers' rights, 284
  inequalities in employment contracts, 295
  musicians' access to money, 153
  online music teaching during COVID-19, 282
  payment of marginalized musicians, 288
  visa restrictions, 159, 282
Woods, Simon, 87

Yang, Mina, 7, 39, 96
Yatsyuk, Sofia, 243

yellowface, 106, 108
"Yellow Peril," 7–8, 166–69
YOLA. *See* Youth Orchestra Los Angeles
Youth Music, 119
Youth Opera Company, 206, 209

Youth Orchestra Los Angeles (YOLA), 81, 84

Zhang, Subaiou, 241
Zisso, Yfat Soul, 241
ZKM Center for Art and Media Karlsruhe, 274

Printed in the USA/Agawam, MA
February 5, 2024

860636.001